STUBBORN OUNCES — JUST SCALES

With Witness For Peace
In Nicaragua: A Gringo's
Reflections, Observations
And Sermons

BY DONOVAN ROBERTS, Ph.D.

Fairway Press
Lima, Ohio

STUBBORN OUNCES — JUST SCALES

7900 / ISBN 1-55673-417-4

The Texas Roberts
especially Essie Lee Roberts Music
Gras Fyddo Gyd Â Chwi.

Table of Contents

THE SERMONS

"What Time Is It?" Ecclesiastes 3:1-9
"Time for Dancing On the Promises!"
    The Beatitudes — Matthew 5:1-10

Introduction

In June 1988 I traveled in Nicaragua with Witness for Peace. A year later, in Port Townsend on Washington's Olympic Peninsula, I began sifting through the 400 pages of notes scribbled during that powerful experience. I cannot shed the memories of my simple presence in a land beautiful beyond the telling, among friendly and hospitable people. I will not forget their courageous struggle to survive in the midst of a war that is nasty, brutish, and not short.

The result of that sifting is a journal; a topology of observations and reflections driven by remembrances that linger and a gritty passion for peace that refuses to lay down and keep quiet.

The journal entries are composed of two parts. Observations chronicle the lore that we swapped, tales of the road, notes on the terrain, descriptions of the people, and faithful recapitulations of our many formal and informal interviews with the Nicaraguans. I have attempted to record their words with verbatim accuracy; let the Nicaraguans speak for themselves, a minimal gesture of respect since for 134 years other people have tried to do their thinking and speaking for them.

In stark contrast, Observations are followed by Reflections — descriptions of the territory of spirit I was passing through on this journey. They are purely subjective, the meanderings of my meditative muse. While I am apt to call it a process of distillation, others see it as catharsis. My family unambiguously call them Roberts' Ruminations — cud-chewing.

Well and good; they are all of that. Reflection space alternately serves as battleground and bedroom, a place where the mind and heart lock-up to fuss or tryst with each other. They are an effort to make sense out of observed reality and determine the relation I will take to it.

Within my spirit, observation and reflection function like the systolic and diastolic beats of the heart or the inhalations and exhalations of breathing. By itself, one movement doesn't do you much good without its counterpoint. Apart from finding a complimentary rhythm and collaborative cadence, my spiritual system lurches toward catastrophe.

Together they represent the polarities within which I search for a point of contact between the groundswell bass of personal piety and the recitativo of prophetic demands for social justice. In that sense, I am unabashedly an old-fashioned Wesleyan Methodist. Martin Marty locates it within the constant symbiosis between mysticism and politics.[1] In the parlance of Witness for Peace and liberation theology, it is called the Action and Reflection Circle of Praxis. If the imagery of the dialectic is helpful, it is the point mid-sweep in the pendulum's swing twixt inner spiritual discipline and outward political engagement.

My reflections are generated out of the desire to discover some thread that weaves toward intimation of kingdoms yet-to-be tugging at those already within our midst. Like stalking a fresh track to the water's edge, the spiritual pilgrim must stop often, hunker down, be quiet, and open all senses to a calm and vigilant alertness. Consequently reflection precedes rigorous academic analyses. Those who thumb the following pages looking for a scholarly treatise of that stripe look in vain and won't find it here. In my experience, reflection prefaces the task of planning for social change through the labor of developing strategies and negotiating tactical systems.

While the Observations are straightforward, Reflections are obviously something else. A description of that process is appropriate; how I move from observing the suffering, witnessing the transformation, and listening to the hope-filled commitment of the Nicaraguans, to my cogitations, the occasional prayer or poem, and finally the six sermons that a friend called, hard-lovin'.

Before the gospel is a word, before it is an action, it is silence. Spiritual journeys begin at a still-point; in the words of the psalmist, "Be silent, [still] and know that I am God, saith the Lord" (Psalm 46:10). It is the germinal silence in which we are invited to 'stop the world;' to stop the world of all business-as-usual; to stop the world of all taken-for-grantedness; to stop the world of our preoccupations with hyper-rationality. There in the silence, beneath the raucous or the routine claims of persons and a hurting world, the spiritual pilgrim 'centers down' and attempts to locate themself in the presence of God.

I take this time and enter these spaces simply because I must. God is neither above, nor beyond, nor outside of time. God is at the heart of time. The spiritual disciplines of meditation, contemplation, and prayer allow me to enter a pause within the eternal moment. It is the sacred silence underneath my being and my doing. It is where I encounter the presence of God, the creative nerve within each present moment, the master storyteller who cares about the story I am creating with my life, moment by moment, breath by breath, heartbeat by heartbeat.

I have no gnostic crystal ball. I cannot penetrate the veil and experience the mind of Christ during those periods when he took himself apart from the disciples and crowds for unaccompanied intervals of intimacy with God. I do sense something of the passion that attended those moments, that emerged from these observances.

Remembering those stories that have made us a people, that map the track of our past with its sacred places and special gestures, I note, and regard it as as significant, that solitariness prefaced Jesus' ministry of teaching, his acts of healing, and the assertive stance he took in confronting the 'principalities and powers' of our world. In my imagination I sense that these disciplined intervals became a creative isthmus through which his clarity of mission was perceived, were moments for cleansing the lens of his perception, became channels through which the resolve of his commitment flowed.

For those of us who purpose to follow him, it is not light work to see the duty demanded and to call things by their right name. We receive our orders — feed the hungry, shelter the refugee, comfort the afflicted, release the captives. We are to work for peace and pray for miracles. And while we are sent forward to do things and speak words in his name and for the sake of his kingdom, we also see the cross. In that ominous moment we touch our own fears and pray for his power, lest we become misers of miracle and penny-pinching guardians of grace.

In the silence with the glimpse of that cross burning its way into our brain, we learn a hard lesson. The encounter with God at the still-point of a meditative center does not always leave Christ's followers in the happy estate of sanctified bliss. Remembering his stories, or having lived part of them ourselves, we know that the tryst with God puts an inescapable claim upon our lives. The orders we receive at the center may afflict us with terror as opposed to granting us comfort. The seal or sepulcher of our well-ordered lives may be broken under shafts of light that send us forward into hard struggle.

Stopping the world of 'business-as-usual' invites dealing with an angel that leaves us scarred or lame. Blemished or alternately-abled may be the short of it. The indelible image etched into consciousness during that encounter was that of a cross with its implication that it is in our own bodies that the grain must be ground and the wine pressed before our lives incarnate the spirit and sacrament of Christ.

The silence within stopping the world of all 'taken-for-grantedness' is of a different kind. Here the gift correlates with a grace capable of honing our faculties of discernment. If the first 'stopping the world' opens us for dreaming dreams and seeing glimpses of holy vision, this interval is the crucible in which the tools of kingdom building are forged. Whispering hints and shimmering glimpses are long gone. In their place this silence is invaded with the brash commands of prophecy and strong words of ultimatum. I hear the voice of T.S. Eliot's "Choruses From 'The Rock:' "

> *"Much to cast down, much to build, much to restore:*
> *Let the work not delay, time and the arm not waste;*
> *Let the clay be dug from the pit,*

Let the saw cut the stone,
Let the fire not be quenched in the forge.''[2]

I am silent.

Long- and short-range goals, the strategies and tactics that stake out and shape up the territory of the kingdom begin to emerge from the words pounding upon the stillness. An Old Testament brusqueness carries on the wind. We ready ourself, brace, and prepare.

Then, another silence, a re-envisioning of that cross and we remember something else: Christian shepherding, vital to the praxis of mission, commands that we care for our allies and those whom we must confront. While the propsect of kingdom building taxes our reservoirs of strength, the latter always puts us hard up against our capacity for compassion. Heidegger called it a 'meditative thinking,' that rare mode of recollection that begins with listening to the logos of the other, to the spirit within the situation, and to the voice that the other hears in their own stillness.

With all this said, however, the silence at the still-point has another purpose. Sometimes the work of strategy or tactics, the labor of assessment and deployment, sometimes all of this is forced to a halt. We do not always soar like eagles. We grow faint upon the march. As movements for social justice become embattled, its warriors grow weary, are wounded. The cultivation of quietness and the savoring of silence is also a time for repair. The ancient stories and ours as well bespeak of brokenness. The children of Exodus were also the same whose journey took them into wilderness. The territories of borderland and wasteland are also our own. At some point we all become refugee. We seek sanctuary where wounds can be bound. None of us are far distant from our needs for respite, for shalom. The practice of Christian spiritual discipline invites us to step into the spaces between the tics of our clock, to listen and move with the unique rhythms of our time, our life, our body, and open ourselves again and again to the tender mercies of God.

Sam Keen said that the human spirit is a pilgrim, only at home on the road. And the paths of our Journey are unique, for each of us are one-of-a-kind items. The challenge of personal integrity is to be 'true to the grain of our own wood.' The calling of discipleship is to be faithful to the Christ that claims our service. The grace of Christian-mindfulness helps us wrestle with the dilemmas and sometimes recalcitrant stuff of our life and work and sense the dignity of our struggle.

As a preface to the journal, I offer the following Observation and Reflection. Not only do they suggest the format that follows but they tell the story of why I went to Nicaragua in the first place.

OBSERVATION: "Four Proddings, One Decision"

Grace Paley — artist of the short-story, poet and feminist peace activist — was the honored guest at the Resource Center for Non-Violence's 1988 annual banquet. Home-based in Santa Cruz, California, hundreds of us were gathering in support of the Center's global work.

Chatting-up friends and waving to others, I meandered toward my assigned table and found a seat. Public social events find me wearing an obliging smile while inwardly buckling in for a tricky ride. Sometimes that demeanor is mistaken for arrogance. I count it more to an introverted nature than one hinged to ego. Socializing in large groups is for me about as pleasant as a ride on the Big Dipper at the nearby boardwalk.

That particular evening was an exception. The folk in the hall were old mates — fellow travelers in the spirit, confreres in deeds of social justice.

Within a few moments the empty place next to me was taken by a woman whose colorful Guatemalan blouse and skirt were complimented by a smile so vigorous and ebullient that my shyness vamoosed. Dorothy Granada has a penultimate and enchanting charm. Moreover, I was probably the only person in the room that did not know her. A former Witness for

14

Peace Long-Termer in Nicaragua, she listened as I spoke about the Pledge of Resistance's plans for a vigil to be held at the Main Gate of Fort Ord.

Forty miles down Monterey Bay on Highway 1, this 'home base' is the training center for the U.S. Army's 7th Light Infantry. One Bay, two points; the Center at the north end spurred an opposition to the federal government's interventions in Central America while the Fort at the other end sent its infantry and Special Forces into the jungles of Honduras to implement those policies. Like Mohammed and the mountain, while the Fort was a stranger to the Center, most of us at that evening's celebration were not strangers to the Fort.

During a lull in the program, Dorothy delighted our table by reciting Giaconda Belli's poem "What Are You, Nicaragua?" Offering it first in Spanish and then translating it to English, this *chicana* mirrored the passion within her Nicaraguan friend's verse. In the quiet that followed, she seized the moment; fastening her eyes to mine, she leaned over and said, "Donovan, why don't you go there yourself, with Witness for Peace?"

George Baldwin was a United Methodist pastor, formerly a professor at St. Paul's School of Theology in Kansas City. Now he lives in Nicaragua. Trading the pulpit and podium for working with a building materials and construction cooperative in the war zone, the documentarist Bill Moyers interviewed him in Paiwas, his new home. Watching Moyer's "God and Politics," I listened carefully as the soft-spoken Baldwin, wearing old Levis and a T-shirt, remarked that he was fulfilling his 'calling' by standing in solidarity with the Nicaraguan poor.

Early in 1988 his cousin, Don Baldwin, like myself a United Methodist minister serving a church in Santa Cruz County, invited me to join him for dinner. Not so unusual. Don and I have been friends most of our lives. Both our fathers were Methodist clergy. But the company at this supper would be unusual; his cousin George was visiting from Nicaragua. I wanted to meet that man.

Once again I found myself seated next to a person who called Nicaragua home. As the conversation moved into the night, George offered me an invitation: "Come to Nicaragua. Visit me, be with the people. See for yourself."

Where Nicaragua is concerned I do not consider myself a 'doubting Thomas.' Yet twice in the space of a few weeks, I had been invited to come, see, and touch.

Why not? I was due for a study-leave. The congregation would be supportive. In 1983 our parishioners raised the funds to send two of our members on a similar fact-finding tour. The project was aborted when the U.S. Passport Agency misplaced and finally boggled their documents; an appended note cited complications pertaining to the men's 'high security clearances,' another souvenir from their years of service with the Army in Vietnam.

Running before me or standing side by side, our three grown children would share their encouragement, or, as sometimes happens, chasten me the words, "Stand up, Speak up, Don't fool around!" My wife, Dianne, also a founding member of the local Pledge of Resistance, had twenty years of experience campaigning for world peace and inserting herself like a wedge against walls built to keep the poor from exercising their rights. In two decades, the only change in her quarrels with the exploitations that profane and separate persons was the wording on the top layer of bumper stickers fixed to her VW — 'Grandmother for Peace.' With all its sham, drudgery, violence, and broken dreams, she knows in the marrow of her bones that ours is a beautiful world. And whether she was leafleting at Fort Ord or fasting and standing with Charlie Litkey and Brian Wilson on the tracks at the Concord Naval Weapons Depot, her prayers for those who inflict suffering on people and the planet are not diminished by bitterness. A rare and radiant lady, this gentle warrior of the spirit inspires me with the truth that the price of hating others is to love oneself less.

Finally, during an early morning coffee with our Religious Committee for Peacemaking, A. V. Coyle announced, "I'm going to Nicaragua in June with Witness for Peace." A. V. and I are old sidekicks. A member of the Order of Veronica, this Roman Catholic sister and I have organized and politicized on behalf of poor peoples and Hispanic concerns throughout our village on the Bay. The banality of affluent culture, a church that aggrandizes the status quo, the chauvinism of nations, obsolete barriers that keep us from seeing eye to eye and working side by side, all that bogs us in the ruts of remaining unconsecrated selves, when our prophetic sister speaks, bishops and city councils take note. So do I!

As ever, A. V. turned up the heat. She has a knack for that. With one wife, two sisters and one brother on the prod, what had been a gently percolating idea, sort of half-on and half-off the back burner of intentions, was fired to a rolling boil. Silently — it's that old introversion again — I resolved to make an inquiry and see if there was an available spot in her delegation.

The regional staff person for the Witness was quartered at the Resource Center in Santa Cruz. Discovering that there was another space in the June delegation, I processed the papers quickly. Announcing my intentions, the family, the church, and my friends contributed their approvals. The gears for this journey were sliding in a greased groove.

The first opportunity for meething other members of the delegation occurred in Berkeley at the Quaker Friends Meeting Center. We were an assorted lot. Including myself and A. V., there were nine other persons. David Roberts (no relation) was the youngest member, completing his sophomore year at University of California Santa Cruz and majoring in political science with an emphasis in revolutionary movements in the developing world. Bard Henry, a solid and callused-hand general contractor in his thirties, was from Mendicino County. Laurie Ruben had completed work for her State of California teaching credential and was going to Nicaragua in-between writing a curriculum text. Laura Doyle held a Masters in Public Health from Yale and had recently been employed by the AIDS Education Project in Berkeley. Bill Simonsen held a Canadian passport but had lived in the U.S. and Marin County for many

17

years and was a retired businessman formerly wholesaling electrical lighting fixtures. Carol Carr, an RN emergency room technician, took a leave from her staff position in a hospital on the coast north of San Francisco. Sara Wright worked as an administrator in one of Stephen Jobs high-tech graphics corporations while completing a Master's degree in cultural anthropology. Ellen Schewe, a West German citizen, was a student of theology at the Pacific School of Religion in Berkeley. Shuji Ohyama is Japanese and had completed a year of post-graduate study at Union Theological Seminary in New York City; he would return to Japan following the trip.

What did we have in common that would bind us in kindred cause for this journey? Not all of us were anglos, neither were we citizens of the same nation-state, nor believers in the same religious creed. Our economic and educational backgrounds were mixed. Politically, some were journeying to gather facts in the formation of opinions, and others were going to stand on the facts already at hand and make a witness to their convictions.

Our experiences with non-anglo and poor peoples varied. Laura had recently completed two years of living and working with Native Americans at Hopi in Arizona. Carol had served with the Red Cross in the Ethiopian famine crisis. Bill had the most experience traveling in Latin America. Shuji had spent the most time in jail as the result of his work to evacuate political prisoners in North Korea and relocate them to Japan. A. V. was the most proficient Spanish speaker given her work with Hispanics and teaching in an Adult Education program. For five years, while Chaplain at Boston University, I worked with the New England Boycott of the United Farm Workers and wrote my Ph.D. dissertation on the social ethics of Cesar Chavez.

REFLECTION: "Violence as 'Midwifery,' 'Blowing Dust,' 'Evangelism?' "

Immediately prior to my departure, I wrote the following 'Open Letter' to the members of the United Methodist Church in Watsonville, California, a congregation of remarkable compassion and gritty social conscience. I had been their pastor for five years:

By the time you read these notes I will be in Waslala, a small village in Nicaragua's northeastern Matagalpa District. Sister A. V. Coyle from the Holy Eucharist Parish in our neighboring Corralitos will be there too. Together with the other eight members of the Witness for Peace delegation, we shall listen and learn, work and worship, with our sisters and brothers in this land that has absorbed so much violence over the years.

And they are long years, years numbered in decades. Leave us not indulge ourselves in the West's penchant for amnesia. For if we are intermittent in memory, we shall also be fragmented in conscience. The odyssey of struggle in Nicaragua is not new, is not limited by current combat between Contras and Sandinistas. No. These struggles are old, as the years are old. President William Howard Taft first sent in the Marines in 1911-1912. They remained there until 1932 and left only after inserting the dynasty of Anastasio Somoza who called Nicaragua, "my farm," a 'farm' he cropped for profit and irrigated with blood. Yes, the years of war are marked by blood. Old blood and fresh blood. Blood that has always been shed in acts of violence.

Violence! Marx regarded it as the midwife of history. Shakespeare saw it as a restless passivity blowing about our frail dust. Saint Matthew talked about it as a means for establishing the kingdom of heaven.

Midwifery? Blowing dust? Evangelism? Can it be such? What manner of grandiose insanity lurks within our human condition that passive or active violence should have this power over persons?

I think of World War II and recall the horros of Nazi concentration camps, the internment of our own Japanese citizens, Soviet Gulags, and the atomic bombing of Hiroshima and Nagasaki. I remember Vietnam. No person, no family, no race, no culture, no religious tradition has been exempt from the universality of violence during this century. It seems as pervasive as the air we breathe. Asians, Anglo Saxons, Mediterraneans, Africans, Latin Americans, all of us are afflicted by its perfidity.

Beyond accounting for its origins, how do we calculate its cost? In dollars spent or dreams destroyed? In victories of battle, or crops and pasturage rent asunder? In the joys of homecomings, or tears beside graves? However the count be done it has cost a lot; a lot of bullets, a lot of bombs, a lot of words, a lot of insults, a lot of despair.

The old sage had it right; "Never ask the sword what the wound feels."

On April 17 of this year Neris Roble died a violent death. Why? Because this thirty-six year old unarmed civilian disobeyed a Contra order and attended Mass in Waslala where an Italian priest, Father Ubaldo Gervasoni, was preaching political sermons critical of the counter-revolution. His throat slit and his pants and shoes stolen, Roble became another victim.

Of what? Of history's midwifery? Of passive blowing dust? Of Christ's kingdom a-coming? Perhaps President Reagan and the Contras have an answer. Perhaps Daniel Ortega and the Sandinistas have an answer. But both sides are standing in pools of blood with bloody hands. And whatever answer they offer, we won't know how Neris Roble felt about it laying there in the dirt 200 yards from the chapel.

"Never ask the sword what the wound feels."

Someone once said to me, "Death ain't so bad. It's getting there that's hard." Whatever his politics or his faith, to die by having your throat slit must not have felt very good to Roble. Christ hanging on his bloody cross, a tortured mass of brutalized humanity, would not have said that such dying felt very good.

That's what vexes me about violence. And it doesn't matter whether the battlefield is defined by the geometry of war between nations, or the lingering hard places between once-upon-a-time lovers, or the geography between a person's ears. Whenever violence inserts its pornographic presence into affairs of state, or the diplomacy of relationships, or when it begins to unhinge the sancturaries of the mind and soul, always something is going down to the bad death. Something is saying 'No' to life and not loving it. And if you don't love life, you kill it. And if you kill it because it doesn't have the same politics or the same color or the same faith or the same dream, if you kill it because it's convenient to have some other person or place or thing to blame something on, well, finally it's all the same. There's a little more hate and a little less love in this hard and hurting and beautiful world. And pretty soon there will be a little less of us in the world, too.

The man said it right; "Those who live by the sword, die by the sword." And it's not simply the sword that slit Roble's throat. Or the bullets fired and bombs dropped and missiles launched from under the wave. It's the angry curse, the gesture of derision preceding the fist, the arrogant sneer of supposed superiority. It's all those active little violences of spite and spirit that kill love as sure as the sword kills life. And those who are apt to call things by their right name, call the 'No' to life by another four letter word — Evil!

But evil has another face, a passive face. It's not only the acts that we Do, but those we Don't as well; it's the risks we don't take, the things we don't stand for, the words we don't speak. And the man had something to say about that, too: "Let your Yeas be Yea and your Nays be Nay." Take a stand. Don't equivocate. Spend less time covering your backside. Spend less energy trying to get ahead at any price. Wherever there is disdain for life, call it out. Wherever there is an atmosphere of death, don't adapt to it. Say 'Yes' to life, to love, to justice. And then put your poke where your mouth is.

The same man had compassion for wounds. He tended them and healed them. And that compassion for pain also had a plan for swords. Turn them into plowshares. And that's why I am going to Nicaragua. To back my prayers for peace with a gesture of hope. And I do not deceive myself. Hope doesn't have a blessed thing to do with believing that you are going to win anything; not a war, not an argument, not a sliver of sanity in a world that seems to be heading for hell in a hurry. Hope is divorced from optimism and pessimism. Thank God! It is simply doing something decent while muttering a prayer that God will serve up a jolt of underserved integrity that keeps your foot to the fire, at the right time, in the right place.

Our little efforts and funny hopes may never be enough to sway the balance between war and peace. But I have chosen the side that shall feel the stubborn ounces of my commitment. It is the side of reconciliation; the side that attempts, by the grace of God, to stand there looking both directions and saying "No more war," the side that shall attempt by its witness for peace to encourage belligerents to lay down their arms, to extend the right hands of forgiving fellowship, and then stoop to pick up the tools of reconstruction. Yes, tools that will once again build schools instead of barricades, clinics instead of ramparts, instruments that will prepare the soil for crops instead of destroying it by mortars. We yearn to build a place where the laughter of children will echo across the valleys instead of the din of mourning, a place where lovers can stroll in meadows without fear of snipers, a place where Contra and Sandinista can be grasped by the vision and pledge themselves to life and one another, honoring the words of old Isaiah, that "none shall hurt or destroy in all my holy mountain." So be it. God help us!

THE SERMONS: "What Time Is It? Time for Dancing on the Promises!"

Witness for Peace requests its partners to 'go public' on their return, to proclaim however they can what it is that they have seen and heard. The process of making application for the delegation includes a section for envisioning how that will be accomplished: Public speaking, lobbying Congress, media contracts, convening small groups for living-room discussions, lecturing . . . all of that and more, as each is able.

A preacher with a pulpit has the medium of the homily at hand. Therefore I have appended to these notes the six sermons delivered at my parish upon coming home.

Like Observation and Reflection, the sermons follow a similar two-step pattern, but music instead a motion might be a better analogy. The words of Ecclesiastes — "A time for . . ." provide the rhythm, a searching and percussive throb asking the question "What Time Is It?" The words of Jesus' Beatitudes suggest the melody as "Dancing On The Promises" scan the horizons of Scripture for his responses; blessed are the peacemakers, the meek, the merciful, those who mourn, the poor in spirit, the persecuted and reviled.

Point . . . Ecclesiastes. Counterpoint . . . Jesus. One-two, One-two. Inhale the question, exhale the exclamation. It's that old beating heart again.

The first sermon was written and delivered within seven days of my return and the others followed week upon week. Arguably, I may not have left enough time for 'simmering,' letting the dust settle, time to ponder before thinking. If the results are murky, so much graffiti on walls bearing up under too much evidence of Kilroy's having been there already, they do, however, suggest a sense for linkages between observation, reflection and proclamation.

The journal with sermons reflect something of the faraway music that Nicaragua, with all its beauty and alarm, has inscribed upon my heart. I went to make a witness for peace. I came home with the melodies of a struggling and hope-filled people inspiring me to thanksgiving for the Witness for Peace that they are.

Flight To Mexico City

June 11, 1988

The distance from San Francisco, California, to Managua, Nicaragua, is roughly four thousand miles. This journey, however, would entail more than a simple flight south from thirty-eight degrees latitude to twelve. In a sense it resembled a cartwheel in the spirit. I am a gringo, born and raised in that lovely California city by the bay. Now I was flying toward the capitol of a nation that my government regarded as the enemy.

The enemy! As a child growing up during the Second World War, the first international enemy I recognized by name was Germany's Hitler and the Aryan Nazis. After Pearl Harbor the name and color of the enemy shifted to include Hirohito and the Japanese. During my grade school years, Senator Joseph McCarthy's House Un-American Activities Committee declared that the enemy was amongst us as they sought to identify and harass domestic Communist sympathizers. The face and place of the enemy shifted again. When the North Koreans invaded Seoul, I thumbed through my atlas and encyclopedia to discover who and where the enemy was now. By the time I was in high school the enemy was Stalin, the sadist slaughtering the kulacks, the perpetrator of tragic purges, the imperialist plundering the peoples of Eastern Europe in the creation of a Soviet hegemony. Another enemy. But when Khrushchev became Premier of the U.S.S.R., the Kremlin launched a de-Stalinization campaign and our former Soviet ally was declared the enemy of his own people.

The 'enemy' business was getting complicated. During my college years Khrushchev backed Fidel Castro's rebels and their revolt against our 'friend' Batista, the dictator and President of Cuba. Nikita and Castro were in cahoots; both were the enemy. We failed to neutralize Castro, witness the Bay of Pigs disaster, but we blockaded his Soviet collaborators from establishing missile sites on the island using the threat of nuclear retaliation to check and checkmate our adversary. The chilling prospect of nuclear war between the super powers meant that the list had indeed become Hydra-headed, ugly.

Then came my generation's war. Neighbors and friends my own age were shipped out to the old and blood-soaked killing fields of Vietnam and Southeast Asia. The new foe was Ho Chi Minh, another former ally during WWII, a man given to quoting our Declaration of Independence, the writer of no less than six letters to President Harry Truman declaring his admiration and affection for the U.S. Nevertheless, once again we were in it for the long haul; another deadly war.

Crisis upon crisis, the identity of the enemy changed character and visage as quick as a high-fashion model shifts through a wardrobe. Rapid changes, too, enemies popping up here and there faster than moving targets zipping across the line at a carnival's shooting gallery. The news remained riveted to scenes of soldiers moving east or west, off on another crusade of holy war in the grand battle with evil totalitarianism.

History, during the adult years of my life, is an interruption of war by truces. In the intervals between raging battles, the time-outs to catch a second breath, it seemed as if the enemy list was hidden under a shell waiting to be manipulated by sleight of hand. Shuffled in dizzying convolutions, the flim-flam artist would hoist the pod and announce the foe of the day: Iran, Libya, Palestine. We waited. Mostly we were surprised. Grenada. Of all places!

Inevitably alliances were respecified with a speed that boggled the mind and just as fast, borders were redrafted. The net result — a condition of perennial confusion in the 'friends' versus 'enemy' business; stupefying, plus the fact that last year's atlas became as obsolete and useless as last year's headlines.

But my cart wheeling leap was taking me into a different horizon where the people were neither Arabic nor Asian. I was soaring toward the Central Americas and the lethal shell-game being played out over the heads of our hemispheric and

Hispanic-Indian neighbors. Our violence-obsessed Administration determined that Nicaragua belonged under that shell and most especially the people who called themselves Sandinistas. And among those people, one in particular stood out in bold relief as 'the enemy;' an intense, brown-skinned young man with black hair and black glasses over a black mustache. His name was Ortega — Daniel Ortega, leader of the *Frente Sandinista* and President of Nicaragua.

I have not been to the oracle, have not read the tea leaves, nor have I consulted the bones. Consequently I am no more in the light about this enemy business than anyone else. But you don't need a soothsayer to realize that our political and social culture is obsessed with enemies and possessed by violence and the frenzy of war.

During the two terms of President Reagan's Adminstration, Nicaragua's Sandinistas have persistently been portrayed as a threat to our national security. Threats must be confronted, restrained, contained. Threats prompt the defensive and reactionary language of vilification. Enemies, on the other hand, require a stiffer treatment, a stronger and more forceful strategy; ultimately they deserve eradication. Consequently our President stated, "If we cannot defend ourselves there, we cannot expect to prevail elsewhere. Our credibility would collapse, our alliances would crumble, and the safety of our homeland would be put in jeopardy."

Thus in 1981 the President asked for $19 million to support 15,000 C.I.A. recruited and U.S. Special Forces trained Nicaraguans. These anti-Sandinista counter-revolutionaries were called the Contras. We would defend ourselves by using Nicaraguans to kill Nicaraguans; after all, it's never too painful to fight to the last drop of someone else's blood.

I remember seeing a bumper sticker at Fort Ord: "Join the Army; travel to exotic, distant lands, meet exciting, unusual people, and kill them." Using someone else to 'defend' ourself 'there' — somewhere far away and remote, a place with strange sounding names, a place allegedly inhabited by demons — when would 'there' be defined as the end of our nose, conceivably a place worth defending?

27

As children, we would draw a line in the good honest dirt. It marked the border of 'our turf,' a boundary we would superintend and protect with vigilance against invasion. This side of the line we would puff ourselves up and parade our funny ferocities. Bravado and ballyhoo were the order of the day. But our threats and intimidations seldom resulted in a scrap. Fighting is hard business. It hurts. Noses bleed, eyes get black and blue, and your hands get scraped. And then you usually caught hell at home. Right after the iodine and a Band-Aid, you got either a lecture or a spanking for the buttons that were missing on your shirt or the new hole in your jeans.

A line made sense. It created space for coexistence. I could ponder that line, and, for that matter, I could study my own nose, the one this side of that boundary, the one that didn't like to bleed, that didn't want to get broken. And from a safe and respected distance I could regard the nose of my neighbor. Was it like my own? It didn't take me long to conclude that both noses breathed the same air.

So what was all this 'defend' talk? And why was our line somehow drawn in Nicaragua? Or was I to believe that Sandinista noses were marching toward the Rio Grand? Would they lay siege to the Alamo in a tired old rerun of Colonel Travis and Davy Crockett histrionics?

I doubted that even the President could believe such drivel. But given his adulation by the main-stream masses, he might be able to sell that pap to suckers if he added a little spice. So he embellished the scenario. This Sandinista named Ortega was in cahoots with the bolsheviks. Terrorizing decent Nicaraguans, the god-less Sandinistas repressed the practice of religion, engaged in extra-judicial killings and torture, 'disappeared' their adversaries, and were eliminating entire cultural and ethnic groups. President Reagan's menu was serving up more than thin gruel; it was a rich and racist stew complete with chunks of cold war ideology floating in a broth of fear.

Once again I found myself growing old and weary listening to other old men tout the verities that inevitably fuel the engines of war. It was a mega-dose of superficial platitudes and flimsy generalizations, of propaganda and dis-information and outright lies.

Who was terrorizing whom? Their killings were extra judicial, but ours were legal? If torture is morally and legally verboten, what dispensation made ours permissible? If eliminating cultural and ethnic populations cannot be sanctioned, why were we trying to 'disappear' these people? If atheistic Sandinistas were squelching religion, why did they use the Bible as the teaching tool of choice in their historic literacy campaign?

Something didn't make sense. And neither did the fact that what we were leaving in the bloody wake of defending that line were more widows, more orphans, and another experience of the hideous calculus called 'body counts.'

Propaganda is like a colander; what goes in doesn't resemble what comes out. It changes form, texture. The final product may be similar, but only at the molecular level. Once again it was time to probe the propaganda for the truth behind the party-line. I knew whose hand was behind the colander; now I wanted to see the reality being squeezed through its tiny holes and paraded to our nation as 'truth' and the 'whole picture.' Beneath the rhetoric of war, it isn't only truth being forced through a sieve; it is a nation.

The only secret about this 'secret war' against the Sandinistas was what it looked and felt like from the underside, from Nicaragua. I wanted to listen to the Nicaraguan people; not the expatriated elite living off the federal pork barrel in their Miami condos while lobbying Congress for luxury in the name of Reagan's Contra war. I suspected that the barrel the majority of Nicaraguans were looking at was the one pointed at them as a result of our federally financed terrorism.

I am the kind of partisan that insists on creating larger holes, gaps, fractures in the propaganda colander. A reprieve from ignorance was in order. I was going there to see for myself.

As our jet began descending to Ixtapa for an unscheduled stop at this resort on Mexico's west coast, in my mind the images and hoopla of war were dense, like a San Francisco fog.

29

Connected to the main by a small tidal peninsula, a mountain gouged into the sea just beyond the landing strip. A lone sentry, it resembled Moro Rock on our own coast. Perhaps a mile off shore other rocks were domed with white; guano islands.

The sight of the white-capped islands stuck in my mind. I was vaulting out of the 'land of the free and the home of the brave' whose triumphant symbol is the magnificent white-headed bald eagle. During this handspring I was abandoning my place on the comfortable beach in the cabana of my affluence where my security was protected by the iron-taloned fist of that magnificent bird with lightning in its claws. I was flying toward a land that my government was laboriously trying to convert into a guano island, a place over which the eagle was demanding the right to fly, a place over which the eagle was screaming, a place that was the target for those deadly lightning blots, a place that this winged-bird was trying to isolate and white-out with the droppings of its foreign policy.

MEXICO CITY

OBSERVATION: *"Casa de Los Amigos"*: **Place of Power in a Flying Wedge**

June 11

Before proceeding to Managua, our twelve member Witness for Peace delegation would spend three days in training at the *Casa de Los Amigos* in Mexico City. The sprawling megalopolis of 17 million was congested with people and careening traffic. I braced for a lung-clogging bout with smog as viscous as rubber cement, but on arrival the sky was bright and clear. The reprieve was defintely a good omen.

A Society of Friends or Quaker meeting center and guest house, the *Casa* serves as checkpoint, layover, and seminar center hosting persons moving between tension points in the hemisphere and around the world. It's a place of action and stillness, for search and discovery, where the yang and yin of hazard and tranquillity settle down to nurture each other.

30

Originally built in 1941 by the Mexican muralist Jose Clemente Orozco, the *Casa* is situated in a triangle-shaped neighborhood bounded by *Paseo de la Reforma, Avenida Insurgentes,* and the *Plaza de la Republica.* No wonder the *Casa* is a place of power, situated in the center of that wedge where the spirits of 'Insurgents' and their demands for 'Reform' commingle.

During the days of training, Orozco's two-story studio with a wall of glass on the southern exposure became our center for Meditation. Normally it serves as a library and meeting room for Friends worship and contemplation. His salon in the adjacent building was used for the work that would confirm us, gird us, for becoming gentle warriors of the spirit on a non-violent mission of peace.

And through the west windows, the sight of the imposing copper domed 76-meter-high arch marked the base of that triangulated wedge at the grand *Plaza de la Republica.* The arch is the tomb for representative heroes of the Mexican Revolution. The bones of Francisco [Pancho] Villa and Emiliano Zapata lay beneath its massive stoneworks. But their spirits are strong, seething in the underground, moving in the capillaries of pre-consciousness, working their way through the fissues of old dreams refusing to die, hungering for fresh incarnations. Indeed, the vigorous and vibrant heart of *Insurgentes and* Reforma beats strong in the land south toward which the cartwheel was taking us.

REFLECTION: "There Is A Place"
> There is a place,
> Somewhere,
>> Between the Valley of the Sun
>> And the Valley of the Moon,
> A place where phantoms come
> To brood and conjure.
> You sense them in the not-quiet darkness,
> Hear them in the vaults of a tomb not sealed.
> Shimmering, shattering, voices eloquent and brash;

Pale phantoms,
    Wrestling with possibility and limit,
    Coiling at the Casa's windows like whispers of
       smoke
    Murmuring Quaker prayers for Peace, Peace;
  Vivid phantoms,
    Blazing with the raw rage of life,
    Sparks bolting from the revolutionary wedge,
    Moaning and hissing Zapata's demand for Justice,
    Justice.
Moving through the Valley of the Still-Small-Voice,
  Climbing up the mountain,
    Standing on the promises,
Do you see them? Hear them?
  Haunted, driven,
  Vexed with cowardice,
    The little challenge
    The small risk
    The nothing ventured-nothing gained
    Middle of the road
      Taken-for-grantednesses and
      Business-as-usual . . .
  Those vagrant spirits
    Of the small life.
Lingering in the quiet mood of Quaker contemplation,
Motionless beneath the rebel's arch,
  Spirits catch the updraft
  Heading for the volcano's rim,
    Disappearing over the top,
  And in the silent spaces of wonderment —
  Caught in the ambitions of ancestral pride —
    Suddenly you muster the dare
    To love the struggle, and
    The second wind of commitment finds it backage.
You are not now a soul
  Caught like a trapped animal,
  But a lusting spirit

Dancing between the known
And the yet-to-be,
Obliged, dedicated
To the fine art
And warm dance
Of balancing between
The terror of being alive
And the wonder of being
A special child of God.
There can be no finer tryst
Than to share such power.

OBSERVATION: "Training for Accompaniment"
June 11

Sue Severin accompanied the delegation as far as Mexico City to facilitate our training. A former Long Termer with Witness for Peace, she worked in Bluefields on the Atlantic Coast.

A petite blond woman, Sue radiates a powerful presence. In fact, she reminds me of George Fox's 'Angel with the Flaming Sword,' a compelling archetype. Hovering there at the rim, in the borderland between the known and the yet-to-be, the Angel's light beckons us to name the center of being, the flame within the fire. The brandishing sword threatens separation, the cleaving of conventions, a breach from old securities — the dogmas, the habits, and the comforts of the familiar. Conflagration, fracture, my sense of trepidation is appropriate.

I am here to go to Nicaragua. But the Angel suggests that the journey begins at the edge of my own center. I fear the crack of thunder, the jolt of lightning, being pushed over the abyss toward my hidden self. But in another part I feel alive, aflame. There are some things more vital than comfort and safety.

Sue, a medieval scholar, provided relief from the tedium of the flight by reciting alliterative lines from the 9th century epic, "Beowulf." Strong in accent, full of guttural force, it was a remarkable tour-de-force. A powerful and urgent woman, Sue is an uncanny intermingling of a passionate blazing gusto that alternates swiftly, effortlessly, to an eerie calm and still-small-voice. She is the conscience for our training, the guardian of the working values of the Witness. The keeper of its seal for our mission, during our training she is the wisdompole sharing reflections from her past toward our future. Through her we sense the higher meanings of a spirit that may protect us against wrong-headed dissolution as a group.

The work of team building involves the quest for stability as a group against the background of our sense of self as individuals. The personal question, "Who am I?" must reach out to embrace its sequel, "To what, to whom do I belong?" We need to develop a primary sense of belonging, of counting, of participating in situations together as a group. And among near strangers who hardly know one another from Adam's house cat, this shall be no quick accomplishment. A host of positive and negative exchanges will be generated in the task of developing an other-than-self reference. If the process works, we shall fashion and fortify a new family. Our choices, decisions, and actions as a group will be taken in the light of their bearing upon our mission in Nicaragua. And in the process we may open to hidden gifts; a new dignity, an enlightened self-respect, status calculated collectively as contrasted to being fixed in ego, and enhanced or enlarged sense of self.

Sue talked about the work of discernment. I remember the first time I ever heard that word — Discernment. Years ago Dad admonished, "Two things are necessary. Make love with integrity and reflect with discernment." I'll spend a lifetime unpacking and struggling with the implications of that admonition. What do I discern? About my own sense of self, about the group?

Sitting in Orozco's studio, the sensation came on strong and clear; we were sojourners in a foreign land. Home is a memory, distant and fading. Strangers to this billet and one another, we have no place to hide. We are in exile; from the familiar, from comfort, from easy conscience. It is a humbling awareness. We are on the road and will not linger to pitch tents or sing the songs of Zion. The simple must be sufficient. Today we are a live and funny conglomeration of guts, gumption, and grace. Tomorrow it may all be different.

The sounds of laughter infiltrate the silence of our fears. Then it is quiet until someone begins the murmurings of song, a whisper of prayer, the sounds of moving on. So this time and space and our way of being in it are good. I think of Father Jim Carroll's words; "Whatever forms of jeopardy or risk this meeting of flesh and spirit leads to, whether large or small, we shall never be the same again. Nor is anything."[3]

He's right. If discernment is at all like contemplation, it is not seeing a different thing but a different way of seeing. And if that happens — transfiguration! Buffy Saint Marie sang it: "Mystery and magic are afoot!"

REFLECTION: "The Pace of Prayer"
11:30 p.m.
The spirit moves at the pace of prayer,
    Neither a sprint nor a jog,
    Maybe six miles per hour, an easy gait;
        Quietly, slowly, gently;
        A no-rush stroll of complete simplicity
        Requiring nothing less than a willingness to pause
        In-between the tics of our clock,
        As in the lull twixt two waves upon the sea.
Point-counterpoint,
Rhythmic, undulating,
Like the motion of the heart or lungs,
    Summonsing,
    Always beckoning with invitations
    To dance between the solitaries of reflection
    And then forward to prayers of Nay or Yea,
        Our bidding prayers prefacing the doing of deeds.
The heart cradles my mind through the search
    For something beyond preoccupations
        With business-as-usual, With taken-for-grantedness,
        With fatuous western hyper-rationality.

Alone, yet together, we are searching
    For some connection with our depths,
        For inward tranquillities that bodes for peace,
            For assurance that the universe is indeed
            Unfolding as it should.
    The Feelings emerge,
    At once breezy and exultant,
    Then bittersweet and scary —
        We are pilgrims with one foot in
            The securities of our world
        While tentative toes point toward
            The promises and terrors of another;
    Stretched taut between the Now and something
        Yet To Be.
Indeed we are a kind of tryst;
    Laughing, silent, pondering, planning,
    Trying to see things as they really are
    And call them by their right name.
Moving up mountains of dreams and
    Becoming transformed or transfigured;
        Now we pause to remember and reflect
            On who we are,
            On whose we are,
            On what it is that we shall become.
We are not brazen nor filled with heady arrogance:
We are the penitent hope-filled,
We are the accompaniers and the accompanied
    Who do not suspect that the inspirations of our heart
    Or the convictions of our resolve
        Will auger sufficient to turn the wheel
        Of justice full circle to completion.
    But we are resolved to take time
        And discover the place that will feel
        The stubborn ounces of our commitment.
In these great waiting moments
    We are quiet, renewing our spirits,
    Recreating our convictions,

Hands and hearts open to receive gifts of strength,
Expecting to be sent forth to tomorrow,
Neither reluctant nor diminished.
For ours is the journey road of compassion,
A sojourning on the high road
To a new day a-coming.
And we move on,
With our prayers,
With our doubts,
With our resolve,
Until again, like tonight,
We make pause to remember and reflect.

OBSERVATION: "What is Witness For Peace?"
July 12 — Mexico City

At 6 a.m. I left the Casa and began walking the side streets toward *Paseo de la Reforma*, the edge of that wedge. I enjoy watching a city awaken, stretch, shake sleep off its pulse. In the soft morning light I savored the sights and sounds and smells; garbage collectors fracturing the quiet, slamming cans into the belly of a diesel truck bellowing at the idle; women working over fires in cut-down barrels, the odor of chorizo and green chili opening my nose. A cup of coffee and pack of cigarettes in hand, I returned to the Casa.

Acción Permanante Christiana por la Paz is the named adopted by Witness for Peace in Nicaragua. An alternative to 'Witness' had to be found to distinguish WFP from the Jehovah's Witness that formerly roamed the countryside proselytizing for converts.

Witness for Peace is in Nicaragua by invitation of CEPAD, the Evangelical Committee for Aid and Development, an ecumenical coalition of forty Protestant Christian denominations in Nicaragua. WFP is a faith-based organization attempting to accompany the Nicaraguan people in their struggle for survival and self-determination. Their strategy of accompaniment is elegant in its simplicity. Since 1983, over 170 Short-Term delegations have brought more than 3,500 persons to Nicaragua. Together with a grassroots network in the U.S.A., friends of the Witness stand to speak these words to the political powers of our nation; "This is what we have seen and heard in Nicaragua. Our eyes do not lie! Repair the damage. Change the policy."

In order to see and hear from the Nicaraguans themselves, during the initial orientation that occurs stateside several weeks before departure, each Short-Term delegation creates a list of persons and agencies they would like to interview. WFP regional coordinators send the list forward to the Long-Term staff in Managua who begin the work of making these arrangements. When the delegation arrives the schedule for interviewing is reviewed and, if necessary, amended by mutual consent. The spectrum of briefings for our delegation included clergy, educators, health-care professionals, trade unionists, co-op organizers, Nicaraguan feminists, and representatives from the opposition, including an editor at *La Prensa*, and a diplomat at the U.S. Embassy.

Witness for Peace headquarters is in Managua but most of its Long-Term staff live with Nicaraguans in the cities and rural hamlets, from Chinandega on the *Pacifico* to Bluefields on the *Atlantico* and in-between in the districts of Matagalpa, Jinoteca, Esteli, and Chontales.

The objective of Witness for Peace is to render accurate non-partisan information describing the impact of U.S. foreign policy on the people of Nicaragua. Its commitment to the diplomacy of non-violence involves staff members in the work of investigating and documenting all incidents of harassment, terrorism, and violence against the people, including acts of FSLN as well as Contra aggressions. Only testimony from eyewitnesses is acceptable and used to document these episodes.

The 1986 Witness for Peace on-the-scene testimonies, **"What We Have Seen and Heard in Nicaragua,"** includes these reports:

> *"On a Sunday afternoon 20 men were kidnapped by the contras from the countryside surrounding Achuapa.*

The bodies of 13 were found in a ditch a week later. The campesinos who found the decomposing bodies, covered with rocks and logs, located them by their smell. All the remains showed signs of torture: cut out tongues, stab wounds, empty eye sockets, severed fingers and toes, castration. Most of the dead had been so badly tortured they were difficult to identify."

"Natividad Miranda Sosa was kidnapped and held for nine months along with her four daughters, ages 20, 15, 13 and 11. Her oldest daughter Aureliana, was delivered to the contra leader known as 'El Gato.' The rest of the women were held captive by the contra leader called 'El Gavilan.' They were given little to eat or drink, were constantly guarded, and raped again and again.[4]

The Sandinistas neither facilitate nor frustrate WFP investigations. Its findings are communicated to the Nicaraguan and U.S. governments and to international human rights organizations without the burden of censorship. As a consequence of the WFP's even-handed commitment to justice and nonviolence, Miguel d'Escoto, Nicaragua's Minister of Foreign Affairs, credits the Witness for being a significant part of the barricade against a wholesale invasion by United States military.

While the WFP lives and works in Nicaragua with the permission of the government, that authorization does not include any assurance that its members are entitled to special Sandinista protections. Over the years, Long-Term personnel and Short-Term sojourners have been allowed into sections of Nicaragua where others are forbidden, including the war zones. When its members have been kidnapped by the Contra, there are no dramatic interventions by the Nicaraguan army to hasten their rescue. Again and again we were reminded that the Witness does not travel in the *campo* with military escort, eschews any protection other than that afforded the ordinary *campesino*, and under no circumstances will tolerate its members carrying weapons.

Permission for unrestricted travel and exemption from the censorship of reports is not evidence that *Acción Permanante* is in cahoots with the Sandinistas. WFP is no unwitting puppet, or unsighted apologist for Sandinista programs and policies. It receives no financial assistance from the government or other perquisites that would make living and working in a nation at war some kind of tantalizing proposition.

REFLECTION: "All Wars Are Civil Wars"

Sociologists use the German word 'Weltanschauung' when referring to a person or culture's 'world view.' It's a coherent conception of the world, including society and its institutions, as seen by a person or group from a particular value system. As a philosophy of universe, it is the lens through which we see life, interpret it, and try to make some meaningful sense out of the hodgepodge.

World-view lens crafters are the traditional institutions of culture; families, schools, churches, mass media, and that magisterium of temporal power — the government. Obviously this business of creating and polishing a Weltanschauung is an important enterprise, a powerful project. And it is not immune to abuses. It ceases to be lens polishing and becomes a deceptive and leveraged ax grinding when the tutors tell students what they are seeing instead of comparing notes and allowing each to suggest what that means for them. Korea was a 'Police Action.' Vietnam was a 'Conflict.' What I saw were wars. A trifling with nomenclature? I wonder if it feels less fatal to die in a Police Action, or in a Conflict, as opposed to a war? Dead is dead, verbal subtrafuge notwithstanding. Interpretation leaves room for the freedom to debate the messages within perceptions and to haggle over meanings within the social construction of reality. It's sacred space, since the signification of reality is always arguable.

But when someone puts their glasses over your eyes, that's meddling. Be it a parent, a peer, a pastor, a lover, or Uncle Sam, the bottom line is the same; someone's tinkering with your lucidity. When you can't say with any self-confidence,

'I spy with my little eye . . .' you are disposed of a selfhood. Consigned to the status of a non-fully functioning and dependent person, you become a victim. You are weak while others are strong, powerless against the controllers of even your most precious personal environments — the faculty of sight and the interpretative function of mind. Persons become authentic selves when they learn to see truly through their own eyes. They become discerning when they trust their mind and senses to detect the real from the unreal.

Discernment involves nit-picking your world view. It means discovering how that lens has been ground. It notes the conditionings that have formed the bailiwick of that value system, the impulses that flesh-out what is esteemed to be the good, the true, the beautiful. Discernment invites radical doubt, invites questioning what we have been conditioned to take for granted, invites keel-hauling the basic assumptions of value that impregnate our world view with meaningfulness. Is more always better? Is bigger always best? Is happiness hinged to having? Is pleasure morally preferable to pain? Is suffering always to be avoided, at all costs, whatever the costs? Is self-denial sick? Is my nation always right and its critics dangerous enemies? And if my answers to these questions are 'Yes,' is that because I am discerning? Or is it because I am enchanted with affluence and the economics of consumerism, betwitched by power, drugged by the politics of hedonism, and rather enjoy the privileges that are mine as a product of the Western mirage-making world view machine?

Discernment implies that we come to terms with the limits of that lens, the blind sides created by human frailty; our inclinations to pettiness, our foibles, lusts, and cruelties. In the social matrix, discernment demands that we locate ourselves within networks of prejudice; our racisms, ageisms, sexisms, classisms, and jingoisms. Simply put, it is a quest for critical self-consciousness, from the underside, the shadowside. Inevitably it is a slow and particular process; a day-labor that comes bit by bit, a scrap here, a scrap there. And it hurts. Nietzsche said, "All truths are bloody truths for me."

41

Fear and trembling are the gut reactions to this precipitate shakedown, this shaking of the foundations. Typically it is a dance that you put on your card reluctantly. On the other hand, if the lens through which you look at life and your place in it generate impressions that look like the reflected imagery from the funny mirrors at a carnival, you may wish to fashion one afresh, grind one free from old distortions. And if that's the decision, welcome to the dance!

But the dance of discernment is no frivolous fandango. It is frightening in its prospect and lonely in execution. Taking off the glasses of the old world view means that you find yourself alone in a strange place where fear is the master of ceremonies calling the tune. Moreover, the dance floor is poorly illuminated. It's dark. Shadowy. Unable to see, you feel doomed to a perpetual clumsy bumping around, hitting walls, falling down into cellars, until feelings of uselessness and futility preside like unwelcome ghosts. Nothing you possess, no relationship, no job, no reputation will put a candle's worth of flicker onto that bleak arena. They aren't worth spit when you're naked, when you're alone, when you're vulnerable and witless. Eventually you begin to suspect that you've suckered yourself. Played the fool. John Wayne isn't riding to the rescue with a lantern in hand. The undaunted don't trifle with the gutless. Superman won't trade you his eyes. Besides, what have you got that's worth bartering? The Kryptonite of your blind fear? If he's not cornered in some closet, he's too smart to trade-down.

No more smug certainties. Pretentious arrogances have evaporated. Mythic fantasies are futile. Toughness flees, surefooted confidence vanishes. As you braille that lonesome domain, the impression grows that the reconnaissance maps of the old world view were the very charts that brought you to this unlit place. So what's left? With a blind past, a confusing and perhaps unknowable present, when the word 'future' does not find its way toward the tongue, what's next?

Collapse. You've hit the big wall. Bottomed out. And when that's accepted, you have a choice. A bullet in the mouth is one of them.

Another option is to begin re-focusing through a new lens. Christians call it *metanoia*, turning around. Break-loose begins with breakdown. The old eyes that gazed on old maps have got you nowhere. Nowhere but boggled and bogged, lost and lonely. So you confess it. Reluctantly, at first, but with the grudging resolve of the jinxed, you accept it. And that admision of powerlessness and helplessness is no mediocre event. But it is a beginning.

On the Damascus road, Paul was dramatically knocked off his high horse. The man was shot right out of the saddle. And when the fellow hit the ground, his weltanschauung glasses fell off. Moreover, the mule stepped on them. Glasses shattered, the bottom he hit wasn't only the one tucked under his belt. The one undergirding his world view was also gone, and with it, his identity, his mission, and the old life. The man was ready for conversion; for new eyes, a new dance, a new life. And since God is insufferably gracious with fools, finally he was offered light and power sufficient to pick himself up, dust himself off, and set out on a new road. And he didn't stop hollering about it until the moment he died. He's probably still screaming about being 'born again.' "Once was lost but now am found, was blind but now I see!" It's the hoot called Amazing Grace.

And if conversion is resisted, what are the options? Persisting in fear? Living in blindness? Death? I remember the old Texan lore about rattlesnakes in August, that period when the reptile allegedly sheds its old skin. During this transition the snake is immobile and blind while the skin comes off, like when we pull a sweater overhead. At the slightest nearby movement the snake is stricken with terror. If an object touches its body it lashes out blindly sinking its fangs into the spot that has been touched. The deadly venom is released into its own body. The result is death, the bullet in the mouth trip, suicide. That's the price paid for deciding to remain blind.

And it's as apt an analogy for a nation as it is for persons. Out on the dance floor, fussing with the lenses, wondering about this business of *metanoia*, I ask the question born of

43

that snake story: How long can my fear-driven country continue to strike out blindly, destroying itself piece by piece? We were the blind snake in Vietnam. And what do we have to show for it? One long wall of names in Washington and more walking wounded than there are tombs in Arlington's garden of stone. Do we really hanker for more?

Have we so perfected freedom, justice, and the American-way that we have a righteous mandate to compel the nations of earth to memorize our ideology, mimic our political economy, and wear the glasses of world-view U.S.A.? Ask those who live in the blind-spots, beyond the sighted range of our much touted mythic image, those for whom the 'business of America' is the no-business end of a hard stick. Ask our homeless living on the streets with no warm or safe place to lay the head. Ask our 20 million hungry for whom the empty belly is the norm and not the exception. Ask the farmer whose land has been foreclosed what he thinks about the world's rural poor and their demands for policies of land reform. Ask the welfare mothers living in hovels with diminished support for food and health or child care. Ask the under-employed and the unemployed if they would rather have decent jobs or $70 billion's worth of B-2 and Stealth bombers. Ask the foot soldier at the Army's Fort Ord, without adequate housing or paycheck sufficient to feed his family, ask him what he's fighting for as he boards a plane for a midnight flight to Honduras. Ask the man in an over-crowded prison what he thinks of white-collar crime, Wall Street scandals and Milken's bilked billions. Ask the junkie going through the hell of Jones-coming-down what it means to join the First Lady in a chorus of 'Just say no.' Ask the woman whose been raped whether it felt like a degrading sexual experience or a criminal and profound violation of her person in an act of violent assault. Ask the elderly who get to choose between one out of three; food or shelter or health care. Ask the families whose loved ones are hostage in Lebanon why Colonel North can maneuver illegal weapons deals with Iran's Iatollah to finance Contra war when they remember Reagan's rant about not negotiating with terrorists.

Only a blind snake could be so easily self-deceived, so obsessed with folly, as to believe that ours is not only the best, but a perfected world view. An Old Testament vengeance carries on the wind.

I am a North American patriot and a partisan. Only the lenses I wear see it and define it differently from the likes of the President and Colonel North. Their definition of patriotism is none less than a strategy to renovate the 19th Century sphere-of-influence politics whose single aim was world dominance, the protection and expansion of our nation's fragile affluence, the propping up of our international prestige — our superpower mania.

I dispute these ambitions and I refuse to be a cheerleader for our foreign wars. The War on Poverty was lost before a second shot was fired. The War on Drugs is a duplicious smokescreen. The War Against Terrorism is a hypocritical scrimmage. And the wars against unemployment, inflation, the pollution of our global environment, what are they? Skirmishes. Any numbskull knows that war on our staggering national debt has not even been declared. My sense of justice is outraged. And against Reagan and North's patriotic fervor, a profound mood of shame and humiliation sours my spirit and gravels my temper.

Small wonder the peoples of the world resent our posturings and resist our murderous assaults and thinly veiled clandestine interventions in their affairs. Small wonder that a growing number of people at home are dissenting, protesting this subversion of the democratic principles on which our republic was founded. Williams James said, "God may forgive your foolishness; the nervous system never will." I doubt that God is prone to overlook such blatant hubris and its concomitant self-destructive obsessions. These infatuations carry a heavy tax that bankrupts the spirit faster and more assuredly than it wrecks similar catastrophe on the treasury.

The only Weltanschauung worth a shout is the whole earth, the entire human family. Anything less is too small, too obsolete, too lethal. The humane fact is that we are one people; there are no decisive separations between us. By my reckoning

45

of the Christian understanding there is neither east nor west nor south nor north, dark nor white, Jew nor gentile, male or female, and certainly no alien or foreigner in Christ. And 'in Christ' means not only those who belong to the Church, but all those for whom Christ died: The whole human family.

All wars are civil wars, wars within the one human family, wars against sisters and brothers. And while we are called to be one another's keeper, this does not imply that we are ordained to be their policeman, their Big Brother, or their lens crafters. It means to be concerned for their good, for their life — not their death — for their right to choose their own form of life, a life the way they see it, even when it does not resemble the choices we make for our own.

OBSERVATION: "The Work of Non-Violence"
June 12

There in Orozco's salon, we began the training exercises designed to probe the spots where as individuals we have a tendency to lose our nerve. Most of us had been through equivalent procedures before; in the movements for Civil Rights, in anti-war actions, demonstrations in support of a new environmental consciousness, resistance to the proliferation of nuclear power technologies, standing with Cesar Chavez and the United Farm Workers. Selma, Chicago, Delano, Diablo Canyon, the Naval Weapons Depot at Concord; such were the places where we tested the grit of our commitments to non-violence, put our feet underneath our mouth and stood to the line.

Albeit, that line is harder for those who do not enjoy access to the comfortable and gracious life of the law's protection and comparative wealth. Mostly we are complicitors in a world of violence; seldom its willing perpetrators, and even more rare, its direct targets. Deprivation, brutality, imprisonment, these are not our daily portion. Our risks are small. Symbolic. So we make a gesture, risk a little, to stand for a moment beside people for whom life is indeed nasty, brutish, and short. Together on that dance floor we hold a candle against the darkness and pray that someone will see its glimmer. Maybe turn on the lights.

46

We remain fledglings in this work of non-violent resistance. And we stand present before our need to remember and recondition the character of our commitment. We ask ourselves, where are our pressure points — the powder kegs — the private places where the candle might ignite hidden combustible materials? What are they?

In the case of this Celt it would be a loss of temper, the masquerading twin of fear. Forced into a corner with my back against the wall, caught between a rock and the hard place, in a situation riddled with danger and panic mounting, would I forget, weaken, abandon my commitment and erupt in a flash to lash out with violence?

A team member was instructed to stand before me, his nose a scant four inches from my own. That posture alone is guaranteed to clinch my gut and send Code Blue messages throughout my system. Like a Marine Corps Drill Instructor, driven with hostility, words of derision spattered against my face. The air between us filled with distempered belligerence.

I knew it was a set-up. This was an exercise. We were play-acting. He was posturing, trying to get his finger on my buttom. "Stooge," "Dupe," he snarled. Decide, Roberts. Would I retaliate, catch him in the groin with my knee? If his right hand so much as quivered, would I pre-empt the blow and slam my own fist into his face? It was showdown time, Gary Cooper at "High Noon." This artifical adversary was calling me out, calling my bluff. Would he succeed, finger that irrepressible nerve, or was my commitment to non-violence more than a callow bluff, something deeper, locked in the bedrock of my faith?

Maybe the saints have it down pat, but for most of us there remains a potential and a possibility for retaliation. Few are exempt. Perhaps it is an automatic reaction of the nervous system, the heritage of the gene pool. What sudden and crucial decisions involving our own safety and that of the group might cause us to implode? Or explode? What fears, stark and precipitate, might flood us with desperation, have such a dead-weight advantage over us, become so deeply terrifying that we could be seduced into deadly combat? After all, we are the product of a panic-ridden culture, a political society gone mad in its obsession with 'security.'

Other exercises seemed less combustible. The intent was to create within us a sense for what it felt like from the underside, the non-Anglo, non-affluent, non-powerful side. But for most of us this would be only a 'sense,' not a full-bore understanding. I can never be poor, not in a real way. Even if I relinquish the tight grip on my possessions, the fact that I can choose to do so marks me as a person of privilege. At best I can only imagine what that feels like. I resolve to increase my capacities for compassion. I nudge myself in the direction of places generally occupied by shadows, the place of the 'other.'

We began to identify in ourselves the non-obvious and non-public fragments where we resemble the targeted persons of the world. What does it feel like to be a minority? To stand with the back against the wall alongside the disinherited? To share the space of the weak in the midst of a larger dominant group? To find oneself unprotected when confronted by the controllers of political, economic, and social life?

Sue Severin instructed us to cluster together at one side of the salon. Furthermore, she insisted this exercise would be observed in total silence. No snickering, no conversation, no questions. Silence!

Several statements would be made, one at a time. If they applied to us we were to move out from the group and stand in the center of the hall. Then we were to look at ourselves, those who stood with us, if any, and those who were now separated from our midst. The Haves and the Have-Nots. The Majority and the Minority. The Over-Class and the Under-Class.

It began: "Those who are non-white, move to the center." Shuji and Dorothy separated themselves from us. I watched them go. After a long minute, Sue called, "Those who are not citizens of the U.S.A., step to the center." Dorothy returned to the larger group but Ellen, the West German, and Bill, the Canadian, joined our Japanese friend who stayed put.

Sue continued calling us out, her statements pounding the ear, the slow cadence of a deep drum. "Those who grew up in poverty . . ." "Those who have spent time in jail . . ." "Those who are over fifty years old . . ." Two members in that small circle. "Those who have ever been the victim of racism . . . sexism . . ." On and on. "Those who have ever been called fat . . ." "Those who have been abused sexually . . ." "Those who have lived with alcoholism or other drug addictions in the family . . ."

Early on I wore my tough-guy posture, thumbs hooked into my belt. Soon the arms were hanging limp at my side. Powerless. Vulnerable. Defenseless. Would the next statement apply to me? The distance between the groups there in Orozco's salon could not be measured in feet. It loomed like a chasm.

What if I were too embarrassed to speak the truth with my body and move out if the call caught me at a tender point? Would I lie? Why share this information with strangers? It's stupid, no, it's dangerous folly to offer some information into the hands of persons who, at some later time, might convert it into ammunition. Damn these California-type encounter games. Be gone this pre-fab and pseudo-intimacy rubbish. To hell with the forced march into so-called authenticity.

Again and again we were reshuffled like cards in a deck, each statement ringing in our ears, waiting for the one bearing the imprimatur of a piece of our identity, who we were. In the silence, underneath a layer of resentment, I could smell my dread. What if the Joker in my own deck were called? Who wants to be branded, wants to come out of their secret closet, wants to abandon the safety net of being in the majority? How many times did I make that trek? Two? Three? Maybe more. I lost count.

Finally it was over. "Lay down," was the instruction. "Breathe slowly." "Stay quiet." "Go deep within." "Brood on how you feel."

Flat on my back on the hardwood floor, emotions were going over me like a rusty chain through a dry winch. There was information about me, who I was, where I had come from, that was now the property of the group. But strangely enough, breath after breath, I began not to care. It wasn't an abject resignation, the capitulation of the looser. It felt more like a relief. Keeping secrets requires energy, constitutes a drain on the resources of the emotional life. When they are voluntarily exposed, put out onto the table top, they lose their threatening power.

It was mysterious, but it worked. Now, if someone wanted to cajole or mock me with that information, I could not be molested with bitterness. Cold, hard, and deadly fears were being replaced with a sense of fellowship. No deception here; I had not magically ceased to be male, affluent, a privileged citizen of the most powerful nation in the world. But there were parts of me, generally hidden, where a sense of kinship allied me with the minority; I had been divorced, was no stranger to addiction, bore in my body the working process of chronic illness. But around that, my bundle of resentments was shrinking, and with it, the desire to justify myself, defend myself, to strike back.

REFLECTION: "A Weapon Seldom Selected-Love"
June 12 9:00 p.m.

Time to 'center down,' that Quaker phrase made all the more appropriate by our presence in the Friend's meditation room. Time to cease from that which wearies the spirit. My mind was fatigued from over-working. The lectures and exercises of the day had worn down my alertness; nothing was left but numb edges. Opening to a moment of plateau in Orozco's studio, in the hush of quietness I allowed the heart to cradle the intellect. No more focusing on the labor of our team-a-birthing. No more preoccupation with the sufferings of war's violence, the hunger of the starving, the ache of the widow, the loneliness of the orphan. Even Jesus took time for ingathering, separating himself from the crowds and disciples to spend moments in spirit-nourishing solitude. To press on at this point would be foolish, would invite a drought to settle over the soul leaving in its path a withered and parched heart.

50

Following moments of silence, we shared descriptions of the territory of spirit that we passed through during the afternoon, swapped the lore of the road we traveled during the day, paused to 'love ourselves with integrity and reflect with discernment.'

The Lakota referred to themselves and other Native Americans as 'human beings.' The White Man was something else; Homo sapien, yes, but not yet human.

Millennia ago, farther back than the records of history reveal, *Australopithecus africanus* appeared on the sky-swept savannah of the African highlands reaching north from the Cape to the lakes of the Nile. Children of all animal kind, we inherited many a social nicety from the predatorial ways of these killer apes, our immediate forebears. Even in the first long days of our beginnings we held in our hand a weapon, an instrument somewhat older than ourselves. The man-ape used the humerus bone of an antelope as a cudgel to kill its prey. Systematically, effectively, efficiently, and repeatedly the creature used this bone and bequeathed it into history as the first tool; a weapon, a blunt instrument intended for inflicting death, for killing.

Discernment. That which differentiates us from our ape forebearers, the distinguishing nobility of genus Homo sapien, is located in none else than a demonstration of rational capacity. And the first evidence of manifest intelligence was the deliberate and calculated use of a tool. A weapon. Indeed, we've come a long way. More and more Homo sapien all the time. First we extended our arm with a club, then developed spears and bows, invented gun powder, and, finally, nuclear arsenals. Now we prepare for war in the heavens; 'Star Wars!' From feeding ourselves to defending ourselves to destroying ourselves. Yes, we've come a long way!

The applied sciences of physics and engineering advance upon the human stage diverse instruments of war. We marvel at their complexity, the genius behind their research and development. The human mind is capable of astounding ingenuity. But what about the spirit? Is it likewise able to comprehend and adapt to these devices that destroy and threaten annihilation? What moral calculus suffices to becalm the soul agitated by these prospects? And what feat of ethical engineering stands adequate to the task of quieting the conscience in the face of modern war? How do we balance the faculties of mind with the need for nurturing the heart, for honoring the quiet but persistent cry of spirits that hunger for the gentle touch?

While Homo sapien revels in master works of technology, the disciplines of meditation and contemplation need be cultivated if we are to enter the realm of becoming 'human beings.' And the distance between these levels of being requires a quantum leap of soul. What must we learn if we are to walk gently upon the earth with reverence in each footfall and in graceful thanksgiving for the company of our sisters and brothers? What must we learn if we are to leave no scars on our path, but the lingering sweet bouquet of a loving touch?

The Buddhist monk is a master of careful walking, touching the earth gently, caressing it non-violently with deferential respect. But these same monks were also among those who quietly, dramatically, and ever so fatally surrendered their own bodies in non-retaliatory objection to the wars in Asia.

Deep Is the Hunger is a collection of meditations from the marvelous searching spirit of Howard Thurman. One of them tells the story of an ancient Buddhist monk and it carries to me a lesson about non-violence.[5] A village lived in fear of a violent cobra that persisted in dealing death to its livestock and families. On arriving in the village the itinerate monk was surrounded by people telling the story of their plight and beseeching his intervention. The compassionate holy man went forward to address the snake. Petitioning the cobra to spare the village, the snake agreed and ceased its destruction. In the following days the villagers noted the snake's change and began to no longer fear its deadly wrath. The people likewise changed. Now their attitude was driven by a desire for retribution. With the balance of power in the hands of the villagers, they wreaked a cruel revenge on the cobra. At long last the monk returned. Upon encountering the pitiful and suffering snake, the cobra protested its plight with bitterness. Pleading that it had obeyed the monk's command, the holy man remonstrated, "You failed to carefully heed my words. I never told you not to hiss!"

This side of the Kingdom, it is an affirmation of life to oppose with voice and body that which seeks to destroy our right to life. To do less is to be stripped of dignity, to acquiesce and sign a pact with death. So I will stand with the people of Nicaragua, refusing to take up weapons, and hissing like hell in protest of my nation's attempt to demean, thwart, and destroy them.

Against hatred and violence we must find a stronger power, a more substantial courage, a life-affirming vitality that leads to Shalom: Peace within ourselves, between us, and spreading like a blanket of benedictive grace over the daughters and sons of Life.

The exercises of the day were well crafted. Appropriate. If there are experiences that seem overwhelming and fearsome dark valleys through which we must pass, we must endure these situations without panic and without rage. Non-violence, both the moral commitment of the heart and its practice, is a style of prayer, the deed before the doing. We put aside the shibboleths of the past, stop the sorry wheel that grinds out wars, and stand still in silence. It's a twilight zone, a place for cease-fire within, a time to cultivate visions, a chance to breathe the air of hope.

It is also a time to reflect and remember. What has human history gained in the attempt to establish peace by using the tools of violence? Have we succeeded? If so, to what advantage? When I lay my head against the pillow tonight, will I feel safer and sleep more sound knowing that the enemy is kept at bay by Tridents prowling the submariner depths? When the sun rises, will I feel more secure because airborne armadas payloaded with nuclear weapons soar in the supernals, out of sight, but seldom out of mind? When I walk to the Plaza and set foot on good honest dirt, can I take comfort from the fact that soldiers numbering in the millions around the world tread the same good earth carrying M-16's and AK-47's? I sleep on a pillow turned to stone against which the head finds no rest; I dream of rainbows in the sky overhead and cringe at the thought of screaming fireballs; the earth under my feet is a pot of gold, and a graveyard.

William Sloane Coffin, speaking of 'The Theological Imperative to Act,' observed that "Power always invites greater power." Historically it involves a curious chronology. The invention of the stirrup provided the mounted warrior with superior power so armor was fabricated as a rejoinder. Large guns sank wooden ships so iron plate was applied to their sides. Machine guns multiplied firepower so tanks were invented. Aircraft begat anti-aircraft artillery and big bombs became superbombs. Finally, the net result in modern times has been an arms race costing humanity five-trillions of dollars. Again, we've come a long way!

No. The fact or prospect of war's violence is not comforting. Not now, not ever. Its strategy is too old, its history too grim, its future too feeble. Any cursory glance at human experience confronts us with the fact that there is an iron law of relationship between ends and means; direct, immutable, unadulterated. We reap what we sow. The attempt to create peace using the contraptions of violence is a contradiction; it yields no basic gain. Like dullards, again and again we try to bend that law or crack the iron of its inflexibility until the impression grows that we are indeed slow learners, perhaps non-learners.

Repeatedly we unfurl the patriotic banners, mobilize the military, accelerate the industrial impulse, and beat the drums of war as we go forward to engage the adversary. Like King Kong, we pound our chest, bare our fangs, make all manner of gruesome threatening noises, and then unleash violence in a torrent of destruction.

We reasoned that we could stampede the North Vietnamese with a deployment of overwhelming kill-power. Surely our rampage would resemble the wrath of God, strike fear upon their hearts. It was only a matter of time until they would cry

'Uncle.' But they didn't stampede in gutless disarray; they went underground to time and target their retaliation with precision. Not dissembling in fear, they converted trepidation into the fuel of resistance. And the only cry of Uncle that could be heard was a term of endearment, an affectionate homage paid to 'Uncle' Ho; it was never accompanied by the white flag of surrender and a plea for mercy.

So what makes us think that variations on the King Kong strategy will work against the Sandinistas? It hasn't worked for us in Nicaragua for 134 years. Why should it now? How many times do we need to make world-class chumps of ourselves, parade our capacity for self-deception, and demonstrate once again the painful, deadly, and costly futility of not learning the simple lesson about sowing and reaping?

But if we must pick up a weapon, I believe there is an alternative to the ones Bill Coffin described and lamented. We can choose another weapon. Perhaps the authentic moral stature of a person is determined by the choice of weapons they select. Non-violence is to choose an armor; one that does not inspire fear, though it's opponents despire it; one that does not breed retaliation, though its challengers resist it; one that can confront evil, though the realists dismiss it; one that has created social change, though the practical distrust it.

But it does require significant spiritual maturity to risk its use. Nobody denies that. Of all weapons, love is the most powerful and disarming. Few there be who dare trust their fate into its hands.

OBSERVATION: "Tortured in El Salvador — Revolutionary Nurse or FMLN Guerrilla?"

June 12 — 11:30 p.m.

Sitting on the curb in front of the Casa, smoking the last cigarette of the day, out of the side of my eye I noticed a man walking in my direction. When it appeared as if he would pass behind me, I decided to stand, move two steps into the street, and turn around. No need to present myself as a hapless target for a mugging. Did he sense my uneasiness? Either out of politeness or caution, he stopped in the middle of the street, a safe distance for both of us. With an informal salutation, he asked permission to join me for a cigarette at the curb. I agreed.

His Spanish hit me like white-water rapids. Telling him that this Yankee spoke only second-hand Tex-Mex often salted with inadvertent and clumsily inserted French, he smiled and agreed to speak slowly, distinctly.

Asking if I was staying at the Casa, I nodded. Immediately he inquired if I was a member of *Accion Permanente Christiana por la Paz* heading for Managua. Who was this man? How did he know about Witness for Peace?

His name was Mario Ossamu Nomura. The El Salvador delegation of the International Committee of the Red Cross recently secured his release to Mexico City. He needed surgery for the removal of part of his right lung and medical treatment for Paragonimos Westermanis, an exotic parasite he contracted during twenty-eight months of imprisonment and torture in El Salvador. Having said that, straight away he requested that I deliver important documents to John Long at the Witness for Peace house in Managua.

I hesitated and did not consent immediately to be his courier. Why was I being solicited for this mission? What was the urgency? Quickly he added that I was free to examine the papers and make a final decision in the morning. That would not be difficult. He was also staying at the Casa.

We went inside and Mario disappeared to his room to retrieve the documents. I waited in the library, tired, perplexed. He returned and handed me a spiral-bound file containing photocopies of various letters, statements, and medical records.

On the letterhead of the '*Comite Internacional de la Cruz Roja Delegacion en El Salvador*', a letter signed by Lucienna Annichini, the Coordinator of that Red Cross agency, stipulated Mario's name, nationality, date of birth, and the dates, plus locations of his imprisonment in El Salvador. The letter was dated, January 8, 1988. He was Brazilian, born December 11, 1952, and had been imprisoned in *El Desta Camento Militar No. 4 de Morazan* on January 24, 1985. He was subsequently released from the **Centro Penal de Mariona** on September 11, 1987. CICR physician, Dr. Jacques Stroun, confirmed the severe impairments to Nomura's health and agreed with doctors from Medics of the World that he needed care that only an advanced center of medical technology could provide.

Leafing through the binder I read fourteen pages of testimony which Nomura offered on April 15, 1987, to the Non-Governmental Commission On Human Rights (CDHES) in El Salvador. This affidavit was made from his bed in *Hospital Rosales*, in San Salvador.

Reading the document was a passage through a chamber of horrors. The details of his arrest, the two plus years of electro-shock and hallucinatory drug applications, multiple beatings around the head and genitals, isolation and food and sleep deprivation, it was a loathsome scenario. At one point his hands and feet were tied and he was lowered head first into water mixed with urine, cockroaches, and the floating corpses dead rats.

Accused of being a North Korean mercenary, the affidavit alledged that former U.S. ambassador to El Salvador, Thomas Pickering, and Colonel James Stealer of the CIA interrogated him on at least two occasions. The following bill of particulars stipulated their charges against Nomura:

1. That he was a Brazilian communist member of Batallion America.
2. That he was a mercenary communist contracted by Daniel Ortega and sent to El Salvador.
3. That he had been trained in Libya, Cuba and Nicaragua and was a specialist in explosives. That he had the rank of a guerrilla commander and among other things he trained women and children in guerrilla acts.
4. That one of his principal missions was to destroy the country's economy, dynamiting bridges and electric plants, schools and hospitals.
5. That Ortega in the next few months was going to send groups of Palestine trained suicide commandos to El Salvador.

6. That as a commando he earned a thousand dollars a month and that he had participated in the destruction of Puente de Oro.[6]

In Part III of the document, Nomura contended that during one of Pickering and Stealer's interrogations, they were accompanied by Colonel Ricardo Aristides Cienfuegos, Director of COPREFA, who presented Nomura with the above allegations in the form of a confession. He was to commit them to memory. El Salvador's President Napoleon Duarte was scheduled to present this infamous guerrilla commando to the national and international press. If Mario fessed-up to the charges and renounced his loyalty to Batallion America and Daniel Ortega, he would be released, given 100,000 U.S.A. dollars, and a plane ticket out of the country to the destination of his choice. On the other hand, in the event that he refused to cooperate, his future was bleak — more torture and death.

Nomura wanted to know the meaning of these accusations. One of the gringos collaborating with Pickering and Stealer attempted to offer an explanation:

> *"That the U.S. Government had been fighting an internal battle with Congress, to put into effect 100 thousand [million] dollars in aid to the contra but that the government needed proof and testimonies against the Sandinista regime with the end result of changing the North American public opinion to believing that the main enemy of democracy on the Central American continent was Daniel Ortega and Nicaragua. And that furthermore, Daniel Ortega was the supreme commander of the Salvadorean and Guatemalan guerrilla armed forces. Ortega sustains the terrorists in El Salvador with arms and dollars and he has a plan to take terrorism to North American territories. If the U.S. Congress approved the aid to the contras, the Reagan government would be helping the Nicaraguan people as well as the Central American isthmus and in this way would prevent the exportation of the Marxist-Leninist revolution by Daniel Ortega and his*

*alliances. The CIA had proof that Ortega was going to
send suicide commanders trained by the PLO and
financed by Kadafy to El Salvador to commit attempts
on lives of high political officials, military officials and
U.S. Embassy personnel which represents U.S. interests
in El Salvador. After all this, all of Latin America would
be in danger and it was because of this that the aid to
anti-Sandinista forces was so vital to the interests of the
U.S. Government.*"[7]

According to the affidavit to the Commission, "He
[Nomura] said he had never been a guerrilla or a terrorist.
Rather, he was an International Brigadista who had come to
El Salvador because of the need to help thousands of civilian
children, women, and elders who were victims of brutal and
irrational air bombings, beatings, massacres, and tortures. He
said he had come to El Salvador as a nurse to help the civilian
population affected by the war."

When Nomura refused to cooperate with their scheme, the
persecutions began again. In his testimony he said that Lieutenants Cisneros and Quinanilla, his principal torturers, threatened to kill him with a rifle, fastened electrodes to his penis
and left ear and shocked him repeatedly, injected him with
massive doses of drugs, pulled teeth from his mouth with pli-
ers, broke his ribs, and removed his toenails from both feet.

Eventually, the CICR (International Red Cross), Amnesty
International, the Non-Governmental Commission on Human
Rights of El Salvador, the Archbishop of San Salvador, the
Brasilian Embassy, and other international agencies succeed-
ed in negotiating his release.

I agreed to deliver the file to John Long in Managua. He
thanked me and we said goodbye. I also decided to xerox the
documents and keep a copy for myself though I had no idea
what I would do with them.

REFLECTIONS: "Death isn't bad: Getting there can be hard."

Certainly there are fates worse than death. Shortly before he died, my father was the one that said, "Death isn't bad: Getting there can be hard." Dad was not trying to be cute or amuse himself with a clever turn of phrase. He looked me straight in the eye when he said it and neither of us chuckled. His Christian faith assured him that death was neither the final enemy nor something to fear. And he knew that getting there could be hard. Late in life he developed multiple sclerosis and struggled with progressively diminishing capacities for eight years before dying. He knew about hard.

I believe that Mario knew in both flesh and spirit just how hard getting to death can be. I wondered if he ever prayed for death, the arrival and touch of a benevolent reprieve, the merciful release into a domain beyond suffering and unremitting pain.

I do not know. In truth, there is much about him that remains in the shadows, that hovers there on the borderlands beyond all knowing of facts. I suppose I know his name, perhaps where he was born, that his hair and beard and eyes are black, that his nose is *aquilino* and his mouth is normal. All of this was apparent to the eye, was the description on the *Título De Nacionalidade* prepared by the Brazilian Consulate in San Salvador. And I believe he has suffered; the lines of lingering pain were deeply etched into the creases around his eyes, so much so that he squinted in the near darkness sitting there on the curb.

But what about the cultures that wove themselves into the fabric of his experience of living? What were the anvils upon which the principles of his political loyalties were pounded out, the crucibles where his faith was forged? Of these I knew little. What was it that impelled him to risk throwing his life like dice onto a table where all that he knew and loved and cherished could be gambled and in an instant lost? Why become a nurse in an International Brigade, or a soldier in Batallion America, which ever? What took him to the battle fields of

60

El Salvador? How had he chosen the purposes along which he determined to live his life, sending it like a rifle shot down a bore towards a destiny that prospected adversity as contrasted to security?

I knew nothing about this intensely private world behind the black eyes, beneath the black hair. These were the precincts of his heart, the hidden recesses wherein lay his uniqueness, his distinctiveness, his unrepeatability. I think of twenty-eight months of imprisonment and torture. To endure such an ordeal suggests that somewhere inside, intimate and exclusive, he had been able to fasten to a teather that secured his life to a purpose beyond mere survival. How did he grasp or touch this thread? With words spoken in meditation or prayer? Through exercises of breathing? Rekindling memories of family or the cherished touch of a lover? Something created a synthesis of resolve that stood him well in coping with his tormentors, in addressing the pain of torture from which there was no outer protection and only faint prospect of reprieve.

I asked questions about Batallion America, his feelings about Ambassador Pickering and CIA Colonel Stealer. Were I to see him again I would ask different questions. How did he choose his path? What were the values that compelled him, that drove him to his feet in speaking aloud his Yea or Nay?

Mario used the word 'revolutionary' and I think of Jesus. Before he was born his mother foresaw that he would 'put down the mighty from their seats and exalt those of low degree'; he would 'fill the hungry with good things and send the rich away empty.' [Luke 1:52] Jesus said of himself that he came to preach good news to the poor and release to the captives. He preached his first sermon on racism and nationalism and the congregation ran him out of town intending to throw him over a cliff. [Luke 4:16-31] His early disciples were dragged from their homes in a riot and charged with "turning the world upside down." [Acts 17:5, 6]

Of all persons, Jesus was a catalyst for revolution. He rebelled against established customs, narrow mentalities, and stiff rituals that passed for religion. To the picture of him as the meek and mild shepherd with lambs in his arms, I oppose the

61

picture of him in the rough dress of a carpenter. He walked hard and dirty roads and had no place to call home. As a teacher, he rode roughshod over the prevailing ideas of property and patriotism. It was no milksop but a rebel who threw moneychangers out of the temple. Jesus was an outlaw who ate with tax collectors and drank with sinners, a dangerous agitator who was put to death as a public menace.

Revolutionaries are not always pleasant people, probably not congenial weekend guests in the homes of polite society. They do not conduct happy revolts and are not led by the sane, the housebroken, the inoffensive. And neither true religion nor rapid social change comes about on the heels of that which is tender, but in the hard currency of sacrifice for human betterment. The Church is meant to be a company for revolution whereby the Gospel is released for the transformation of society. I wondered if Jesus' Church ever opened its arms to embrace and uphold this man named Mario?

OBSERVATION: "The Data is Never All In"

Once again we were reminded that the team leaders have the responsibility to make the final decision about who goes forward to Nicaragua and who does not. If necessary they will cull the herd, separate the sheep from the goats. In all other matters effecting the group, decisions are made by consensus. Schedules, interviews, chores, these are determined corporately. The bottom line is that we must discuss and debate matters until we achieve a common mind, a single focused agreement. Our enthusiasm around a decision may vary, may run hot or cold. But once we offer our individual consent, we pledge our willingness to freight the weight of its consequences with the team.

Yet the consensus process includes an option; we can refuse to collaborate, withhold our approval. One person blocking consensus and the process comes to a dead halt. Obviously this ought not occur for flip reasons or be foisted upon the delegation for light and transient cause. But in the event that someone's inner light causes them to declare a veto, the buck stops there. The group must reconnoiter another path.

That applies across the board — save for the decisions about who will constitute the team. This remains the sole prerogative of the leaders and Long-Termers. These days of training have constituted the third screening of team members. The first occurred when the regional and national staff reviewed our written applications and support documents. A second winnowing took place the day we met as a team for the first time in Berkeley. One potential member elected at that point to join the Veterans Peace Convoy in Texas. Having completed training in Mexico City, the staff would make yet another decision.

If those decisions were mine, how would I make them? Some might be obvious: a person's health fails, suddenly and dramatically, and requires specialized treatment; an individual's commitment to the goals and processes of the Witness is manifestly inadequate; under the stress of training a person collapses emotionally, becomes inordinately dependent, or violence erupts through a fault-line in their character. These would be obvious.

Since none of the more bold impediments to our success have surfaced during the past days, discernment necessitates a keener intuition. Would I have sufficient good will to be fed by facts and remain open to a careful understanding of them — concerning life, my fellow sojourners, myself? How would I energize the imagination so that it might savor all manner of creative possibilities for our fellowship and mission? How to familiarize myself with the flavor of people and their possibilities? Discernment!

REFLECTION I: "The Work of Discernment"

The work of discernment was again on Sue and Dorothy's agenda. I reflected on that process. Roughly put, discernment as a method is akin to the process of decision-making: observe, judge, weigh-up, decide, and act. It's a trip down the rational and intuitive funnel that ends by going through a sieve.

I begin by listening, watching, and using my senses to gather relevant data. Eventually the sensate systems push over and make room for the faculties of reason. It's the mind's turn to sort out patterns, to put order on the chaos. I make preliminary judgments; what's relevant versus irrelevant? Among the left-overs I separate the crucial from the merely important. Options begin to appear. The spectrum of choice narrows. Discernment is taking me through the hoops. I throw each option against the screen of those values around which I purpose to live my life. Some fit, others are discarded. The ones that are left go onto the balance wheel to see if they auger to support my objective or deflect from it. Finally, when the heart and mind are in sync, I decide. When they are not, I go back through the hoops again. Or maybe they resist coming into stereoscopic focus, refuse to move in parallel lines. Sometimes I have to decide whether to follow the intuitions of my spirit, play the hunches, or defer to the rigors of the mind. However that's resolved, finally I must act. I put my words, or my resources, or my body on a line. The line in the dirt is my own, drawn by my hand. It is neither vague nor the handiwork of impersonal fates. I own the process. I am willing to back it personally and take responsibility for the fall-out consequences of my determination. Always, I pray that my observations will combine accuracy with sensitivity, that judgment will be tenderized, my hardness softened, my justice merciful, my actions faithful.

Most decisions, however, are made on the basis of evidence that is never obviously conclusive. Whatever the polestar, seldom does it yield unwavering light in bright and sufficient beam for making easy decisions. Judgments have to be made without complete knowledge of the facts involved. Values compete and contend, array themselves in shades of gray. The temptation is to postpone or defer decisions. I recall the dictun, 'Not to decide is to decide.' This is the precarious burden of power, the anxiety underlying responsibility.

Archibald Macleish said there were only two kinds of people; the Pure and the Responsible. How do I narrow the gap between them in myself? How sweet it would be to see the proper course with surety and navigate with confidence according to those bearings. The burden of justification would be simplified, the lines of cause and effect rendered traceable. But that is my hankering for safe bets and the luxury of a simplified life.

REFLECTION: "A Chicana with Soul"
June 13

I decided to shift moods and begin the day with a quiet prayer of thankfulness for the leader of our delegation, Dorothy Granada.

A former WFP Long-Termer, Dorothy is fifty-seven years old, Mexican-American, and a Registered Nurse with considerable experience in a wide variety of medical and clinical venues. With Charles, her carpenter/author husband, she lived and worked in rural Nicaragua during 1985-86.

Long raven-black hair streaked with gray, skin the color of burnt sienna, she conjures in my imagination the mature version of an enlarged photograph exhibited in Mexico City's Museum of Cultural Anthropology. The black and white photo was taken during their revolution. As I recall the image, a young *compañera* is poised on the steps of a train. Her short-sleeved peasant blouse is gathered at the waist with a sash, a bandoleer with cartridges in the loops hangs over her shoulder. A rogue gust billows her full skirt and flutters the bandana covering her hair. Looking forward, her lips slightly parted over a squared jaw, one foot on the step the other reaching earthward, one hand gripping a handrail the other ranging outward, the glint of anticipation sparkles in her dark eyes. The aura of that alert expectation fills me with inexpressible admiration. Her future squints at her like an ever longer unending question.

I think of the words of Teilhard de Chardin; "I am afraid, too, like all my fellow men, of the future too heavy with mystery and too wholly new, towards which time is driving me."

I am silent.

Seven years ago Dorothy was 'born again,' converted. Married to a physician, she lived on the treadmill of rising expectations and possessed the affluence to secure them. They

65

enjoyed the 'good life;' a euphemism for disengaged decadence. The assignation is her's, not mine. But at some point she realized that values are not neutral and those around which she postured her life where not worth the effort. Asking herself the classic 'Alfie' question, "What's it all about?" on reviewing her life she felt only emptiness. The corroding impact of North American domestic unrest and betrayal, the monotony of her daily round, something felt raw and empty at the place where the desire for wonder and purpose ache for lack of soul nourishment. People get sick at heart not simply because they are not loved; they get sick at heart because they do not give love, do not waste themselves, or expend themselves, or invest themselves without calculation.

The reassurance of a secure income, the quiet security of working inside a respected institution in conventional ways, the sense of well-being that comes from acceptance by everyone because one's thinking is sensible and safe, well, it does bode for a kind of tranquility. But not for the restless heart. There is apt to be no growing edge and very little of the tang and zest of aliveness that only the adventurous spirit knows. It is no accident that the messengers of the ancient gods were symbolized as humans with wings; this, long before Homo sapien ever thought of taking to the air in machines. No, the Mystery of life is an adventurer. And those who would affirm their kinship with the liveliness of life, must ride that train, like the *compañera* of the photograph.

Being 'born again' means that you sense an irresistible impulse to risk yourself for unprovable goals. It means to say 'Yes' to the invitation to commit your life and fortune to an enterprise worth having a legitimate claim on your final devotion. Beginning to see differently and hear the sound of a different drum, Dorothy's feelings and her thinking shifted. No longer was she content to be a spectator throwing the dice at the foot of the cross gambling for trivia. Instead she would live in accompaniment with the poor and oppressed and gamble that the man on that cross would graft his power and strength onto her soul.

To say her life changed would be an understatement. Working with the Mothers of the Murdered and Disappeared in Guatemala, interposing her own body between targeted leaders and Death Squad thugs, identifying friends and children in morgues, being invited by Nicaragua's Foreign Minister, Fr. Miguel D'Escoto, to attend him personally during the Lent 1986 forty-day fast and 'Stations of the Cross' walk from the Honduran border to Managua, yes, her life changed.

Dorothy has a lovely voice, one that would ring clear in stone cathedrals or waft like coiling smoke across valleys; it's a resonant glorification of creation. Her reflection this morning began with the reading of Nicaraguan poetry. Perhaps the words Nicaraguan and poet ought to be taken as synonymous. Is there a woman or man-child of this culture that does not put feeling into the lyrics of words? She shared a poem written by a man imprisoned for his role in the assassination of the elder and first Anastacio Samosa. The poem was composed and smuggled out of jail prior to his being taken to the home of Samosa's son where his execution provided the entertainment for an evening of drunken party.

The poem was recited in Spanish. The haunting beauty of his words, his passionate love of life and family, his dream for a free Nicaragua, my spirit filled with sadness and love. Tears tracked their way down many a cheek in that quiet circle, my own included.

Once again I am reminded that there are many things in life far worse than death. With all its apparent finality and the sting of it, this man anticipated death and felt no dread, no panic. He seemed to know that death is implicit in the fact of life. Even the bullet smashing into brain could not detach him from the dignity he achieved with his living and loving.

While it was not his prerogative to resist death, he did seize the power to determine how he would present himself to the inevitable. We were becoming the beneficiaries of that passion and that spirit which death could not swallow, could not vanquish. His words continue to gift us with an expression of the aliveness of life. And over that, neither the tyrant's hateful cruelty nor the fact of death can prevail.

OBSERVATION: "Signing the Witness for Peace Covenant"
June 13

Sue and Dorothy achieved consensus. All of the team members would continue to Nicaragua. The mid-afternoon schedule will include a ceremony of Covenant, the formal and solemn agreement binding upon those who venture forth with Witness for Peace.

The Covenant includes twelve articles and by chance that equals one for each member of the delegation. Each person elected a portion of the pledge to be read aloud before kneeling in the center of Orozco's studio and signing the corporate document.

The Covenant of Witness for Peace is as follows:

We commit ourselves:

1. To prayerful biblically-based reflection, and unity with one another as the foundation for this project;
2. To non-violence in word and deed as our essential operating principle in Witness for Peace;
3. To honesty and openness in our relationships with one another and with all parties in the conflict;
4. To maintaining the political independence of Witness for Peace;
5. To act in solidarity and community with the Nicaraguan people, respecting their lives, their culture, and their decisions. We will respect guidelines worked out with the Nicaraguan government in regard to our presence and mobility in areas of conflict;
6. To commit time and financial resources as we are able, to Witness for Peace;
7. We commit ourselves to regular communications documenting our witness both within Witness for Peace and to the broader public;
8. To participate in the selection process, training, orientation and evaluation;
9. To participate both in non-violent witness and constructive work projects;

68

10. To be responsible and accountable in our actions to the community of which we are a part and to the principles of leadership which have been established;

11. To record-keeping and documentation of our witness, including reflection on our process, journal keeping, and a final summary analysis before departure;

12. Upon return to the U.S., to share our experience in WFP by participating as best we are able, in the followup programs of press work, public education, and political action.

Someone balked at number six, taking issue with the request to share our time and resources with Witness for Peace. They felt this was unwarranted, onerous, an infringement on their liberties, and inappropriately coercive. They were reminded of the "as we are able" clause that lodges this firmly in the discretion of each individual. We struck a truce, achieved consensus. All of us were willing to sign the Covenant.

REFLECTION: "Ritualizing Our Resolve"

A graduation of sorts. A rite of passage. We ritualized the accomplishment of our days in training by signing a pact. Once again we paused to linger in the re-membering of who we were, whose we were, and what it is that we were to be about together. It was neither sentimental nor immature. The act of kneeling to sign the Covenant summoned the memory of children pricking fingers with a pin, pressing them together while swearing oaths of loyalty unto death; a ritual of fellowship sealed in blood. Even children sense the power within formalized bonds of fraternity. Is that not, finally and at the core, the mystery of Eucharist?

Standing arm linked through arm in a circle, I prayed that among us there would be no Gordian knots to untie, no insurmountable barriers between us during the weeks to come. The candle flickered above the page with our signatures and I was chastened by the power of simplicity; simple props, simple stage, simple gestures, none of which should be underestimated in their not-so-simple significance.

The ceremony of Covenant calls attention to the moral power of fellowship, even as it recognizes the essential aloneness of human life. Perhaps we shall have the integrity of our witness tested against pressures that threaten to devastate. Perhaps we shall find occasion to confirm our commitment to non-violence under withering assault and discover hitherto undisclosed reservoirs of fearlessness. Perhaps in the days to come our reverie will return to this simple ceremony and be nourished by its secretive power. And whether these women and men who are now my sisters and brothers, bow the knee before any altar or confess any creed, in the final analysis, the ceremony alone is authentic, its inner meaning universal.

MANAGUA I

OBSERVATION: "Entering the Land of Nicaro"
June 14

The flight to Managua included a stop-over in Guatemala City. Piercing the veil of clouds, our descent through the mist revealed a city spread out over hills with deep ravines in-between. The turbulent air made for a rough landing on a strip that appeared out of nowhere. When the jet reached the end of the tarmac and turned toward the hanger, I noticed that this ribbon of asphalt looked more like the catapult for a roller coaster. The point of initial touch-down was no longer visible, having disappeared behind one of the summits drifting across the runway. Passengers broke into spontaneous applause, a very audible thanksgiving for having successfully survived this tricky maneuver. One of our delegation, visibly upset by this adventure in aerodynamic gymnastry, swore that if the pilot was going to perform four-point-rolls and hammerheads, on the flight to Managua he was going to ask for a six-pack of beer and stockpile the anesthesia.

Someone remarked that the AeroNica fleet is two time-worn Boeing 727s, both bought used from Greece. Paint peeling off the fuselage, threadbare carpets, emergency air lines falling indiscriminately from the ceiling, it looked haggard. So did the pilot. I wondered if he came with the bargain, thrown in for good measure by the Greeks. Cropduster, stunt pilot, combat jet-jockey — whatever his background — his 'top gun' days were long since past. Perhaps he couldn't shake the notion that this Boeing wasn't designed to dance on the head of a pin.

The flight into Managua made the approach to Guatemala City feel like a kite luffing in a gentle breeze. Wheeling in wild gyrations of pitch and yaw, the 727 was slam dancing through a storm. Below us Lake Managua lay in the crater of Apoyeque, a vague mass black as an ink blot. The city itself stretches from the lake's western shore and climbs upward toward the old volcano's rim. The handful of lights flickering in the distance offered little indication that this sprawling metropolis contained over half of Nicaragua's population of three million.

Descending toward Augusto Sandino International Airport, lightning darted at the wings in intermittent flashes, glaring through the port windows to create an eerie strobe effect in the cabin. It was time to hand it over. I found myself imploring the compassion of God's tender mercies more than trusting the talents of the man at the helm. The storm persisted, gained in intensity. In desperation I invoked the spirit of the revolution's grandfather himself, General Augusto Cesar Sandino.

For seven years between 1926 and 1933, the General's guerrillas harassed and eluded the U.S. Marines. This master strategist and military tactician gave both the leathernecks and Somoza's private army, the National Guard, their first lessons in the helter-skelter of counter-insurgency warfare.

Where the Marines and the National Guard failed in the field, Somoza succeeded with treachery. When the leathernecks departed and Nicaragua was free from U.S. military intervention for the first time in twenty-two years, Sandino and President Juan Bautista Sacasa negotiated a truce. Early in 1934

71

Sandino and Sacasa were dining at the Presidential Palace when Somoza's Guardia disrupted the banquet and kidnapped the General. While Somoza alibied his role in the conspiracy by attending a poetry reading, his troops took Sandino to the airfield we were now approaching. There they executed the rebel leader.

Though Sandino's body was never recovered, it was not inconceivable that a residual of his spirit remained underneath the runway below. When fueled by fear, my imagintion knows no bounds. Perhaps the General's spirit might look kindly on these gringos seeking reconciliation between our nations. After all, I reasoned, if we were to carry the work of peace back into the jaws of the behemoth, the petition for a safe landing seemed altogether sane. My fear-inspired solicitation of Sandino's assistance may have been superstitious nonsense. Nevertheless, it was genuine and timely. Whatever the intervention, *'espiritus dios,'* or *'Sandino vive,'* or the tested and adequate skill of the pilot, something worked! Litanies of 'Praise the Lord' were muttered by a neighboring passenger when the tires squealed on the runway.

Nicaragua! It was a scant four centuries ago that the aboriginal Chief Nicaro extended hospitality to the Spaniards who ventured north from Panama, their nose open to plunder profits. In innocence and pride the chief was an exuberant host, ostentatiously displaying his gold to these guests. Modesty is surely a virtue! These pirates would subsequently relieve him of his wealth and leave little but his name as an inheritance of memory for subsequent generations. And 'in the course of human events' the rest resembles the 'begets' in the Pentateuch's Book of Numbers: gold fever begat Spanish colonialism throughout the Central Americas, which begat British and North American interest in the natural resources of Nicaro's land, which begat the disenfranchised and dissident Nicaraguans, which begat the spirit of Sandinismo and finally the Sandinistas who repudiated the whole bloody begetting business and said the buck or last falling domino stops here!

By the time the raging storm in the clouds reached Sandino's asphalt grave it was transformed into a gentle misting rain.

72

Perhaps even the weather refused to play rough with Augusto's spirit. Through the warm tropical evening air, the sky beyond the western mountains was a deep indigo. In the distance a lone soldier lounged along the siderail under the canopy leading into the terminal. Obviously there are soldiers and there are soldiers. This one seemed young and fatigued, his 45-automatic hosltered. Both arms were comfortably folded across his chest. Threatening no menace, I felt no urge to give the man his space and pass on the wide arc. It would have been an obviously clumsy detour. Besides, it was unnecessary.

Lines! I had been standing or sitting in little else all day; in airports waiting to board the jet, in the aisles waiting to deplane, lines to pay the tax for leaving and then again for entering, customs' lines, passport lines, luggage lines. Purgatory is a long line of waiting. For Godot. For the toilet. For a chance to sit down and smoke a cigarette. Perhaps this was some form of spiritual boot camp, preparation for what lay (I almost said 'in wait') before us. The land of Nicaro is allegedly famous or infamous for its queues. You wait at bus stands, to make a telephone call, at the gates of the Embassy, or before the doors to a Ministry. I don't recall Jesus every saying in the Beatitudes, "Blessed are those who wait; theirs is the Kingdom of Patience."

In the lobby beyond we noticed three friendly faces; Julie, Tito, and Rhonda were the three Witness for Peace Long-Termers who would trek with us for the next two weeks.

Julie Knop is the *responsable*, the person you want to talk to whenever you want to know what's happening or about to happen. The lead WFP Long-Termer from Waslala, she came to Managua from the mountains in order to turn around and take us back into the District. Young, maybe twenty-five, her light brown hair was gathered in a long braid that hung plumbline straight over a hand embroidered Guatemalan peasant blouse.

Peter Davis, in his book **Where is Nicaragua?** reported an encounter with Julie in December 1983 at the border near Jalapa. At that time she was a WFP Short-Termer having come to Nicaragua on a mission such as ours. Back home in

73

Americus, Georgia, she lived and worked on Clarence Jordan's Koinonia Farm. She told David, "If you work for justice, you want to live it out, so I'm here."[8] It also explained why Jordan's experimental Christian ecumenical community was her U.S.A. home. The lady was no stranger to either radical politics or 'put your body where your heart is' faith. Jordan, that feisty renegade Southern Baptist preacher, was creating Liberation Theology and base-community-churches in the bowels of our South about the time she was born. A student at the University of Wisconsin in Madison, she drifted toward Jordan's Koinonia experiment after her spiritual creek ran dry in the Campus Crusade for Christ. Koinonia Farms was a spring-board for her life and work in the land of Sandino. Soon after her Short-Term trip, Julie left Georgia and returned to Nicaragua with Habitat for Humanity. A year of construction work and she joined WFP for the long haul.

Had he not been standing between Julie and Rhonda, Humberto 'Tito' Laurel could easily have been taken for a Nicaraguan. Average in height, coal-black hair, a wide brimming smile that curls upward toward dark eyes circled by black rimmed glasses, Tito is Latino, a Mexican-American from Laredo, Texas. Studying for the Roman Catholic priesthood in San Antonio, he left seminary with two years remaining for ordination and closed rank with the Witness. He was within three weeks of his own return stateside and the resumption of preparation for Holy Orders. But first he would accompany us back to Waslala, the town that had been his home during the year. Comfortable with his Latin roots, Tito was first with the hugs, quick to break into song and passionate in his solidarity with the impoverished poor. Tito was already my kind of priest; tender without being soft, gracious without being officious, kind without being condescending. In the days ahead, he would stimulate many of us to touch our own essential worth. To call him a friend raises a shout of thanksgiving in my heart.

Rhonda Collins was comparatively new to the WFP, but not to Nicaragua. Blonde and disposed to chain-smoking brown cigarettes that were about as long and thin as she was, Rhonda projected the aura of a wiry cool. Something about her suggested a person who has seen much, understood even more, and is hard to frighten. Ask her where she's from and she tells you, "New York City, the Nevada desert, all over. But I took a degree in video art from U.C. Santa Barbara." When not in the field monitoring the war, she's at the editing board in the WFP media office making videos for use in the states. "Nica's reality can't be left to fantasy or hallucination. 'The camera never blinks,' to quote Dan Rather," she offered with a wry smile.

Like Julie, Rhonda also came to Nicaragua as a *brigadista* wielding a hammer with a women's construction project. Now she wallops her convictions into celluloid in the hope of stirring the North American conscience into building and not destroying her Nicaragua home.

And home it is and shall be. "There's nothing left in the states that's worth my sweat. No cutting edge. The struggle to become human there is harder than it is to stay alive here."

I asked her if she planned to become a citizen. "No way. I'll keep my passport. That way I can go home to visit family. Someday, if they stop making war on us, I might reconsider a return." The language made me wince. When I hear it at home, 'they' and 'us' talk always catches me up as being divisive. It's the vocabulary of 'isms,' speaking of other persons as if they were a separate species. But then again I haven't been shot at or driven to the ground by in-coming mortar fire bought and paid for my own tax dollars. If she didn't 'walk the walk' I would be more critical of how she 'talked the talk.'

REFLECTION: "If you can't fight or flee . . . flow!"

We were spent; the tedious flight, hauling luggage and heavy boxes from pillar to post, the continual waiting in lines, underneath the din in the airport lobby you could hear the muted mutterings of our complaints.

In off-hand fashion, Rhonda remarked that a motto for the WFP might be, "If you can't fight or flee — flow!" Her amusement was obvious. Our fatigue and the mild frustrations of the day's travel was obviously not much by comparison to what we might face in our acts of accompaniment. It was neither a slap nor a rebuke. A chuckle.

Flow. Like a meandering stream that spreads itself thin across a delta and is dissipated in the sand? Or like a river deep in its banks, channeled toward some powerful destiny?

These committed Long-Termers have made a decision. They are not building sandcastles at the banks of a quiet stream; they are in the gorge, riding the white water. Products of the traditional North American world-view, they accepted as morally compelling the myths about democratic society and its promises of freedom and justice for all. But the hard realities of political power were something else. The polarization of rich and poor, the fact that those who wield economic and political power offer not a handshake but a half-nelson to those who are its target — these abuses were intolerable.

Furthermore, they determined that these disparities and oppressions were not isolated occurrences but the result of a total system — a coherent network of attitudes, institutions, styles of relation, and power alignments. Joe Matthews defined a cynic as an idealist whose ideals have vamoosed. Long-Termers are not cynics. Neither are they left-wingers full of high-flown talk about the demonic capitalist system but dodging the work of doing anything to change it. Instead they are willing to share in the shaping of a new vision. And they would do it as exiles from the old order.

In the process they were developing an authentic selfhood, a type of maturity that repudiates all oppressive and paternalistic relationships. Perhaps this will succeed in doing little more than discovering and mapping the terrain of an alternative form of personal existence. But they refuse to be boxed in by the old logic that accepts as inevitable the existence of 'haves' and 'have nots.' Whatever the outcomes, they were sloughing off the extraneous conveniences and securities that we regard as necessities back home. If you are unable to leverage the monkey off the back of the dispossessed, at least you don't have to add your own weight to that burden. So they don't. And they do what they can to unfetter the bondaged. That's no pissant mission.

In their presence I was beginning to detect a fresh lift of spirit, a quality of relentlessness and constancy. But at their center, a penetrating sense of calm radiated from their core. It is a gift to those who dare to ride the white water.

I thought of Tito's impending vows: poverty, chastity, and obedience. In their life with the Nicaraguan people these might well be translated to knowing one thing, willing one thing, doing one thing. The ability to bring all the transient impulses and desires of life under the control and direction of a single dedication is of no small significance. As hard as it is to bring our passions and wandering curiosities into the focus of a single purpose, it is even more tricky to find and fashion such a purpose. What an arduous challenge. Finding a goal lofty enough to challenge the spirit and worthy enough to command the consent of both the mind and heart is difficult at best. Despair is the condition of double-mindedness resulting from the heart saying 'Yes' and the mind saying 'No.' The result is worse than simple divided loyalties; it is none less than a distemper of the soul. When a person is at war in their most intimate inward parts, life becomes an uninterrupted tragedy.

When I think of saints, I am tempted to recall people like Polycarp who faced the lions at age 80 rather than throw a pinch of incense on Caesar's altar. Or Joan who heard voices, accepted her calling, and was burned at the stake for her obedience. Or Francis, playboy turned pauper, the friend of creation. Plaster statues painted in pastels, perched in the alcoves and niches of sanctuaries and gardens with bouquets of flowers at their feet, most of the saints are the objects of sentimental piety, obscure in their reality.

Hell is no pastel, quaint, isolated, or obscure reality. I defined it as the condition where people feel no pain, where they are blind to beauty. What makes these times so hellish is the desensitizing of our emotions; we are so callused by violence that we lose our feeling. Indeed, we have gone straight to hell when we become insensitive to human hurt, insensitive to brutality, insensitive to beauty.

The New Testament word 'hagioi' designated saints as persons set aside for special service in God's purpose for humankind. The work of saints is to resensitize our human feelings, to quicken our sense for beauty, to seek a life-affirming balance at the core. For Christians, the communion of the saints is a company of persons who seek a quality of life that they find demonstrated in Jesus. Then with their blood, sweat, and tears the saints try to live it. In this company they see life steadily and see it whole. And if we are bold to count ourselves among their number it is not because we are wild-eyed raving mystics preaching a moldy gospel. We are simple women and men. And we are simply convinced that you cannot kill casually without injuring yourself, without vandalizing eternity, without destroying beauty. Remaining anesthetized to the pain of violence is to sign a pact with the devil.

In this land afflicted with the horrors of war, living among these people struggling to assert the dignity of self-determination, I sense that Nicaragua is indeed giving these Long-Termers a gift. They are among the rare few who have found a purpose worth the focusing of their spirit, a challenge that focuses the rallying of their exertions, and a coherence capable of coupling their mind and heart in common cause.

OBSERVATION: "Managua — City Atop a Graveyard"
June 15

Managua is the capitol of Nicaragua, a nation about the size of the state of Oklahoma with a total population about one-sixth of Metropolitan New York City. It is also a city sprawling around its own cadaver. A vast emptiness prevails at the core of this urban megapolis. Two days before Christmas in 1972, a series of earthquakes centered at the lakeshore leaving roughly eighty percent of the city in ruin. An estimated thirteen-thousand Managuans died instantly. A quarter of a million lost their homes. Factories and large department stores disappeared into deep crevasses; the entrepreneurial backbone of the city virtually collapsed with the buildings.

Sixteen years later Managua still resembled a spoked wheel hanging on around a hollow broken hub. In this sound-stage unreality, the suspicion grows that perhaps a neutron bomb exploded leaving behind the skeletal carcass of towering and disheveled empty buildings flanked by lots covered with vegetation. Block upon block of wasteland and rubble was slowly and reluctantly reverting to dust and weeds. No center and a destroyed past, the visual and visceral impact was chilling.

Immediately following the earthquake, over $300 million flowed from the international community and relief agencies throughout the Americas to assist the Nicaraguans in rebuilding their homes and lives. Tacho, the nickname for the reigning Somoza, skimmed nearly $100 million off the top and banked it in his personal accounts. The oligarchy and the National Guard hoarded commodities flowing toward the disaster. Beans and rice were not freely given to the stricken victims but sold for yet another profit. Emergency shelter and tools for rescue and reconstruction were given to the government without cost by nations rushing to Nicaragua's aid; once again these were sold to the people. For a marginal compensation, international corporations leased construction materials and trucks to the government which never used them for public purposes. It was a vulture's banquet. The profit to those who preyed on the dead, the dying, and the dispossessed was, obviously, one hundred percent! To salt the open wound, Somoza left the rubble undisturbed.

In the face of such an unconscionable and bewildering rip-off, businesses that survived the catastrophe opened their stores and warehouses giving assistance to the poor who were hit the hardest. Against this dramatic solidarity — this compassionate neighborliness — the unvarnished fact of Somoza's greed was self-evident. Out of the ruins a link was forged between elements in the middle-class and the growing revolutionary anti-Somoza alliance. The quake was an exclamation point, an 'act of God,' injected into a desparately fragile political situation.

In 1979, during the final stages of the Sandinistas' revolt, the World Bank loaned the Somoza regime $56 million. Immediately prior to the entry of FSLN troops into the city, Somoza's planes strafed and bombed many of the remaining buildings while the tyrant conducted a raid on the National Treasury. When Tacho and his cronies finally high-tailed it, there was less then $20,000 in the nation's coffers. The Sandinistas inherited an exuberant but financially bankrupt nation and a capitol reduced to rubble. And, as if the new government hadn't enough on its reconstruction agenda, from 1980 to 1982 the World Bank, under pressure from the Reagan Administration, forced the Sandinistas to repay a total of $29 million on the World Bank's development loan to Somoza's Nicaragua. While that works up to a good definition for 'adding insult to injury,' it also stands to the Sandinistas' credit that they had the integrity to make good on an obligation from which the people of Nicaragua derived no benefit whatsoever.

Without funds for repair and reconstruction, central Managua remains a hopscotch of grassed-over blocks and derelict buildings interspersed with shopping districts, government offices, and small businesses. And sandwiched in-between are the working-class barrios and shanties hobnailed together from beaverboard and scrap metal.

REFLECTION: "Life goes not backward nor tarries with yesterday"

Beyond the brute force of a natural cataclysm to unhinge life in the personal or public domain, I am repeatedly awed by the counterpoint; there is another power throwing its stubborn weight against catastrophe to repair and sustain us. In the case of this crisis, the dangerous earth opened to swallow life. The city was reduced to a wasteland with all vestiges of health compromised. But there was at work another impulse pressing forward from nooks and crannies; an urgency to survive, to rebuild, to press forward. Some cumulative momentum refused to stay put in desruction. Life was yet alive. Better yet, life itself is alive! Disintegration is not the last word.

Against the counsels of despair there are deeper affirmations expressing the will to go on, to pick up and grow. Life neither tarries with yesterday nor fixes its gaze in the rearview mirror. This is the core of the core; this is life's own declaration that it is continuous. What a glorious outreach of the spirit.

OBSERVATION: "INSSBI — Sandinistas and Sandalistas"

There are exceptions to the bleak landscape of downtown Managua. In the distance, the fifteen-story former Bank of America building thrusts skyward, a lone sentry on the otherwise low-slung urban horizon. Testimony to an odd justice, the skyscraper now houses government offices and the National Assembly.

To the west, the Intercontinental Hotel survived the catastrophe. Looking like a sawed-off concrete pyramid dug into the side of one of Managua's hills, it failed to collapse.

Our bus rumbled on, its wheels chattering against the cobblestones of Somoza's own bricks. Following the earthquake, Tacho decreed that Nicaraguan city streets be paved. Since the 'Family' owned the brickworks, the materials specified in reconstruction plans called for nothing other than what they could supply. Mile after mile, ten-inch square by four-inch thick pieces of aggregate, shaped like a Jerusalem Cross, were laced together to form a network of roads. During the insurrection, citizens and armed rebels pried these very bricks out of the ground to build barricades thwarting the maneuvers of Somoza's National Guard. And when they weren't stacked to block tanks and bullets, they were broken up and flung at the enemy by hand.

In Managua it's easy to lose all sense of direction. Street signs are noticeable in their absence. Avenues and boulevards converge in traffic circles then disappear. Even the lone skyscraper played hide and seek with my mental compass. There was nothing familiar from which to take or check a bearing. Small wonder that Managuans appear to give circuitous directions. The WFP House is, for instance, *"De donde fue el viejo hospital OCUN, una cuadra abajo, media al norte."*

81

If you don't know where the old hospital is or the block below it, or where to begin going the half block north, well you end up lost in the neighborhood. With so many directions hinged to 'old' versus 'new' or 'was' versus 'is,' you nearly have to tap into the collective memory from Managua's past if you want to find any place in the present.

While street signs are scarce, large billboards abound. In a curious juxtaposition, Hewlett Packard advertises its computers and across the street Aeroflot commends its jets for flights to the Soviet Union. How many Nicaraguans can afford computers? And, of the ones I talked to, most would rather fly to Disneyland than Moscow. Other billboards drove their point closer to home, into the bedrock of transnational reality. One board pictured a woman suckling an infant to her breast, pointing up the fact that mother's milk is superior to synthetic formula. In the other direction the silhouette of a family caught my eye, especially the conspicuous absence of a man. Dad hasn't been lost to the war. The rhetorical question, "Where's the Father?" is answered by letters in bold face; "*El Alcohol*!" Again and again this accent on recovery; from the multiple devastations of war, from natural calamity, from the destitutions of economic poverty, from addictive disease. The Nicaraguan propensity to "tell it like it is" with boldfaced candor was arresting. That itself is the first step in recovery.

It is this aliveness of life that throbs in the Nica spirit lending a rich vitality to everything it touches. Always and anytime, I'll join in solidarity with a person or a people who repudiate our Western penchant for denial, avoidance, and flight.

The bus passed what someone mistook for a maximum-security prison. Walls of concrete fifteen-foot tall and crowned with coils of razor sharp concertina wire surrounded an encampment about one square city block in size. Sitting in a reinforced sentry box and behind thick bullet-proof glass, men in civilian clothes observed traffic on the street through high-powered binoculars. Wall-mounted cameras scanned and photogaphed the flow of vehicles and pedestrians passing the checkpoint. A large and electrically operated steel gate was further reinforced with iron grates. Surveillance equipment mounted on the exterior walls looked like pimples on an already ugly facade. It resembled San Quentin. But over the wall, an American flag fluttered in the breeze and a Long-Termer announced, "That's the U.S. Embassy!"

The Embassy was also destroyed and one employee killed in the earthquake of 1972. The extreme defensive precautions at the new Embassy are not unique to Managua. Following the assault on the Marine barracks in Beirut, Lebanon, U.S. Embassy installations in 'hot spots' around the world were retrofitted with similar protections. As for the Marines, four days after the tragedy in Beirut, President Reagan unleashed them on Grenada, giving them a bone to chew on to vent their rage.

Across the street and fronting the Embassy from the north, vacant lots were oozing mud from last night's rains. Broken down and useless abandoned vehicles littered the quagmire like so much discarded trash. And behind the lot, a barrio with its crooked streets and makeshift shelters hastily thrown together presented a stark contrast to this headquarters of *Norteamericano* diplomacy.

Finally we arrived at the *Instituto Nicaraguense de Seguridad Social y Bienestar*, [INSSBI], or the Social Services and Public Welfare Institute. We had an appointment with the General Secretary.

Due to a late departure from the WFP House, we were ten minutes behind schedule. The General Secretary left to attend another appointment but her Assistant would meet with the delegation. A distinct courtesy. So much for racist jokes about 'Nica time!'

Senor Carlos A'Jorge Mendosa received us in the Executive Board Room. Two woven tapestries hung on the pine paneled walls, both depicting smallish Nicaraguan *campesinos* with white doves of peace hovering near their shoulders. Quite a contraste to Mendosa who was big, urbane, and who looked at us through very dark, very still, and very self-controlled eyes.

83

Mendosa spoke slowly and distinctly; "The Nicaraguan economy still responds to the capitalistic system and is unable to react to its own needs. The principle export products are cotton, coffee, and cattle but our ability to produce these commodities and present them to the international market is frustrated by rapidly inflated prices for the machinery, fertilizers, pesticides, and petroleum that must be imported for production. A negative downward spiral results where production increases while net income to Nicaragua decreases."

Mendosa's voice became even more serious as he lowered his bulk over the table and started accenting his words with animated hand gestures; "Nicaragua is involved in a Revolution. For the U.S.A. to make war on us as we build our nation is a crime. Since 1981 this war has cost Nicaragua $4 billion in damages, 250,000 refugees, 50,000 dead, 60,000 displaced children including 12,000 war orphans, and 2,500 combat injuries. The *campesinos* who should be involved in production must serve in the military and consequently production suffers. We build health centers and schools and the counter-revolution destroys them before they can serve the people. Fifty-percent of the national budget must be diverted to the military at the expense of health and education and welfare programs. The masses of people flee the war zones and come to our cities that do not have the infrastructure to support them and their demand for services. Instead of remaining in the countryside and being producers, they now become consumers. The result is obvious; long lines, and shortages of food."

Demand bumps up hard against supply. During the Somoza dynasty, the masses were not aware that they were entitled to what we regard as normal goods and services. If you were poor and unconnected, health-care, education, affordable housing, and land were unavailable. Period. Furthermore, to desire more than subsistence was not only impractical, it was immoral. As a result of Sandinista initiated programs, the people were beginning to awaken, were fashioning a new world view. Neither God nor any rudimentary conception of justice as fair play demanded that they be treated as dogs, cowering under the table begging for scraps off the plates of the rich.

Childcare was an example of a new program developed to serve the people. Mendosa observed that "INSSBI has created 190 Child Development Centers. We do not call them 'Child Care.' We assist families in the 'Development' of 35,000 children. Fifty-percent of the cost for our programs for children comes from European nations. Many of the Centers are staffed by *internacionalistas* from Norway and Canada. The European Economic Community also contributes food for these programs."

It was time for a vocabulary lesson and a good example of Nica humor. I was familiar with most of the terms. *Sandinistas*. That's obvious. *Brigadistas* are persons coming in to work as groups, brigades, in the coffee harvest or on construction projects. Both Julie and Rhonda were *brigadistas* prior to joining the WFP. *Internacionalistas* come to Nicaragua with specialized skills and expertise. They may be employed in health-care, education, agricultural, or industrial sectors. But then he used a term that I had not heard before — *'Sandalistas.'* It sounded enough like Sandinistas that I thought I misheard the man. Asking for clarification, he repeated himself. When a bewildering look remained on my face, he smiled and pointed to his foot, *"Los Birkenstocks . . . sandals."* But a *Sandalista*? These are the sandal-wearing North Americans and Europeans who came to Nicaragua, not out of sympathy with the Process or to work in solidarity with the people, but for kicks, because Nicaragua was the 'in' spot for the adventure set, because the exchange against their currency was favorable. When the going got tough, as in February when the Sandinistas tried to put a bridle on inflation, the *sandalistas* pushed off in search of other ports-o-call.

Mendosa resumed talking about the economy. "In our Pension System employers must pay 12.5 percent of a worker's annual wage into the retirement program. We now have 30,000 pensioners each receiving 10,000 Cords per month on the program. This includes workers who labored all their life without benefit of any pension security. Both the U.S. and Canada owned and operated gold mines in the Waslala District like the Rosario Mines in Siuna. If a man was killed in a mining accident, before the corpse was cold the boss would inform the family that he had violated articles 18, 115, and 119 of the Labor Code and had been fired for not fulfilling his contract. Therefore the company was under no obligation to the family. In 1979 these mines were nationalized. The workers who had no pension benefits, many of whom suffer from brown-lung, are included in our plan. We also have military pensions and death benefits for families."

Returning to the WFP House, we joined Daniel Erdman on the porch for a lecture on the history of *Acción Permanente Christiana por La Paz*. Erdman, one of two chief coordinators on the Long-Term staff, is a citizen of the U.S. who was born and raised in Mexico. During the twenty years that he lived in New Mexico, he worked with Salvadoran and Guatemalan refugees through the United Presbyterian Church Hunger Relief program. Motivated by the persisting question, "Why is there hunger in this world?" he joined WFP in 1984 as a Short-Term delegate to Jalapa. A year later he returned as a member of the Long-Term staff.

Witness for Peace began in July of 1983 when 150 U.S. citizens of differing faith persuasions went to Jalapa. This area in the Nuevo Segovia District was the scene of intense Contra war with aerial bombings and guerrilla attacks being mounted daily from military bases in neighboring Honduras. The population of this agricultural valley was pro-Process, supportive of the Sandinistas. The intent of the Action for Peace delegation was to link arms with the Nicaraguans in a nonviolent vigil protesting the invasion. In fact they literally stood arm in arm with Nicaraguans, interposing themselves against agressions mounted by Contra troops. The WFP logo was taken from a photograph of these women and men standing on the battle line, taking a risky stand for peace through nonviolent direct action.

Their gesture caught the attention of the North American peace community and the Nicaraguan government. Both wanted it to happen again. A permanent action was called for. By the end of the year, Long-Termers were placed in Managua to coordinate the visits of Short-Term delegations. However, the tactic of standing arm to arm against the Contra was abandoned. The Contra were not persuaded by these dramatic gestures of non-violence. Persons standing together on behalf of peace and desiring nothing more than to be left alone to live under a peaceful sky were simply easy targets. Sitting ducks.

But the presence of the Witness found other expressions, some equally dramatic. Like David facing Goliath, a shrimp boat was motored into the path of a U.S. warship in Nicarguan waters on the Gulf coast. Unlike the biblical story, this Goliath did not surrender the field. Another boat maneuvered down the Rio Coco positioning itself between Honduras and Nicaragua as a witness declaring that these nations should be in conversation. Not war. While some tactics were abandoned, the work persisted. Non-headline-making efforts continued to encourage the Contras and Sandinistas to begin negotiating for peace. On occasion, high-risk interventions were performed by Long-Term teams to secure the release of Nicaraguans held hostage by Contra forces. Mostly they succeed.

Erdman reminded us that our journey to the Waslala District would take us to the political and geographic edge, the frontier of the war in its current phrase. In 1985 it was Esteli. In 1986 it was Jintoega. Always the WFP was there. Now it was the mountains of Waslala which for the past two years have been within the Contra's zone of control, the window through which they organized and mounted their attacks on the center of the nation.

Located on the strategic boundary between the states of Matagalpa and Zelaya in Region 5, the FDN forces of the Contra join ranks with Pastora's ARDE to produce what is euphemistically referred to as 'Low Intensity War.' The military planners who packaged the scenario for Vietnam forsook this mode when they opted for classic full-scale and high-profile strategies. The results are common knowledge. Now the advocates of LIW were having their chance to prove the viability of an alternative theory which substitutes economic destabalization and guerrilla terrorism for massive frontal assaults. Daniel assured us that in the mountain districts we would have an opportunity to observe the impact of these revised tactics at close hand. In addition, upon returning to Managua we would have a tutorial on the subject from one of the professors at the university.

OBSERVATION: "One Cathedral Plus One Tomb Equals Two Graves"

June 15

Despite arriving ten minutes early at the office of the Non-Governmental Commission on Human Rights, our briefing did not occur. The Director had an 'unavoidable schedule conflict' and was unable to reach us because the telephones were not working. Fact or fabrication?

Noticing that one of the secretaries was using a phone, my suspicions peaked. There's enough of the old Saul Alinsky style in my temper to prompt an immediate protest. Julie asked permission to check the phones. The lines were indeed dead. The secretary was talking on an intercom.

In the lobby of the Commission Headquarters, one entire wall was posted with copies of articles from the international edition of the *The New York Times*. Without exception, each article was critical of the Sandinista Government. Salient denouncements were underlined in red. One article reported the recent resignation of the Mayor of Managua following a dispute with President Daniel Ortega.

What a curious display. Finally it occurred to me what was wrong. It should have been obvious from the outset; all the articles were in English!

For whom were these displayed? The walk-in-off-the-street average Nicaraguan? Hardly. They were posted for the benefit of persons like ourselves, visitors to the Commission deserving a gander at the 'real picture.'

Outside on the walls of the Commission an abundance of graffiti proclaimed "*Vive Carlos Fonseca*" and "*No Amnesti.*" Perhaps some *compas* had read the bulletin board and were posting their equally graphic reply. In red, no less.

With nearly two hours of unscheduled time on our hands, the group had to decide between touring, shopping, or swimming. Lake Managua is one of the most foul bodies of water in the hemisphere. During the Somoza dynasties it was used as a dump for the city's garbage, raw sewage, the toxic industrial pollutants from U.S. corporations like Penn-Walt that discharged mercury from its battery factory straight into the lake's seething depths. The consensus was for touring; specifically, we wanted to visit to the National Cathedral and the National Palace.

The Cathedral and Palace stand at the edge where Managua meets the shore of its lake. From a distance the Eighteenth Century tabernacle appeared intact. An illusion. The cathedral is a burned-out skeleton of its former gothic glory. The roof is gone. So are the windows and doors. Grass and small trees grow helter-skelter throughout the nave where pews once were arranged in precise formation. The Madonna and Child carved above the main entrance survey real estate that now looks more like the barnyard around the stable in Bethlehem than when the church was in its heyday. Statuary and art fixed to the walls depict the saints leading the crusade for Christianity atop horses in battle and from the helm of boats tossed upon tempestuous seas. Frothy oceans and clashing conflicts they may command. Earthquakes are another matter. I don't recall a patron saint for *El Temblor de Tierra*, unless, perhaps, it was Saint Vitus. Now the plaster saints review oblivion and disarray with birds and mice for their congregation. The place where the Somozas once knelt in prayer echoed with the laughter of a few noisy children, their merriment skittering across the rubble, bouncing off the walls.

Nicaragua's Cardinal Obando y Bravo is adamant that the old cathedral be restored on this historic site. The Sandinistas countered with the offer to build one elsewhere in the city. Sitting directly on top of that lethal fault in the earth's crust, it was the epicenter of the earthquake in 1972. The government claims that any attempt to rebuild on the spot would be wasteful and improvident. Why beg for an invitation to repeat history? The Cardinal argues that relocation equals defamation. After nine years debating the issue, neither side has budged. Nor has the cathedral.

West of the cathedral, the National Palace is another rugged survivor of *El Temblor*. Hung on the Doric columns of this pretentious Parthenon are two formidable banners. Each is an icon, significant in the lore of Nicaraguan history. On the left is the familiar portrait of the Revolution's namesake, General Augusto Cesar Sandino. It's not his serious face that immediately attracts the eye. Rather it is the tall ten-gallon cowboy hat. In fact the image of that hat is perhaps the most potent symbol in the story of the Revolution. On fences or walls, in the *campo* or the city, that hat appears, a half-circle with a straight line drawn underneath. Wherever you see it, you know that the ghost of Sandino is lurking about.

To the right is the banner of Carlos Fonseca who founded the Frente in 1956. Representations of the *comandante* typically picture him looking upward, his eyes and jutting jaw cantilevered in an angle of expectancy, of forward motion, of hope. Side by side these banners silhouette the father and eldest son of the Revolution. Between them the air seems to reverberate with the sounds of *"Patria libre! O Morir!"* A Free Homeland! Or Death!

Together they stand sentry at the main entrance to suites of government offices. The guard in the doorway stepped forward and asked for my camera. A revolver on his hip suggested that the request was serious, but his smile was friendly. The camera was placed in the top drawer of a rusty file cabinet. If someone had been that cautious ten years ago, history might have been different. One midday in August of 1978, a handful of FSLN guerrillas led by Eden Pastora and Dora Maria Tellez, seized the National Palace while Somoza's legislature was in session. A number of the nation's leading senators were hostaged for a $500,000 ransom and the release of Sandinistas held prisoner by Somoza. To the dictator's everlasting chagrin, Daniel Ortega was one of the commandos returned to the rebels as a result of this daring-do.

Over the doors to the great hall of the deputies on the second level, a mural painted by Belkin illustrates the history and spirit of struggles for liberation. A gift to the people of Nicaragua in celebration of the 65th anniversary of Mexico's own Revolution, it is a testimony to the passion and anguish of martyrdom. The images of Zapata and Villa and Dias at the left begin the historic trek and end with Sandino and Fonseca at the opposite side. Generations of those who matched the hope of their dreams with the blood of their flesh are captured in violent primary colors, frozen in moments of victory or pain, their souls exploding like the colors, full of emotion, responding to a different gravity. The expressions on their faces catch the spirit of these two peoples who lived under volcanoes and felt the boot heel of despotic tyrants. They reconciled to nature. They repudiated the oppressors.

Standing in the open-aired courtyard of the Palace, I looked up to a sky that was saturated with gray, a dramatic contrast to the mural before me. In a moment the clouds burst and the cobblestones were pelted with rain. It was a scouring downpour. Not a shower.

Across the plaza and opposite the cathedral, a tenacious flame licked away at the driving rain. Set in a shallow blue tiled-pool, a white concrete block contains the physical remains of Carlos Fonseca Amador.

Spanish naming is logical and informative; it incorporates both the father's and mother's last names. So, as in this case, Carlos is the given name and the first surname belongs to his father, the second to his mother. Generally the mother's name is not used save for signing legal documents or, like now, on a tombstone.

The tomb is square at the base with triangular sides moving toward a flat top. A bronze plaque facing the cathedral identified the dead warrior and underneath, the single word, 'PRESENTE!' Beside the tomb, a white cylinder emerges out of the pool and at the top, the stubborn flame.

REFLECTION: "A Flame for the Living Dead"

I was struck by the symbolism. The hard driving rain neither dampened nor extinguished the flame. The pyramid is top-less, without a point; it does not achieve a pinnacle. The surface of the pool was agitated under the force of the torrent.

Nicaragua's spirit is a combustible desire for liberty that achieves its flash-point when utter, raw, and undisguised poverty can no longer be ignored or tolerated. The work of that fire is to burn away the cause of human misery and then to heal, to cauterize the wounds of subjugation in the flames of freedom. It is the bush that burns yet is not consumed.

The pyramid reaches toward a destiny that is always in the process of becoming. The year 1979 marked the 'Triumph,' the overthrow of the Somoza dynasty. At that junction, the 'Revolution' began — the 'Process,' as they choose to call it. Incomplete, still unfolding, moving onward to achieve the destiny that lays in wait, it hungers for fulfillment. Nicaragua's spirit moves through the purgatorial fire of a conflagration that obliterates the old boundaries of slavery. The apocalyptic fire burns through the bonds of the old serfdom. The sacrifical fire consumes any scabbard that would contain it.

The surface of the pool roiled in ferment. Nicaragua is a cauldron seething with a heady brew: Life! The crypt of the old order is broken, like a volcano erupting to vent the force of dreams that can no longer be contained. There is no encounter with life until that which has repressed it is broken. The possible confronts the womb and at the irrepressible breaking point, an abrupt birth through the suffering pain of a hard labor.

It is impossible to wander the streets of Managua without feeling the accompaniment of Nicaragua's ghosts. *Sandino Vive!* calls to the onlooker from graffiti on the walls. *Presente!* announces the voice from the writing on the tomb. Hospitals, boulevards, schools, stadiums, all bear the names of memorialized martyrs and heroes. Fifty-thousand, maybe sixty, persons have died; gone, but not forgotten.

Why? Because there are things in life far worse than death. With all of its apparent finality, death itself is not the ultimate oppression; ask the poor, ask the disinherited, ask the dispossessed. In death the physical body achieves complete cessation of all human activity. It may have been stripped of all defenses by the ravages of war; there may remain no surface expression of dignity or identity. Cadavers return to nourish the earth from which they came. But something remains, something that is untouched, something not exhausted by the fact of death.

That 'something' is what stares at you from the banners and the piercing eyes of Sandino, or the upward lift on Fonseca's jaw. From the side of your own eye you catch it in the lick of the flame or the dance of rain over the waters. It's a brooding presence that the event of death cannot contain. It is the spirit of life, the aliveness of life that refuses imprisonment. These ghosts infect us with the contagion of hope. And that hope rides on the horizon beyond simple objects of sacred homage and veneration. It is that hope which has struggled with the fact and the shadow of dictatorships forcing them to yield. It is a wedge applied against tyranny until at last it begins to open up, to yield, to break down, to disintegrate. And in its place, a new reality is born of new facts. In the face of that hope, the sting of death cannot prevail.

Nicaraguans hang on against long odds by the threads of that stubborn hope. They do not despair. They will not go down again. Be it a Sandinista, another Nicaraguan political party, or an outsider attempting a new imperialist colonialization, no principality or power on earth shall make them prisoners in their own land.

This is the "Yes!" they exclaim to the infinite creative possibility of life. And therefore I am not affected with disgust by what some regard as their morbid cultic infatuation with the dead. It is not death they have fastened onto. For they know that not even death is capable of telling them what it is that God has to say about life. The life they have received as a bequest from these daughters and sons of Revolution has gifted

93

them with a pulsing spirit that is vaster and greater than anything they have ever known before.

And some of us standing on the margins with them, say, Amen!

OBSERVATION: "Diplomats, Vampires And Vendors"
June 15

The rain disappeared as quickly as it arrived leaving the plaza awash in streams rushing toward the lake. A small coterie of young FSLN soldiers emerged from the cover of a gazebo and meandered back toward Fonseca's tomb. Polishing their dress-parade helmets and rifles with white gloves, their banter was peppered with laughter. To the man they appeared to be in their late teens or early twenties.

In the distance I heard the wail of sirens and soon a motorcade appeared lead by three motorcycles with flashing lights. Sandinista Police cars followed, blaring, filling the plaza with screeching noise. The air reverberated with two notes, one high and the other low, jumping back and forth like a shrill fog horn speeded up. Sandwiched between the police vehicles were three limousines. The procession stopped behind our bus and the sound and light show came to a halt. The soldiers were no longer lounging and had moved into position around the parameter of the pond and its tomb. Standing in rigid attention, rifles snapped across their chests, their unblinking eyes were fixed on some distant object.

A corpulent man in a loose fitting dark suit emerged from the limousine. A tripod was removed from a trunk and a man wrestled an ornate wreath of flowers. The procession formed moving in silence toward the tomb. Obviously some foreign dignitary was about to pay his nation's respects to this Revolutionary hero. The wreath was set in place and following obligatory moments of silence, the man from the limousine offered words of homage. His language was neither English nor Spanish. It sounded Slavic.

I searched for something that would identify the nationality of this compatriot delegation. A flag appeared as the group

huddled loosely at the foot of the pond. It was Czechoslovak-
ian. I balked. Anger combined with nausea creating a confusion of impulses.

Like a flash-back, I remembered camping in Prague during the summer of 1968. An uncommonly beautiful city, the
Czech capitol was alive and vibrant with the commingled high
spirits of a people whose own liberation had been paid for at
substantial price in the currency of blood. Alexander Dubcek
successfully navigated the path toward reform and among the
Eastern-block peoples, the Czechs achieved an unparalleled
independence from Soviet domination. The spirit of Masaryk
and Benes thrived in the pulse of that liberty which is the
hallmark of the open society.

On leaving Prague and driving toward Austria, the evidence
of Soviet and Warsaw Pact preparations for invasion was obvious. Troops, tanks, and light artillery were arrayed in formation, poised for invasion. And then it arrived, on August
21, full of vengeance and terror, leaving only the broken shell
of a valiant people who once again would feel the heartache
of a familiar tyranny. Dubcek was deposed, evacuated into
the belly of the Soviet bear for retrofitting, for reprogram-
ming, for silencing. Once again it was censorship, the dissolution of non-Communist political groups, the publishing of
lists of unacceptable persons, the installation of Soviets into
the machinery of government.

On a return trip to Prague, the streets were silent. The
sound of laughter no longer rippled from cafes and bistros.
Children were not at play over the cobblestones and in the parks
lovers no longer strolled hand in hand exhanging glances of
endearment. Everything was locked up and battened down.
Grim-faced troops patrolled with rifles at the ready. Gone, too,
were the harassing and resisting crowds. In its place there was
quiet, a mood appropriate to mourning. Prague shared the fate
of Budapest.

But this Czech presence in Nicaragua troubled me. If this
diplomat was Czech in the tradition of Dubcek, then his
presence was understandable, commendable. If not, it was

hypocrisy. Perhaps the vigilant surveillance of Sandino and Fonseca's spirit would indicate his lineage. If he was a ward-clerk of despotism, pretending to do oblation and feigning solidarity, I hoped that Carlos' bones would rattle in defiance of the contradiction. Or maybe the General's hat would slide off the banner and transform itself into a banana peel heading for the foot of this pompous dignitary. Not all tyranny comes from the North. The East is also culprit. And not only Central Americans suffer the brunt of despotism. Or was it the Fabian policy of 'forgive and forget' as long as Czech-made supplies flowed into Managua's mercados?

I resolved that if he quacked '*Vive Sandino*' or '*Viva la Revolucion*' I would counterpoise my own cry, '*Viva Dubcek*!' and watch for the look on his face. Talking revolution while practicing repression is more than a corruption of vocabulary. It is the counterfeit spirit that will always betray the hopes and dreams of those people whom it panders to serve while destroying their life. Targeted minorites in the U.S. are familiar with this strategy of deception. Ask the Blacks, the Chicanos, the Native Americans in our homeland. And if their answers are not clear enough, ask the Vietnamese, the Grenadans, the Salvadorans . . . hell, the list would be too long. I turned on my heel and left.

Behind the plaza the husk of a department store and an arcade of former shops stood as roofless as the neighboring cathedral. Across an empty lot the carcass of a derelict office building stretched its bear beams toward the pitiless sky. Peter Davis reported that somewhere in the vicinity were the remains of the '*casa de vampiros*' (House of Vampires.)[9] It's a humorous reference to the once prosperous *Plasmaferesis, Inc.* In a good example of what is meant by the word symbiosis, prerevolutionary Nicaraguans sold their blood — really their plasma — to the United States. Unemployed or under-employed poor peoples sell their blood so that *Norteamericano* hemophiliacs and indigent visitors to our hospital emergency rooms can survive. Is that symbiosis or solidarity?

Once the 'vampires' extracted the blood, it was centrifuged to separate out the plasma. The donors were reinfused with the residual red cells in a saline solution and the plasma was shipped north. In return for their contribution, Nicaraguan donors were fed a hot meal and provided with a regimen of vitamins and foods. Their health was monitored and supervised by the only free medical care Somoza offered the people. Participants were paid for their services the equivalent in Cords to what their U.S. counterparts were paid in dollars. Depending upon the market, it fluctuated between $5 and $10 per visit, which could be as often as twice a week. The center's three buildings held 250 beds and on a good day processed 15,000 donors yielding 20,000 liters of plasma a month, or fifteen percent of the world's supply. No plasmapheresis center in a U.S. city could compete with the volume. Perhaps more interesting is the fact that at the New York City inspection, no U.S. center could compete with the quality of Nicaragua's disease-free plasma. Since North Americans needed this blood it was in their interests to keep the Nicaraguans alive and healthy. Times change.

The glitch in the story is that the operation was owned by two partners; Dr. Pedro Ramos and Tacho Somoza, the ruling dictator. It was Tachito that remarked, "I am a businessman, but humble." A businessman? So was Al Capone. Humble? Like Duarte and Pinochet. Ramos and Somoza put a 300 percent markup on the plasma they sold north. Their annual profit was $12 million. No longer was 'bleeding the people' a mere figure of speech.

In 1977 the editor of *La Prensa*, Pedro Joaquin Chamorro, exposed the plasmapheresis process in Managua for the exploitation that it was. An otherwise legitimate, needed, and healthy arrangement was contaminated by greed, corrupted. Dr. Ramos fled home to Cuba, filed a libel suit against Chamorro, and lost in Somoza's own courts. Nonetheless, the aggrieved doctor bought a contract on the editor's life. Following the successful assassination, 40,000 enraged Managuans followed the funeral procession to the headquarters of *La*

Prensa where some split from the crowd and turned back to burn the '*casa de vampiros*' to the ground. A full year and a half before the Sandinista Triumph, Somoza lost a profitable business, the plasma connection between Nicaraguan donors and North American recipients was terminated, and what had been fragmentary support for the FSLN began to coalesce with a vengeance.

The irony in that last sentence is strong. Carlos Fonseca Amador was the founder of the Sandinista Front. Fausto, his father, was the Administrator General of Tacho Somoza's vast estates. In the name of patriotism the son worked hard to undo that which the father struggled to secure for the richest man in Central America.

Between the corner of the Palace and the tomb, a vendor opened his two-wheeled store, an old soda pop machine with the familiar Pepsi logo on the side. The paint was chipped but the sweat beading on the metal suggested that inside there were *gaseosas* (bottled soda pop) on ice. Julie, Dorothy and Rhonda wandered in that direction.

Julie has a marvelous knack for drawing folk into conversations dancing between humor and politics. Two of the vendor's sidekicks joined the cluster. Noticing Bill's WFP shirt, the man remarked that all *Norteamericanos* in Nicaragua were guests of the Sandinista government. So far so good; WFP is there with permission of the state.

Then he remarked that Ortega and his ministers provided us with food, shelter, and our transportation. His conclusion strayed from the facts. On being corrected, he broke into a smile and asserted, "Nicaraguans have to work to eat."

Julie's reply got a round of laughs, "North Americans not in favor with Reagan's policy have to come to Nicaragua to eat and sleep out of the rain."

"Just like here," the man replied. "All political parties are really looking out for themselves; they skim the people for their private gain. Including the Sandinistas. What we have is a bureaucracy of hunger."

98

Behind the tranquillity of the scene, an atmosphere of increasing weariness and cynicism intensifies as the daily frustrations, inconveniences, and the humiliations of economic hardship mount.

One of the other men removed his cap to scratch his head. His dark face was wrinkled and hadn't seen a razor for several days. "We want peace," he offered firmly. "Peace and the return of U.S. companies. They bring the jobs. We need work and parts for our machinery and cars."

The third man joined in, "Maybe the next President after Reagan will allow peace." "Maybe yes, maybe no," the other replied, displaying his broken teeth in a wide smile.

Standing underneath the gaze of those banners and not a stone's throw from the grave of Fonseca and the Sandinista security police, these Nicaraguans felt secure enough to talk openly and freely and critically of their government. With strangers from the U.S. no less.

Smile, Sandino. Loosen up to a grin, Carlos. This is what you fought for. "Vive Nicaragua!"

REFLECTION: "The Radical Contingency of Life"

The vendor at the National Palace remarked, "In Nicaragua we have to work to eat." Food nourishes the body so that we might know that life itself is alive. Through its energy we come to feel whatever portion is ours of vitality and power. Some say grace before they eat. Silently as individuals or with the group, we pause. An old Western Shoshone friend of mine unobtrusively takes a small morsel of food from his plate and places it on the earth before eating. Perhaps what we do is not gestured from an immediate sense of gratitude to God for our daily portion. At least it signals a deference to the fact that some other form of life has been yielded, sacrificed, in order that we may inherit the strength of its resource.

Life feeds on life. It's that simple. Something has to die in order that we may live. The meat that occasionally finds its way to the platter at the WFP House, the bean, the vegetable, the fruit — life consumes itself in repeated acts of sacrifice. If life is to continue it must do so at the price of giving itself away. 'Soul food' is not some exotic fare served in ethnic kitchens. All food consists entirely of souls; animal, vegetable, or fruit.

So we pause and make a rest of motion as we salute its leave-taking from life. And we remember that life is never ours alone. Nor is it our own. It is the after product of that which has preceded it and surrended itself that we may inherit for a moment that which we too shall bequeath in similar fashion to those who follow us.

The lingering question is double-edged: What must I die to in order to really live? And second, what must I die for in order that something or someone in a following path may live? Death is always hovering there like a coiled spring waiting to pierce us through and through so that something else may be lifted up to life.

I remember my parents. I recall the images of Sandino and Fonseca. Each were quickened by a restless desire to stand and work and live and make of that life something worth all of the struggle and sacrifice of the lives that had preceded theirs, that formed the geography of their dreams, that nourished them in body and spirit. They desired vibrancy, craved purpose, would not settle for the haphazard or trifling after nonsense.

My father's people were sharecroppers; my mother's father was a laborer on the railroads. Yet both of my parents received graduate degrees, one in theology and the other in education. Why? Because, in part, of the struggles and dreams and sacrifice of people who said 'No' to the little vision, the small destiny. They accepted the challenge to make good in their own lives that which was worth the offerings of the past.

Self-consciousness is to be aware of such contingency, the startling magnitude of our indebtedness. Stewardship is to accept the gift and the responsibility for making of our lives a thanksgiving for that which has been spent for us. To do less is to forfeit self-respect, to abandon our claim to integrity.

I remember the words of Octavio Paz, favorite words:

> *"Death is a mirror which reflects the vain gesticulations of the living. The whole motley confusion of acts, omissions, regrets and hopes which is the life of each one of us finds in death, not meaning or explanation, but an end. Death defines life. If our deaths lack meaning, our lives also lacked it. Death, like life, is not transferable. If we do not die as we lived, it is because the life we lived was not really ours. Tell me how you die and I will tell you who you are."*[10]

Someone once said that the only relevant question about death to ask a Christian is, 'On what field of mission did they find your body?' What we are willing to die for is an accurate gauge of that which we have lived for, worked for. What must I become, must I do, in order for my life and my death to be a 'witness for peace?' How can I become an instrument of compassion, a conduit of benedictive grace?

To stalk answers to such ponderings and have the scent of a response opening the nostrils is to feel in the gut that life is truly alive. It is to feel the lift of the spirit into heights of understanding that have clarity. It is to walk and not faint in the strength of a faith restored. It is to run and not be weary and to soar into the supernals on the wings of eagles. It is to look up the long trunk of a cross and see a man hanging there and then fall on the knees before the humbling truth that self-sacrificing love is more powerful than hate. It is to accept that a body may be broken, but, if we choose it, the spirit can never be vanquished. It is to empty yourself and wait in the conviction that while tyranny may carry the day, may grind lives into dust, finally you can feel a vibrant hum in the world's tension and hear the single chorused note 'Vive!' It is to give life's length to listening for the givenness of God and become aware that love is at the core of universe. To know this thoroughly is to rob death of its terror and life of its fear.

101

OBSERVATION: "Hard Day's Night — A Team Crisis"
June 15
7:15 p.m.

Following supper, Julie, our *responsable*, briefed us on what to expect in the laboratory of the Nicaraguan 'Process;' hints for survival in the mountain war zone. She reminded us that the conditions of the unilateral cease fire are unstable. In fact, dialogues between the belligerants broke down Thursday the week before. FSLN troops were under orders not to fire on the Contras. Nevertheless, violations of the truce have occurred. While the villages of Waslala and Zinica are well defended, the jungles and mountains are staging areas for the Contra and combat often spills over onto the roads.

The town of Waslala is divided in its attitude toward the politics of the war. Most of the commercial people in the village are 'non-political,' which means they are opposed to the 'Process.' Evangelicals from the Assembly of God congregation are adamant in their opposition to the government's program of involuntary conscription. Their opposition to the draft is the only point where I find myself in sympathy with the social ethics of the Assembly! I take it that Assembly Pastor Pat Robertson does not share his denomination's aversion to conscription; some of the Contra troops he review and blessed in Honduras are not there voluntarily but through kidnapping. Roman Catholics in the village are 'pro-Process' and the Pentecostals are mixed in their attitudes. Some families have loved ones fighting with the Contra and other households have sons and husbands in the Frente. Julie remarked that you can usually tell the difference between Contra and Frente soliders by their uniforms; the Contra are better equipped and their camouflage fatigues are a brighter green, newer.

Waslala is the current frontier of the war. A majority of its inhabitants are there because they were ousted from their homes higher in the mountains, deeper in the jungles. Their cottages burned and their crop destroyed, they fled in search of safety, shelter, and food. Unfortunately, the amount of goods available for sharing is limited, both for the refugees and other inhabitants of the borderlands. Finding little to sustain their poverty, their attitudes toward the government in Managua are skeptical at best. Others flee to the village to avoid being press-ganged into service with the Contra.

We were warned that although there is small chance of being ambushed on the road during the day, there have been searches and seizures and tragedies. Within the past ten weeks two civilian vehicles have been stopped, its passengers robbed and wounded, and their trucks destroyed. Except in Honduras or Costa Rica, Contra guerrillas have no need for trucks. Without dependable access to the roads, trucks are useless in the jungles, worthless in the mountains. For them, this is a foot soldier war.

Julie reminded us that the hardest test facing delegations is their response to poverty. Aside from portable generators at the Roman Catholic Church, the district hospital, and the FSLN army base, there is no electricity in Waslala. The power and telephone lines connecting Waslala to Matagalpa are rarely in service. Our host's homes have dirt floors and animals roam through the dwellings at will. Some have privies. Others use the bushes. Or the trails. Or the river. Toilet paper is scarce and there are no Sears catalogs; bring your own or use leaves, and of those you must be careful which ones you choose to put against your backside. The water supply is contaminated and we must always force our drinking water through the carbon filters at the trucks. The families get their water from the river or streams and for us to use it invites illness.

The group was invited to share their own agendas. Fears and trepidations hitherto cloaked were to be put forward, exposed. Friction between members of the team or irritations with the Long-Termers were to be identified and called forth. We began to ventilate. The rocking chairs circled on the veranda of the Witness for Peace bungalow created an interesting pattern of motion. Some rocked faster when the discussion heated up while others paused or stopped moving all together. Our words were counterpointed by a symphony of squeaks as the rockers' wooden runners scraped the polished tile.

One member of the group announced her strong reservations about continuing into the mountains. In Mexico City she expressed a fear of stepping on land mines; an appropriate dread. Prior to the signing of the Covenant, she objected to the wording of Article Six: To commit time and financial resources as we are able to Witness for Peace. Now that same issue resurfaced. Once again she was reminded that the language of the article did not carry for force of law, did not constitute a legally binding contract. Signing the pledge was an affair of the heart, perhaps binding at the moral level, but not enforcable except as conscience intervened. She was not consoled. Perhaps it was in the jurisdiction of the spirit where she was having her real dilemma. Someone suggested that she could 'discern out,' remove herself from the delegation.

During training in Mexico City, Sue Severin asserted that if a person had serious qualms about continuing into the mountains, it was best to handle that then and there. Opting out in Manaqua created problems. The Long-Termers assigned to headquarters were few and already overburdened. There was neither facility space nor staff time available for helping someone sort through basic ambivalences about being in solidarity with WFP. Discontinuing in Mexico was dealable. Administering such a decision in Managua was difficult. Coming to closure and opting out while in the *campo* invited a crisis. It would require one Long-Termer and one truck with its driver to transport that person back to the city, a heavy and perhaps dangerous price for the team to pay. We were prepared for that contingency in the event of serious injury. Evacuation was possible. But reservations about the mission were something else. Should we risk it?

We were in Managua, hours away from departing for the mountains. Sitting on the porch, the slow motion of the rocking chairs came to a halt while this young woman continued to profess her inability to understand either the philosophy or the process of Witness for Peace.

To claim that kind of ignorance meant that something was very wrong. The fear of stepping on a land mine I understand;

or being caught in a cross-fire, hit by a sniper, being taken hostage, getting some wormy little parasite knitted into the gut. The women feared being raped like I cringe at the thought of similar violent torture.

But ignorance of the purposes and goals and procedures of Witness for Peace? That was something else. Dozens of pages of background materials outlining the history and methods of the Witness were provided to us when we requested our application. Others documented what to expect as we traveled, in Managua, in the mountains. We were told what to bring, and most important, how to prepare ourselves emotionally and spiritually for the experience. Signing the application itself was a specific indication of our understanding and acceptance of the very principles and conditions which she now was challenging as unfamiliar and unmanageable.

Someone spoke up affirming her honesty; how beautiful it was that our group had become authentic, genuine. We could speak freely with and to one another. We had achieved the sacred benchmark of forthrightness. Ambivalent or hard feelings were being expressed.

I maintained silence. We were in Managua, not Esalen on Carmel's coast. The Californian penchant for 'sensitivity groups' was becoming, for me, a close encounter of the third kind. When honesty skirts the edges of manipulation it comes perilously close to the ragged brink of hypocrisy. For me it wasn't beautiful. It was tragic and one unredeemed by likening it to a sublime madness of the soul.

Inwardly, my emotions were transiting from confusion to irritation to flat anger and indignation. This was not a case of someone being a 'slow learner.' It felt more like monkey-wrenching; the deliberate toying with the group to test our capacities for endurance, for charity. As to the former, I was running thin. Of charity, the ache in my gut and the throb between my temples indicated that my quotient on this scale was a cold zero.

Silently I repeated Reinhold Niebuhr's prayer, the Serenity Prayer, like a mantra: "God grant me the serenity to accept the things I cannot change, the courage to change the things I can and the wisdom to know the difference."

Consensus does not imply undifferentiated unity. I like contrasts, the possibilities inherent within blending, the strength associated by multiple voices and the collection of differences. And I don't flee from friction and negative emotion — it's that Celtic temper. That too can be a sign of vitality and health in relationships. Accountability and confrontation are important disciplines in the nurturing care of spiritual growth. In a healthy context they signal that there is life in our new family, something between us matters, is alive, has full and forceful feeling.

But sitting there I was smouldering with ambiguity. I was not certain whether the points of contrast, the substance at issue, were my feelings, differing values, personal perceptions, or whether something was surfacing that signaled a real and risky problem for the delegation.

I was feeling nervous, then I remembered someone saying, "Nervous isn't a feeling; it's a jumble of feelings that you can't sort out." I wanted time to sift and sort. The squeaking rocker next to me sounded like a metronome reminding me that time was not an unending commodity.

Finally I decided to speak. I wanted to be as specific as possible in order to be understood as accurately as possible. I did not want to complain, be glib or sarcastic, or mind-rape. I opted to state as clearly as I could what I had heard her say and how I had observed her behave on the three occasions when she presented these concerns to the group. Then I unfolded my own feelings about these perceptions. At the bottom level, beneath confusion and incredulity, were the stronger apprehensions of feeling manipulated, deceived.

Sitting on the edge of her chair, her head bobbing foward, back, sideways, her eyes looked empty, her gaze blank. The woman was dissembling. Inwardly I debated with myself whether to back off and let it go, or proceed. Choosing the latter, I challenged her sense of corporate responsibility by putting the group at risk and possibly hazarding our assignment.

She had teetered on the brink of indecision twice before and now on the eve of our departure was attempting to put us through the same hoop a third time.

No longer was it simply a question of how she felt or what she wanted to do. The decision had become the property of the group. Her despair or double-mindedness — her equivocation — was having a negative impact in me. The balance of my fellow-feeling was tipping against her. Our camaraderie was endangered, becoming precarious.

Confronting me, she said I was being hostile. I willingly fessed-up to being angry. It did not feel as if I had vented animosity upon her, or was dumping my emotional refuse on her. Telling another that I am angry is not, for me, the same as feeling pugnacious or wrathful. These are emotions I associate with hostility. But I was willing to take responsibility for my strong reactions. She offered that we could either work it out in a one-to-one, or in the circle of the group. I figured it was the property of the group. Let them decide.

Tito suggested we sing a song. In the moment I could not tell if it was a denial-avoidance-flight tactic or simply a temporary measure, space for a cool-down. Some folk simply do not like heat. I thought of Harry Truman; "If you can't stand the heat, get the hell out of the kitchen." Anybody who doesn't like the heat ought not be in Nicaragua.

To her credit, she was not willing to be deflected from the issue at hand. The song was sung with less than half a heart and immediately she asked how the process of discernment would work in this instance. It felt pre-emptive. Too quick. In two minutes she had transited from 'let's work it out' to a flat, decide! Perhaps she had arrived at her own decision.

Rhonda retrieved the WFP policy guidelines from the office and read them aloud to the group. Three levels of decision were involved. One belonged to the individual themself. The second belonged to the group. The third, final, and binding decision was the prerogative of the Long-Term team and Dorothy, the delegation leader. It was decided that in the morning WFP personnel. the group coordinators, and this woman would meet to negotiate a decision. Since WFP operates by a principled commitment to consensus, it would take only one dissenting vote to block her continuation with the delegation.

We stood to form a circle before going to bed. The day had been long, the discussion tiring. Following silent prayers I made my way toward the door. Standing beside the doorway, each of us received a hug from this woman as we retired, a friendly gesture that felt more like the acknowledgment of tension than lobbying.

Climbing up to the bunk, I was nearly asleep when Dorothy came into our room wanting to walk and talk. Since the team had elected me to serve as their Chaplain, she didn't apologize for awakening me and I didn't think twice about it. Pulling on my Levis we went out into the dark streets. There was much to wrestle with.

My first line of interaction with the world is intuitive. Analysis comes later. I feel life before I think and reason my relationship with it. That arrangement is simply a fact of who I am psychologically. It's my path and I choose to accept it. Moreover I respect it methodologically. It's okay for Donovan's heart to cradle his mind. And now I needed the time with Dorothy to sift and sort, to put the focus of reflection on the habits of my heart. There were many undercurrents of tensioned feeling roiling around. For instance, where I felt betrayal others saw courage in the woman's attitude and behaviors.

In Mexico City during a group session I suggested that her attempt to be the group's interpreter was the deportment of a co-dependent. I did not elaborate the concern. But now her preoccupation with acceptance and being liked suggested weak internal boundaries. The need to control events and other people felt obsessive, especially when I felt the hot breath of that treatment blowing on my neck.

The walk with Dorothy might open something inside toward the light of clarity.

I chattered away into the warm darkness. Did her behavior exhibit craftiness, a word implying maliciousness, or was it an obsessive/compulsive style that suggested an emotional imbalance? There seemed to be a truth here that eluded the data. What was being required of us? Accountability or mercy? Or both? How? There was a hauntedness about all of this that begged for healing. Like the words of the song, it was becoming "A hard day's night."

Dorothy has a gift for triage and she quickly came to her bottom line. It was a bell ringer for me. The issue here was not one of limitations, the sister's or the group's. Nor was it one of proportions of feeling or 'symptoms.' While those were no doubt important, in this instance they were out of place. They should have been addressed and resolved in California during the application process, and, if not there, at least in Mexico City. If they were present in Managua they would probably materialize in the *campo*. Here in Nicaragua they were inappropriate by virtue of our mission and the constraints of time. We had covenanted with WFP to participate in an important gesture of solidarity with these people. We would learn from them and stand beside them. But it was to be a short sojourning. That which deflected from the mission deserved our serious attention. If it was contrary to covenant then it needed to be called forth and separated out. She was going to recommend that the woman remain behind and not proceed into the mountains. If necessary she would block consensus. Hopefully during the morning session the sister would discern herself out.

Realizing the power inside the decision she had made, Dorothy added these words; "I'm not a careless woman. I don't make this decision lightly. If it seems I'm playing God with the life of another person, I know that love demands hard decision. Hopefully God will give me humility in equal measure to my responsibility."

I agreed with Dorothy's decision. When it comes to struggle, this *chicana* has grit blended to grace in balanced combination.

I thought of the meeting that would happen a few short hours later. Would Dorothy or anybody be able to speak in

109

a language that the sister could understand and at a level where she was capable of operating? I resolved to pray for them during that hour. We gave each other a hug and headed toward home. In the distance the outline of the mountain behind the WFP house could be seen, and on its slope the large white letters FSLN carried into the night.

REFLECTION: "Denial and Self-Deception — Hell of a Twin"

It's bloody hard not to deny in myself what I challenge and criticize in other people. Their vices and defects of character are inclined to become virtues, or at least benign, when seen in my own behaviors. What I am so quick to call pose or pretense or dis-ease in others comes under the hand of a lighter and more charitable scrutiny when applied to myself. I hope never to take-for-granted or minimize my own tendency toward self-deception.

Was I criticizing and confronting impulsively, in anger, or out of annoyance? Was I saying she was off kilter or broken because I am centered and whole? Was I seeing things clearly, or was my limited vision blinding me to self-serving motives? I wanted to be scrupulous in this self-examination. If I was unfair, I wanted to know it before any further words or actions on my part would drive with fearful accuracy to create more harm.

This is not theological rant, psychological cud-chewing, or the intellectual chatter of the fore-brain. The way of self-doubt and self-examination is very much the sum and substance of the reason I am standing here in Nicaragua. I am here because of my peoples' and my own capacity for self-deception and the willingness to trade parochialism for coherence — to settle for narrow self-interest instead of social justice. An example may be suggestive.

In July of 1986, Nicaraguan President Daniel Ortega appeared before the United Nations and charged the United States with gross violations of international decency and law by forming and supporting a mercenary army called the Contras. Under

110

orders from the National Security Council, the Central Intelligence Agency, and the U.S. Southern Command, they have destroyed Nicaraguan property, mined the nation's harbors, killed or kidnapped its people, and fanned the flames of rebellion among the indigenous Miskito Indian populations. A law suit brought to the World Court in 1984 found for the Sandinistas and ordered the U.S. to cease and desist from these actions. President Reagan refused to obey the order of the court and told the U.S. public that he acted in accord with a 'higher law' that compelled a greater cause; 'stopping world communism.'

There should be nothing surprising about that information. It's public knowledge, not 'out of the loop.' What is startling, however, is the short span of memory it displays; that and the capacity for self-deception. Saul Landau is an astute observer of international affairs. In his recent book **The Dangerous Doctrine**, he reminds us that in 1776 the British Crown acted in response to its own perceived 'higher cause.'[11] In reaction, our own Thomass Jefferson charged King George III with gross violations of decency and law. Specifically, Jefferson charged that the King had "plundered our seas, ravaged our coasts, burnt our towns, and destroyed the lives of our people." In fact, the Declaration of Independence accused the King of "transporting large armies of foreign mercenaries to complete the works of death, desolation, and tyranny, already begun with circumstances of cruelty and perfidity scarcely paralleled in the most barbarous ages and totally unworthy of the head of a civilized nation." This same document also expressed indignation at the British policy of stirring resentment among the Indian nations against the colonial settlers.

What a remarkable parallel. King George III and President Ronald Reagan both responded with imperial righteousness against 'upstarts' who evangelized nationalism and mobilized for revolution. That message and mission is guaranteed to fibrilate the hearts of the rulers of Empire. Each potentate attempted to justify their denials of sovereign rights to fledgling nations by picturing a parade of horror should these insurgencies succeed. Communists from the independent and sovereign state of Nicaragua marching across the Rio Grand is the current propaganda of dementia.

In any case, the only 'falling dominoes' on the horizon are the credibility and integrity of those who arrogate to themselves the prerogative of being 'king makers' of the world. Revolution, which was once an inalienable right, is now rendered pornograpic. Those who would pander 'national liberation' are fiendish enemies out to profane the very liberties which we cherish as sacred. The republican principles of democracy are menaced if not undermined by such political double-speak. That is the banality of evil. That is the price paid for self-deception. It's as true for nations as it is for individuals. Only the order of magnitude is intensified. In either case the result is tragic.

It is for good reason that we include in the historic Christian liturgy 'The Office of Confession.' I recall those words in the 'General Prayer of Confession,' the vague and abstract summons to contrition. It is familiar and I repeat them by rote . . . recalling the myriad ways I have "offended against Thy divine majesty by thought, word or deed; I am heartily sorry for these my misdoings, the remembrance of them is grievous unto me." That's deductive. It moves from the top down. It's also dangerously abstract. The poor but well intended spiritual pilgrim can get stuck in the stratosphere fretting over how 'divine majesty' has been offended. Up there where the air is thin you have a tendency never to get down to basics, to the nit and grit of real harm, the kind that aches and bleeds.

Then I remember Step 8 in the program of recovery as suggested by Alcoholics Anonymous; "Make a list of all persons we have harmed and became willing to make amends to them."[12] That's concrete and specific. Moreover, it's inductive, moving from the bottom up. The difference between the two is enormous. By my life, my will, my actions, I may indeed harm 'divine majesty,' but until I determine the particular persons on whom I have inflicted pain, 'divine majesty' will have to lick its own wounds. First things first. I inflict pain on particular persons, humans with names, with feelings, persons who breathe the same air I share no matter how far the miles that distance us. I need to inventory those abuses and make my list of amends and ask forgiveness or make restitution there before 'divine majesty' can have its crack at my sinful hide.

Finally, what I condemn in society has its genesis point on my own turf. To ferret out that which is tawdry and evil in society requires me to first endeavor wholeness and righteousness in my own heart and life. About this there can be no equivocation, no settling for second best, no failure of nerve.

OBSERVATION: "Fernando Calomer — "Miskito, Moravian, Pastor — Three Strikes — Not Out!

June 16

Reverend Fernando Calomer is short, a bare hand-span over five feet tall, with a full but not overloaded frame. A Moravian pastor, Calomer is a Miskito Indian from the *Atlantico* and has a touching, uncalculating friendliness about him. Born in the north-central mining region in a camp named Bonanza, he was one of fifteen children. Not assigned to a local congregation, Calomer's ministry of social work is targeted to community development projects which he directs throughout the Atlantic Coast. His friendship with the WFP began in 1983 which has twice sent him to the U.S. as a spokesperson for peace in Nicaragua.

A Moravian Miskito; twice a minority, twice familiar with persecution. In the lineage of Jan Hus, Fernando's religious roots go back to that Fourteenth Century Czech religious leader. Professor, rector, and preacher to the University of Prague, Hus was excommunicated by the Roman Curia for his reformationist teaching. However, he had not fallen out of favor with 'Good King' Wenceslas IV who continued to grant him patronage. But when the renegade reformer denounced Pope John XXII's sale of indulgences, Hus went one step over the line and forfeited the King's protection. Tried for heresy, he was subsequently burned at the stake. There is something about the unbridled Czech spirit that appeals to me.

German Moravians brought pietism to Nicaragua in 1847 via the Caribbean islands of Jamaica and St. Thomas. They were the first Protestants to settle in the land of Nicaro, making their home in the province of Zelaya on the eastern seaboard. U.S. Moravians took over their missionary work and eventually handed the church's leadership to Nicaraguans like Calomer.

Calomer provided a short-course in the history of his people. The man was an encyclopedia of information. Pointing to the copy of *El Nuevo Diario* laying on the porch he said, "In today's paper you see that article about the MISURA guerrillas meeting with Tomas Borge here in Managua but today the dialogue is canceled because Borge is ill. Nicaraguans are negotiating with Nicaraguans for a treaty of peace. Why? On a map you note that Nicaragua extends from the *Atlantico* on the east to the *Pacifico* on the west. In 1502 Columbus landed on our coast, the *Atlantico*, at a place that he named *Cabo Gracias a Dios* — Cape Thank God — near the mouth of the Rio Coco. But the Spanish didn't settle the *Atlantico*. Instead they conquered the Mayan-descended Indians of the *Pacifico* during the Sixteenth and Seventeenth Centuries. About a hundred years after Columbus, French buccaneers arrived and fifty years later English pirates established a trading post which became the British protectorate of Mesquitia from 1678 to 1894. Shortly after that a Portuguese ship carrying African slaves sank offshore and the survivors were taken by the Indians. A new race was the result, the Miskitos. Our names reflect our roots; Indian, German, Spanish, English, even Chinese."

He continued; "What we have are two Nicaraguas about equal in size. One Spanish and the other Miskitia. Each has been taught to hate the other. Our geographical isolation is matched by our political isolation and the distance between us is great; in language, in ideology, in culture. The language of the West is Spanish. The peoples of this Nicaragua abandoned their own native tongues. In the East we still have our languages. And our own cultures."

114

The Zelayan half of Nicaragua is largely low-lying, hot, swampy. The inland area is a combination of tropical jungles, pine forests, and marshlands networked by waterways. Of its roughly quarter-million population, the racial homogeneity of the Spanish west is noticably absent. As well as the Spanish speaking *mestizos* that comprise fifty percent of the population, there are Creoles and three different varieties of AmerIndian tribes — the Miskitos, Ramas, and Sumos. Calomer mentioned a fourth grouping, a small community of Garifonos or "Black Caribs" whose proper home is north in Belize. The Bristish used the Miskitos as puppet monarchs, many of whom were educated in the West Indies or England. The Sumos and Ramas currently number less than a thousand each, in part the result of oppression by the Miskitos. The Black Creoles were the petit-bourgeoisie imported by the British to serve as overseers and clerks.

The picture emerged of a distinctively different Nicaragua, one that encompassed 57 percent of the nation's geography, 10 percent of its population, was 80 percent Protestant (Moravian), where a substantial portion of the people were English-speaking, and where 90 percent were unemployed. The culture and the people were different, distinct, remote. Neither were they connected to one another or the Spanish west by conventional linkages like roadways or an abundance of telephones. There is no coast-to-coast highway in Nicaraga. The highway from Managua becomes a road in Matagalpa and turns into a trail from Waslala to Rama in the east where it ends. From there to Bluefields it's a boat ride when the Contras have left something on the water that floats. Sandinista television doesn't cross the mountains so the locals watch programming from Costa Rica. Both Puerto Cabesas in the north and Bluefields in the south have airfields and the occasional flights to and from Managua are booked weeks in advance. If you were fortunate, a telephone connection might be managed, but it would take a penultimate amount of luck.

Calomer continued to elaborate on the 'two Nicaraguas:' "The English left in 1894. What followed was a neocolonialism as the Spanish *Pacifico* attempted to impose its order, its values, its culture on the peoples of the Atlantic east. They also imposed another occupation on us. The English were followed by the *Norteamericanos* as the transnational resident imperialists and the U.S.A. took up where the British left off, exploiting the remainder of our natural resources. The English took our forests of precious hardwoods and the U.S.A. mined Nicaragua for our minerals, our rubber, and our bananas. We were resource rich, cheap labor abundant, and company-store poor. And who was it that invited this into the lives of my people? The Spanish Nicaraguans of the West.''

There was no malice in his voice, no undertone of resentment. Instead, he was laying on the line his version of cold, hard, and unpleasant facts.

By the time of the Sandinista Triumph in 1979, the U.S. banana and rubber plantations were gone and so were the pine and hardwood forests. North American gold, silver, and copper mines were either collapsed or in serious disrepair and the U.S. shrimp and lobster industry had depleted those natural resources as well.

"We used to have very little contact with Managua," he remarked. "Somoza rarely came to the Atlantc Coast. And then only to look for votes and bring shirts and food. Relations between our peoples and the National Guard commanders were basically good. Consequently during the insurrection, we were not much involved because of that geographical and political isolation. Mind you we wanted independence. We have been wanting that since 1800. From the English. From the *Norteamericanos*. From the Spanish Sandinistas. And we fight for it. There has been too much abuse, too long, from too many places. Even from those who call themselves Nicaraguan.''

When asked to differentiate between the counter insurgency of the Contras and the resistance among the peoples of the *Atlantico*, Calomer was evenhanded in his repudiation of all colonizations and imperialisms: "The Contras struggle to overthrow the Sandinistas and re-establish the old system. The Contras are fighting President Reagan's war. It is hopeless. Our

116

people do not accept them. Not willingly. They are ambitious for power but only want to re-establish the hard class system of the old Somoza dynasty. That is no solution. It is only more suffering and death.''

He continued, ''The indigenous struggle is radically different. We want peace. But a peace with sovereignty. We want autonomy. Not a return to some old order. Not to become pawns in someone else's game. We are not slaves and we will not be hostages. The MISURA are here to enter talks with Borge; they are not CIA Contra. They are one of several indigenous guerrilla groups of the *Atlantico*. The peoples of our Coast want a federation of states, separate but one. Like you have in the United States. So we propose three points in conversations with the Saninistas: First, we want to develop our own international relations with foreign states. The government says No. Second, we want an Atlantic Coast Army and Police that will work in cooperation with the *Pacifico* but without the Spanish Sandinistas being in control. We continue to dialogue on this aspect. Third, we want administrative control over our own natural resources: petroleum, fish, agriculture, minerals. We have some agreement on that too.''

He looked like a man who felt the weight of life, anticipating the future and all that must be accomplished, his feet planted in the present, feeling weary. Unhurried he continued, ''It is a slow process. When the FSLN came to power they wanted to do everything very fast. They made many mistakes. They admit this. The Miskitos and Sandinistas have negotiated a separate treaty to extend the cease fire. Our relations are improving. We have many dialogues.''

Calomer had a knack for understatement, somewhat on a par with his announced need for an English interpreter. The man's focus was hawk-like, attentive, and observant of detail as Julie translated his Spanish. The charade was over when he began correcting her translations; in English, no less.

The FSLN's mistakes in the *Atlantico* were numerous and disastrous. Small wonder Creoles and Indians became alienated to the point of armed resistance. Young Sandinistas from the west arrived singing songs of victory following Somoza's ouster. Simultaneously, Somoza's local henchman decamped. Since they had been the operators of the company-store economy in Zeyala, the bottom of the barrel disappeared. The quality of local misery intensified. As if to compensate, the Sandinista cadres were lavish with promises of new hospitals, schools, and transportation systems. But the new government could not deliver. There was the matter of distance between Managua and the inaccessible far coast, the scarcity of materials, and the fact that very soon there was another war to be fought.

Calomer was emphatic: "In the United States you have political wars. In Nicaragua we have strong military and ideological wars. And every day, like this morning, we wake up to a new economic crisis."

The Sandinista's dealings with the Miskito people were a chronicle of errors. In mid-February 1981, the FSLN arrested popular Miskito leader Steadman Fagoth and claimed he was a Somoza agent. Beginning in January 1982, some 8,500 Miskitos were taken from their land along the Rio Coco and resettled forty miles south of the border. Their homes, churches, livestock, and crops were destroyed to deprive the Contra of refuge or supplies. In less than a year another massive relocation occurred as another 7,000 were taken from their homes along the Rio Coco. This time they were sent into central Jinoteca and farther south into Matagalpa to work the crops on state coffee farms. Infants, the elderly, and the infirmed were transported by helicopter or trucks. The others made the trek on foot. I remembered the Cherokee 'trail of tears.' The third wave of Miskito relocations occurred in October 1983 when 5,000 were again forced from their tribal homes in the Rio Coco when it was rumored that the CIA would commence massive bombings.

Cuba's revenge? Puerto Cabezas is the Miskito community of 20,000 on the north coast. During World War II, the U.S. built the landing strip there and developed the port. Following the war they turned them back over to the Nicaraguans.

But not quite. Puerto Cabezas was the launching point for the CIA directed assault against Cuba in 1961. The Bay of Pigs flotilla began in Nicaragua. Small wonder that the Sandinistas saw the potential strategic value of the Atlantic Coast to the United States. It is that part of Nicaragua closest to Cuba.

Following the Triumph, Sandinista troops began to appear in the *Atlantico* until Puerto Cabezas had two garrisons making up about one tenth of its entire population. For a people few in number scattered over small hamlets, this concentration of uniformed and armed military seemed excessive. It far outnumbered the National Guard that Somoza kept in the region. Once again the sleepy port was transformed by thundering troop-transporting IFAs, darting jeeps, and modern weapons of war.

Since the bulk of the Nicaraguan middle-class bolted with Somoza, the medical and educational infrastructure was left in a vacuum. Had it not been for the massive influx of Cuban health-care professionals and teachers, the period of transition would have been much more difficult.

Unfortunately, Cuban medical teams displaced their professional counter parts from the University of Wisconsin who had been working in Nicaragua staffing clinics and hospitals in Puerto Cabezas and Bluefields. Complaints charging the Cubans with malpractice, discimination, and a general disinterest in Miskito health circulated throughout the Indian culture until the local population boycotted these services choosing instead for tribal practitioners.

Castro sent two thousand teachers to Nicaragua, half of whom were deployed throughout the Zelayan department. The Sandinista National Directorate soon determined that the Miskito were ideologically backward. When they attempted to remedy the situation, parents complained that political propaganda had replaced education. The culturally religious Miskitos, who generally regarded themselves as 'more Christian' than people in Managua, took sharp offense at the atheistic rhetoric of teachers; they objected to the proliferation of classroom posters depicting Ho Chi Minh and Lenin.

119

Sandinista militia drilling on school grounds, including dangerous sessions of target practice while school was in session, prompted an exodus of students from normal instruction.

In the early 1930s Sandino himself claimed the northern part of Zalaya along the Rio Coco for communal farming territory. Far from being an experiment, this conformed well to Miskito culture and practice which held many types of property in communitarian arrangement. Forest lands were usually owned and worked communally. Social class distinctions between the Miskitos were negligible. If a people do not acknowledge these differences, it is difficult to mount an ideological program oriented to class struggle through progressive stages. To the Miskito it was literally nonsense. Absurd. Furthermore, while the Sandinistas were restricting private ownership of property on the *Pacifico*, they were reluctant to permit the communal ownership practiced and advocated by the Miskito which did not include state control. In the first instance the Miskito reacted to notions of social class by pleading ignorance. More obnoxious was the Sandinistas' refusal to honor their communal property holdings; ideologically it was a bald-faced contradiction; in practice it constituted an unwarranted theft.

When it came to dealing with the Miskitos, for a while it seemed that the FSLN put a new spin on the Midas touch. Everything they put their hands on turned to chaos; not gold. The result was a complicated evolution of indigenous *Atlantico* resistance movements and splinter movements. Their abbreviations look like alphabet soup. Fagoth and Brooklyn Rivera founded MISURASATA [Miskitos-Sumos-Ramas-Sandinistas] in 1979. Within two years Fagoth declared open war on *sandinismo* and its refusal to consider autonomy for the Atlantic and created MISURA in Honduras while Rivera took the movement to Costa Rica and aligned it with ARDE. In 1984, thirty-three Miskito communities formed MISTAN seeking dialogue with the Sandinistas and a peaceful solution. A year later KISAN was created by Wycliffe Diego under the FDN to unite MISURA and MISURASATA and then broke itself into two splinters; K-WAR which favored opposition to the April 1985 cease-fire and **K-DIALOGUE** which, as the name implied, favored negotiations with the Sandinistas.[13]

The dialogues that Calomer referred to were attempts to establish a pattern for reconciliation. The Sandinistas' priorities were political control and military security. The Miskito priorities focused around communal rights and religious freedom. Neither side saw their claims as negotiable.

The evacuation of the Miskito from the Rio Coco was reversed. The government's policy of Amnesty was attracting weary warriors from the Contra ranks and other dissident forces. Perhaps most promising was the program known as the Autonomy Project.

Autonomy would eventually provide Zelaya with some of the very objectives Calomer discussed. The cultural rights of all ethnic minority communities in the province would be guaranteed. Zelaya would have a large measure of self-government but it would require the federalization of powers that Calomer mentioned. According to the proposed division, Managua in the Spanish west would retain responsibility for foreign relations, international defense, internal security, and general budgetary economic strategy. The remaining work of governance would be the responsibility of a regionalized executive and assembly. What some Managuan politicos decried as Balkanization seemed a plausible strategy for fresh alliance. Work with them or fight them. Where's the choice?

Calomer touched his shoulder. He was nursing a gunshot wound. About three months before, late Palm Sunday evening March 27, he was attacked by thugs as he returned home from worship. They stole his wallet. Street crime is trans-ideological, capitalist and socialist allegations notwithstanding. Poverty is also trans-ideological. Nonetheless, I felt safer on the evening streets and in the barrios of Managua than I do in my own urban village on California's Bay of Monterey.

Recently returned from an international assembly of indigenous peoples held on the Pine Ridge Reservation in South Dakota, Calomer had participated in a sweat lodge ceremony. The Lakota medicine chief informed him that the bullet in the shoulder would emerge naturally and safely within six weeks. Fernando had a month to go.

My eighteen-year-old son was working on a farm about one hundred miles from where Calomer had been in conference at Wounded Knee in the Paha Sapa.

Sitting on the veranda, within days this man had been physically closer to my son Darius than I had for two months. It was a strange feeling. We stood to hold hands and close with prayer, for all our peoples, for this one very beautiful and small world, and for peace.

REFLECTION: "Trust — An Endangered Spirit"

God, we make a gesture of hope toward all human kind,
  Sioux and Sumo — Miskito and Spanish —
      Anglo and Creole,
  Where tensions brood and mistrust lingers —
  Come, Peace, for tempest-tossed days.
God, we make a gesture of mercy toward all grieving hearts,
  Mothers of Heroes and Martyrs and Disappeared,
  Where death abounds and sadness is unremitting —
  Come, Peace, which the world cannot give.
God, we make a gesture of serenity
      toward fears ever present,
  As despair keeps watch against dreams ever threatened,
  Where we sense the evilness of evil
  And the goodness of good —
  Come, Peace, confirm thy will in our spirits.
God, we make a gesture love toward friend and foe,
  Soldiers and peacemakers, the poor and their keepers,
  Where fortitude abounds as strength in weakness —
  Come, Peace, with justice to ease heavy burdens.
God, we make a gesture of trust toward all of life,
  That all my savor the urgency of growth,
      the strength of laughter,
      the vitality of friendship —
  That all may sense the joy of understanding,

the blessing of fulfillment,
the moments of delight —
That all may share the offerings of faith;
the gifts of variety,
the blessings of peace.

OBSERVATION: "C.E.P.A.D. — Launching Pad for Mission"
June 16 11:10 a.m.

C.E.P.A.D. is the Spanish acronym for Evangelical Committee for Aid to Development. In their usage, Protestants are 'evangelicals'; Roman Catholics are something else. As I interpret the word, 'evangelical' refers to preaching the gospel and preparing to act on the commitments of faith. In that case, it's hard to justify the exclusionary practice. Reading and pleading the Gospel through the lens of liberation theology is the hallmark of Nicaragua's base-community Roman Catholicism. These sisters and brothers neither live nor die as if there is some barrier separating Christ-devotion from Christian Action. The divisive use of the term irritates me.

Headquartered in a non-descript two-storied office in a bustling barrio, CEPAD's store-front operation is not one of the gadget-driven agencies of bureaucratic Christendom. Its message would ring hollow and its influence decline if it kept one more penny for itself than it takes to keep the lights on, the telephone working, and support for the poor flowing.

Roger Valesquez welcomed us into a conference room. Maps were pinned to the walls; Nicaragua, the West Indies, Central America, the World. Think globally, act locally — the cartography of mission, the dialectic of discipleship, the terrain of tension . . . I like it. At the head of the table was a large blackboard; Valesquez has chalk dust on his fingers. I settle in for a lecture.

Born Roman Catholic, Valesquez converted to Protestantism during a preaching mission at the First Baptist Church of Managua. Called by God to the Christian ministry, he studied at Santa Monica City College in L.A. and studied theology at the California Baptist Seminary and Union Theological Seminary in Pennsylvania, a Presbyterian school.

Returning to Central America he pastored the First Baptist Church of San Salvador for eighteen years. Two years ago he came home to Nicaragua. U.S. Congressional funding for acts of aggression against his people convinced Valesquez that Contra war was something more than an Oval Office debacle, something other than a vicious experiment in National Security Council slight-of-hand. He returned to share Nicaragua's pain and join the struggle. Working as a CEPAD volunteer, at first he drew no salary from the coalition. In 1987 he accepted the position of Director of Church Relations.

A brief history of CEPAD followed. The 1972 earthquake destroyed 600 blocks of downtown Managua. Thousands were buried under the rubble and more were left injured, lost and homeless. The infrastructure of the capitol disintegrated. The dust had hardly settled when, four days later, six Protestant leaders met in the Baptist Church. There was one item on the agenda: How do we stop the Somoza dynasty's theft of international relief funds flowing to Nicaragua? The pastors concluded that over the long haul, Nicaragua was far more endangered by the criminal acts of Somoza than by natural calamity.

Eventually, forty-six denominations shaped a coalition for the responsible and strategic application of international assistance. CEPAD serves as a conduit that over the years has supported self-help programs in housing, agriculture, medical health, and small business management. It provided grains to initiate farming collectives and sent agronomists to share information on pesticide use. On examining one group's proposal, they provided 100 bags of cement and negotiated another 70 bags from the Sandinista government to launch the dream for a cooperative bakery. A recent grant from the Norwegian Church helped establish a fishing cooperative on the Atlantic Coast. The current U.S. economic embargo has not halted incoming aid from North American or European churches.

Valesquez described CEPAD's ministry as twin thrusted: "The Diaconial work of development proceeds in agriculture, housing, sanitation, health-care, and small business cooperative programs. The Ecclesiastical thrust involves Concillar programs on human rights and inter-church relations including training adults and youth in techniques of Bible study and theological reflection."

Of the major Protestant denominations working in Nicaragua, only the Assembly of God, in response to pressure from its American headquarters, is not represented at CEPAD. Apparently they do find Christianity and Revolution to be irreconcilable. This decision, however, is not directed by a strict sense of limits. They do not anathematize violence as a tool for gaining or inhibiting rapid social change. Simply put, the sensitive conscience of non-violent spirits like Gandhi or King are not a working part of their theological/political disposition. Too often the Assembly take the 'one necessary thing' of the Gospel as a mandate to violently oppose Communism at any place, by any means, and at all costs.

Valesquez continued; "We enjoy the support of our Roman Catholic churches, too. Only 54 of the parishes in Managua are obedient to the Cardinal in not working with us. They fear him. And it's a pity. The Assemblies and the Cardinal are relics that choose against the 'Process.' They only hurt themselves and their people," he says without a visible trace of resentment.

Valesquez and CEPAD assert that the Christian Church is and shall continue to be the midwife of the Sandinista Revolution. In this regard, Cardinal Obando y Bravo is not far wrong in his accusation that CEPAD is the religious arm of the Sandinistas.

In August of 1982, twenty churches belonging to Mormon, Seventh Day Adventist, and Jehovah's Witness congregations were seized by Sandinista 'neighborhood committees' and charged with being accomplices of the CIA. Elliott Abrams, then Assistant Secretary of State for Human Rights and Humanitarian Affairs, assailed U.S. groups sympathetic to the

Sandinistas for their "deafening silence" in the face of these totalitarian assaults against organized religion.

Nicaragua's fundamentalist sects and churches are even-handed in their open hostility to Roman Catholicism, mainline Protestantism, and the Sandinista government. But the expulsion of the twenty pastors and the confiscation of their congregation's properties was a morally obnoxious error and a tactical blunder of the first order. However, the U.S. State Department's assertion that this unseemly act constituted an epidemic of religious persecution was an extravagant stretching of the facts.

It is a fact that Nicaraguan authorities have grave suspicions about the work of sectarian evangelicals opposing the government. Three years later in 1985 the DGSE (state security organization) detained and questioned several evangelical leaders. Eight were released after several hours and three were held for several days. Once again the U.S. State Department heralded this as "a holocaust against evangelicals in Nicaragua."

President Ortega's chief of staff, Rene Nunez, indicated that these persons were questioned concerning their relationships with the U.S. Embassy, the CIA, and anti-Sandinista organizations in the U.S., namely the Institute on Religion & Democracy and Open Door.

One man in particular, Boanerges Mendoza, was detained a second time. Mendoza denied rumors circulating in the U.S. that he had been tortured by the DGSE. Upon agreeing not to involve himself with the counter-revolution, he was assured of complete freedom to carry forth his evangelical, ecclesiastical, and educational work.

Valesquez smiled and remarked, "If the Sandinista government was a totalitarian regime, I would not be here working with the churches and organizing in the communities. And neither would you be here with Witness for Peace." A close working relationship exists between the coalition and Minister of the Interior, Father Miguel d'Escoto, and Minister of Culture, Father Ernesto Cardenal, these revolutionary Roman Catholic priests.

Neither does CEPAD chafe at the fact that the Revolution identifies itself as a combination of three ideological elements: *Sandinismo, Marxismo,* and *Christianismo.* With respect to *Marxismo*, Valesquez is unabashed; "Nicaraguan Marxism is of the humanitarian sort. 'Hard-line' Marxist/Leninist types that deny the significance of spiritual values are a distinct minority in Nicaragua; they have only two elected seats in the National Assembly. Nicaraguans are deeply religious. Without the participation of Christians, the revolution would never have been able to take hold. It would be like taking an aspirin to cure cancer."

Mario Vargas Llosa, the Peruvian novelist, likened the Sandinista political party to the discrete dictatorship of the Institutional Revolutionary Party in Mexico. Another literary giant and son of the hemisphere, Carlos Fuentes, observed that if Cuba and the USSR were to disappear and sink into the sea, there would still be revolution in Central America.

It is well to remember that not all Marxists are Stalinists. William Solane Coffin drove that point home when, in his own inimitable fashion, he remarked, "Stalinism is to Marxism what the Klu Klux Klan is to Christianity; a manipulation of symbols in order to deny reality; I've yet to meet a Stalinist in Central America." Oppressed peoples are attracted to the promises of Marx, not to the power of the Soviet Union; after all, capitalism has not been kind. And while Managua hardly resembles Moscow, neither does it resemble Mexico City.

Nicaragua is attempting to synthesize Marxist historical analysis with Christian social ethics, and Western democratic principles with socialist economic objectives. The result is a process as fragile as it is innovative. Considering the fact that they are conducting this experiment while struggling to survive an undeclared war foisted upon it by the world's greatest military power, well, the effort is as formidible as it is precarious.

REFLECTION: "Christians and Politics"

Six church leaders huddled to pray and plan following a natural disaster. Christians caucusing to yoke spirit and muscle into ministries of compassion is normal enough. In this case, however, the wounds of natural calamity were being salted by the blatant greed of tyrants. Somoza was exploiting the victim's plight to reap personal profits. Consequently the caucus was set on a hazzardous edge. To stand against oppression would require more than compassion; it was to enter the risky arena of dangerous politics.

I do not know what they felt. I can imagine that the shock of the earthquake's devastation continued to chill their sensibilities. Furthermore, I'm certain that Somoza's ruthlessness in dealing with adversaries was a known fact, one worth a shiver of fear.

In a situation where things were quite literally falling apart and people were in panic, they did not lose nerve. Instead they made a decision to commit themselves and their destiny to a project that would have a long-range and far-reaching impact on the lives of their people. Under the stress of the moment they were capable of nerve and firmness.

Revolution is the product of a terrible anger and a deadly despair. It cannot be reduced to stories of courageous guerrilla warriors and legendary battles. Before that, it is the story of radical faith. Radical faith is the decision to stand and be counted. It refuses to relax allegiance to the ideals and values that reflect decency. It is to be dedicated to a high purpose with a deep resolve. It is to let the Yeas be Yea and Nays be Nay; it does not cut or trivialize the difference. It is to say No to the threats and thievery and treachery of Somoza and Yes to the invitation to the corporeal works of mercy: feed the hungry, clothe the naked, shelter the homeless, release the captives, and proclaim the acceptable day of the Lord.

And radical faith demands that to be responsible we must purpose to stop the routines of our lives. There can be no more business-as-usual. A decision of this caliber commits a person to actions reaching far beyond the boundaries of their little world. It involves risks foreign to the old temperament, the established life plan, the securities of habit.

It is good for me to meet people like that. It reminds me that Christian faith and the Church were born in politics and abandons the political life only at its peril.

What does it mean to say that "Churches should stay out of politics, that religion ought not mix with affairs of state?"

Imagine what we would have to delete from our Biblical studies if we were to eliminate the political order and political strife from that instruction? In the Old Testament it is good to recall that Joseph was an office holder in the court of Pharaoh; that Moses himself was reared in a palace and became a revolutionary; that Joshua combined political and military aggression to occupy Palestine. Remove institutions and politics from David, Solomon, Elijah, and Elisha and what's left worth studying? Isaiah was a statesman and Jeremiah preached quite explicitly about foreign and domestic policy in the midst of a crisis that shaped Judah's statehood.

Turn to the New Testament. Without politics there would have been no census bringing Joseph and Mary to Bethlehem. Neither would King Herod have sent the troops on their bloody mission to slaughter the Holy Innocents. Without politics, John the Baptist would not have lost his head. There would have been no zealots among the disciples, no messianic issue, and no trial of Jesus. Certainly there would have been no crucifixion. Neither would Paul have appeared before Agrippa or appealed to Caesar. The remarkably political Book of Revelation would never have been written, which might suit quite a few as just fine. Politics, even bloody militaristic politics, is a very biblical reality.

All religious language is symbolic; we have no vocabulary restricted for holy things. The God of the Judeo-Christian biblical witness is a political God, as much of its language bears witness. The vocabulary of political life saturates the text: God is 'lord,' who is known as a 'ruler' or 'king.' The faithful respond in 'obedience' and become 'citizens' of God's 'kingdom.' God chooses a 'people,' delivers them from 'slavery,' gives them a 'land' and enters into a 'covenant' or compact, the requirements of which hold with the force of 'law.' The 'good life' is not defined by reference to the religious life of ritual or ceremony but by the terms 'justice' and 'peace' which are words of political vernacular.

In due time, from David's line, there comes the Christ, the 'Anointed' one who was born 'King of the Jews.' Prior to his birth his mother experienced a revelation that can hardly be regarded as anything less than political. In strident, if not hardcore, terms she sees him as destined to 'put down the mighty from their thrones,' to preach 'good news to the poor,' to 'release the captives' and set at liberty 'those who are oppressed.' He itinerated preaching the 'kingdom of God' and was regarded as speaking with 'authority,' a man having 'dominion and rule' over 'principalities and powers.' If these aren't political images then I'm plainly stumped.

Yes, both the Bible and Christian faith are political. The church in its prophetic witness must press its place in the community and hold both itself and the state in accountability before God. For neither she nor the state are absolute. The church must teach and insist that all history is under the judgment and redemption of God. Moreover, the quality of community life which the church represents has a conception of peace and justice that transcends radically that of the political community.

Christians are called to be political, even radical. While that frightens at least a few, it confuses even more. We see phony radicalism that is so much riotous foolishness. Our ears ring with mindless invective and the rhetoric of exaggertion and vilification which bears no resemblance to serious thought. Some confuse violent means for shallow ends with non-violent means to profound ends. Single-cause radicals take insufficient stock of the complexity of life in which their cause is embedded. Interest-laden radicals are often as arrogant or tyrannical as the despots they seek to overthrow. There is much about radicalism that is confusing, sometimes sad, sometimes sorry.

The radicalism of St. Paul, by contrast, was rooted and grounded in love — a love that was full-orbed, all-including, embracing not only one's self but others. It was a radicalism reaching out to encompass the whole inhabited world. It repudiated the 'we-them' mentality. And what deserved such a love? God! For whom and to whom is such a love to be directed? The neighbor. And who is the neighbor? Humankind.

WASLALA

OBSERVATION: "Departure for the Mountains"
June 16

Leaving Managua and heading toward the mountains and Matagalpa City, we are on the same highway the revolutionary army used to enter Managua in 1979. The clog of city traffic behind us, the road stretches around Lake Managua. A gentle climb in a north-easterly direction and the countryside resembles scenes from the U.S. southwest. Tall cacti blend to scrub and further up the flanks of the foothills, pine forests are visible. The low-slung mountains themselves are a combination of buttes and mesas. Even the colors resemble the pastels of the high desert around northern Arizona and the canyonlands; purples and lavenders, dusty rose and terra-cotta. But nowhere in the southwest have I ever been able to shift my vision from high-desert to tropical with the mere quarter-turn of the head. Here I see, literally in the same field of gaze, saguaro-like cactus on the one side and moss hanging in clumps from tree limbs on the other. Bromeliads cling to the telephone lines. It's an environmental conundrum. In fact it's easier for me to imagine lions laying with lambs than to suspect that scenes from Florida's hanging gardens could crowd so close to those from the Arizona wilderness. Nicaragua is a strange place.

We arrived in Matagalpa City and drove to the city center. A farm worker hostel two blocks off the central plaza was a gift in 1981 from the sister city in Holland. Depositing our gear on bunks, we walked to the city cemetery before dark and supper. Ben Linder and other *Internacionalistas* are buried there. It was time to pay our respects.

This was an especially significant pilgrimage for me. In May of 1987, I placed a white wooden cross in the front yard of the parsonage. Ben's name is inscribed on that cross. Now, fourteen months later, I was standing above his grave looking at the tombstone.

BENJAMIN ERNEST LINDER
Internacionalista

Nacido 7 Julio 1959
San Francisco
California
U.S.A.

Caido 28 Abril 1987
San Jose del Bocay
Jinoteca
Nicaragua

LA LUZ QUE ENCENDIDO
BRILLARA PARA SIEMPRE

Ben Linder was an electrical engineer. In 1983 he made his home in Nicaragua. Supervising the construction of a small hydroelectric plant in the town of El Cua, the project was complete in 1985. At the time of his death he was designing and building another power generator to serve the small village of San Jose del Bocay.

Linder knew that his work was hazardous; he joined the ranks of those marked for death by the Contras — health-care workers and doctors, ministers and priests, school teachers and others laboring to build and reconstruct this poor and tired and torn land. Nonetheless, he persisted with his work.

Ben looked at the clock of his spirit and saw that it was time to build: A time for placing stones together, for making a dam to generate electricity; A time to place a candle in the darkness; A time to pump water and bring light into homes, into schools, into hospitals.

Ben was a gentle friend of creation, a builder. Not a destroyer. Ben was not a violent man. He was a dedicated man. A compassionate man. And now he is a dead man.

132

On the morning of April 28, Ben and his two Nicaraguan co-workers, Pablo Rosales and Sergio Hernandez, were working along a stream when twelve Contra soldiers made their attack. Hand grenades were tossed onto the work site immobilizing Linder with wounds to his legs and left arm. Both Pablo and Sergio were likewise seriously wounded. Crawling toward the jungle, they were overcome by the gang. Linder was shot at point-blank range with a bullet through his skull. Sergio suffered a similar fate. Pablo Rosales was fatally stabbed in the chest. The bodies of all three men were recovered from the Contra and brought to Managua for a period of national mourning.

Ben's desire was to be buried in Nicaragua, preferably at his work site. The government asked the Linder family for permission to bury him in Matagalpa. Two reasons were compelling: it would prevent Contra desecration of his remains and it would make it possible for Nicaraguans to join in offering their gestures of appreciation at his interment.

Standing in a circle and holding hands around Linder's grave, a woman approached accompanied by her children. In her arms Señora Elsa Aleman cradled a bouquet of cut blue flowers and asked if her family could join Ben's friends. She had seen us walking through the town and suspected that we were North Americans heading for the cemetery. Following silent prayer she crossed herself and knelt to pull a handful of small weeds from the earth covering the tomb. The cut flowers were placed in the sign of the cross over the grave.

In the quiet talk that followed, we discovered that Elsa was Ben's 'Nica Mother.' She hosted the Linder family when they came to observe the first anniversary of his death and they continue to be guests in her home when their travels bring them to this place. Every week Elsa's family climb the hill to this simple plot and decorate Linder's tomb and those of five other *Internacionalistas* killed by the Contras while pursuing their development projects.

Contra leadership announced that foreign workers would be regarded as enemy agents and then killed the Frenchman

Joel Flueux, the West German Bernard Erich Koversteyn, and Claude Leyvraz, a Swiss citizen. William Blandon and Mario Acevedo were Nicaraguan FSLN killed in the same ambush. The Europeans were buried on the hillside near Linder. In order to protect their lives, all *Internacionalistas* from the war zone were evacuated. We paused at their graves paying silent tribute to the spirit of their sacrifice.

"No more *Internacionalistas*. Please. They are so young, so talented, so beautiful. They risk their lives for us. They end up being murdered. Such a waste in the eyes of God. Such pain for their Nica families." Señora Aleman's words conveyed love and deep pain.

I looked at Julie and Rhonda who were standing beside each other. Was Elsa speaking to them? They were taking turns translating, an effort because each had found their own tears. Small wonder. These are the graves of their friends, their comrades.

Julie remembered the unicycle that Ben rode into the villages attracting people to meetings or to clinic programs. Children flocked to him, fascinated and dazzled by his clown routines and juggling. She also spoke of seeing his body at the memorial wake in Managua, the bullet hole in the head with the powder burns from the shot, the shrapnel wounds in the legs from the grenade. Nicaraguans and *Internacionalistas* joined mourners from the U.S. and around the world in their homage to the peaceful young man. And she was here when thousands made the pilgrimage to stand with Comandante Ortega and Ben's parents as they put his body in the rich soil of Nicaragua.

Sisterhood has many faces. A warm and beautiful smile reached through Julie's tears touching Elsa with a palpable blessing. Neither did Rhonda mask her emotions. But through her tears I saw the cantilever of a hardening jaw. The hand at her side flexed unconsciously, over and again working itself into a fist, then stretching forward into a low-five. I suspect that there comes a point where an *Internacionalista* feels less like a Belgian or a German or a *Norteamericano* and more like a Nicaraguan.

The country of our birth is a fact. We do not control it. But we can leverage the option for where we die. These six chose to risk making this land and it's people their last home. They earned the right to be called Nicaraguans. I sense that these two sisters have likewise crossed that line.

Elsa stood and straightened her dress. The little boy in diapers wanted water that the older brother carried in a jug for irrigating plants on the graves. Lifting him to her hip she invited us to join her beside another grave. This one belonged to her daughter.

In 1979, Martina Aleman was a second-year student at the University Medical School in Leon. As the Revolution moved toward Managua, she joined fellow students at the barricades and there met her death.

When Elsa received the news she was too shocked to cry. It was necessary to be strong; for the remaining children, for her husband. Matagalpa was itself under attack. By night Somoza's artillery and mortars rained bombardments down upon the city from behind Cross of Calvary Mountain in the far distance. Silently she pointed to the crest of its ridge. By day the planes of the National Guard circled overhead swooping to strafe city streets and parks.

She has since wept. One of her grown sons is within two months of completing his two year military obligation and is now in the mountains resisting the Contra. The other son serves with the Ministry of the Interior and is assigned to Matagalpa.

The thought of sacrificing another child to this war prompted the shedding of fresh tears and she knelt to place cut flowers over Martina's grave. "My daughter would be proud that we speak these words and stand together at her grave."

These people are different; strong, opinionated, and fierce in defense of their liberty.

The six-year-old stood to the side. In good Nica fashion he was learning to spit. A slug of water from the jug relieved his cotton-mouth and he wandered off sluicing indiscriminate targets. Darkness approached and the western horizon was an odd color of blue and white. The blue fit my mood. White inspired a thought of resurrection.

135

Elsa inquired about Brian Wilson and the convoy stalemated at Laredo on the Texas/Mexico border. She knew that the State Department acted to prohibit the caravan from bringing medical and school supplies to Nicaragua. Brian is with the convoy and has been a guest in her home on a previous visit. She asked, "Why won't President Reagan allow them to share these simple things that we need so badly for our children?"

What could we answer? It was a hard-hurting silence that stopped our mouths from chattering explanations or castigating the banality of such evil. Some grief is best accompanied by silence. And in that silence the unanswered question lingers, What time is it?

REFLECTION: "Ben Linder: Hero or Fool?"

Ben Linder is dead. Standing at his grave there in the cemetery at Matagalpa one cannot escape that fact nor deny the reality. During the circling moment of prayer, someone said that Ben was a victim of this war. But it is likewise true and a worthy 'fact' that Ben was not a victim of war. He was not a victim of war at his center, which is the tragedy of modern life.

Ben was not a person condemned to the desperate and exhausting dance of a life lived at crossed-purposes. His destiny cannot be described as some kind of isometric always catching him in the process of working against himself. Nor do I count him as one immobilized by choice and drifting on the misty flats refusing to come to decision.

Were that the case, he would not be here in this grave. Nor would I be standing beside it. No. This man whom I never met but much admire is a symbol for the power that comes into human life when the force of the spirit is concentrated in a thrust to care, to build, to share. It is the assertion through the quiet strength of centered conviction, "This I do — this one thing — with all my heart and soul and mind and strength!" It becomes the secret power undergirding the spirit.

Other claims against time and talent may be authentic, may be convincing. There may be no precedent for the dream and its endeavor. But mysteriously the dreamer is dreamt by the dream, sluffs off the extraneous, and yields to the absorption of a fresh dedication.

Ben knew that he had been marked for death by the Contra. Nevertheless he did not choose the easier way out. He did not opt for the less costly or more convenient thing. Some say that his decision to continue with a second project was tantamount to suicide. And in the saying, he is bitterly judged and grossly misinterpreted. I choose to believe they are mistaken. I do not sense that Ben was the victim of pride or arrogance or conceit, the three horsemen of egotism that afflict demagogues and tyrants who abuse and exploit persons for their own gain.

Ben's single holy purpose was to say YES to life and to love people. It received the consent of his mind and heart. He was not paralyzed with uncertainty, not neutralized by equivocation. His deepest desire shaped the choice of his goal and directed the labor of his life.

I do not know of his faith or what god he may have worshipped. I do believe that at his death he had no reason to be either afraid or ashamed before that which we all stand accountable.

Some say the Contra killed him because he was a clever engineer. I wonder. We will find others who can build hydroelectric plants. But that spirit? It remains the living and final enemy of those who took his life. And against that, in the long run, Contra war is a futile subterfuge.

OBSERVATION: "Circles Robinson — Union Man"
June 17 Matagalpa City

Circles Robinson is in his early thirties and slight of build. Beneath a hank of dark curly hair, his tortoise-shelled glasses suggest the look of a man who spends his life in library stacks. Maybe in another life. A faded denim shirt, old black Levis and scruffy leather work boots mark him for a man familiar with Nica earth. Circles arrived in Nicaragua to serve as a translator for TourNica. Later he spent five years farming though he never studied agriculture at home in the States. Since 1986 he has worked for U.N.A., the National Union of Farmers and Ranchers. Founded in 1981, the Union represents small landsmen at the regional and national levels of government. Circles' area is the north central Region VI which includes the districts of Jinotega and Matagalpa.

Leaning forward with his forearms on his knees, he spoke softly but not slowly. "Of the region's 616,000 population, 72 percent live in the rural sectors. Sixty-five percent of Nicaragua's coffee is produced here which accounts for 60 percent of the nation's total export revenue. The North Central region is second in national corn production and vies for third in rice and bean yields. Some vegetables grow at higher elevations."

Since Region VI is Nicaragua's major agricultural heartland, it has been a prime target for Contra activity. Over 20,000 families have been displaced by the war; their farms are no longer in production. Overall, a quarter of a million persons or eight-percent of the entire Nicaraguan population have become refugee during the war. The result is a massive drain on the national system of social services. For the victims it constitutes nothing less than wholesale trauma. Physically, economically, socially, and spiritually they join the swelling ranks of the destitute. They left behind their land, its graves, and their kidnapped with whom they may never connect again. Now they are separated from all they have ever known and loved.

He continued; "Prior to the Revolution, 110,000 farm families did not own the land they worked. Another 51,000 *campesinos* owned 3.5 percent of the arable land. The Somoza dynasty of 95 families owned the remainder. On this land the privileged and prosperous grew their coffee and cattle and cotton. The national network of highways and roads were mapped, constructed, and maintained to link these 95 families with each other and the domestic and international markets for their products. National programs of credit were created exclusively for them. Small acreage farmers seeking production or development loans from these banks were forced to place their lands in collateral. Invariably the loans were foreclosed and the confiscated properties were joined to the holdings of the 95.''

Many of these displaced families retreated into the mountains of the outlying districts and attempted to begin again. But their slash and burn flat-land style of land preparation violated the highland's ecologic system. Heavy seasonal rains washed out the crops and the land eroded away in floods. The catastrophe was humorously referred to as 'Somoza's Agrarian Reform Policy.'

Typically, farmers accept natural calamities as part of the risk package of life on the land. When their bond with the earth is jeopardized by human connivance, that is another matter. Patience disappears. Tenacity and the grit to endure in the struggle converts into the mood of insurrection. ''Cheat a person, lie to them, steal their land, and at that point they do not need sophisticated ideological tutorials in the theory of exploitation,'' Circles insisted.

The minority rich unscrupulously schemed to defraud and displace the majority poor. Once they owned a little land. Now they owned none. The land barons already owned large estates. Now they were larger. It was not necessary to convince them that the Dynasty's 95 families were bleeding the multitudes. They wore the mark of that experience in hot memory. And sometimes on their bodies. The Frente Sandinista promised redress of grievance.

In 1986, Ortega challenged his Central American neighbors to a competition with the goal of achieving 'integral democracy;' the holding of periodic elections, free public education and health-care, decent housing for the poor, and a just and equitable redistribution of land. Already in 1984 an open and democratic election had been held, one year in advance of the Sandinistas' original schedule. In the estimation of international authorities it was an uncorrupted polling of the people. Now the president was challenging the presidents of neighboring nations to follow suit.

Circles continued; "In 1981 the government instituted the Agrarian Reform Act. Within two years of the Triumph, 40,000 families were given clear title to lands that they once held but had been taken from them by Somoza's fraud. Another 72,000 families were given their own lands for the first time. In 1988 only 12 percent of the arable land under production in Nicaragua is owned by the state. During the nine years of agrarian reform, a total of 4.9 millions acres were redistributed to dispossessed campesinos, a figure that compares favorably to the 3.4 million acres diverted to the poor in all of El Salvador, Guatemala, Honduras and Costa Rica combined."

Article One of the Reform Act guaranteed the right of land ownership by private persons. Article Two mandated that all arable land must be put to efficient use. Confiscation was the penalty paid for non-use of otherwise productive land. Small farms were protected from confiscation whether they were used inefficiently or not. On the Pacific side, a small farm was anything less than 860 acres. On the Atlantic, the line was drawn at 1,720. By 1984 the government claimed and redistributed over a million acres under this law. Article Three set forth the laws protecting agricultural workers, among which were a guaranteed minimum wage, protection from being fired for sickness, freedom to unionize, insistence on the provision of adequate housing, and schedules for overtime work and pay.

Three types of co-ops exist in Nicaragua: Credit and Service Co-ops, Sandinista Cattle and Production Service Co-ops, and Dead Row Co-ops. Participation in the co-ops is entirely voluntary and each is an organization of private citizens, neither state owned nor managed.

A description of the various co-ops followed: "There are 542 Credit and Service Co-ops in Region VI made up of ranchers and farmers who own their own lands. Some have held onto their fenced land since before the Insurrection. Others received their lands as gifts from the state and others subsequently purchased their titles. Each farm is worked by individual families. A non-paid Board of Directors governs their common interests. The co-op negotiates loans from the government and then makes funds available to members. Credit is established on an individual basis. Participants are eligible to purchase seed or sell their product cooperatively or individually as they choose. Some of the more sophisticated co-ops purchase trucks, tractors, and other farm machinery and share their use between member farms or with other co-ops. Similarly, the large coffee pulpers cost more than a single family could afford to own or operate by themselves. Without them a family would be able to wash and husk, pulp and prepare enough coffee beans for their own use but it would be impossible to produce the volume worth presenting to the commercial market.''

Robinson took a deep breath and I flexed my hand that was cramping from the vigorous notetaking. Then he resumed; "Another 171 C.A.S. or Sandinista Cattle and Production Service Co-ops provide displaced war refugees a chance to start over. Land ownership is held in the name of the Co-op and its members participate with equal shares. The Board of Directors determine the type of crop or livestock to be produced and assign tasks to individuals and families. Coffee and cattle are the major products. Deliberating to consensus, the Board sets wages and makes decisions involving priorities for capital improvements. Wages are set according to an agreement for the amount of effort that constitutes a fair day's labor. This becomes the standard unit against which each person's contribution is calculated and reimbursed. The C.S.N. or Dead Row Co-ops get their name from the 'dead row' or unplanted space that separates member's parcels. As with the C.A.S. Co-ops, members of the 66 Dead Row Co-ops in Region VI also have their names listed in the title to the land. While families may work the land as they choose and develop the crops of their choice, normally a significant portion of each parcel is given to at least one co-op specialty. The co-ops are allowing small parcels to be used for private cultivations of beans and corn. That which is not used by the family is donated to the co-op's communal kitchen to feed workers during the harvest or may be sold in the village market for personal profit.''

141

Robinson works in the international relations and special projects division of the Union. Writing project grants and funding proposals for various co-ops, he submits them to the government or agencies like CEPAD. When San Francisco's Institute for the Practice of Non-Violence or the Veterans Peace Action Teams organize brigades, Circles is responsible for bringing them into Region VI and coordinating their work on construction projects, in the coffee harvest, or providing non-specialized labor to co-op farms. Twenty-five of these brigades came through Matagalpa and Jinotega during the past twelve months.

U.N.A. is a private co-op, and for Robinson's services he is paid $3,000 a year or $280 per month — when he gets paid. There is talk of a 30 percent pay increase for teachers, healthcare workers, farm organizers, and inventory workers. However, that raise will not yield a break-even against the Cord's recent devaluation.

According to Robinson, "What we now have in Nicaragua is a mixed economy, a blended capitalism. At different levels in different parts of the economy you will see evidence of three models at work; state ownership, private ownership, and mixed patterns that blend the two. For instance, the Nestle factory in the hills above Matagalpa is a combination of state and private ownership. We are doing the same thing with the economy that we did with the Constitution. We took the best from all the available models. If we think it will work, we try it out. We don't do this to conform to some ideological strategy for development. We don't have that luxury. This nation is at war and this is a 'survival economy.' And we're hurting. All of the Central Americas are in economic crisis. But we are the only one that must devote 60 percent of its Gross National Product to defend itself against external aggressors. Our economic picture won't improve until the war is over and we're learning some important if not expensive lessons. For instance for the past six years farmers and co-ops have found it easy to receive credit and federal loans. But the spiraling devaluation has made this ridiculous. You borrowed money to buy a cow. Then the currency devalued and you were able to pay off your loan for the cow with a chicken. Great for the farmer. Lousy for the economy. Or the fact that in 1987 we lost 30 percent of all our production because of inadequate storage facilities. You can't get ahead when you lose that much of your crop to rats and other animals and rot.''

Circles closed the morning session with these observations: "When Somoza fled the country in 1979 he took $1.5 million from the National Treasury. He left $3 million behind that he could not get his hands on in a hurry. [That figure varies with each report.] He also left behind an incredible national debt that grows by $500-700 million per year in interest on the unpaid principle. I believe the total debt is now between $5-6 billion. The Sandinistas vowed to pay back Somoza's debt and made good on part of it. Not because the money had been used for the people. It was already in Somoza's Swiss bank accounts or in Florida real estate developments. No. They figured the money was loaned in 'good faith' for development and the fact that it was taken in 'bad faith' or stolen did not absolve Nicaraguans from a moral obligation to repay the loans. Odd, isn't it. Most of that money is owed to the very nation that is doing its best to destroy our economy and any means we might put together to pay back the billions we owe. It shouldn't surprise anybody that there will be no payments or negotiations for payment until we have peace.''

REFLECTION: "Stubborn Ounces on Just Scales"

I'm cogitating on *Internacionalistas* like Circles and our Long-Termers. The word vocation comes from the Latin *vocatio*, to call. Spiritually, it's a fundamental idea. God calls you by name to a responsible life. God calls Adam, "Where are you? Are you hiding?" God calls Abraham, "Go out!" To Moses, "Go down." To Jeremiah, "Tear down and destroy, then plant and build." To the enslaved peoples of Israel, "Come out." Jesus called as disciples, Matthew from the tax collector's table, and Peter from his fishing nets. The *convocatio* are called-together.

143

I believe these fellow peacemakers have been called. And I suspect there is evidence of the consecrated in the handiwork of that calling. That suspicion rests on three assumptions: One, they are doing necessary work. It contributes to something needed. Stripped of frivolity and absent of luxury, they are not engaged in 'Trival Pursuit' while trading their talents for the superfluous.

Assumption Two. What they do is morally right. John Woolman hired out as a clerk and was then ordered to make out a bill of sale for a slave. Young Woolman mustered his courage and told the boss that buying and selling people like property was "inconsistent with the Christian religion." He refused the task and left. Some assignments cannot be tackled if a person has to reckon with their conscience.

Assumption Three. The work must call forth an individual's best efforts. Income is no substitute for satisfaction, at least at the level where the soul is nourished. If you work to the highest level of your competence, you don't cut corners, hedge bets, or fixate on the clock. You throw your shoulder to the wheel and push toward heaven letting the sweat go to hell.

How did these *internationalistas* hear that call? What keeps their shoulders to the wheel? Their answers must vary, but living in the arena of crises must have played a crucial part. It provides them with a gift of information about themselves. It may be something like the wheat and the tares of the parable. Come harvest and the rigors of threshing, the two are separated, their worth assessed. The value of the tares is negligible and they are cast aside. Only the wheat is taken; only the wheat has worth.

Another analogy may yield a better perspective. Following the driving winds and pelting rains of an evening storm, the jungle floor is littered with dead branches and smaller debris. In truth the dead has been separated from the living. On a sunny afternoon looking up into the lattice of the jungle canopy you would not be able to distinguish the one from the other. But in the turbulence of the storm, only that firmly attached to the vitality of life remains secure.

If we resolve to live our lives beyond the reach of the storm, isolated from tempest and tribulation, we forfeit the opportunity to reconnoiter the 'dead' from the 'not dead' in us. The storm distinguishes the 'called' from the 'not called.' When survival demands that we muster all available strength, the useless and trifling becomes apparent. It is seen for what it is. Extraneous. A dangerous cargo. Continuing to freight its weight is a fool's option. The prudent person seizes the chance to let go of all that is not connected to a life-serving core; they abandon the dead, the lifeless, the sterile. The detritus is blown away.

To have the system purged is a godsend. What remains is not only that which has been chastened, but that which has been confirmed. There you find a new sensitivity to a neighbor's need, are alive to their hurts, feel deeply, sense pain, and are indignant at wrong. You're apt to get mad once a week, be angry at evil, and become aroused by flagrant wrongs that defy all justice.

I think of the *Internacionalistas*. I remember Wendell Phillips. Leaving home one evening he was going to an abolition meeting in those days when that cause was risky. His wife, standing in the doorway, called to him, but not what you might think, "Don't stir up trouble and make a fool of yourself." Rather she said, "Now Wendell, for heaven's sake don't shilly-shally."[14]

Movements abort and great moral causes flounder because too many shilly-shally. Not Phillips. He did the right thing, the costly thing, and his words are worth keeping in mind:

> *"You say the little efforts that I make*
> *   will do no good:*
> *They never will prevail to tip the hovering scale*
> *   where justice lies in balance.*
> *I don't think I ever thought they would.*
>
> *But I am prejudiced beyond debate*
> *In favor of my right to choose which side*
> *Shall feel the stubborn ounces of my weight."*[15]

145

OBSERVATION: "A Sandinista Comandante's Briefing"
June 17 La Dalia

We returned for breakfast to the same *comedor* where we ate supper the night before. Our typical fare in the *campo* would be *gallo pinto*, [the spotted rooster], red beans and rice — without the egg. In a *comedor* you don't ask for a menu. If they have food, you eat. Period. Being curious or cautious is to press your luck. Finicky folks shouldn't stray far from the buffet at Managua's Intercontinental. Strong Nica coffee abounded. If you drink it like the natives, it's a 50/50 mixture of sugar to coffee. The dextrose rush and caffeine jolt are guaranteed to shock the system and start your starter.

Sprawled over the tarps covering our gear in the truck beds, we left Matagalpa on the road heading north and east. Coming to the edge of town, a bright red pedestrian foot bridge crossed the highway. Across its steel sideboards were the words, *"Aqui No Se Rendie Nadie*!" (We will never surrender here!) In 1988 this was the national slogan. The phrase banners the headlines of the *Barricada*, the Sandinista daily newspaper. It is also used to cancel stamps on posted letters and you may hear it chanted like a mantra during political rallies. Next year the slogan will be different. They'll have to repaint the bridge.

One kilometer out of town and the paved road ended. So far we had been lucky. Now the dust began to fly as we put a new definition to the phrase 'bump and grind.'

We stopped at La Dalia, a compact community smaller than a village but larger than a *comarca* or a thin collection of homes and farms. The district headquarters of the FSLN was small and nondescript. Revolutionary graffiti covered the whitewashed adobe walls. To the left of the open door, Sandino's hat was stenciled in silhouette over the image of a machete. This icon of the Revolution evokes strong feelings of solidarity with *La Causa*. That 'ten gallon' hat, like the one Tom Mix wore in the old westerns, is a good image and meets an important qualification for being a movement symbol. Nobody is confused by its meaning and everyone from the smallest child can reproduce instantly; a half circle with a line slashed beneath it.

Fernando Torres is the Secretary of Political Education and Propaganda for the Frente Sandinista in the Waslala District. He clarified the term 'propaganda.' "We understand the word literally. It means to get the word out, to spread information. Not to deceive or manipulate the truth."

Torres is young, maybe in his early thirties, and handsome with a neatly trimmed dark beard. Wearing slacks and a short-sleeved white shirt open at the collar — no fatigues or Colt 45 in a leather holster slung off a webbed belt — he didn't look like a guerrilla. Within minutes it was obvious that he was bright and intense, a determined person exuding a kind of confidence generated from some layer deeper than the knowledge of facts.

The small office was commonplace. While Laura introduced our delegation, Torres listened with a widening grin and Laura smiled through her words. Maybe they both knew that this pro-forma piece was not necessary; only a polite gesture. On the other hand, every gesture that North Americans make in the direction of appearing peaceful and decent is not pro-forma. This man has been in combat against Contra armed with our weapons. Perhaps he has lost relatives or neighbors to terrorist kidnappings. Besides, he was sharing his afternoon with us. We were grateful.

Torres nodded his acceptance of our salutation and commenced to tell us about his world, the world we were entering, the world of Waslala. "The Waslala District is 140 kilometers in length and 46 kilometers wide. Since you have talked with Circles this morning, you know there are 32 state farms in this zone, 220 Sandinista co-ops, 140 other co-ops, and more small private farms than we can count. You may not know that there are 52 Catholic Churches in the district and 46 Protestant Churches. Not bad for a government that is the enemy of religion!"

He grinned broadly, taking pleasure in goading the popular myth of our own propaganda that does trifle with truth.

"We have the District hospital in Waslala and two major clinics; one in Rancho Grande and one here in La Dalia. The services of INSSBI are available throughout the district. When the Contra haven't cut the lines, we have telephone service as far as Waslala. Right now the lines are down."

Torres paused. "But we have greater problems in this zone. The war and infectious disease. Tuberculosis and infant mortality due to diarrhea and parasites are hard health problems for the poor."

He looked down at his hands and became quiet for a moment, a sad frown on his face. Soldiers know how to confront the enemy armed with rifles and grenades and artillery. Going up against the unseen enemy that poisons the system and steals life is another kind of battle. In the mountains, parasites are companions for life, needling their dim ways into the hidden tissues of their host, in the lung, in the sinewy gut, breeding, hatching, devastating. They steal and suck life away. And in their track — the injury beneath a blank look in desolate eyes. I ache for the sense of helplessness that *Comandante* Torres must feel. Again I wonder if perhaps he lost a child. Then I reflect, "Ask not for whom the bell tolls . . ."

Torres brought himself up and out of the silent moment. "Since the Esquipulas Accords were signed in Guatemala, 112 Contras have accepted amnesty and surrendered their arms. This has happened because the people have gone out and talked with them, trying to emphasize the difference between who they are as brother Nicaraguans and who it is that is behind them. It happened because soldiers of the Frente have gone into their units with physicians and nutritionists to talk and bring aid. They risk ambush and kidnapping but the message is worth the mission."

Hostile contact with the Contra has diminished since the Esquipulas Accords. Only 62 incidents known to Torres, and that includes the destruction of four trucks, two belonging to the State, and two which were the property of private co-ops. The Frente has made 250 attempts at dialogue trying to demilitarize the situation. Protestant pastors, Roman Catholic priests, and Delegates of the Word are encouraged to celebrate peace vigils and do all within their power to make it safe for Contras to return to their villages and attend worship. Land is offered as an opportunity for them to resume participation in normal productive society.

In areas where the Contra wield a powerful influence, FSLN negotiators stage small fiestas to attract them into dialogue. "We provide beer and dancing; we want only to talk," Torres insisted. "And we will never capture or harm them where we put forward the hand of friendship. But on the other hand, Frente members have been kidnapped on their missions to talk to the Contra in the mountains. Their troops move through Waslala returning to Honduras and they need to replenish their ranks with hostages and take them back across the river for training. They always loose some by desertion, or by sickness, or combat injury and death. Many of the kidnapped are teachers or health-care workers. Nine days ago we lost another teacher. That makes eight since the dialogues stopped. We have another dialogue scheduled for tomorrow near Waslala but we don't know if they will meet with us."

Contra leaders currently working in the Waslala staging area are Rojito, Johnson, and 'Strong Wind.' Troops moving south from Honduras meet the units coming north looking to hook-up with replacements and fresh supplies.

Torres ushered us into the adjoining room and over to a large map stapled to the wall. Frente and Contra troop movements and staging areas are indicated with different colors. He assured us that Frente intelligence is very accurate and up to date. "Right now, coming from the north out of Honduras, 1,600 Contra troops were arriving with fresh supplies. They are due north of Waslala. Coming from the south are 800 Contra that will join with these troops about here," and he pointed to a mountain ridge just south of the village of Waslala. "The fresh troops will receive information about the zone from those coming recently from combat and will then be deployed toward their missions."

He smiled. "Today it is calm. Traffic on the road is proceeding normally. But only during the day. We allow no travel over the roads after 3 p.m. or at night. The only movement on the road after dark is Frente troops or the Contra who are there to mine the road or destroy bridges. So far they have sabotaged four bridges between here and Waslala. You will see that we are rebuilding the major bridge, but now you must cross through the rivers. Fortunately the water runs low and slow. Later the ferries will carry people and cargo across to connect with vehicles on either side and you hop-scotch your way to Waslala. When the heavy rains come there is no crossing the rivers without the bridges.''

The friendly smile disappeared. ''Last week there were four hostile combats between us and the Contra. They were chance encounters, accidents. Soldiers meet each other coming out of the jungle onto the road or a clearing and they begin firing without thinking. Sometimes the combat is not accidental. Last week five Contra were drunk and made a solo action, not under orders. One killed himself with his own grenade. It is forbidden for a Frente soldier to drink while in uniform.''

I asked Torres if the Sandinistas can compete with the U.S. in offering incentives to persons contemplating becoming Contra. ''The Contra are composed of many youth and kidnapped persons. Mostly these are people from this zone, natives. We cannot make unrealistic promises. They know the truth. In the past we made promises that we could not keep and it hurt us. The Contra offer uniforms and boots and weapons. All of these are out of reach for the average *campesino*. They can't always provide food or health-care, but recruits don't know that. What we do propose is this: We will provide them with land and assist them in building a home. We do this for refugees so it is not unusual. Free medical care, a pension, education, and food. Again we offer this to everyone, so there is no difference. Medical care is crucial. We had none during the Somoza years. Now we take teams into the hills and vaccinate the Contra and the children if they have them in camp. Food is shared as we have it to share. We make a special case for Contra leadership. Since they are fighting for Dollars, we offer them Dollars if they will come over and bring some of their comrades. That cuts back on the funds we have for building schools and other programs. But if they join the Revolution there will be fewer schools we will have to rebuild because of Contra sabotage.''

One of our team commented on the posters hanging on the walls in the outer office. Underneath one is a quote from Ecclesiastes; "There is a time for Peace, a time for War, a time for Hate, a time for Love.'' Another is a paraphrase from Isaiah; "How beautiful are the things in the mountains that make for peace.'' All seven posters accented the same theme. It's worth mentioning that they are permanently mounted to the wall; not thumb-tacked, hastily put up for our benefit. And they are in Spanish!

One of the team, impressed by the theme of forgiveness on the posters, remarked, "That's a strange way to conduct a war.''

Torres' reply was chastening; "We have a nation to rebuild. It will require the efforts of all the people. The Contra troops are *campesinos*, our brothers. We must restore the unity. Some will never return. Their leaders who had land before the Triumph and were better off, they resent their losses. Some will never return because we have harmed them with the errors of our own troops. There is much to forgive. On both sides. And work to be done in peace. Together.''

REFLECTION: "Amnesty, Clemency, Pardon"

Torres spoke of the Amnesty. Amnesty means forgetting, amnesia, or as the Supreme Court defined it, the "abolition and forgetfulness of the offense.'' The American Civil Liberties Union suggests that amnesty is the discretionary action of a sovereign state deciding to abstain from prosecuting groups of citizens who may be in conflict with the state for political reasons. It wipes the slate clean. It restores the guilty to a condition of innocence. It is not earned. It is the act of goodwill undertaken by legal authority.

Clemency, on the other hand, relaxes the penalty. It is leniency, 'going easy' on the offender. This may be earned, as good behavior in prison brings early pardon, an earned re-entry.

Pardon means the remission of penalty; it cancels punishment. Pardon forgives the offender. It implies guilt. Those who accept pardon, like former President Richard Nixon, admit their wrongdoing.

The Sandinistas are proposing amensty. In Fifth Century Athens, the nation had been divided by a conflict of principle and the children of the defeated tyrants were restored to membership in the state by a declaration of amnesty. Subsequent historical precedents suggest that it has been extended not only to deserters from armies but also to those who engaged in acts of insurrection, piracy, and acts of rebellion by enemies of the state. Typically it is offered following victory as a generous act of grace to those who were defeated in the struggle.

If amnesty is truly a forgetting, an erasing of the enemy's deed from the nation's memory, it is well to remember what a remarkable feat this is — for the Sandinistas who propose amnesty, for the people of Nicaragua who must live with it. The devastations of burning and bombing, the routing of hundreds of thousands from their homes to be set on the road as refugees, the thefts, the assassinations, the torture, the rapes, the kidnappings . . . not to remember these is a large order indeed. It would be easier to forget the offenders than to forget the offenses.

So perhaps in the strict sense of amnesia as forgetting, amnesty needs to be hinged to a preceeding work; remembering without resentment, without the smoldering desire for revenge. Here the genius of Jesus becomes pivotal. Instead of punishment or pardon, the mandate is to love the enemy, to pray for those that spitefully use us. And before that can happen there must be forgiveness, radical and unconditional forgiveness. This is not conditioned on repentance for there is no implication that the offenders must become contrite, stand before authority with hat in hand reciting their *mea culpas*. Repentance is required before offenders can feel forgiven, but that is the intimate and personal work of their own journey in the spirit. What is necessary is that the governing authority forgives. As the 103rd Psalm reminds us, God does not deal with us according to our iniquities. Before God we are not given our just desserts. Were that the case we would beg for clemency, leniency, or flat pardon.

Forgiveness bridges the gap of our reluctances and makes reconciliation possible. All are brought together asking and receiving forgiveness from one another, not waiting for repentance one from the other. *Comandante* Torres was right; all need forgiveness — those who made the war from whatever motive or intent, and those who fought with whatever if any regrets. Reconciliation brings the family back together, restores relationship. It does not gloss over the issues that separated them in the battle. It puts them on the same side of the table for solving problems together, non-violently.

Finally, the issue is not the intent of the Contra to return or their desire to return or even the legal status of their right to return. Amnesty as forgetting may simply be a change of status which is important. But amnesty as forgiveness begins the challenging work of reconciliation. It is the first step in the direction of removing rancor from the ranks of the common life. Amesty restores self-respect; it's a decent thing in a time when all need to do a decent thing.

The words of President Lincoln come to mind; "With malice toward none, with charity for all, with firmness in the right as God gives us to see the right, let us strive to finish the work we are in; to bind up the nation's wounds."

On the road again and heading for Waslala, my mood turned. Amid the noise of the laboring diesel and the buffeting we were taking over this tattered road, I made an act of prayer:

"The smell of life is very much upon us now, O God. And the fact of death. Torres' words trouble my mind and make anxious my heart. War envelops this earth where brothers lift the sword against brothers. The panic of fear and the torture of insecurity rekindle ancient hatreds and prompt the shedding of blood. Surely Torres is right. There is much to forgive on both sides. Neither are we without guilt; for the sins of our pornographic affluence, our aggrandizement of it, our complicity in the terror of this war, our spiritual poverty.

"But it is right and true, O God, that now I seek room in my heart for peace. Already there is room enough for the chaos of my confusion and my bewilderment. Ben's death, the tales of Contra torture and rape, murder and pillage, this savage terrorism breeds a heady bitterness within that erodes my peacefulness while building a rampart for revenge.

"Center me and calm me down. Reveal to me a peaceful path. Then give me the wisdom to choose it. Bend me that the product of my mind and the resources of my spirit may be purposed to peace.

"No, I would not lead death to any person's door. And yes, I would join in common cause with those who work to build a friendly world of friendly neighbors beneath this beautiful Nica sky. That is the desire of my heart. Open unto me, Lord."

OBSERVATION: "Smiling Young Soldiers — Grimacing Old Guerrillas"

June 17

The road to Waslala is treacherous. Foothills lift into mountains of staggering beauty. Across the broad panorama, rugged peaks jut into the sky with columns of rock gathered at the scarp. Sporadic growth clings to the crevasses like an intrepid technical climber. At the base of the shears, a dark line is drawn where the lush jungle terrain has been halted in its march to the heights. Swerving or folded, the valleys below are verdant, glorious. How different from anything I have seen before. The jolting granite of the high Sierras at the Sonora Pass would be similar. But there is no comparison between pine forest and this tropical jungle.

The road skirts the mountain like a cow trail, jungle above, jungle below, a thin wobbly ribbon carved through rock and hardwoods. A stream plunges out of a fissure, becomes airborne, and crashes to earth disappearing in a misty spray at the roadside. The pool at the base of the falls looks inviting. Television commercials could be made of that scene; the jungle, cascading water, a collection pool, it lures like a Siren. The trucks grind on dodging the boulders but hitting the pot holes.

Convoys of IFA transporters rumble past moving in the opposite direction with their cargo of young soldiers in their late teen-age, about as old as my sons. Noticing the women on our trucks, they broke into large smiles and waved or flashed the 'V' sign. Others frolicked making flirtatious gestures, calling to the sisters, whistling the two-note universal code of attraction. The team shouted '*Adió.*' Nicaraguans mostly clip the 's' and use the word in greeting passers-by as well as on leaving.

Twice we passed columns of foot soldiers coming out of the jungle and walking beside the road. Unlike the young men on the IFA's, these are older and war-weary. No smiles, they do not wave or flirt with the women. Weather-beaten, their skin dark and tough, eyes bitter and penetrating, their features strong, they moved with the dangerous menacing dignity of men who have killed and not flinched. Laden with a full compliment of weapons and supplies, one hefted a rocket launcher and behind him other men toted the anti-personnel missiles that feed the lethal tube. Each carried a pistol, a machete, an assault rifle, and bandoliers worn in both directions across the chest. Overhead, a blurred colorless brightness forced their eyes into a squint. These are men at war. These are the guerrillas of the FSLN, the core of the Sandinista army.

Five times we forded rivers where the Contra reduced the concrete and steel bridges to tangled masses of rubble. Where the highway crosses the Rio Yesseca in a broad valley, construction crews worked cutting steel with acetylene torches while cranes hoisted huge beams over pilings reset in the riverbed. Some of the spans over canyons in the mountains are intact, guarded by detachments of heavily armed troops patrolling the highway with clusters of men and light-gauge artillery sandbagged into battlements on the mountain side.

The accent here is on rebuilding. Not building. Restoration. Repair. Not creation. Work on the trans-national highway is halted while the previous work is redone. So much Sisyphusing around. What should have been invested in building schools and hospitals and industry or homes is deferred and postponed. Caught in the whirlpool of war, when you cease being a developing nation what's left? A dissembled nation?

Wisely so, where the investment is, there is also its protection. It's not the soldiers that I see that concern me. I am becoming accustomed to the sight of uniformed troops standing in the road or sitting on trucks in the hunkered-down posture of waiting. Considering the alternative, as far as I am concerned they can wait all day. Until the Second Coming, for that matter. I am in no hurry to get caught in a firefight.

It's the soldiers that I barely see or merely glimpse that are unnerving — like the wizened and unsmiling guerrilla with an AK-47, the one looking at me with the keen eye of a hawk observing the pullet. Or the one suddenly standing there almost within arms reach when my head jerks around at the sound of a whoosh and the jungle's green screen parts to reveal a man with a machete in hand. Or the one that you think you see out of the side of the eye, and when you turn to look there is nothing there; only a whisp of motion, a shadow fading in the dusty rays of a blistering tropical ball of fire hanging due overhead.

War is the trickster of sanity. Not only is it a maddening waste but it tinkers with fundamental perceptions of reality.

REFLECTION: "War, the Trickster of Sanity"

Laurel Desnick, a former WFP Long-Termer, shared a story from her experience in the *asentamiento* of MuluKuku. A remarkable community of determined and hope-filled refugees, they succeeded in creating a model of corporate life that reflected democratic leadership and efficient production. While the war succeeded in turning much of their old life into garbage, they had the knack for converting it into compost. No small achievement.

Successful co-ops and *asentamientos* are a Contra target. MuluKuku was high on their list for a hit. A unique strategy of terror was executed that is worth the telling simply because it deviated from the norm of ruthless slash-and-burn terrorist tactics.

For several days, Contra laid a small number of landmines in the area surrounding the village. These, however, were not concealed, were not obscured with a thin covering layer of brush or earth. Easily seen and handily avoided by the villagers, their sole objective was to inspire terror. Each device presented a visible and lethal reminder of the enemy's lurking presence. Each night the landmines were carefully relocated until the villagers gained the reasonable impression that they were living smack dab on top of a deadly mine field. Stress levels accelerated as the tangible, concrete, and familiar patterns of their well-ordered lives began to disintegrate once again. Would the Contra mount a frontal assault, lay siege to the village, or take them out one by one with kidnappings and assassinations?

The co-op militia was put on alert. Individuals were assigned to stand watch through the night. One evening a single Contra quietly broke into the village store. Only a small amount of cash was stolen; no supplies disappeared. A note impaled onto the door with a knife reminded the villagers of what they knew already; they were vulnerable prey.

On discovering the note, the villagers calculated that the visit from the Contra occurred during the watch assigned to a particular old man. From there the situation deteriorated quickly. The old fellow was not dependable; he was lazy and not to be trusted. Furthermore, he had been slack in attending to other chores.

Their equanimity shattered, the traditional vehicles for settling disputes became useless. The grievance committee failed to operate with customary competence. Delegates of the Word were unable to facilitate a healing of the wounds that set family against family. The mechanisms of self-goverment and cooperative production stalemated and ground to a dead halt.

Unable to sort out the real over and against the unreal, they felt powerless. None were able to see that this was the calculated impact of the Contra tactic. The securities and confidences occupying a central place within their hearts were evicted by confusion and chaos. Why?

The threat of violence, a fact of their experience and never deleted from memory, is a powerful weapon. Without so much as firing a shot or exploding a landmine, the prospect of brutality produced a war of nerves that wrecked havoc upon sanity and soul. Whatever prop the mustering of a reconstituted militia might add to their shaken foundations, the fact of fear and the prospect of death was standing its vigil. It gnawed at their private ambitions; it eroded the fabric of community life.

I thought of those incredibly fitting words of Jesus in the tenth chapter of Matthew: ''Do not be afraid of them. There is nothing covered up that will not be uncovered, nothing hidden that will not be made known. What I say to you in the dark you must repeat in broad daylight; what you hear whispered you must shout from the house-tops. Do not fear those who kill the body, but cannot kill the soul. Fear him rather who is able to destroy both soul and body in hell.''

When the balance-wheel of sanity begins to wobble, when dangers from without infiltrate the fragile web of normal human relations, when our world churns and everything tied down starts coming loose, it is there, just there, that we need to stop.

In the British Royal Navy, an emergency onboard ship prompts the Captain's signal for the bosun to pipe 'The Still.' During training, the crew is conditioned in body and spirit to stop in their tracks upon hearing this call. It triggers an automatic reaction intent upon forcing them into a moment of lull, a moment of halt to reconnoiter the situation. It creates an interval enabling them to gather their wits and proceed with extreme care.

However a person stops the spin of a crazy world — through an act of deliberate breathing, a prayer, a personal affirmation — opening the spirit to some centering moment helps us detach from the emotional shackles of crisis. Confronted with overwhelming odds we find a sanctuary in which fear cannot survive, where we can redefine, reshape, and refocus our lives.

I think of the Contra soldier, the man who inflicted this havoc upon the villagers. He and his comrades are also victims. Hatred of that caliber destroys the mind and degenerates the spirit of the perpetrator. Like a boomerang, it turns against the executioner as surely as it threatens the victim. Consequently the Contra are casualties in the predicaments of their life, products of their own frustrations and trainings, and the insidious collective pressures commissioning them for this demonic work.

I do not excuse them. I would understand them, break the walls that isolate us from one another. If I refuse to keep this in my heart, I make room for retribution and the desire for vengeance. And once that happens, I too have been poisoned by evil and join in sharing company with wickedness. Both of us deserve to live in a friendly world. Neither of us can afford to abandon that dream or leave it to mere chance.

OBSERVATION: "Waslala — A Western Sound-Stage" June 17

The village of Waslala sits perched on a bluff overlooking the broad meandering Waslala River. Crossing on a one lane bridge, a steep climb takes you into the town proper. A litter of sagging windowless shops, a *comedor* and a *cantina* with their acrid sweet smells, a red-brick bank, mud, weeds, stagnant ditches — it looked like a sound-stage for a Clint Eastwood 'spaghetti western.'

Small tired horses tied to rails in front of plank walkways, gaunt cows, scrawny bent dogs and thin chickens, everything alive enough to move scrambled to avoid our diesel trucks. Main Street, the highway, was cratered with potholes big enough to swallow a tire. Generously pock marked with animal dung, the pigs scavenged the mire for want of better fare. Little children scampered behind posts and then peeked out at us with furtive glances. Listless adults paused to review our entry, occasionally waving, but more often simply observing us with quiet quizzical looks on their faces. How many times have they seen a caravan of *Norteamericanos* coming through this outpost?

159

East of the shops and toward the far edge of town, the Roman Catholic church compound sits directly across from the school and the military post. The five-acre complex is surrounded by a cyclone wire fence set on a concrete foundation. Two strands of barbed wire were strung on the top. Large swinging gates at the entrance were normally chained and locked. By comparison, security around the army camp looked feeble.

The church itself is a gangling patchwork of four by eight sheets of galvanized zinc and odds and ends of plywood. Twin wooden towers to the right and left of the front doors resembled silos for a barn. Corrosion and stain marred their metal skin and oozed down onto the sides leaving a patina of rust. An attempt to dress up the exterior with white wash failed. The tropical rains scrubbed the cosmetic work into the ground leaving a chalky and flecked residue. To the left of the entrance and piled on the grass, a stack of heavy steel re-bar in twenty-foot lengths lay on the ground oxidizing into orange flakes. The church is in the process of rebuilding, this time with reinforced concrete.

We would spend the overnight in the *campesino* bunk houses behind the rectory and old church. Tomorrow we will disperse to the homes of our host families. Pulling our gear off the trucks, we flopped onto the lush carpet of green grass. Our repose was cut short when someone leapt skyward in a clumsy wiggle slapping at the seat of their pants. Red ants. Now for the mosquitoes when the sun sets.

The hostel is a layover for construction crews when work is underway on the new building. Alternately, displaced families take emergency shelter there prior to being moved into hastily built shacks on the fringes of the village. Twenty sets of bunks lined the edges of the room with a narrow passage up a central aisle and between the beds. Men and women chose their bunks indiscriminately. Three men at the far end were playing guitars and singing nonchalantly, the gentle lyric poetry of Nica folkmusic.

Deciding to bathe and swim before dinner, we took laundry and soap in hand and walked down the trail heading for the river. An odd sight, this column of gringos. Julie, who lives in the village, took the point leading us beyond the last house on a low-slung bluff overlooking the river. The scragglers in the rear of the column, myself included, failed to see the gate only twenty feet away and squeezed through barbed wire at the head of a trail zigzagging down the cliff.

Twenty-feet away, in broad daylight and not concealed by jungle or anything else, and we missed the gate. If it had been a Contra we would have had an immediate short course in vigilance. The trick is to keep alert to what is around you as well as what lies under foot. I have that old primal fear of snakes. Ordinary enough. But those critters generally skedaddle, hiss, or rattle a warning to avoid being tromped. We were not cautioned about stepping on reptiles. Instead we were reminded that this is a war zone. Land mines don't slither away. Moreover they are curiously silent. Until they go off.

At the foot of the cliff a broad meadow stretched toward the river, a bowl of green under a canopy of sweet loamy air. The grassland was veined by thin cow paths meandering between thickets of brush and disappearing in stands of trees at the water's edge. In the rainy season when the river overruns its banks, this is either a swamp or underwater. In the distance, children played and cattle roamed freely. Across the trail a swath of ants proceeded in jiggling lines each toting bits of green leaf luffing their way into the tall grass where they disappeared.

The serpentine river moved slowly, gently lapping at the banks. Perhaps a half mile from the cliffs we found a spot in the shallows beneath two towering silk-cotton trees that vaulted into an umbrella of shade. Across their broad bottoms the trunks were buttressed in flanges, perfect for laying out our drying clothes or as a recliner for lounging into a nap.

The opposite river bank disappeared in thick jungle. In the distance two young men hunkered down, watching us intently. Our fair-skinned *chella* sisters must have presented a remarkable sight. Julie swam downstream with deft sure strokes, passed the men and stopped to shake out her long hair before making the return. The crawl back against the strong current was more difficult. A frisbee appeared and a game of toss and fetch evolved. Across the meadow, small boys rode barebacked pushing their horses at the gallop into switchback patterns through the grass; as good a ride as any Lakota I've ever seen on the Pine Ridge of Dakota.

Suddenly, two shots fired in the jungle broke the air and stopped our frolic. The report was muffled by the dense growth. The men downstream vanished and so had my relaxed disposition. Quiveringly alert, I waited for secondary sounds, shouts, bushes being pushed aside. To hell with the frisbee, bathing, the laundry, and napping. If there's a time for all things under the sun, this was not the time for drubbing with soap or housekeeping chores. I searched the trees in a vain attempt to locate the source or the target of the discharge. Nothing ricocheted off the water's surface so perhaps it was a bad shot, or a warning shot. The thought that we weren't the quarry didn't occur.

A *compa* emerged from a trail in the jungle. Carrying his AK-47 high overhead, he slogged across kicking up a wake. His companion appeared but paused to remove his boots before crossing at the shallows. Julie suggested that the men were hunting. Stands to reason. Ammunition is too precious for target practice. Besides, if they had just come from a tete-a-tete with the Contra they would be moving a lot faster than they were. So would I. There are times when I know without doubt that I too can walk, hell, run over water.

High in the trees across the river a bird screamed and took flight into the hot hammering sky. Its eerie sound trailed off in a slow muffled widening. Startled, the wet hair on the back of my neck shivered again. The cicada in the tree above us seized their cue and began that hollow shrill grind filling the air with a plaintive mysterious urgency. The sound rocked back and forth between the jungle and over the meadow, an anarchistic cacophony. My tension remounted like a low-grade fever; always with you and only momentarily put out of mind. Then David yelled for the soap. I was about to tell him to find

162

his own damned Ivory when everything suddenly stopped in a tremendous mindless silence. The jungle, the cicada, everything turned off, shut down. It seemed as if the river slowed down, turned to molasses, stalled. The air quivered then became still. My inclination was to lay low, become inconspicuous, and put as much distance between me and this place as feet and strength would allow. I was in the market for some un-North American anonymity.

REFLECTION: "What You Seek from Beyond, You Must Find from Within"

Dusk settles upon the valley,
cicada cease their clamorous cacophony,
the tranquil river murmurs, 'Lift your eyes unto the hills,
What you seek from beyond, you must find from within.'
In the soft highlighted after-glow,
the deep breath, the long look,
a heartening gaze, and I yield, open to life's moving light
casting its shafts down the corridors of my spirit.
Poised at the zenith of its arc,
time changes guard in the darkish isthmus
bridging sunlight and moonlight,
this portal through which together we must pass,
this arena for dancing gods and mystery.
I stop my world to wait and watch,
standing between the tics of the cosmic clock,
humbled before nature's celestial tryst,
honoring this interval of the sacred,
accepting the gift of raw spirit.
Sweeping across the savannah of my lifescape,
dusk — the holy architect —
kneads eventide with mysterious power,
embracing my fears of war,
absorbing all fractious business-as-usual,
quieting bankrupt babble,
mending fractured dreams,
succoring the bastardy of affections,

163

hushing my galvanized insecurities,
collecting all traces of fevered life into
an indescribable tenderness stealing into my fingers
with the delicate disciplined touch of a gentle lover.
In the Great Quiet,
beneath a glowing firmament and limitless landscapes,
reason is nonsense and faith stands the watch alone,
deeding to God the yesterdays, these moments,
and all tomorrows.
At day close, grant a blessing of serenity,
a benediction of peace,
reminders that neither crisis nor catastrophe are eternal,
cannot eclipse dusk's wonder,
nor diminish its splendor.
The river shades to indigo, byzantine silences,
ripples brailling primeval wisdoms
more ancient than breathing;
'Lift your eyes unto life, for lengthening shadows
veil the seeds of the morrow;
Open your heart to love, and touch with tender hand
dimness and death, your pale laughter
and abounding tears;
Cast me the cargo of your cares, your dreams,
that together we may flow to our sacred source.'

OBSERVATION: "Enrique Blandon — Maverick Priest"
June 17

Darkness overtook the village. In the parish's communal
kitchen, above the conversation around the supper table and
the buzz of insects, the drone of the portable electric generator filled the night air with a rumbling hum. Three facilities
in the Waslala enjoy the luxury of electric power; the district
hospital, the military base and the Catholic church. The rest
of the villagers use kerosene lamps or set their schedule according to available natural light. At night we were the only
ones on the streets and trails with flashlights. Either the villagers

know the paths by heart or don't mind bumping into trees and animals or sliding off embankments.

Then that lore about the third man on the match bumped into mind; six inches behind the glowing light and you might be in a snipper's cross-hairs. Inadvertently kissing a tree or a cow would be welcome by comparison. The *comandante* warned us against using the roads by night. Does that include paths through the village? I chose to use my flashlight sparingly and at odd and irregular intervals. No reason to tempt the devil. In any event, Waslala is not an appliance-driven settlement. Electricity is a luxury appreciated by a few when it is available, tolerated when it is not; most do without it altogether.

Father Enrique Blandon looks to be in his middle thirties. A handsome man, he displayed the powerful melancholy mien of a priest who understood dying. Waiting for us inside the church, he looked tired and perhaps a little peeved. In Levis and a T-shirt he had the countenance of *Comandante* Omar Cabezas minus the scar on the right cheek.

For the past seven years he has been the priest assigned to the districts of Waslala and Siuna, this zone where the war has been intense and unremitting. These are the mountains, the combat terrain, that Cabezas described in his book **Fire From the Mountain**: "In Waslala there are mosquitoes all day long, mosquitoes everywhere . . . That's why your face becomes lined in the mountains — your expression is always pained."[16] And these are the same mountains in which Cabezas contracted lesymaniasis — mountain leprosy.

Blandon shifted in his chair and began to speak: "For two years I have worked with the *campesinos* in Waslala. I have learned how to evangelize in war. Not in seminary. And, as you can see, I have been privileged to enjoy an important relationship with the brothers and sisters of the Witness for Peace. Over the years I have been threatened by the Contra because of the kind of work we do in this parish. But during the past two months we have been breathing the air of peace; we have great hope for peace."

165

He added quickly, in an effort to be precise, "But it is only a relative peace. The war has not ceased. Remember that the cease-fire is unilateral, a significant gesture of good will on the part of the Sandinistas. The Contra have not agreed to it. In that two months there have been 12 combats, 49 kidnappings, 8 murders, and 2 ambushes. All have been documented. Ten days ago a new truck was ambushed and burned. What's left of the truck is here in town. You can see it."

Where's the peace?

Blandon continued; "During the past ten weeks we have had 28 Contra come back and accept Amnesty. Four different dialogues have occurred between Contra and Sandinista leaders and 36 group meetings have been held to provide the people with information about the Accords and how the Process is developing. These group meetings are the work of the Christian community. We receive the latest information from Managua and take it into the hills and countryside. The war has not paralyzed the work of the church."

There are 60 resettlement communities in the Waslala District. In the past four months, 9 kilometers of new roads have been built connecting these outposts. Over these roads and on trails passable only by foot or horseback, Delegates of the Word move into the war zone reactivating schools and offering instruction. Blandon said that the lessons are functional; basic health practices and grain and crop cultivation. "In the time of Somoza there was no education for *campesinos*. If they received any instruction at all it was the Church that did the teaching. And the Church was instrumental in the great literacy campaigns. Many learned to read with the Bible as their teaching text book," Blandon said with a smile. "In fact, in the war zone most of the educational materials are provided by the Church. We teach the people using religious literature."

"You look puzzled?" he asks. "We do this to protect the teachers. If they are sent from the Ministry of Education, they ae singled out and targeted by the Contras. But the Contra respect our teachers and let them pass. If they were carrying

Ministry of Education materials with their heavy political content they would be killed. So now when the Contra examine their books and lessons they see that they are not carrying dangerous literature. Their safety is not jeopardized." He broke into a hard laugh. "They have no appreciation for the revolutionary message in the Gospels."

One of the teams asks if he has been kidnapped.

"Twice. The first time with Sandra Price, a *Norteamericano* from California. We spent three days under strong interrogation. The last time was from October 9 to 21 the past year. Three of us, myself, an Evangelical pastor, and a Seventh Day Adventist pastor, were invited by letter from the Contras to meet with them and dialogue about the Sapoa Accords. But we were betrayed."

Blandon made a fist of his right hand and stared at it for a long drawn-out moment. "They had no interest in dialogue. It was a mask for a major Contra offensive. A group of twelve Contra kidnapped us and accused us of being Sandinista politicians and communists. They said we were trying to persuade their troops to surrender. This was one of five simultaneous operations and Waslala was being harassed by mortar fire. The vehicle bridge leading into the village was destroyed in that assault. Even the military base was under attack and there was intense combat in the hills.

A look of disgust crossed his face. "Our Contra interrogators kept repeating a long list of questions like they were parrots. They didn't understand what they were asking. The dupes!" The frown turned into a broad smile. "Well, they didn't know what was going on. Here they had three clergy two of which are conservative evangelicals. When the word of our capture got back to their families and congregations it went quickly to the U.S. and around the world. 'Contra Attack and Kidnap Clergy,' is bad press. The pressure put on the U.S. State Department was decisive. A North American conservative Catholic Bishop demanded my release. Finally the Contra received a direct order from Washington D.C. to let us go. It is interesting, but our kidnapping did aid the

Contras in one respect. Many of the people in the mountains knew me as their priest. They brought us food as we passed through their territory. But the Contra took the food for themselves without giving us any and for days at a time we went hungry.''

Father Blandon's mother was in Wisconsin during this period. The State Department and her Bishop called to report on his condition and assure her that Enrique was alive. Following his release he joined her in the States and compared notes. ''The reports to my mother of my condition during the interrogations were true. In fact they were exact. And the U.S. says it has no direct participatory role in this war?''

On a sad note, Blandon reported that the Roman Catholic hierarchy in Managua offered no support whatsoever. ''They said I was worth more dead than alive to the Sandinistas. In fact they blamed the Sandinistas for the kidnapping saying it was a publicity plot. Actually the Contra kept us in positions of danger. They forced us to the head of moving columns where we might step on landmines or be shot by Sandinistas if we encountered their patrols in the jungle. Then the government would be blamed for our murders. When the Papal Nuncio in Managua met me following my release, he asked me, with no shame at all, if it was really the Contras who were the kidnappers. There are no worse blind than those who do not want to see.''

Living under the threat of Contra violence is accepted as part of his ministry. Three times he has been ambushed on the highway. On occasion they have interrupted the Mass with gunfire or entered the sanctuary to stand beside the pews with their rifles pointing at members of the congregation. Neris Roble was one of his parishioners. On April 17th, Neris was found dead two hundred yards from the chapel, his throat slit and shoes stolen because he defied a Contra order and attended worship at Blandon's church when Father Ubaldo Gervasoni was preaching.

I recall that the Contra's marching slogan is, 'With God and Patriotism we will Fight Communism!' Threaten the priest, kill the parishioners, disrupt worship. In the name of God? For Nicaragua? To rescue democracy?

"Communism is not the issue for them," Blandon continued. "They would not know how to define it. They are angry with the Sandinistas because there is not enough food, no sugar or oil for cooking, and they do not have boots. They refuse to accept that there is not enough of these things for all the people."

Father Blandon's first experience with Liberation Theology occurred in college. He has been practicing it for the past seven years of his ministry. "In college I learned the stories of the great Christian martyrs of Latin America. To be a Christian and committed to share the life of people means that you will be persecuted. I accept this. At one point when I was being interrogated, a Contra soldier asked the commanding officer for permission to kill the priest. Well, they can kill me. And other priests as well. But they can never kill the faith or the spirit of the people."

A team member solicited, "What is your Liberation Theology?"

Blandon replied, "It comes from our reflections and prayers and study of the Bible as we work to build the Reign of God. It develops as we promote the practice of justice and peace and love. Our theology is a product of what we share, here, in Waslala. It does not come to us from the Vatican or the Cardinal in Managua. We are not passive. We do not wait. That is a corrupt deception, to believe that the Reign of God comes in the afterlife. The *campesinos* are not fooled. They know that poverty and oppression are created by humans. So they must be resolved by humans. And that is what we do. We are the architects of the Reign of God."

Inevitably the question of violence was asked; "What kind of violence do you support?"

"Many pacifists react negatively to the fact that movements of national liberation cannot avoid the evils of war and killing. But the Bishops of Latin America in 1968 reminded the world that there are other kinds of violent death: Death from landless poverty and the facts of hunger and unemployment and no health-care and no education. If you count these deaths, those that died by armed violence would be far fewer in number.''

He did not address the question of whether or not, in his view, a Christian is justified in using violence as a tool to win freedom from exploitation. The hour was late and he was tired. I suspected that his mind resisted diving into abstract reveries. Perhaps he would return to the subject at a later session. Unfortunately, he did not.

Later during the week Father Blandon and I spoke privately. I decided against questioning him on theological justifications for the use of violence. I doubted that we would agree. Instead I questioned him about the Sandinista's treatment of Roman Catholics, specifically three incidents. While these occurred some years earlier, I was curious to see if they reflected patterns in the government's dealing with the Cardinal's strident opposition to the regime.

"In 1982," I began, "the government prohibited the release of a Papal letter to the bishops of Nicaragua in which the Pope advised against the politicization of the Gospel. Do the Sandinistas normally censor communications from the Pope when they are hostile to the Process?''

Blandon cocked his eyebrow, looking stern and perplexed, as if to suggest annoyance at my ignorance of the facts, "First, the Pope's letter was read immediately in all the parishes before it became an issue of censorship. The issue was whether or not it would be printed in *La Prensa* and read over the Church's radio station. The Archdiocese decided to offer the letter only to that paper and when the censors got their hands on it they interpreted it as an attack on the 'popular church.' The Vatican believes that churches supportive of the Process are deviating from accepted religious teaching and work. Second, the censors created a delay, but not two weeks worth; it lasted for two days. *Barricada* and *Nuevo Diario* published it right away and *La Prensa* never did. Yes, it was an error to censor the letter, but in my judgment it was an error for the Pope to send it in the first place. We simply do not agree with each other on these matters of faith and the work of the Gospel. Fortunately Rome is a long ways away. So is Managua, especially when the telephones are not working." The frown had changed into a broad smile.

Remembering that the head of the Catholic radio station had been caught in a scandal worthy of our own *National Enquirer*, I asked whether the Sandinista police marched this priest naked through the streets after cathcing him in bed with a woman.

Perhaps my impertinence was worth the two-eyebrow hoisting it received. The preist's alleged *flagrante delicto* received televised exposure in Nicaragua and was covered by the Sandinista press.

"Does the government regard itself as having proper authority for the policing of a priest's morals?" I asked.

"What happened in that situation is not clear except that it was an embarrassment to the priest and the church, and especially for the woman. Personally I believe that it was set-up. The government had nothing to do with it except make a bad situation worse by allowing it to be publicized. Initially, the censors prohibited the showing of the television film and banned the story from the press. But *La Prensa* violated the restriction and sensationalized the incident. What happened and who was responsible remains debatable. Was it a coincidence that the police just happened to be waiting outside, that the television people just happened to be in the neighborhood? Did the woman's former husband actually interrupt Father Carallo having an affair? Or did he force them to undress while they were having a meal and then push them into the street in an act of vengeance? There are too many coincidences here. I believe they were victimized by someone out to create trouble for them both. But who . . . I do not know."

I sensed that Father Blandon was tiring of this gringo's inquires but I pressed my third question anyway.

"Monsignor Jose Caldera was a popular priest in Managua's Santa Rosa parish. When the Archbishop transferred him because of his work with the Sandinistas, his

171

parishioners protested and occupied the church. An Auxiliary Bishop arrived to confront the congregation and was beaten by what he called a mob. If the Cardinal were to reassign you out of Waslala, would his representative meet with similar treatment?''

At last I managed a question that did not stir the Father's ire.

Smiling broadly with a twinkle in his eye he simply remarked, ''Caldera called himself *'una cura de barrio y no de salon.'* '' (A neighborhood priest, not a drawing room priest.) ''Again the reports differ. The Auxiliary said he was cursed and pushed to the floor, others insisted that he tripped in the confusion and was not beaten. Nevertheless the Archbishop excommunicated all those involved in the protest. The point is that the government did not get involved in the incident. It had no business there and this time they were smart in staying away.''

Would something like that happen here if you were reassigned?'' I pressed my point.

I hope I am a priest of the Gospel and the people. That's what the Process is all about. As they say it in the U.S., 'Power to the People!' Would it happen here? Managua is a long way from Waslala. We are poor and we are small. Why should they bother?''

It was time to go. Besides, it was good to leave with a warm handshake and laughter between us, two clergy from distant parishes, both committed to the power of one Gospel and 'power to the people.'

REFLECTION: ''Architects of the Reign of God''

The light from the Coleman lantern flickered. Between the hiss of the gas light and the buzz of insects in the night, hard silences lay into the intervals between Father Blandon's thoughts. He is neither a consummate theologian nor perhaps much of a contemplative. Neither is his religion wrapped in a cloistered spirituality. There is dirt and blood on the man and a touch of the rogue. His mission is clearly that of

172

Christianizing Nicaraguan society by confronting the forces that corrupt and oppress, from without — from within. And he will not be a spectator.

"We are the architects of the reign of God." Architects dream of what might be, conceive forms, fashion models, and make a blueprint for construction. The objective is to transform ideas into material realities, to put order on the chaos.

The Kingdom of God is a dream. Ultimate in its essence, perhaps as an ideal it is beyond our farthest reach. In the glimmer of that dream, in the faint momentary glint caught out of the side of the eye — for Father Blandon, for me — some things are certain. When the Kingdom comes, much will be noticeable by its absence. The landscape won't be littered with bomb craters and children won't forage the dumps scrounging food. Infants won't be held to the dry breast while their tummies distend — not because of plenty but because of parasites. Young widows will not cry themselves to sleep on pillows turned to stone and men will not stand on corners gazing with blank stares into nothingness with hands listlessly dangling at their sides or gripping a bottle of bootlegged liquor. Nor with another lay upon a hospital bed searching for feet that are no longer there while dumbly shaking a head that cannot get shed of the muffled roar of a landmine exploding.

Ask Father Blandon what the Kingdom is about and he'll tell you what won't be there: not the sordidness of the struggle, nor mindless life-crushing brutality.

Peace and justice are the keepers of the Kingdom. Love is the inspiration of its dominion. Its common ground is everything that says Yes to life, quickens the pulse, and inspires hope. It is the magnet that tugs at the heart of the race pulling toward fact that which cannot be left to fancy. That Kingdom is that which cannot be abandoned either at the time of prayer or in the sweat of labor. For without such dreams we wither and become very poor and wretched indeed.

The source of Kingdom dreaming is a mystery. It is the best of life yet it comes from somewhere beyond life. I sense it when I see this young priest who will not yield to the intimidations of guerrillas, when he breaks into smiles as young children gather in a tangle at his feet, or as he stops dead in his tracks when an old woman hesitatingly asks for a moment of his time and you know that as he bends to listen there is nothing more important, no war, no meeting, nothing.

But Kingdom-consciousness is more than a feeling, more than a response to distant music, or a poem on the wind. Kingdom ideals take form as Blandon listens to that old woman's words, for architects must deal with stubborn realities. If it is to be a place fit for humans, then it must be crafted from the stuff of life, the raw materials of her experience, and the children's, and mine too. There must be about it something recognizable, a place where we can celebrate the character of the living spaces of our daily place. Close at hand. Something to which we can belong. Something that informs our striving. And although we are damn short of getting there and prone to fail again and again, we are not alone. We are not only the keepers of the dream, but we are kept by it as well. And each step toward humanness in the midst of monumental insanity is in fact one step closer to the nearer end of that far-reaching Kingdom.

What we seek in Kingdom dreaming, if we seek it at our best, from where we are, when we are most ourselves, is the very stuff that God is seeking for us, through us. Yes indeed. Daily bread, a humble heart, our portion of justice, an inclination to mercy, and forgiveness for our sins.

OBSERVATION: "Commodity Shortages — Hope Surpluses"

June 18

Walking down the main street of the village, two things surprise me. One is cheerful. The other is not. Apparently Waslala is the center where the region's sewing cooperatives market their garmets. On both sides of the street small shops display assorted dresses and shirts with bright primary colors beautifully embroidered onto cotton so white you would think it bleached. Conditioned by tourism, I expect to see lavish

174

clothing at city boutiques and airport shops. I am surprised to find them in a mountain outpost. Odd, too, is the fact that few of the villagers are wearing the fruits of their labor; most make do with patched-over hand-me-downs.

Other stores sell medicines, hardwares, and a minimal assortment of farming supplies. By my reckoning, if you took all of the goods and furnishings off all the shelves from every shop and stacked them in the street, you would be able to put them into a medium size U-Haul truck. Not even enough for a corner convenience store in the States. This, for a commercial center that serves a district of 30,000 population!

Three men comprise the Waslala *Junta* and are responsible for the government of the municipality. Jorge Martinez is the Coordinator of the Junta; call him the mayor. Don Valverde is the Coordinator of Finance, the municipal treasurer. Rauel Fonseca, the brother of Carlos Fonseca Amador, is the Registrar responsible for recording births and deaths, marriages, and land titles.

Fonseca is rumpled by age and hard years, his voice low and deep, intense but friendly: "Fifteen years ago Waslala was a village of four houses. Until 1979 this was a remote outpost of Somoza's National Guard. Many of our revolution's guerrillas trained and fought in the surrounding mountains. My brother Carlos was not the only *comandante* killed near here. Claudio Chamorro, Edgar Mondia, Rene Tejada Peralta also died here. Tello was killed nearby during the December 1974 attack on the Guardsman barracks up the street." He seemed lonesome and beaten, his head teeming with tragic memories.

He continued, "In 1979 after the Triumph, the National Assembly called for the administration of justice in the departments and I was appointed *responsable* to Waslala. I was happy to serve here. There are too many people in the west. This is Nicaragua's frontier. I served until 1982 when the Junta was formed and we elected the officers of our government. In this department there are 126 small communities and maybe 30,000 population. Only 5,000 or so live in this town."

One of the team asked the Coordinator of Finance, Don Valverde, how the devaluation of the Cord would impact the affairs of the district. "It hurts. Projects like a water system for the town began in 1985 but are now on-hold because of the war and the unstable Cord. The things we need for our families, they go up in cost but as state employees our salaries do not increase as well. But these problems are not so big. Our greatest probems are how to provide homes and food and jobs for displaced persons. We do not have the resources to do this for ourselves. But Dorstan, our Sister City in West Germany, is involved in a project of building 40 dwellings for these families."

Eventually Fonseca closed the session with the following words: "We as Nicaraguans and residents of Waslala express our deep sincerity and appreciation for your coming to us. We hope that you will see that our people do not carry in our hearts and minds any hate for the people of the U.S.A. Unfortunately we have political differences between our governments. But we want peace between our peoples. Precisely for this reason we are in national dialogues with the Contras. To my way of thinking, and to my brother Carlos' too, people who desire war are unbalanced. They are crazy. It would be a good thing if the rich and powerful people would sign a treaty for world peace. In the battlefields of today it would be better to plant basic grain under a flag of peace. While you are in Waslala, feel you are in your own land."

Back at the Church, Josephina Radia and Santos Molina were waiting in the sanctuary with Father Blandon. Each shared accounts sketching their experiences with the Contra.

Following introductions, the priest introduced Josephina Radia. A soft tragic quality shone from the pain in her eyes. "My father had a farm in the rural village of Saffana, about 50 kilometers from here, a one and a half day walk. We grew cacao and sold it here in Waslala. The Contra passed often through that zone and across our land. Then they began to accuse us of collaborating with the Sandinistas because we came here to sell our cacao. On October 17, 1984, they came to our home early in the morning and took me away. They were led there by an informer in the village. They took me to a Contra house and kept me there overnight. On the second day I was brutally tortured, raped, and accused of working for the Sandinistas. It was not the first time I had been raped. That happened when I was fourteen; the men belonged to Somoza's National Guard.''

Tears dribbled over her cheeks.. Fourteen years old and stripped of her exuberance as casually as dandelions are ruptured by the wind. "By the end of the week, the Contras took me into Honduras to the military base called Las Stregas. I was kept a prisoner there for three years. Eventually I discovered the reason they kidnapped me; my brother Juan Jose Rodriquez was a soldier in the Frente. When they beat me and raped me they said that he would get the same treatment. It was a lie. He had been killed earlier during an ambush. Every day I wanted to return to Nicaragua and my three children but I did not try to escape. I feared that I would be killed by the Contra, or by the Sandinistas if they thought I was a Contra sympathizer. Following Esquipulas II last August in Guatemala, the border opened at Las Manos and I was allowed to go there. I did not know where my children or family were but someone in this church heard I was at Las Manos and told my mother to come and see me. She brought a letter from the Sandinistas guaranteeing me a safe return home.''

Senora Radia brought her young son to her side. He looked to be ten or eleven, caught up in a silent holocaust, mute, shriveled. "He has not spoken a word since the Contra kidnapped me. Even now that I am home he does not make a sound.'' She hugged him close and joined her son in silence.

My noisy mind stopped working. So did my heart. Each had become frail, exhausted. Sometimes it costs a lot to remain alive. Josephina Radia paid some heavy dues for the privilege. What kind of memories invaded that family's dreams during the night? Did she remember the laughing faces of violent lusting men, the sounds of their demented passions? Or was God generous enough to allow these haunting remembrances to dissolve like salt in the seas?

And the boy? If his muteness was hysterical, a reaction born of terror and the trauma of witnessing his mother's abduction, what would it take to loosen him up? To a laugh? Or a shout? Or a murmured, 'Mama?' Tears don't need a voice. Would he have to take a knife in hand and slit a Contra throat before the sight of blood on his knuckles would free up his tongue? Or would God provide a miracle, get on the block again and start taking care of business?

My bewildering muse vanished. The backdoor of my mind slammed shut like a steel trap and I half hoped that God got a paw stuck in its teeth. As far as I was concerned, the time was long overdue for that Mystery to be put through the double-ringer.

Santos Ochooa Molina is a sad little whip of a man. Short, gaunt and sickly, earlier Father Blandon mentioned that Santos struggles with many demons. One of them is more invisible than the Contra; Santos is alcoholic. Sitting on the bench with his wife, Santos began to remember things that do not need to be remembered; they remember themselves.

"For us it is sad to be in Waslala." He was almost whispering. "I was taken from my home on November 7, 1987. The Contra said they were going to kill me for being a Communist, a Sandinista, a '*peri quako*' (mad dog). Before that, Contra collaborators took one of my cows, a pig, and some of my chickens. Always they were leaving me less and less. They left receipts saying that they did this for the Contra and that I was suppose to trade the paper for cash at Contra headquarters. One receipt was for my pig. It said they owed me 60 Cords. When I went to the Contra for the money they said they were going to kill me for not supporting the liberation of our country. Later they came to my farm and I became their prisoner."

He dropped his head and licked his lips before continuing. "Some of the Contra were dressed like *compas*. They tried to make me believe that it was the Frente that really wanted to kill me. I escaped by running through the coffee *fincas* and forests until I found a real *compa* who took me to the *asentamiento* on the Rio Blanco. Finally, I was taken to Matagalpa and the Bishop's office. He told me I was too involved in politics and sent me back to Enrique here in Waslala."

178

Like a man who has hit bottom and not bounced, he said, "My wife and family are here, but the farm is gone. We are mountain people. To live here in Waslala with no land is hard. The old life was so good. But now we have nothing. I gather firewood and peddle it to make a little money so we can live. Our youngest daughter died since we have been here in Waslala. She starved to death. That never would that have happened on our farm. The Contra and their collaborators have my 7 cows with calves. They took 120 pounds of rice and 7,200 pounds of corn and 70 pounds of beans, 12 pigs, and 2 horses. The *correros* [informers] even sold some of our dishes here in Waslala."

Was life trying to slip him a daily does of Mickey Finns? He was near exhausted, spent. "But I am a Delegate of the Word," he said with a jumpy assertiveness. "For twenty years I have been a lay leader of this parish. When Father Enrique was kidnapped I tried to get others to assist in his release. The Contra accused him of being a Captain in the Frente and those who worked for him are Lieutenants." He spat on the floor and stopped talking.

When the Contra kidnapped Santos, his wife was in town and the children were at home. An older daughter is a novitiate with the Brazilian nuns at the parish. The mother was working in the Sewing Cooperative which is organized through the church. The Contra claim that working in community cooperatives is a violation of political neutrality.

And then it was over. Father Blandon stood, motioned us to remain seated, and spread his arms like wings around his families and gently took them to the door.

REFLECTION: "Going Through the Double Ringer"

No banalities, no cliches, no polite wheezings of the forebrain that put a foundation under most conversation. How many times had the priest listened to these narratives? Perhaps on the first hearing he erupted in a paroxysm of rage, the visceral involuntary ferocity of a father on being told that his children have been violated. But now it appeared as if his internal temperature had dropped thirty degrees in as many minutes. And what was left . . .? A compassionate but rugged revolutionary hardness that will not falter, weaken, or wear out.

To ask him about his endorsement or participation in defensive or retaliatory violence seemed impertinent, an invitation to join me in speculations from the safe and detached vantage point of the armchair. When I break the bread and pour the wine at the communion table, these are substitutes for my body and blood. Not Christ's. When this priest consecrates the elements, he does so in the presence of people for whom the sacrament is no metaphor, who kneel at that table making the sign of the cross over their own broken flesh, who drink from that cup and remember the taste of their own blood. I ritualize the death and resurrection of my Lord as an act of intensely private devotion, this side of the barricade, celebrated with clean hands and a modestly clean conscience. What must it be like for those who do not die a little or suffer minimally?

OBSERVATION: "Fidel Ventura Hospital: 'War is the first illness we must treat!' "

June 18

Fidel Del Ventura was a young medical doctor and Frente guerrilla. Killed fighting beside Carlos Fonseca, the District Hospital in Waslala bears his name and honors the memory of his sacrifice.

Dr. Jose Francisco Umana is also young, Nicaraguan, and has as smile that opens as fast and wide as a switch-blade. He is the Director of the Hospital and one of the 'new breed' — doctors who trained and graduated during the 1980-1986 cycle. Between the 'Triumph' in 1979 and his 1986 graduation, some 700 physicians and 900 health technicians fled the country. Having tendered their services through Somoza's conspicuously elitist system of restricted care centers and private practices serving the middle and upper classes, they didn't get going when the going got tough; they got out! The 'new breed,' the medical personnel of the 'Process,' bring their talents to bear on the 90 percent of the population previously ignored or excluded from the old medical marketplace.

When Umana gets paid, this physician and hospital director earns $50 a month. The likelihood is scrimpy that he will ever become a member of a rich or privileged caste. The vacuum created by the exodus of his predecessors was being filled, slowly and painstakingly, by women and men willing to trade material incentives for compassion.

Umana greeted us and introduced his Italian associate, Dr. Claire Castana, who smiled at us bemusedly. She has worked in Nicaragua for five and one half years, half of that at this hospital in Waslala. Except for the stethoscopes hanging around their necks, there was no other evidence that either of them were physicians; no badges or special clothing to rank and separate them from their patients.

The Director has a flair for lecturing. He seized a piece of chalk and stepped to the blackboard. A flurry of words and typical physician's scrawl followed; "*Curanderos* have been the traditional healers in the Nicaraguan rural areas. They are a cultural institution that ought not be dismissed. They were trusted by the *campesinos*," he remarked. "Furthermore, they had at their disposal a vast pharmacy of medicinal leaves, powders, and potions that often brought effective treatments to the people."

Since 1985, the impact of the war on supplies of modern therapies prompted a renewed interest in the craft of these 'primitive' healers. Bread for the World, the European Economic Community, and Oxfam U.S.A. provide funds for researching the lore and materials of Nicaragua's traditional medicine. The resulting inventory of herbal resources classifies 325 as medicinal plants, 72 of which are regarded as 'clean,' meaning they demonstrate proven results in the treatment of benign illnesses. Botanical pharmacies established by these grants use garlic, eucalyptus, mint, mango, and guava as medicines for diarrhea and bronchio-respiratory diseases.

"Modern medicine brought pills and hypodermic needles and advanced surgical skills. That was progress," Umana added. "But when sales representatives from transnational pharmeceutical corporations attached themselves to the physicians, together they flooded the country with medications and progress became a problem."

The transition from the *curanderos'* potions to bottled drugs was swift and indiscriminate. The supply was excessive, the demand inordinate, and the penchant for self-diagnosis and self-medication resulted in abuse. Since the average *campesino* is unable to consult an equivalent to our **Physician's Desk Reference**, typically they opt for the rare, the exotic, and the expensive elixirs.

"Aspirin and Milk of Magnesia are on the shelves of stores in our village," Umana reported. Well and good. "And right next to them, six varieties of ampicillin for the flu and Valium for nervous tension." The latter is little more than powdered alcohol, the drug of choice for the North American suburbanite looking to get stoned without the tell-tale of boozy breath. Nicaragua produces the world-class rum, *Flor de Cana*, and each region distills its own bootlegged liquor. Consequently they have problems enough with alcoholism and cannot afford to become a society of genteel addicts.

The problem of health-care became more complicated. Umana continued, "If a *campesino's* physician determined that an illness was best treated with undramatic methods like bed rest, avoiding caffeine, and drinking plenty of water, the patient concluded that they had not been treated. Without being given handfuls of pharmaceuticals, they reasoned that the doctor was either not taking them seriously or was incompetent."

Curandero care, self-care, no care. The options were hazardous. Against that, however, Somoza's health programs were a paltry and usually non-existent option.

Umana continued; "The Somoza government was paternalistic, among other things, and they regarded health-care as so much welfare." Charity. "Minimum was sufficient," he grimaced, "and when that was available it was provided by foundations and humanitarian causes administering the sparse resources provided by the state. But twenty days after the Triumph, the new Sandinista government instituted the Single

National Health System (SNUS). Health-care for the people was a top priority in the program of the Revolution. The guiding principles of SNUS were sixfold, three of which were accented: (1)Health is the right of all and the responsibility of the state; (2) Health services should be accessible to the whole population with priority given to the mother/child relation and to workers; (3) Medical services have an integral character; both individuals and the environment are to be treated. Specialized treatment for the few was replaced with the goal of comprehensive care for the masses and the attitude of paternalism and charity was transformed into one of rights and duties.''

Rubbing chalk dust off his fingers and onto his pants, he continued; ''Nicaragua was divided into health areas each having between 20,000 to 30,000 inhabitants.'' The image of a triangle appeared on the board. ''Hospitals like this one preside over scattered health centers which are the fundamental unit of health-care. At the base we have health posts staffed by nurses' aids and *brigadistas* serving smaller sectors of 3,000 inhabitants. Within a year of the 'Triumph' and the SNUS declaration, the first team of university-trained doctors and nurses arrived in Waslala establishing a medical station that operated out of tents set up in the street in front of the school and across from the bank. A year later, in 1981, the first building on the present site was erected with bamboo and built by the people of the village. By 1984 a second unit was built within the scope of the Carlos Fonseca Project, itself a gift financed by the European Economic Community. In recent years, Cuban and Ecuadoran physicians have worked as staff members of the hospital's surgery and clinics. Two other medical doctors are assigned to the hospital. They are completing their two years of mandatory national service in compensation for their free university medical training. In addition to the physicians there are 74 workers in the hospital including 26 paramedics.''

Currently the hospital and five satellite health centers serve, on the Director's count, 36,233 persons in the 867 square kilometer area of the Waslala Department. Dr. Umana smiled when mentioning this statistic. "It's hard to tell who has died or who has been born in the mountains." Between 30-35 health care *brigadistas* work out of the hospital in the rural mountain areas, but it would require 70 more to do all the work that needs to be accomplished.

'Women and children first!' The etiquette of the lifeboat. SNUS picked up the axiom and consequently the triangle of treatment accentuates prenatal and postpartum care including gynecological therapy, birth control options, and procedures to detect and control cancer in women. Eighty percent of Nicaraguan children suffered from malnutrition and illnesses like measles, whooping cough, and chronic diarrhea which produced an infant mortality rate of 120 per thousand at the beginning of the 1980s. Massive immunization campaigns and the establishment of Oral Rehydration Centers provided effective treatments to imperiled infants. By 1986, infant mortality dropped to 69 per thousand. Polio was effectively eradicated. Incidents of malaria were reduced by 50 percent. When support for the counter-revolution became a U.S. White House priority in 1983, Nicaragua's gains in health care were impacted severely.

Umana pushed on: "Beyond the treatment of war casualties, our main medical problems in the District continue to be malaria and tuberculosis and infirmities preventable by vaccination. We have also seen episodes of rabies. Right now thirty *brigadistas* and Delegates of the Word are in the third and final phase of training to go and vaccinate against an epidemic of whooping cough."

As he spoke, ashes from his cigarette fell to the floor. He didn't seem to notice and kept lecturing. "Many diseases here are preventable. Sixty percent of our children are still malnourished and many will die from parasites and dehydration from chronic diarrhea. What does it cost in U.S. money to save a child from diarrhea? Ten cents? Twenty-five? We fight to save our homes, our families, our nation. Meanwhile we don't have the money to save our children."

Preventable disease? In 1985 Managua was afflicted by an epidemic of dengue fever which was accompanied by outbreaks of measles, German measles, diarrhea, spinal meningitis, and malaria. Granted, Lake Managua is literally a cesspool, one of the most polluted and foul bodies of water in the world. It is a rank and toxic lake, the recipient of untold quanities of raw sewage and industrial wastes. Granted that in its sprawling barrios, garbage accumulates and drainage ditches are but the breeding cultures of disease. But the dengue epidemic was curious. The government suspected foul play.

Steven Donziger, a journalist for the *Philadelphia Inquirer*, interview representatives from the International Red Cross and consultants with the World Health Organization. WHO statistics showed that Cuba in 1981 and Nicaragua in 1985 were the only two nations in the hemisphere to suffer epidemics in the hundreds of thousands magnitude. Odd. Even more curious was the fact that they were the only ones hit with the rare and fatal hemorrhagic dengue. Mexico, in 1982, had the only other outbreak of dengue and it affected less than one-tenth as many people while its population is much greater than Cuba and Nicaragua's combined. Conversely, Haiti and Honduras, notorious for having the worst of hygienic conditions, these nations were spared the plague. Was the dengue another facet of 'covert actions,' a disease implanted by stealth and the heinous subterfuge of bio-chemical warfare?

Dr. Claire remarked, "In Nicaragua, the primary causes of death are diarrhea among children and the war among adults." Quoting Comandante Dora Maria Tellez, the nation's Minister of Health, she was adamant; "The war is the first illness we must treat." Indeed. War-wounded and disabled — the blind, the amputeed, the brain damaged — constitute a high human and social cost. War is an immoral and bastardized exercise in double-jeopardy; it cripples persons and puts an unjustifiable tax on already scarce resources. Four out of the thirty Nicaraguan hospitals are designated for extended care and specialize in psychiatric and rehabilitation treatments for veterans.

Umana provided a tally on the hospital's bed-count: "In the pediatric section there are 14 beds, 8 in the men's ward, 12 for women, and 7 for surgical recovery. The occupancy rate is 75-80 percent. It varies according to the state of the war. During crises we treat the wounded and in-between, during the truces, other patients take advantage of the quiet and come in from the mountains.

On a walking tour of the facility we noted that the hospital has a laboratory, a pharmacy, a delivery room, a health education classroom, and a vintage World War II X-ray that is operable when film and a technician are available. Most surgery is performed without its assistance. The X-ray technician, the dentist, and other specialists are susceptible to instant reassignment depending on the needs of the military in the field. Like the staff, medical supplies are often in short supply. One week it is sterile cotton. At other intervals it might be anesthesia. I pictured the doctors standing in a surgery and inventorying what they might need against what was available. One thing they do have is courage. That plus the wit for making-do.

In patient reception areas, down the hallways, in administrative service rooms and in the operating quarters, pictures of human physiology/anatomy and illustrations depicting health-care were painted on the walls. The pictures were vivid, colorful, and suggested basic instruction in hygiene: handwashing and cleanliness in food preparation were emphasized. Intestinal parasites and malaria are common problems as well, each malady accounted for in larger than life simulations of breeding stages and methods of transmission to humans.

"One of my current projects and what I want you to help me with is clearing land for a hospital garden." Dr. Umana was visibly enthusiastic. "We need to plant vegetables. Money coming to the hospital for basic provisions is slow and we must become more self-sufficient."

Waslala is a refugee center in the war zone, the next step up from an *asentamiento* which is the first catchment location for dispossessed families. In both instances, their inhabitants have been relocated from their lands. The cycles of planting and harvesting are disrupted. Malnutrition is the result, especially among the children. A garden made sense;

not only as a means of supply but to serve as a teaching laboratory that might inspire families to follow suit.

There were toilets in the hospital but none worked. Bed pans from the patient's quarters lined the hallways waiting to be emptied. The strong smell of disinfectant wafted down the corridors assaulting the nose. Sink basins were dry, some filling with the butts of crushed cigarettes. No towels, no soap, no water. Where the hygiene? Did anybody read their own graffiti? Take it seriously? Or was the pump broken?

We filed into one eight bed unit with the intent of singing Nicaraguan songs. An assortment of patients gazed at us from their beds looking confused, apprehensive. One woman had recently given birth and nursed her infant, a clear solution inching down the thin tube from a bag overhead making its intravenous way into her arm. The nurse indicated that the elderly woman next to her was in the final phase of dying from tuberculosis. She did not open her eyes. Another woman suffered from mountain leprosy. A young man sat up in the bed near the window, his head swathed in bandages. A long and freshly sutured gash protruded from one end of the gauze. A war wound, we inquired?

"No," was Dr. Umana's reply. "He tangled with a drunken comrade who was handy with the machete. The young man forgot to duck."

We sang two songs and left. The patients who were awake smiled and waved at our awkward attempt at consolation and greeting. The nurse looked like she was glad to see us go. I doubted that she had been trained in the States, but she had that thinly veiled antagonistic stare down pat.

Back in the corridor, Dr. Umana finished his cigarette and in one smooth motion flicked the butt down the dark hallway. It arched over our heads and hit the linoleum tiles coming to rest against a clod of fresh mud tracked in from the trail between two buildings.

I stood there slack-jawed and bug-eyed. Bedpans in the hallway filling the air with a ripe odor, patients jumbled into small rooms where the newborn share close-quartered space with a person dying from TB, not a working sink in sight, and now the medical director flipped his cigarette onto the muddy floor. The mud I could understand; in the tropics it is hard to keep water and sludge from standing in patios and walkways. But the rest of it? Were they trying to repudiate the germ theory of disease as a bourgeois notion?

A Cummings diesel generator in the building near the latrines powered the pump and supplied the hospital with electricity. Why there was no running water in the sinks and toilets remained a mystery. A uniformed guard with a revolver and AK-47 leaned against the wall of the pump house. Both the generator shed and the water tank overhead bore evidence of multiple patchings. Each are prime targets for Contra sabotage.

Hard-by the shed for the Cummings, two ambulances were parked next to our Toyotas. The one that appeared potentially useful stood idle over four flat tires. The other, possibly newer, had a large red cross barely legible on the side panels. The rest was gutted and burned out, the target of a recent Contra attack. Low-Intensity-War is no respecter of relics like the Geneva Conventions; if it's useful and supportive of life, destroy it.

Returning to the hospital at 8:00 a.m. the next morning, we began work on Dr. Umana's garden. One odd shaped section twenty-five by one-hundred feet had been previously cleared. We were to break the ground and turn the earth into furrows. Three of us began to shape it into rows with shovels. Another section about twenty-five by seventy-five feet needed to be clear-cut with machetes and the brush raked into piles for burning. Later it would be turned with hoes. Eventually corn, squash, and tomatoes would be planted. The Doctor had plans for lemon trees in another area.

The Waslala earth is a dark brown clay-like gumbo. Turning the viscous sod into furrows, swinging machetes and hoes to clear the adjacent plot, it was chain-gang labor. If a straw-boss had been pushing the count, he or she couldn't have pressed the crew harder than we were applying ourselves. With the tenacity of pit-bulls, we were going to finish the field or be buried in it. It was a withering pace, a pace driven by compulsion. If the Contra, bankrolled by our tax dollars, were going to destroy this land, we were going to redeem a small portion, and maybe a sliver of sanity, with our sweat.

Overhead against a clear bright blue tropical sky, the late morning sun burned with a savage heat. We were sweating profusely. On several occasions, Nicaraguans warned us to rest and drink lots of water. I was consuming roughly six quarts per day and urinating twice each twenty-four hours, just for the hell of it; once in the morning and then late at night. Out of habit. The rest was washing through my system and out the pores. It was dripping off my forehead into the eyes, running in a constant trickle over my chest and back, down armpits and over my arms and flanks. I was swimming in my own sweat.

REFLECTION: "Death Will Happen; Now to Prepare"

Prior to embarking into the *campo* we were told to brace ourselves for a variety of experiences that shock the ordinary North American middle-class sensibility. We have seen brutal poverty and the ravages of hunger and malnutrition on the bodies and in the eyes of children. The scattered debris and strewn wreckage of combat, the horrors in the blank gaze of people trying to forget what will always be remembered, yes, we have seen that as well. We have heard testimonies of kidnapping and torture, rape and murder — the tragic traumas of war.

Yet nothing disheartened me quite like the visit to the hospital. Am I such a creature of the affluent western model of high-tech professional medicine as to believe that all locations purposed to healing are supposedly sacrosanct? Must they be beyond the thwart of dung and crud? Do I want all my temples pristine and their altars unsullied? This is a field-hospital. Moreover it is here in the mountains of north eastern Nicaragua, here in Central America, the 'developing' third-world. What the hell did I expect?

My eyes squint, the jaws hardens. I think of Jesus raising Lazarus from the dead as reported in the Gospel of John,

Chapter 11. After summoning his friend back from death, he truned to those standing there and commanded them, "Unbind him, let him go free." God alone is the giver of life. Ours is the responsibility to be the binder and unbinder of wounds.

It's not the dirt or the primitive nature of this infirmary's environment that bothers me. Not finally. Rather it's that the effort seems so much like Sisyphus' struggle with that damn rock. I expect that when people have a decent dream and are willing to invest their lives in pushing it into being, you either lend a hand to assist or stay the hell out of their way.

Such is not the scheme within the U.S. program of Low-Intensity-War. Contra snipe at the water tower and electric generator. Both ambulances are down, one permanently. Hospital personnel and health-care *brigadistas* are kidnapped and murdered. Their's is a ministry of binding and unbinding wounds. By direct commission, this is their work, our work. To impede that is not simply nasty, a bad break, the hard luck of war. It is nothing less than a manifestation of the evilness of evil. It is demonic. There can be no more accurate or softer word for it.

But even in these dark places, places marked by all manner of human brokenness and stark tragedy, a bright truth does shine forth. Life is alive. The man with the machete wound, the woman with mountain leprosy, the children with distended bellies riddled with parasites, they are alive. With our varying measures of health and fortune, we all share in the basic aliveness and vitality of creation. God's care for us is resident in the very structure of life itself.

Moreover, as if in our moments of astounding dullardry we need further convincing, the Creator of the life that is us, that is our universe, this Creator has fashioned us in ways that withstand incredible hardship. Our bodies, our minds, our spirits are able to absorb a multitude of harmful and injurious things. Dr. Claire's deft suturing will not return the young man's once openhanded features. But he is not dead. The woman with lesymaniasis (mountain leprosy) finds that the ulcerated and decaying flesh responds to Reprodral and healing begins. Glucose inches down a rubber tube into the arm of a young mother, her infant suckles at the breast. Both are fed. Life is alive!

I recall the hymn, "And are we yet alive!" The staggering miracle is that we are alive. In body and spirit we endure. Within the hidden corners, in the undisclosed interstitial spaces, our own bodies wage silent battle with diseases undetected, undiagnosed.

And yet, while I am inclined to the mood of singing the paeans of life, I am also mindful that life is not all. There is death. The old woman dying slowly of TB will not live forever. Nor will I.

Back home, in these hurried times, most of us are too busy to occupy ourselves with death. We make our wills, keep the insurance premiums paid, perhaps arrange to donate our bodies to science or give useful parts to anonymous survivors. We dispose of death with a polite dismissal. Most people make pathetic efforts to evade or conceal the reality. We camouflage it. Feeling bankrupt before death, we have no resources, no stored-up capital, no income against the outgo: Faced with death we are as poverty stricken as the poorest member of this village.

Death is the power before which all human power is no power at all. Before death all our feeble protests go unanswered, all our longings drift away unfulfilled. Death inspires the poetry of Nciaragua's Dario and the man in the shack next door. Philosophers and preachers meditate on it. But finally it brings both the muse and the meditation to an end. It prompts Drs. Umana and Claire to prolong life, but it will seize them too. In Nicaragua it is impossible to forget that the sight of death makes heroes and martyrs, and at last it drags down to oblivion those it has lifted up. The parents remember the man for whom the barrio is named. But will the children remember? Death takes all the fervent little intersections of human life — the lover's kiss, the friend's embrace, a partner's handshake — and forces them apart and sets such warm gestures into the cold stone and rigid lines of graveyards in Matagalpa, in Waslala, in Hometown U.S.A.

191

In the security of an Ivy-league classroom I recall one pompous professor speculating that soon all internally generated diseases like cancer and arteriosclerosis will be eliminated. He ventured that it would be hard to conceive how anyone could cease to live, save for murders, suicides, accidents, and war.

What frivolity. Death is here to stay. Deprived of the spectacular resources of modern medical science, these people live and die by the rusty nail, starvation, the unstoppable bowel, the invisible parasite, the bomb, the bullet. And when it comes, how it comes, it strikes a blow fatal to body and confidence, reminding us that we are defenseless and mortal, finite creatures.

I think of Sophocles in "Antigone:"

> *"Man the Householder, the Resourceful,*
> *Safe from the drench of the arrowy rain*
> *And the chill of the frozen sky; —*
> *The Inventor of speech and soaring thought,*
> *Against Death only shall he call for aid,*
> *And call in vain."*[17]

Perhaps the most painful sting in death is the partition it enforces. Thousands of miles from home, here in a foreign country where the shadow of war lurks behind every strange element of the terrain, small wonder that the visit to the hospital has prompted my self-conscious awareness of death. I have family at home, grandchildren to watch grow, projects underway, chores that need for doing. I am not ready to leave this world with all its vivid experiences, its intoxicating joys, its love and excitement. I chaff at being reminded that I am neither the master of my fate nor the captain of my soul.

The thought that some unfamiliar voice might reach over the long distance to the ear of a family member and inform them that Donovan's heart has stopped beating, that his lungs no longer pump nor his limbs function . . . this is unsettling. I resist the thought like a child fights sleep or a patient struggles against the anesthesia. I do not want to surrender my consciousness, my aliveness.

I came into this life as nothing, a mere potential. Then I did some things and became a personality. The thought of returning to nothing is worse than speculating on what it would be like never to have been born. For then I would become nothing minus that which I have been. Death is the transaction by which my mixed yet familiar commodity called life is exchanged for an unutterable unknown.

Life is rich: the smell of the fragrant jungle fauna, the taste of fresh tortillas, the sounds of bird song, a little child calling me gringo. I have only a few verses of Scripture to assure me that death is not horrible, not final. But still I feel like Hamlet who dreaded that "undiscovered country from whose borne no traveler returns . . . This puzzles the will and makes us rather bear those ills we have than fly to others we know not of."[18]

I say an emphatic 'No' to be being separated from those I love. The thought of never sitting to table with friends, never to feel the texture of skin touched in love, these frighten me. Inside I feel a looming absence, like sockets in the skull where eyes once danced. I no more want to lose my flesh than the woman with mountain leprosy, or those we have seen who maneuver without arms or a leg.

And there is something else, a final sting that death brings. It chooses its own way and time of coming. I do not choose. Not finally. I say I would rather die quick, without pain. Here in Nicaragua its best not to pray for that too earnestly lest the ground explode underfoot or a sniper's bullet find its target and split your chest. I want neither to confuse God nor tempt the devil.

Maybe I should ask to go peacefully in my sleep. Who has not said that? But was this the final petition of an *Internacionalista* like Ben Linder when the bullet slammed into his brain? I wonder. Wouldn't he rather have died resting in his hammock on a high mountain spring day overlooking lights shining in the village below?

Alas, most do not die that way. Death decides to kill in an ambush, on the highway, or tortuously with the long delay of starvation or disease. Death decides against us how it will come. The sting, the sting!

193

Nevertheless I must come to terms with my own mortality, with all its cramp and pang. My fantasy and my wish are overwhelmed by death's relentless pressure. I do not pretend that I am made of elements other than those as ancient as earth. Grudgingly, perhaps, yet I concede that these are owed back to the web of all living things. Death will happen. I feel it. Now to prepare.

If by alchemy or premonition I knew that I would die Friday of the coming week, what would I do? Scramble out of the mountain district, hitch back to Managua and fly home to Monterey Bay? Would I go see old friends in Boston, long overdue for a visit? Perhaps return to my favorite spot in the Canyonlands of southern Utah and sit by the Colorado River for a spell? Maybe I would simply gather my new friends around me and continue learning these new Nica songs and distribute the clothing and gadgets in my pack. Probably I should ask forgiveness from some of the persons I have wronged and make amends too long postponed. It would be nice to tell my family once again how much I love them. Damn, I do have miles to go before I sleep!

I rather like what Bonhoeffer said in **Prisoner for God**:

> *"We shall not die a sudden and unexpected death for some trivial accident, bur rather in dedication to some noble cause. It is not the external circumstances, but the spirit in which we face it that makes death what it can be, a death freely given and voluntarily accepted."*[19]

Whatever happens to me following my death, it is a gift from God, utterly undeserved. I take it on faith that as a natural man I shall receive my death and then by the pleasure and power of God be re-created in a life new and eternal. That's faith. Not speculation, not provable. And it depends on God's uncalculating goodness. I no more deserve the life to come than I deserved this life before I was conceived. Nor can I know what that life will be like any more than I knew what this life would be like before I was born. Whatever happens, it is the free gift of God; not something due from God as payment for whatever small gestures of goodness or rectitude I managed by grace in this one.

I shall pursue the good in this life, in this world, as if it were all that there is. I must. It is all that I can plan or work in. And I pray to be so fortified that I may face my physical death with stout spirit. God grant me to be made strong, to live in courage, to die in dignity. I need know very little about that undiscovered country that is yet to come, except that whatever it is, God manages it for my good. That is all I know. That is all I can know. It is all I need to know, because "neither life nor death . . . nor anything else in all creation can separate us from the love of God, in Christ Jesus our Lord."

OBSERVATION: "Barrio Claudio Chamorro: Pauth's Finca" June 18

Of the Nicaraguans hosting our delegation, Bard and I were invited to live with the family farthest out from the village, perhaps a little more than a mile. A village street — any dirt road passable by car — went half the distance and disappeared into a two-burro trail and one-at-a-time path. The *finca* of Bertilde Cruz and Juan Bautista Pauth is at the trailhead in the *Barrio Claudio Chamorro*, named for a guerrilla *comandante* killed in the vicinity.

Groping our way with flashlights, we arrived at the Pauth's after dark. Even in the pitch-black it was obvious that jungle and cultivated growth swarmed over the land.

The family ate supper long before we arrived, but Bertilde laid aside portions of rice and beans, fried bananas, cheese, and hot coffee for our meal. We were ravenous. It was no time for grazing or polite dabbles at food. Sitting on wooden stools before planks that served as the table in the bamboo cook shack, midway through a non-stop assault on my plate, everything came to an abrupt halt. In the thin light of a kerosene lamp I noticed the Pauths standing in the shadows watching the spectacle of two North Americans devouring food as if they were starving.

It occurred to me, late as it were, but perhaps each of them had skimped their own portions in order to feed us. It was no stretch on my imagination to conclude that by ourselves we could devour at one sitting what their entire family of eleven consumed at a single meal. Were they in a subdued panic, torn between wanting to be hospitable while fearing that we might well deplete their entire pantry in less than a week?

Pushing away from the table, like Siamese twins joined at the hip, in a single synchronized motion, we stood and said that we would be right back. Fetching ten pounds of rice, an equal amount of beans and a gallon of cooking oil, we attempted to cover our embarassment with meager offerings. How boorish, this taken-for-granted trading on their neighborliness without a thought for their sacrifice. *Imperialismo* has many faces; subtle, pernicious, predatory, and one that sometimes uncomfortably resembles my own. Bertilde nodded her gratitude, Juan's jaw relaxed.

While at my pack I pulled out zip-lock bags of trail mix; a combination of various nuts and dried fruits. Back at the table I opened the bags and extended the mix to Omar and Marta who were ten and eight years old respectively. They backed off shyly. Smart kids. I popped a handful in my mouth and crunched away. Spreading more over my palm I pointed to the raisin and the almond and asked for their Spanish names. The children began to howl . . . "*Mono alimento*!" Moneky food! We were encircled by hands, not grasping or grabby, simply there and open. Their manners at table were better than ours.

Juan and Bertilde kept their distance watching quietly. My first impression of the mother was that of the typical Indian woman; the servant of the clan, silent as clay, no stranger to suffering, bearing much, enduring all, tough as annealed metal. But then she smiled and I noticed a network of deep laugh lines around her eyes and mouth. Mercy, what a beautiful woman.

Juan's demeanor was inscrutable; the terra cotta face of a sunburnt, stern-visaged, tight-lipped man, eyes furrowed with serious intent. That bothered me. Did I inadvertently sit at his place? I let it be. Juan, lean and tightly wrapped — his muscles wound around his bones like copper wire on an armature — he looked like the kind of man who would speak his mind.

When the trail mix was gone, we launched into a game of 'dictionary.' Pointing to objects — hair, nose, fingers, teeth, ears — we asked for the Spanish word. Turning it around we offered the same in English. The fumbling pronunciations finally put a grin on Juan's face. Deciding to add a twist to our tutorial, I produced a small micro-cassette. Holding it forward I indicated for them to continue. They shied from it as if I were holding a snake. Their introduction to the world of high-tech inspired an appropriate reaction; awe fused to fear. On hearing their own voices replayed from the little black box, all reservations gave way to sheer delight.

I felt like Merlin the Magician with a pocket full of magic. The illusion continued right up to the moment Juan came out and joined us on the porch for a cigarette. Displaying a home-made and superbly designed wood-working plane, Bard, a woodworker himself, complimented a fellow craftsman on his prowess. But our Nica host wasn't seeking praise. Instead, as he patiently indicated, he needed blades. The cabinet for Bertilde's sewing machine, the upright dresser drawers which held all of the family's clothes, each was a master-work, mortised and joined with exquisite care. More cabinets were in order but without the blades the tool was useless. Bard promised to send a set from the States.

When I thought of the micro-cassette, Merlin's magic aura faded. If I could trade one superfluous recorder for a worthwhile shaft of steel with a honed edge I would have done so in a New York minute. Bumping into my own paltry 'Ugly Americanisms' is never an encouraging experience.

The Pauths intended for us to sleep in the guest room off the entry way, a small cubbyhole with a single bunk and thin mattress. When we declined and opted for our hammocks, Bertilde did not mask her disappointment. Why would any sane person trade a bed with a mattress for sleeping like a bat suspended from the rafters? Or would it be a monkey? Perhaps she thought we had eaten too much *mono alimento*. Nonetheless, we removed the rice-bag and rope contraptions from our packs. When we moved to rig them on the front porch Juan insisted that they be hung indoors. Sleeping exposed in the Contra dominated jungle was a fool's invitation to danger. The only available space in the house was the large room between the family's sleeping quarters and the cooking area. Oblivious to the fact that they would be an inconvenience in the morning, Bard and I climbed aboard for our first night's sleep in the lofted swings.

Twice in four hours we have given our family cause for consternation; eating before sharing and declining the honor of sleeping in the only private bedroom in the home. Was an appology appropriate? I drifted into sleep praying for an inspiration or intuitive thought that would guide me toward an answer in the day to come.

I awakened at 4:00 a.m., but not to sounds in the house; the rooster was raising a din, crowing like a maniac in the trees outside. Sensing that Bard was awake I shined my light in his direction and played the beam over his face. He nodded. We decided to get up and hang the hammocks out of the way. Swinging my feet to the hard-packed dirt floor, I stood and began fumbling for my pants. One foot inside, two feet, and then up to my waist, cinching the belt.

Something was poking at my toes and Bard was chuckling. The hen and her brood spent the night indoors and the chicks were sampling me for breakfast. No problem. But suddenly it seemed like my groin was being needled with fire. Slapping at my crotch, from his hammock Bard shined the light back to my feet that were dancing a jig, chicks scurrying away from the havoc. I was standing on the path of a line of red ants. When I pulled up my Levis, these feisty little marauders were elevated right along with the denim. I whipped at the clasp of the belt, fell back into the hammock churning my legs wildly in an effort to remove the pants. Suddenly Juan was in the doorway, had sized up the situation and let out a good belly laugh. The attempt at awakening without disturbing the household had failed. Miserably.

Gloria and Aura, in their late teens or early twenties, had cooking fires burning by 4:30 and were pounding tortillas. A pot of coffee on the boil, within thirty minutes we were eating biscuits that tasted like shortbread and sipped the strong and sugary brew while sitting on the porch. The dawn filtering through the steaming mist across the valley was etheral, pregnant with beauty. Even the rooster's crowing sounded like music, a carillon splitting the air in joyful pandemonium. Aloe jell on the thighs was working against the sting of the ant bites. I felt good. Already this place had the ambience of home. In a rush of fine feeling, I didn't know whether to cry, shout, or get on my knees and hit heaven with a broadside of thanksgiving prayers. Maybe I should just give everybody a big hug. Good morning Nicaragua! I was alive — so was Life.

And then Juan appeared on the porch, an AK-47 slung over his shoulder. It was like sliding toward homeplate and when you look up, there's the dude with the ball in his mitt, winking at you, waiting for you. Back to reality, Roberts.

Heading for the gate at the trailhead, we asked to go along. His refusal was firm, non-negotiable. He would take the cattle down to the stream from the corrals where they had been kept overnight near the house. The AK-47 was to narrow the odds should Contra be waiting to replenish their supplies with his livestock. Sometimes they pilfered a cow or pig and might leave an IOU. Never in his experience had they made good on the debt. He preferred not to be a lender. If the area was safe, he would return and after breakfast take us on a tour of the *finca*.

Juan and Bertilde own thirty-eight acres on the side of a hill that falls away to the creek that cuts through the valley. They are neither share-croppers nor *cooperativistas*; neither are they the poorest of the poor. One year before the Triumph they left Estelí and came to Waslala. Their first shack was built with palm and bamboo during the off-hours when Juan was not supervising construction projects in the village. Unlike most of the homes in the village, their permanent home sits on a concrete foundation, has full wooden siding up to the zinc roof, and its doors hang on hinges.

It rains eight months a year here in the mountains, twice daily in June; one deluge in the afternoon, another at night. At each end of the porch, two 55-gallon drums without tops serve as cisterns catching rainwater from the gutters tucked under the corrugated roof. Food preparation, hands and face washing before sitting to table, each of us repeatedly sipping from the ladle, by the end of a twelve hour period, both barrels would be empty. Nearly two hundred gallons a day; a staggering volume considering clothes and bodies are washed in the stream. During the dry season the children haul water for the family and the orchards in five-gallon pails. One look at that hundred-yard hike up a steep 6 percent grade and it's clear that lessons in water conservation are learned the hard way; aching hands and arms and backs are arduous but effective tutors.

Juan is a carpenter and a skilled stone mason. The congregation appointed him foreman for the construction of the church's new sanctuary. His skills were instrumental in building the Military Base and the District Hospital. As a youth, his father told him to travel and learn various trades. His father's advice took him to neighboring Honduras, Guatemala, and El Salvador. Now he is home building a family, his *finca*, and rebuilding his country.

By comparison to others we have seen in the village, Juan and Bertilde are wealthy; at least middle-class secure. In livestock alone Bard and I counted seven pigs, five cows, one bull, two calves, at least two kittens, and three dogs. There were more chickens than could be easily counted.

The *finca* was divided into large, medium, and small crops. Among the large were coffee, pineapple, banana, cacao, corn, and honey. Medium sized crops included avocado, oranges, lemons, apples, mango, guava, papaya, bread-fruit, sugarcane, and plums. Small crops of chili, tamarind, garlic, onions, cumin, cashews and loofah for sponges infiltrated among the other staples. The family sold their crops to the military base and local merchants and beyond to Matagalpa City and Managua. Like a tithe, a portion is given to the hospital and the church.

When I asked if he thought about becoming a member of a cooperative, Juan smiled and said "No." With humor he added, "Most of the farm co-op people here don't know how to farm, do not cooperate, and they don't want to work." To reassure me that the joke was no joke, he pointed to the co-op on the opposite side of the valley. Similar soils, rain, drainage, the co-op crops there were untended and fared poorly by comparison to his own. "I grow what I choose, sell what I want to, when I want, and to whom I want. And I choose my own price." The man sounded like the kind of farmer that is a vanishing breed at home.

OBSERVATION: "The *Misa Nicaraguense*"
June 19th

At the village Roman Catholic Church, Father Enrique stood at the door welcoming parishioners and handing out mimeographed orders of service. Wearing a polo shirt and khaki pants, he did not put on the linen robe and colorful Guatemalan stole until the singing began. The sanctuary was chock-a-block full of people, kids swarming, families bunched together on the benches, youth trading discrete side-eye glances across the crowd. We were among the last to enter. A long pew in front had been saved and we were seated to the side of the altar.

Two troops, their AK-47s slung toward the floor, stood to the rear, not as sentries but as supplicants like ourselves. An old Indian woman, preoccupied and oblivious to the fact that the hymn was over, stood near the altar, her eyes closed as she swayed to the music that must have lingered in her mind. An older man knelt at the corner of the raised platform, hands folded and eyes closed in prayer, his lips moving silently.

The "*Misa Campesina Nicaraguense*' was created by Ernesto Cardenal who wrote the words while Carlos Mejia Godoy furnished the melody. Together they are the liturgical set-piece of Nicaraguan liberation theology. The sermon came close to the beginning of the service, after Delegates of the Word read the day's Scripture. This was no silent and poker-faced congregation. Enrique's homily was frequently punctuated with exclamations of encouragement.

When he asked, "Where do you see the presence of God in your lives today?" a man behind us stood to exclaim, "These *Norteamericano* brothers and sisters from a strange land worshipping here with us!"

Strange land, indeed. The village poor worshipping '*El Dios de los pobres*' said "Amen."

Another blurted out, "Our Contra brother who has accepted the amnesty." A different voice offered thanksgiving for receiving help from the church following a Contra raid that left them homeless and a family member dead.

There is desperation here, more so than formality. They come to have their hope rekindled, their numbed spirits renewed, their strength resurrected.

Given Enrique's striking handsomeness, I expected that he would preside over the Mass with flamboyancy, a dash at the showman's obsession with being center-stage. Not so. There was an absence of theatrical jauntiness. The people of the *campo* were here to plead their cause before God, not be entertained. They know pain and misery and horror. And the priest asks them to look hard and find the face of Jesus in it. Will they find a Risen Christ living close to the bone of the tragic mess to which they must return?

Bread and wine were carried to the altar for the Holy Eucharist. As it happened, Santos and I approached side by side arriving at the priest's hand simultaneously, each taking the wafer in turn. We are both starving men, looking for crumbs. When we reach our lips to the cup like infants searching for the nipple, it is right and fitting that we tremble like the alcoholics that we are; we are looking for nutrient in the only Spirit that will feed our souls. God bless that emaciated *campesino* with fear in his eyes, tears in his heart, dirt on his feet, and corn liquor on his breath. I turn and pass the Peace of God to my brother. "Be not stingy with thy Grace, dear Lord. Embrace my friend with the gift of your serenity and a sober life," I pray.

REFELCTION: "Blessed Are the Misfits"

A Contra accepts amnesty. Praise God. Shelter and food and hope are shared to a war ravaged family. Amen. This was the worship of women and men who come at God from the point of their most desperate need — bare life. They come in the midst of political and social chaos. They come with the bottom having fallen out from beneath the barrel of their private lives, with everything once tied-down come loose. Soldiers with blood on their hands, mothers with infants at the dry breast, drunks with wobbly eyes shaking the stupor out of their head, teen-age lovers worried about a period missed and wondering if there's enough time before death to marry, a band of *Norteamericanos* out of step with the parade of war — Here we were. We came expecting to find Jesus. And if we did, would it be a silent Lord, aloof and detached, caring for our souls but not our maverick humanity?

Lecomte du Nouy suggested that when a species adapts to its environment the species is stabilized, its life prolonged, its numbers multiplied. The price paid, however, is that it no longer contributes to change; it remains the same. Were we the 'masterpieces' of creation or the 'leftovers' of evolution? Which? Mal-adapted to our environments, were we caught in some spieces pool of stagnation or were we the growing edge? Which, Lord?

Adaptation equals adjustment equals the end of evolution. The purpose of nonconformity, being misfit, is to advance progress, be it within the species, be it moral or political. To change the situation, some must refuse to conform. And when that happens the character of society is changed. Gradually, slowly, but changed.

As a person of faith I name myself and profess to follow one of the world's classic misfits, Jesus of Nazareth — a man so maladjusted that his family called him mad, the chief priest considered him a heretic, and the government crucified him as a rebel.

Jesus believed that persons are happy and lead meaningful lives not when they stride confidently through all trouble but when they turn from such pretense and "Grieve, weep with those who weep." The Jews were proud of their race, the Romans were proud of their power, the Greeks were proud of their wisdom. But Jesus said that only those who are humble and struggle for justice and righteousness to prevail, only such can be happy.

Worse yet, Jesus practiced what he preached. When reviled he reviled not in return; when he suffered he refused to threaten or retaliate. He called as disciples men who often became hysterical and would seldom present a healthy showing on the Minnesota Multi-phasic Personality Inventory. Never courting favor with the establishment, he kept company with the ragtag and bobtail of society.

But those who purpose to follow Jesus the misfit must hold fast to certain absolutes. First they must believe in something greater than themself. Calling us into a new freedom, a freedom that includes the responsibility to love, he set vividly before us the terrifying demand that, in Dostoyevsky's words, "hereafter with a free heart, decide what is good and what is evil, having only Thy image before him as his guide."

From this follow many great affirmations: "Whosoever seeks to save his life will lose it, but whoever loses his life for my sake will find it." That's an absolute. "Blessed are the poor, blessed are the meek, blessed are the merciful, blessed are those who are persecuted," because of the justice they have attempted and the freedom and dignity they confer. That is absolutely true. "He who does not love his brother whom he has seen cannot love God whom he has not seen." That is absolute.

Someone complained that Dwight L. Moody rubbed people's fur the wrong way. His reply was simple; "Let the cat turn around." Moody had absolutes. So did Jesus. And those of us who try to walk humbly, do justice, and love mercy will also be misfitted to our society. We frequently rub its fur the wrong way. Lord have mercy. Let the cat turn around!

Bob Hamill was a preacher of rare gift, a storyteller whose imaginative fancy opened many a window in my heart. Apocryphl or not, Bob conjured the vision of Pope Julius ordering Michelangelo to quarry the marble for the Pontiff's tomb out of the high hills of Cararra where the stone is a beautiful white with delicate traces of blue line. The hilltops were miles from the nearest road. In the early Sixteenth Century they did not have the advantage of modern paraphernalia for moving mountains; only rope, block and tackle, and logs. Huge stones, each weighing several tons, needed to be hauled over rugged paths and through deep marshlands. The quarrymen gave up and the foreman approached the old master and said, "I am sorry but I have failed you. Nothing in my experience is of any use to me for this job. I quit." Michelangelo put an arm around the dejected man's shoulder and said, "Yes, Gilberto, you are doing the best you can. I will have to get other quarrymen. You see, I don't have the privilege of giving up."

Michelangelo remembered what his old friend Bertoldi told him years before; "Talent is cheap but dedication is expensive. Dedication will cost you your life."

We live our lives surrounded by persons of enormous talent. But dedication? Dedication is truly extraordinary. A man hung on a cross proving the truth of that simple statement. A man out of step with the parade of his time. And our time. A man totally at odds with many things his society and our society consider true, right, necessary.

When all our little efforts to be other than stagnant, when the results of the struggle for justice seem so meager, when right appears always on the scaffold and wrong forever on the throne, the sight in my heart's eye of that strange man drives me back to my task again and again and again.

Pascal said it is "necessary at times to ask people to demonstrate their greatness." None of us in that sanctuary were there to parade our greatness. Bloodied on the anvil of war, mauled in the battle with poverty, wrung out between the rollers of patriotism and warmongering, we were there to kneel, saturated with silence and trembling. We were there to rehearse once again the drama of our weakness, of our brokenness, before a Mystery, a holy secret, a ghost of a hope. And we were there to confess a deep desire that God would indeed have tender mercy on our leftover conditions. Perhaps, through paradoxes defying comprehension, we would be caught up once again on the wings of a dream and be touched with fire . . . the purging, cauterizing conflagrations of a transforming love.

Simple people. Simply misfit! Sweet it was to be together, knocking . . . seeking . . . asking.

OBSERVATION: "Pentecostal Praise: The Fire This Time" June 19

The team spent the afternoon visiting with the Pauth family and touring the *finca*. Juan, filled with pride for their obvious accomplishment, wielded the machete slicing fruit from the trees and cleaving them into sections which he passed among us. Handing the machete to me for a moment I ran my thumb sideways over the blade and found it sharp as a razor. His eyes gleamed in a wink and he asked if I wanted a shave. The man had been eyeballing my bushy gray beard. The knife's sharp enough but I turned down the offer. A quick shave, a cut throat, no doubt he could do either with a mercuric flick of the wrist.

Later we backtracked the trail over a hill into another barrio and arrived at a one room shack that housed fifteen people. They looked poor, ate poor, and, as one member remarked, even slept poor — five to a bed. Julie introduced us to Estalina, a twenty-four year old woman whose husband was killed by the Contra on the 8th of March.

Estalina looked like a person whose short life has taken her through rotten luck, disease, and general all-around hardship until planting her firmly at the doorpost of hell. "Eleven Contra searched our house, took 3,000 Cords and all our rice and sugar. They even took the soap. Finally they forced us all outside. My husband was sixty years old." Standing beside a woman older than herself, she indicated that Catalina was his daughter by his first wife. "Now she lives with us," she continued. "When they said that they were going to kill him, Catalina attacked the men and was beaten to the ground." Refusing to offer a reason for the assassination, they shot him in the head and then stole the shoes off his corpse before withdrawing.

Abandoning their farm with its crops of rice and beans, bananas, oranges, and coffee, they fled to Waslala. Another widow offered to share her home but there was no land to work so twice a week she and Catalina walk twelve hours back to the old farm to retrieve what they can of a harvest. There will be no planting for next year and no prospect for provisions when this crop is gone.

When asked what her hopes are for the future she responded, "To suffer as God permits." Their bellies distended from parasites and their hair streaked with the bleaching of malnutrition, the naked children clung to the women's skirts as we disappeared down the mountain trail.

I recalled the ancient Athenian observation, "The powerful do what they wish; the weak suffer what they must."

At 6:15 the rain began pummeling the galvanized roof, the tropical deluge splattering like schrapnel. In forty-five minutes we were due at the Evangelical church for evening service. We arrived late, knocked the mud off our boots, and threw our slickers on the floor beneath the last available bench in the rear. The service was already underway. The hand clapping and sing-your-heart-out worship was punctuated with spontaneous testimonials and a gloss of speaking in tongues. The place sounded like the Chicago Board of Trade when the bottom disappeared underneath Egyptian cotton.

David noted that the congregation appeared more wealthy than the *campesinos* at the morning Mass. They also looked more Spanish than the Catholic Indians, and they segregated themselves. We were sitting on the only integrated pew in the chapel. Laura was quick to pick up on two facts: men sat to the left of the center aisle and women remained on the right; and with one exception, there were no children present.

207

The Pentecostals definitely had the edge on music. To the right of the center-staged pulpit, an accordion player was sandwiched in between several guitarists. Vigorous and enthusiastic, they pumped and plucked as the congregation joined in a trenchant version of 'Holy, Holy, Holy,' that old standard extolling the might and mercy of God 'in three persons, blessed trinity.'

I sang away, in English, until my interest waned. I asked myself what any extolling of the 'three person' nature of deity could possibly mean to them, to me, to anybody who prefers to have their worship make one iota of meaningful sense. The trinity sticking in my mind was murder, widowhood, orphanhood. Jesus demonstrated remarkable compassion for widows, so sing me something about that, I pled in silence. The rest is so much dull cant and chatter of the theological forebrain.

One by one, the men seated on the comfortable chairs behind the pulpit stood to offer prayer, read a Scripture, solicit a testimony. Alternately the faithful clapped, praised God, stood to sing, and sat to pray. Up down, up down, it was calisthenics for Jesus!

It had been a long day. I was tired, so I risked being the insulting guest and kept my seat. Julie, who has the forbearance of a saint and the tenacity of a mule, managed a pace with the crowd but the light that shone in her eyes during the morning Mass and the *Misa Campesina* was long gone.

The presiding deacon took the pulpit and launched into the homily. If there was sawdust on the floor and canvas overhead I would reckon this for a revivalist camp meeting. True to form he began to fulminating against the evils of the day, the smokeless air turning blue under the wrath of his stinging denunciations of alcohol, tobacco, cosmetics, lewd clothing, profanity, and *Norteamericano* rock and roll music. There was a broad grin on my face. The parson hadn't missed a beat in excoriating the popular demons that rankle heart of fundamentalist brethren here, there, or anywhere.

As he soared into the octaves I began to sense that this wasn't an ordinary run of the mill lambasting of miscellaneous peccadilloes and generic immorality. The man was doing business, stalking some yet unforeseen prey. His exhortation had gone up out of the larynx and into his bulging eyeballs. It bore down with a cutting edge. But the blade wasn't slicing toward me, sitting there with a half pack of cigarettes stuffed into the pocket of my shirt. I sensed a restlessness in the air, a little too much head bobbing and foot shuffling among the men. The women were a little too quick and loud in the chorus of Amens as the preachin' deacon found his rhythm and stride.

We were witnessing something more than run of the mill admonishments to rectitude. What we were watching moved beyond the pail of reprimands or chastisements. The man's agenda for the evening was rivted to excommunication. Someone was being keel-hauled, being drummed out of the corps of the faithful. I looked around searching to identify the miscreant. I failed to notice any obvious culprit.

The lady seated with her daughter seemed to be taking this especially hard. Something clicked, and inside my mind a puzzle piece moved into place. I wagered that the bull in the pulpit was talking about her husband. Perhaps he was the poor fallen sinner who, during the week past, had infected his life with the debaucheries of alcohol and lecherous living.

Going through the double-ringer is one thing. But underneath the pressing wrath of God's judgment I waited to feel the press of something else from the underside, like mercy or compassion or grace or forgiveness. But not here, not now. Only recriminatory vengeance.

I was seething. And it wasn't any civilized slow burn. My teeth were cracking in anger. Muttering something about the deacon being a self-righteous thug, my mind worked furiously to compose a rebuttal. Guest or no, I intended to stand and deliver.

Laura either saw or smelled my blistering estate and reminded me that we are were here not to judge but to accompany these sisters and brothers. Accompany? Like hell! Not this time. Not this man or his disposition.

Alcoholism is a problem in Nicaragua which says nothing more than to establish as fact that these humans have

209

discovered grain alcohol and some are prone to the disease of its abuse. Addicts know no racial, religious, educational, or geographic boundaries. Give humans time and we'll have drunks on Mars wobbling four-wheel modules and breaking their fool necks in stuporous blackouts. Waslala *campesinos* with their 180 proof corn liquor are no exception. But where there is a problem, there are also solutions and Alcoholics Anonymous reaches out with the hand of hope toward persons with this disese here in Nicaragua as around the world.

The service concluded, not too soon for me, and I stomped toward the door and fumbled for a cigarette. Sara, Bill, and Bard were standing in the muddy road talking and I joined to ask if anybody had some raunchy rock and roll on a cassette. I was clearly in the mood for picking a fight and looked ridiculous. There was a war going on, great stretches of human misery, I was here with a commitment to non-violence, and now I wanted to grab the preacher by the starched collar and mix it up in the street. They chortled at my foolishness. When my temper cooled I stood there deep in humiliation, confronted as if by a flash of blinding light by my capacity for the hasty word, the careless utterance, and my own willingness to inflict deliberate injury on another human being.

REFLECTION: "Smoking Superficialities"

Standing on the edges of my mind, dark or heavy, sometimes light and shifting but usually in the shadows, there is a haunting presence reminding me of the dead places within myself. I ache for that man, the stranger, who may die because there is no oasis of grace in that church, no offering of the only nourishment that can catch his life in its perilous deadfall to oblivion.

At the very point where he needs the vitality of a great resurrection, something to reach in and pierce the madeness of his panic-stricken condition, what deliverance is there in a slap? No, not a slap. That he could probably handle. He probably does guilt real well. What he got was abandonment to the outlands of his hunger, banishment to the loneliness of the lonely, the interminable and unrelieved sickness of the sick.

Hard accountabilities, uncompromising telling-it-like-it-is hard truths, prophetic admonitions — all these are appropriate and sufferable in their place. But the redemptive work here is hinged to motive. If the design is to renew, redeem, and restore, there has to be love at the core, compassion at the bottom line.

Is it supercilious? Perhaps. But I remembered my father, on those occasions too many to comfortably count, sitting me down and in the measured voice that barely masked his strong emotions, telling me exactly where I had crossed the line and was about to get a dose of punishment at the bottom end. None of that 'it hurts me worse than it hurts you' pap. Straight talk. You did this, we agreed that it was not tolerable. Now you get help remembering. And after the spanking, the tears still streaming down my cheeks, he pulled me upright and into his strong arms for a hug and the comforting words, "I love you."

All of us stand before that figure in the shadows with our own mixture of hurt and ecstasy, triumph and nincompoopery, heartache and hope. Even those of us who are creatures of privilege and security.

There is much that casts down and little that uplifts. We run through our lives in tight little circles, minor upheavals, occasional reprieves, always tilting with the wasting of the flesh that fixes our mortality as hard fact. And who among us does not crave, with the hunger and thirst of the dying, a fresh start — something wholesome and unsullied that bespeaks of friendliness at the core of the universe?

When the church, in whatever name and on whatever mission, stubbornly refuses to share that crumb of hope, what's left that's worth a shout, worth touting as 'Good News?' We are left with our fevered spirits, uneasy, anxious and alone, stumbling through the darkness terrified by that haunting shadow.

I started this sitting on the Pauth's porch, intending to work through my tedious mood. I have not succeeded. Remaining recalcitrant and fractious, the strength to forgive has not yet come. If I am stumbling against my ignorance, enlighten me.

211

If it be callousness, soften me. My smallness, little meannesses, the sore spots of my vindictiveness, these I would have purged. I wait. This life is rich with staggering possibility. Guide me and one faceless stranger, yes, even that deacon, to the path. All else is trivia and so much tilting after smoking superficiality.

OBSERVATION: "Ministry of Education — Briefing Interrupted by Mortar Fire"

June 19

The Sandinista Army post at Waslala sits perched on the hill that marks the eastern edge of the village. From that vantage point its artillery surveys the road running west and east and the river valley heading north into Contra territory. A Soviet-built mortar capable of firing forty-eight consecutive rounds, one per second, is shrouded underneath a tarpaulin. The arsenal's set-piece, its cylindrical barrel calls up the image of the old Gatlin rapid-fire gun; the correlation disappears when you compare their respective payloads. Each missle from this mortar can take out a chunk of jungle the size of a barn.

The headquarters of the Waslala District Education Ministry is housed in a bungalow at the foot of this military depot. We had a mid-afternoon appointment with the Superintendent of Schools.

At the entrance to the reception area we were stomping the mud off our boots when a young man invited us to carry folding chairs into the Superintendent's Office. Taking our seats, this same man, perhaps in his late twenties, stepped behind the desk and sat down. Physically small but not fragile, the Superintendent's eyes were as smiling as they were shrewd, unblinking, dark and deep set.

Following the standard introduction, he launched himself into a short-course on the evolution of Nicaragua's educational systems. An avid teacher, not prone to pass an opportunity for pedagogy, his speech came in rapid bursts, an avalanche of facts and dates. I thought of that bloody gun on the adjacent hilltop.

The catechism began. "During the Somoza period, education was 'commercialized;' all students paid tuition for schooling so only the children of the rich learned how to read and write. In the 'Process,' instruction is provided by the state, free of charge, and that includes pre-school through technical and graduate studies."

He reminded us that the experimental and massive literacy campaign sent a 100,000 young volunteer teachers to work among the *campesinos*. "Their work was so successful that in six months it reduced illiteracy from 52 percent to less than 13 percent nationally. Many of the teachers now serving as methodology assistants in the classrooms were themselves students who learned to read and write during this heroic effort. These instructors are barely qualified in their subjects, so a strong emphasis is made for their continuing education."

The system is still heavily reliant on outside aid in the forms of money, materials, and faculty. Many instructors come from Cuba and Western Europe; all are prime targets for Contra kidnap and assassination. Consequently it is difficult to secure staff for satellite schools in the far reaches of the mountain district and at the relocation camps.

More facts: "In the Waslala District there are 2,000 students in primary levels and books for half that number. Approximately 800 adults attend a variety of night school classes; the literacy campaign took them to a fourth level and with one year of night school they can complete their primary education. Grades 1 through 6 are offered locally which include the basic subjects; reading, writing, math, science, history, geography. Those wishing to continue in technical areas such as agricultural or mechanical subjects or prepare for the university, they must go to Matagalpa City. Since the state canot subsidize their room and board they must make their own arrangements or live with relatives in that area."

Samples of various texts were passed around. Someone remarked that the books were printed in Eastern Europe to which the superintendent replied, "All our texts are developed and edited in Nicaragua. But we have no presses to print them so that must happen in Bulgaria and Cuba and elsewhere." As a side-bar, he noted, "Even our currency, the Cord, is printed in East Germany and Italy." The smile broadened, "But when it is re-valued, we stamp on the extra zeros here in Nicaragua." The zero stampers in Managua must be busy these days.

Several of us thumbed through texts that carried the occasional picture; a Sandinista soldier, the Army on parade, guards at sentry around military installations, the AK-47. In the history book there were pictures of Sandino, Fonseca, German Pomares and others. The book, made of stout cover and good quality paper and graphics, was printed in East Germany.

Someone questioned using education as a propaganda tool for the politicization of the people. They also questioned the heavy accent on the military.

The superintendent was about to respond when a volley of outgoing mortar fire thundered off the mountain. The reverberations shook the valley, chattered windowpanes, and hit our ears in a deafening echo. Conversation stopped. Once again we were caught in the sulfurous reality of war. I gazed about the office and noted that the pencil holder on his shelf was a large brass shell casing. As if by plan, the timing of this interruption, like the punctuating clash of a symbol, was perfect.

Without batting an eye, his smile all but gone, he continued on the heels of the receding echo; "We educate to our reality. That is not propaganda. These are the facts of our life. We are a nation at war. When that fact changes, so will some of the content of our teaching. But not all. We teach the history of our nation; the exploitation of our lands by foreign interests, the repression of our people, the collaboration of the Somoza's and their bloody dictatorships, and the history of the revolution that is still in the process of development. And now, defense against counter-revolutionary aggression is a top priority. This must be included in the education of students."

"Why teach Marxist analyses of history and economics?" a team member asked. "We teach other theories as well," the Superintendent answered. "But, tell me, which of these 'theories' has put the blockade, the embargo, and Contra war into our life?''

As happened so often during such interviews, he said this without rancor or recrimination. It is remarkable and unnerving, this willingness to disassociate us from the policies and machinations of our government.

REFLECTION I: "Recycle the Dreams!"

Three images settle in my mind. First, on leaving the Superintendent's office we inspected the carcass of an incinerated flat-bed diesel truck. The blast was hot enough to melt the plastic off the steering wheel and the tires off the wheels. Four months ago it was a brand new made-in-the-U.S.A. $45,000 gift from stateside supporters. Its service life in Nciaragua was two months. Now it was disintegrating into rust.

As the Superintendent told the story, the truck was being used for private non-military business. The driver and his assistant picked up two passengers who rode outside on the flatbed, a small load by normal Nicaraguan standards. One passenger was a courier bringing the month's payroll back to MINCON, (the Ministry of Construction). The other passenger was a woman. They shared the space with a fifty-five gallon drum of fuel strapped to the cab.

Returning to Waslala they were hailed by two drunk Contra who demanded a ride. When the driver refused to stop they shouted, "Sons of whores!" and strafed the cab with machine gun fire before throwing a hand grenade onto the flat-bed. The men inside scrambled out and surrendered. The passengers were caught in the blast when the diesel fuel ignited. Burned and injured by flying schrapnel, the courier reached the safety of the jungle minus his pack with the payroll.

The woman was not so fortunate. Her wounds and burns did not inhibit the soldiers from raping her. The courier returned to offer assistance after the Contra disappeared and together they managed to reach the hospital.

Burned flesh, mangled flesh, these are not beyond the scope of a physician's care. What treatment would they recommend for rape?

The truck was beyond salvaging. Un-recyclable. A total loss. So was the month's 56,000 Cord payroll for MINCONS.

Is it vengeance? My fantasy harbors the notion of the Contras with their financiers and administrators at the Pentagon, Langely and the National Security Council being sentenced to repair and replace that which they have wantonly destroyed. Repair and replace. Repair an orphan. Replace a widow. Restore a raped woman, a tortured man. It may be easier to resurrect the dead.

The second image is more pleasant. Driving to the river we passed a one-room school house. My son did his first grade at a one-room school in Chilmark on Martha's Vineyard. The similarity ends with the fact that each had one room.

Beside the road in a clearing and beneath a large spreading tree a young woman assembled her class. It would be a stretch to call it a 'school house' for there were no walls, windows, or doors. Only a thatched roof supported at the corners by posts. The dozen or so students sat on plank benches facing their teacher. Behind her, a makeshift chalk board was propped on an easel. Instruction ceased as we approached and the teacher smiled as her students waved vigorously at the sight of grubby gringos heading for the river.

At this point we were several kilometers beyond the village. There were no other buildings or persons in sight. Odd. Something was missing, conspicuous in its absence. Schools such as this and teachers like the young woman are targets in the Contra strategy of Low-Intensity-War. Witness for Peace has documented incidents where instructors have been tortured, raped, and murdered in the presence of their students.

Either this was an especially brave woman or I had simply failed to detect the presence of her protection. It could be that she was very capable of defending herself, an AK-47 resting out of sight behind the chalkboard. Perhaps a comrade had taken position behind or up in the branches of a nearby tree and was monitoring us down the barrel of another weapon. I recalled that adage from the '60s — 'If you ain't paranoid, you ain't in reality.'

My uneasiness ebbed when I thought of what it must feel like for them to teach and learn under the constant threat of violence. The mind cannot be completely free to concentrate on a world of new ideas when a critical part must be devoted, perhaps sub-consciously, to detecting danger.

Growing up in San Francisco during the Second World War, and especially after Pearl Harbor, I wore an identification tag on a chain around my neck — name, address, blood type. Periodic air raid drills forced us beneath our desks or out to crouch against the walls in the hallways. Our teachers tried to impress upon us the seriousness of such exercises and the dangers of war. If it happened during recess and forced the interruption of a kickball game it was a nuisance. If it happened during a lesson it was a reprieve. Either way it was no equivalent to the reality these children live with. These students have seen, touched, smelled, and heard the violence of war. For them it is not remote or a concept or something to be imagined. It is real; like a heartbeat or breathing.

The third image. It's an old homemade rag doll, faded and barely hanging together through many patching repairs. It was the only 'toy' in our host's home. There was, however, a shelf in the small room where Bard and I kept our backpacks. On this wooden plank there were five books; the Holy Bible and four works of poetry — even the poor in Nicaragua are lovers of verse. Dust-free and safe from rain and varmints, I sensed they were special treasures and used sparingly.

Not so with the other books that made their way home each day as the children returned from school. Sitting in Juan's hammock on the porch, Omar and I reviewed the day's lessons in his reader, **Los Carlitos 1**. Omar Efrain and his sister Marta Larena shared the text. His homework assignment that night was to write simple sentences using the new words on his vocabulary list.

While Omar searched for his pencil, Bard took a ball-point from his pocket and handed it to the boy. It was a gift for him to share with his sister. The glint in Omar's eye, the pure glee, you would have thought he had been given a ticket to

Disneyland. Wiggling from the hammock he threw his arms around the neck of this general contractor from California. I noticed his mother leaning quietly in the doorway, eyes aglow, proud of her child. After a hug of thanks, Omar settled back into the hammock and began rummaging his sack looking for notepaper.

It was my turn at dumbfounded expressions. He pulled out four sheets of computer forms complete with side perforations. There was printing on the backside and on first glance I saw that it was a list. A closer look and I discovered that it was an alumni directory from Antioch College in Yellow Springs, Ohio. Hooray! We were both beaming when I told Omar that he was using paper from a prestigious liberal arts college in the U.S.A. Antioch recycles its wastepaper and thousands of miles away in a remote mountain hamlet, a young scholar uses North American trash to put a keen edge on an inquiring mind. My heart was quaintly warmed.

Arelis, four years old and the youngest, wanted some attention. Perhaps she fancied a gift for herself. Sidling close to her brother she jabbed at the page with her finger and babbled incoherently. Although the family understands her communications, I was always standing on the outside looking in, puzzled and confused. Omar nudged her away, politely, but she was persistent. When she grabbed the pen from his hand and began to scrawl on the page, Bertilde intervened. Hoisting the girl toward her hip, she retreated to the kitchen amid a squawk of protest. There was a consternated but kindly look in her brother's eyes. After finishing the lesson, he invited us to help him with the chores. Time to feed the pigs.

Returning to the house we noticed Arelis sitting in the hammock the book in her lap and her head bent over the page. She mumbled incoherently. The attempt to mimic her siblings did not go unnoticed. Omar's eyes met mine and carried a hint of sadness.

My suspicions found confirmation; Arelis is 'slow,' perhaps developmentally impaired or retarded. I doubt she is educable; perhaps trainable at simple tasks, but she will never be a student like her brothers and sisters.

I pondered what that will mean for her, for the family. In a life that is already surfeit with the adversities of poverty, another challenge has been added — providing for the long-term care of a person who may ever be able to fend for themself. The earlier glow became muted, this time with the weight of a melancholy sadness. Why the extra burden, Lord?

REFLECTION II: "God Help the Children"

I pray for the children of the world — especially those for whom the ordinary adventures of life are surrounded by a host of tentative shadows, those for whom the mind stumbles because some vital ingredient is absent. Listen up, Lord. What manner of muted anguish must lay beneath the quicksand of never being able to speak a word that registers a clear meaning to the listening ear?

I pray for the children of the world — the hungry, scrounging garbage for crumbs; the thirsty, drinking contaminated water; the naked and shoeless, vulnerable against the evening cold and bitter rains.

I pray for the children of the world — the orphans whose future is bleak, the desolate whose dreams fill with fear and foreboding, the lonely whose lives are bereft of refuge and security.

I pray for the children of the world — those who suffer illness and injury, the unseeing parasite needling the gut, the chills and fevers, the limbs maimed or twisted, the ache that settles deep behind eyes pleading for mercy and compassion.

I pray for the children of the world — adrift without a mooring touch of gentle love that nurtures dreams, that inspires strength to carry on.

I pray also for the students and teachers of the world. In quiet concentration I lift my concern for them into your presence, O God. Embrace their lives, their living moments and their path with vitality and a share of your mysterious wisdom. Nudge their efforts and ours in the direction of 'Thy kingdom come.' Gird all of our pursuits with visions of peace. Direct our efforts toward justice. Inspire our hearts with offerings of compassion.

219

And if this be the pleading prayer of a begging man, so be it. For neither they nor we can persist save that you are with us.

God help us; Help the children. Heal us; Teach the children. Do not defect; Hear our heart's desiring. Through your grace and our grit, together let us salvage these tragic times. Amen.

REFLECTION III: "The Sacred Cow of Nationalism"

Something is bothersome about the concern to minimize Nicaragua's military history in their public school curriculums. It smacks of cultural imperialism: North Americans counseling Nicaraguans how they ought reconceive the foundations of their political culture. Shame on us. They are working to bring into being new models of mind — conscientious means for cultivating intellect and society at large, their own world view. Perhaps this is an historic moment, the birth of a new self-concept, one laden with exceptional intellectual promise. Perhaps not.

Irrespective, their sojourn through pertinent historical corridors is necessary. None of us is granted a reprieve from the imprint of the past. In front of the National Hall of Archives in Washington D.C. there is the bronze statue of a small girl turning the last pages in a book that rests on her lap. Beneath her, a plaque reads, "The past is prologue to the future." Indeed. Remembering the past quickens the awareness of meanings and choices within the present as we continue to live backward and forward in time.

At another level, I feel a pang of embarrassment, one prompting me to set aside defenses against truth. Much of what they will learn in those history lessons will recapitulate the sorry story of our political and military imperialism. The sagas of William Walker and Cornelius Vanderbilt, the 'police' actions of our Marines that first arrived in Nicaragua in 1909 and kept returning like a shuttlecock until 1933, the pilfering of their natural resources, the 1914 Bryan-Chamorro Treaty deeding to the United States exclusive rights to build an interoceanic canal across Nicaragua — the list goes on until we arrive at our most recent belligerent efforts at Nicaraguan containment.

Have we purged our own culture from the bane of militarism? I think of Memorial Day, recently celebrated at the end of last month. Our own rituals of sacrifice and memory, these are fused with militarism and patriotism. What student in our schools will not commit to memory parts of the Declaration of Independence, the Bill of Rights, Washington's "Farewell Address," and Lincoln's "Gettysburg Address" and "Second Inaugural?" Gathered at assemblies, youthful voices will sing the ode to war called our National Anthem, "The Battle Hymn of the Republic." We pledge allegiance to our flag and come the Fourth of July, what ear will not hear orations declaring visions of the U.S.A. as the Promised Land?

And was it not our own beloved John F. Kennedy, who, in his inaugural, stated:

> "Now the trumpet summons us again — not as a call to bear arms, though arms we need, not as a call to battle, though embattled we are — but a call to bear the burden of a long twilight struggle, year in and year out, 'rejoicing in hope, patient in tribulation' — a struggle against the common enemies of man: tyranny, poverty, disease, and war itself."[20]

There is another oath, more familiar in Nicaragua than Kennedy's words. These were probably written by Fonseca and are recited at the point of pledging the Sandinista cause:

> "Before the image of Augusto Cesar Sandino and Ernesto Che Guevara, before the memory of the heroes and martyrs of Latin America and all Humanity, before history, I put my hand on the black and red banner that signifies "Patria Libre o Morir," and I swear to defend with arms in hand el decoro national [national decorum/decency/respect] and to fight for the redemption of the oppressed and exploited of Nicaragua and the world. If I fulfill this oath, the liberation of Nicaragua and of

221

*all peoples will be a reward; if I betray this oath, a shame-
ful death and ignominy will be my punishment.''*[21]

Strident Sandinismo? Decidedly! Militaristic? Yes. Pulsing throughout the Sandinista Oath is an attitude that fuels
the militaristic impulse, the ingredient that needles the conscience of team members. It is an unbridled nationalism, as
perilous in its Nicaraguan formula as it is in any 'My country, right or wrong!' North American expression. That which
begins as Sleeping Beauty all too often ends as Frankenstein's
monster. Militarism is the methodological servant of nationalism's obsession with territoriality. Both are a pure-mined rejection of the compromises of a responsible balanced authority.

Nicaragua fits well into the classic three-stage model of nationalism.[22] In its first phase there is a stirring sense of the people suffering under oppression, a feeling of collective grievance
against foreigners. Sandino initially saw the struggle in terms
of Liberals versus Conservatives. Soon he came to see it as
an effort to repel a foreign invader.

Domination by foreign rule is an affront to human dignity.
As it was for us, so it was for Sandino and others. This revul-
sion against foreign ideas and foreign manipulations launches
a search for an independent political identity. The words of
Sandino are apropos; "You do not discuss the sovereignty of
a country; you defend it by taking up arms."

In the second phase, the centerpiece, armed struggle provides a legend of heroes backed up by the emergence of resilient
national virtues and burgeoning self-respect. In the three decades between the assassination of Sandino and the formation
of the FSLN in 1961 by Fonseca, Borge, and Silvio Mayorga,
there were sporadic efforts at resistance to the Somoza regime.
None sustained itself like "The Program of Popular Sandinista
Revolution" and its 'Triumph' in 1979. The motto for this
stage is familiar; once again the words are those of Sandino;
"*Yo quiero patria libre o morir!*"

The third stage is the work of consolidation, appropriately
referred to as the 'Process.' This phase is seen in economic

222

terms and the challenge to develop a national economy. And here we have a problem. Having achieved independence, the fledgling state is still in danger of falling apart. Struggling with a war that persists in threatening to exhaust national resources, the government must also struggle to maintain national unity and ward off transitions to other kinds of internal politics.

The work of nationalism is now transformed into a device for ruling the realm. By rhetoric and force it attempts to create a homogeneity essential to the survival of the new state, a homogeneity that it in fact does not possess. Struggle is the heritage of nationalism, as useful and precious to the nationalist as thirft is to the Puritan. And struggle is the Siamese-twin of oppression. In unsophisticated fashion, all problems of poverty and partisan political disagreement are seen as indications of external oppression. Breakdown is never attributed to weakness or failings within the model. When this is the case, oppression can be used as a scapegoat for misapplications of an experiment.

I am mindful that things are seldom clear-cut, especially to an observer looking on from the outside and catching not much more than a mere glance. But in this tangled skein I remain sensitive to several convictions: First, patriotic love of country may in fact have nothing to do with nationalism as an ideology. Second, nationalism as a political movement seeking to attain and defend national integrity can easily drift into the tyranny of totalitarianism.

And here lies the bedrock of my uneasiness. Admittedly this is driven by my principled Christian political impulse. The uncritical and zealous affirmation of the nation lacks by its nature a truly humane universalism. It cannot symbolize adequately the unity of humankind. While it is potent in refuting the oppressions of imperialism, it divides the world into those who are on 'our side' and those who are on the 'other side,' between the 'good guys' and the 'bad guys.' It tends to make its adherents view themselves and behave as if they were 'the last hope of earth.' A dangerous hubris always chews at the edges of such talk. God help us!

OBSERVATION: "Neither Sandinista Nor Contra — One Abstention"

June 20

Retracing our steps back around the military post, we slogged through mud puddles but the sun overhead felt like a slap on the neck. MINCONS, or the Ministry of Construction, was headquartered at the eastern edge of the township. Beneath a tower, a D-9 Caterpillar bulldozer, large enough to carve mountains and fell forests, stood immobile, its massive blade resting on the ground, its rear-ended five-foot tall ground-breaker chisels gouged into the mud. No small tractor. But it was going nowhere. Weeds grow through the spaces between the iron-plate treads on its tracks.

Three men stood in the long barn giving their cigarettes a slow smoking. Bent slightly in the shoulders as if yoked to a plow, a man came forward to meet us. Huerta Flores was the engineer Julie arranged for us to interview. After shaking hands he led us into a bare room with benches pushed against the walls. Indicating a chair in the middle for Julie, he took the other for himself and sat down. He looked like a man who had swallowed a nail keg.

Flores is a topographer and has worked for MINCONS for twelve years, the last four of them in Waslala. On March 10 of this year he had his first direct encounter with the Contra. He and four other workers were captured by the Santiago Mesa Command, led by a Contra guerrilla nicknamed Carlota. Two of the five were separated from the others at the outset. After twenty-one days in captivity, four were released. One man was still unaccounted for; some say 'disappeared.' Flores insisted this was rumor and could not be substantiated.

"The Contra told me they were waiting to ambush an Army column but our highway workers arrived first," he said. "They kidnapped us so we wouldn't inform the Sandinistas that they had infiltrated the area. They said they could destroy our machinery any time they wanted to but had not received orders to do so. At least not yet."

Perhaps that is a tactical quandary; risk soldiers and expend ammunition taking-out construction implements or wait until they idle themselves by breaking down.

He was quick to indicate that the men were not harmed during their stay with the Contra. "We were not mistreated. They were good to us. They gave us bedding and even fed us before they took their own meals." That was unusual.

"The road we are building in this area is part of the Carlos Fonseca Project, paid for by the Ministry of Agriculture," he continued. "We built the road to Zinica and Boca de Piedra for the *campesinos* to use to get their crops to market. The road is the only link between the *asentamientos*. Without them we could not build new resettlement centers. The Contra accused us of building roads for the military. We just build the roads. We don't decide who can use them."

Picking up on this hint of antagonism, someone asked if it wasn't a bit unfair of the Contra to conclude that since he wasn't a traffic cop he was therefore a complicitor?

"I have no opinion," came the retort.

We suggested that perhaps the reason the Contra had not destroyed the roads was because they were also useful to them. "I don't know," was his reply. It was a standard comeback that began to resemble a litany.

When asked to share his personal feelings about the Contra he said, "I have no opinion." On pressing the question he relented and asserted, "The Contra are *Nicaraguense* like we are; *campesinos*. They live a hard life, they sacrifice. They live away from their families, get cold, and wet, and hungry like we do. The fault belongs to both sides, the government and the Contras. If there was no war things would be more favorable."

"That sounds like an opinion," someone countered.

"I am not political," he inserted with some force. "I don't take sides."

"Do you have an opinion about the U.S. and its role in the war?"

"No."

"And the Sandinistas?" we inquired.

Flores' flat-line demeanor stopped at this question. He had opinions about the Sandinistas. "In 1978 my salary was 21,000 Cord a year. [The U.S. dollar equivalent at the time would have been $3,000]. I was a happy man. Married, we bought a house, had furniture and appliances. Now all of that is gone. Everything is more expensive. The government says it is because of the war. I don't know. I do know that we produce enough to feed thousands of people who aren't working. Especially the Army."

This was not the only time we heard this remark. In fact the first to make this observation was the *comandante* at the FSLN office in La Dalia. The Sandinistas are clear and vociferous in their insistence that the Army is not a 'producer' but a 'consumer.' Anticipating consternations like Flores', this is stressed to allay tensions between civilians and the military. However it is a bit like the chicken and the egg debate; without the protection of the Army, the workers cannot produce; without their goods and services, the Army cannot protect.

When asked what he disliked most about the current situation he was quick to remark, "When I go to Matagalpa I have to carry papers so that I don't get drafted or sent to serve in the reserves." His look held more sorrow and regret than hatred, bespoke more of emptiness than malice, the fatigue of a man who wakes up asking one question; "Is this the day I die?"

OBSERVATION: " One Loaded Beau — One Loaded Pistol"

Party! Our last night in Waslala called for a fiesta. Host families, persons we had interviewed, everybody was invited. Laura and Sara's host was a young woman named Esperanza. Like these teammates, she was vivacious plus she had that one 'extra thing'; Esperanza owned a combination *comedor* and *cantina*.

Juan and Bertilde Pauth were polite but firm. Declining the invitation for a free meal and night on the town, they would stay home. Probably they had reservations about going to

Esperanza's. Julie mentioned that some families would not attend because the *cantina* had the reputation for being a shady place, an arena staging the occasional brawl, a hangout for miscellaneous desiccated inebriates, a catchment pool for malingerers and social flotsam. The rumors were big, the place was small. The Pentecostals would be a no-show. Neither was it the kind of establishment that would attract the Pauth's as customers, much less one where they would readily send their daughters. Finally they agreed to send Francisco and Omar as the family representatives.

It was pitch dark by the time we started down the mountain, only an occasional glow filtering through the jungle from kerosene lamps in scattered homes. Darkness closes fast in the mountains and with it, the cacophony of noise in the forest. What's left is silence and moist sweet smells, aromas more fragrant than the most seductive perfume, the most intoxicating incense. At the occasional clearing, where the canopy parts and you can see sky overhead, the motionless stars, stark naked and pinned to the sky, mark the borderland where knowledge atrophies and faith begins. The beating heart and whispers of coiling breath remind you that you are your own companion. Own and only! Lest you lose yourself on a blurred and dreamy flight into the Alone, you walk on.

Esperanza's was clearly the brightest and most boisterous spot in town. Crowded inside around small tables, the team and their families bantered while Esperanza and her crew finished preparing supper in the kitchen at the lower level. The Pauth boys did not enter the *cantina*, choosing instead to remain outside and look in from an open window. The village streets were generally empty after sundown but tonight the intrepid and the curious made their way over to investigate the commotion.

I'm not bashful around food. When it arrives I take my share and assume what the kids call my 'Roberts position.' Utensils in hand I lean forward with forearms on the table and begin elevating food to my mouth, the rhythmic steady motion of an industrial conveyer belt. For me, sitting to table is

227

an opportunity for single-minded concentration; no talk, no dallying — I eat! On first meeting my wife, this hunkered-down crouch over my plate suggested to her that I must have been raised in a large or poor family. Barring that, perhaps I had been institutionalized; lived in a place where you protected what was yours, promptly took care of the busines at hand, and gave a clear signal not to be trifled with, disturbed, or poached upon. Ouch. My family was not large, there was always food on the table, and aside from too many years in college, I've never done hard-time in a reform school, prison, or the military service. Where this obstinate and rude posture comes from is unexplored.

For some reason my eye strayed from the plate and I caught sight of A.V. just as I was beginning to burrow a hole into the table. Aware that our guests might not be bold on their own behalf, she elected to serve her host family before taking her own meal.

Damn. Bumping into my own shabby manners is never a pleasant experience. Of all her marvelous attributes, this devotion to unswervingly stand with humble folk is a consistent bench-mark of her character. Back and forth, from the serving table to her family, plate in hand, eyes warm, bending over to greet each one directly and intimately, she offered food, quiet words, a friendly smile. The lady is a priest! Whatever else happened in that room filled with noise and smoke, without pause or preamble, I was witnessing the Eucharist. "Do this in remembrance . . . as often as ye shall . . . Insofar as you have done it to the least of these . . ."

Picking up on her gesture, Bard and I left the table and took plates to Omar and his brother. A soldier leaning through the window with his AK-47 slung across his chest said nothing. He didn't have to; the look in his eyes suggested hunger. Bard brought him a plate and the *compa* virtually inhaled his supper.

Esperanza's man-friend swaggered into the party accompanied by two surly sidekicks. Handsome in a swashbuckling style and well on the way to being looped, his bravado was bearable. The pistol tucked into his belt was not. Drunkenness is one thing, endurable since this was his current home. Being obnoxious and rowdy was perhaps part of his saloon act. But the presence of the weapon tipped the balance; tolerable nonsense now carried nasty overtones.

I watched him closely, wariness taking the edge off my appetite and damping my spirit of celebration. Over his tight smile, his eyes were hard as nail points; this was the bully unrestrained, laughing in short quick starts of violence, driven by anger, swollen with artificially induced power. Too many times I have witnessed supposedly pranksterish horse-play turn into ruinous dueling with fists or broken bottles. Alcohol is cunning, baffling, and powerful enough in its own right. Put a pistol into the equation and it's a formula loaded with menace; now you're here, now you're not. I resolved to close the evening early and get the boys home safely before the affair turned ugly.

Bard joined me outside and noted that we had thirty minutes before the curfew Bertilde established for the boys. By the time we arrived at the Pauth's, only the glow from Juan's cigarette as he lay on the porch hammock gave any indication that anyone was still awake.

OBSERVATION: "Tears Before First Light"

Our sleep was interrupted by a howling dog. When it refused to quit, Juan pushed aside the curtain and stepped between our hammocks reaching for his AK-47 before opening the door. The dog stopped baying when its master stepped outside. The only sound to break the stillness was the snap of spring-loaded steel as Juan fisted a round into the chamber.

I shined my light at Bard and noted that he was wide awake. In a moment we heard voices as someone approached the house and began talking to Juan. Soon Bertilde walked through the room and went outside.

What was happening? Normally I refuse to eavesdrop on other people's conversations. Here in the Contra-occupied jungle and the sight of Juan's weapon at the ready, my curiosity was fueled by fear. Normal courtesies were overwhelmed. The sound of a woman's muffled tears prompted the thought that it might be a neighbor seeking refuge following a domestic dispute. That didn't ring up with the words and snatches of phrases I was parceling together.

Minutes later it clicked. The person who had arrived was neither a stranger nor a neighbor. It was Enrique, their third child and second oldest son. The weeping woman was Bertilde, his mother.

Enrique had been drafted and sent to Matagalpa for basic training. Juan interceded with the base commander to have his son assigned to the Waslala garrison following boot camp. Enrique was studying bee keeping with a priest in the village and his father wanted him to continue these tutorials when he wasn't mustered for duty. Several rows of hives around the *finca* produced a cash crop of honey which was not only profitable but instrumental in pollinating the orchards.

But Enrique's late night arrival had nothing to do with bees or their keping. The young man reported to Matagalpa with another recruit, a life-long buddy from the barrio. On what was to be a routine training patrol, their unit encountered the Contra and a spontaneous firefight occurred. Enrique's friend was shot and killed. It was one of those unfortunate accidents mentioned by the *Comandante* in La Dalia.

Accident or not, grief and fear overwhelmed the young man and he returned home in the middle of the night. It was not clear to me whether Enrique was off on pass following this tragic trauma or AWOL. What was clear was the stark reminder of the horror of war, the fear that riddled Enrique's spirit, and the sorrow engulfing his family.

Bertilde stopped crying when the three came back into the house and disappeared into the family's sleeping quarters.

Bard and I said nothing. What the hell do you say? Tough break? Sorry about your friend? Damn this war? Sometimes the best accompaniment is simply to shut up. Keep silence. Shed a tear. Recovenant to respect their pain. Press on to do our little bit to stop the insanity of such 'accidents.'

My sleep that night was restless. For the first time in a week I couldn't find a spot in the hammock that offered comfort.

By 4:15 someone was in the kitchen but Bard and I waited another 45 minutes before rising to start our final packing. As usual, Gloria brought our coffee but this time there was a dull ache behind her eyes and no cheerful words of morning greeting. Only a fragile smile.

We took the coffee and went to the porch for a cigarette. Neither the strong brew nor the tobacco tasted good. The dull throb between my temples wouldn't shake out and then something else occurred to me. I turned to my friend and said, "I don't know a single word of Spanish. It's all gone. Forgotten. Hell, this morning I couldn't even spit in Spanish."

It wasn't an attempt to be funny. Humor was not on my list of available moods. It had been evicted by confusion, sadness, and the anger that had swept in to set up housekeeping.

Enrique came outside and sat on a bench at the far end of the porch, a webbed utility belt draped over the cinnamon skin of his bare chest. Alternating between his own coffee and cigarette, he stared across the valley, dead quiet as if waiting for the ghost of his friend to emerge from the early morning jungle mist.

Philip Slater called it our North American 'flush toilet syndrome.':[23] Create a mess and reach for the pull-chain that will make it disappear. Disappear the non-whites into the ghetto, the barrio, the labor camp. Disappear the poor into tenements or 'across the tracks.' Disappear the aged and infirmed into warehouses quaintly designated for 'retirement' or 'convalescence.' Disappear a deteriorating marriage with the divorce chain, fade an enemy with bombs and bullets, and if all else fails, disappear yourself and get the hell out. The suckers that have no place else to go can clean up the mess.

Enrique was caught in a tangle that my tax dollars were financing. And now I was about to disappear.

It was no longer possible to postpone saying goodbye. With the worst Spanish I had spoken in days I stammered and stuttered words of gratitude for the gift of sharing their living spaces. Mostly we were thankful for the warmth of their friendship.

But the hearts that were full of gratitude were also cloaked with melancholy. Days spent listening to the testimony of other families as they recounted the impact of the war was one thing. I managed a certain detachment there. Interest, concern . . . certainly. But still there remained an impersonal element in the hearing, some nauseatingly clinical distance.

The events of the last night were closing the gap. Now it was my Nica family being brutalized. Their tears felt too much like my own, the ache in their hearts leaving a soreness at the center of my chest. I was moving farther out of the bleachers. I was beginning to open to a compassion which generated from some layer deeper than dispassionate fact-finding.

REFLECTION: "The Valley of the Shadow — Three Travelers"

Flores dreaded traveling without proper papers lest he be conscripted. My temper was peppery being in the same room with a drunk carrying a pistol in his belt. Enrique's partner was killed by the Contra.

Crowding in upon me during the past twenty-four hours were three unmistakable demonstrations that each of us needed something, something to stand against the fear, to secure the heart against anxiety, to be close and present to us in the face of uncertainties tinged with foreboding.

Flores was midway through a life that he did not want interrupted by military service. Remembering a past that included a home, a family, and the security of a stable income, he longed for a future that included another ride on that merry-go-round. That or a job where ordinary work and common travel would not place his life at risk.

Enrique was midway through basic training and did not want The End scrawled prematurely on the book he was starting to write with his life. His friend had been wrenched out of fact and into memory; he was not anxious to duplicated the experience. Against death he longed for safety, a return to his village, keeping his bees, and perhaps falling in love and having it returned.

I am midway through this sojourn in Nicaragua and I don't want this experience fractured by death, either at the hands of Contra or by a belligerent drunk brandishing a gun. And I too long for safety and a return to the comfortable latitudes of home.

Fear was the common denominator, the shuttle threading its way through the weave of our emotions. Each of us were traveling through the Valley of the Shadow; and, overhead, the looming and sinister threat of death. The result was a war of nerves, the constant tilting with threatening dangers, muted anxiety, a demoralization of the textures of life.

Standing in the Valley of the Shadow, I remembered something Dianne told me years ago; "Donovan, you do human real well!"

You bet! Me and Flores and Enrique. We have brains that work and minds that think, at least well enough to calculate the odds. None of us expect to get off this planet alive. So we choose and leverage options toward the risks we are willing to take against those that are forced upon us. We've had a taste of love and joy, at least enough to know that we like their savor. And we know hate at both ends — how to give it and what it feels like to catch it. We're human enough to laugh and frail enough to cry. Suffering and rejection are there too, but in unequal measure. Mine are bearable enough so I have a smidgen of humility. These brothers stalk the tougher terrain.

Humans learn through trial and error, coming to wisdom in a slow and painful trip through the school of hard knocks. Each of us have made mistakes, ones that involve others in pain, and we suspect that they suffer because of our lunacy. It's that colander again. Often ignorant, humbled by experience, mostly we stand bewildered in the labyrinth like dumb rats in a maze not of our own creation. We squint at the future, and inside, the guts seethe with deep anxiety.

But here in that Valley, at the bottom of the pendulum's swing, we don't feel very well connected. The security of the

233

past is more than an arm's reach behind us while the prospect of a steadying grip on the future is far beyond the grasp of our reaching hand.

What we need is something to support us here in Shadow Land, a vigilant presence to accompany us, something that is unshakable and ready for action, something that will not defect when we call for it out of the trenches of our despair.

Janetta Sagan comes to mind, this woman who was chairperson of Amnesty International. During World War II she fought with the resistance in Italy. In 1945 she was captured and then tortured for six weeks. One night she heard a guard open the door of her cell and fearing that the torture was about to recommence, she began yelling obscenities into the dark. Without a word the guard threw her a loaf of bread. On breaking it she found a matchbox inside that contained a slip of paper on which was written one word; '*Corragio*!' Courage. Her past behind her, the present excruciating, and the future bleak, what Sagan needed was courage.

In our cheerlessness, we search for a presence and a power that will accompany us. Will it be the latest version of some reworked theology? In and of themselves, most are pedantic arguments, dry as a desert creek in July, filled with dusty sedimentations and nary a drop of water. When you are thirsty, academic contrivances are prone to leave you bone dry and fussing with a deeper case of the blues.

Down here in the funk of it, neither were we asking for a dramatic intervention by a kindly and powerful deity. God, here's the nape of my neck. Pull me out. Beam me up. The attempt to manipulate God when you can barely maneuver your own destiny feels preposterous, a balmy indulgence of the ego. Like the novelist/poet Jim Kavanaugh said, "My easy God is gone . . . the omnipotent, manageable one."

What we do need is to let go, to get shed of the fear. We want something that will enable us to stand in the face of the storm, with courage and without panic. No stoic endurance, cold and gray, built of despair, but an endurance warmed by the mysterious confidence that God is willing to work in the midst of our tangled human situation.

Whatever my faith is, I know it is not some exact measuring rod, some detailed set of creeds, some well defined and explicit formula that will pull the whole thing together and get me across this Valley. Life is both pleasant and adverse. While I don't always expect to live peacefully, I do want to live meaningfully. Fear is an impediment, a blockade against my sense for the significance of living.

I think of Peter and the fishermen. Jesus commanded them to launch out into the deep. It was dangerous out there. But to their amazement they caught fish. It was an enormous catch, far beyond their ability to cope. The reality of it shattered their expectations and against the backdrop of his fear born of puny faith, Peter exclaimed, "Depart from me. I am a sinful man." But that is exactly what Jesus did not do. He remained close to Peter, so close that though the fisherman might falter, he would not ultimately fail.

David Livingston spoke to a group of students at Glascow University. When he stood to address the crowd he bore on his body the marks of his years in Africa. Severe illness on more than 30 occasions left him gaunt and haggard. His left arm, crushed by a lion, hung helpless at his side. After describing calamities and catastrophes he said there was one passage of Scripture that sustained him in the midst of an alien land and among people that were frequently hostile; " 'Lo I am with you always, even unto the ends of the world.' On these words I staked everything and they never failed."

Out in the Valley of the Shadow, in the tempest of living where the waters are deep and the waves are dangerous, out where the fish are, where the people struggle, out where God is providing for us and suffering with us, I need to remember and then hand myself over to that promise, "Lo I am with you always." But I wonder, can I say with Livingston, "On these words I stake everything, and they never fail?"

ZINICA

OBSERVATION: *Asentamiento* **In a Mine Field —**
                         Carlos Fonseca's Death Site''

June 21

Juan and Francisco carried our packs to the church. It was a final and appreciated gesture of kindness since the evening rains once again turned the trail into a quagmire of slippery mud. Tito came late to Reflections. This would be his last day in Waslala, the end of eight months of work among the people and a two year tour with Witness for Peace. In August he returns to Laredo, Texas, and resumes seminary studies. In the circle at the close of our morning meditations, we sang *"Nicaragua, Nicaraguita"* but our bouncy song leader could not find his voice for the tears hurling themselves through the great door of his heart.

As the village disappeared out of sight, Tito was looking back with a sad and wistful yearning that clinched my resolve not to turn around. With the events of the preceding evening still hanging heavy inside, my capacity for poignancy had been exceeded.

Heading north by north east, the road to Zinica was more treacherous than the highway to Waslala. It was a white-knuckled hanging on as the Toyotas slammed and heaved their way across the potholed trail.

A river, swollen to its banks, became a test for both the drivers and the vehicles. Nearby, the remains of a bridge dangled in the currents, a twisted mass of steel girders and slabs of rubbled concrete. No need for a 'Kilroy was here' sign claiming this for another evidence of Contra sabotage.

Pausing on a ledge above the river bank, the drivers and Long-Termers caucused. Would we go forward or head back? The four-wheeled vehicles could navigate the torrent, but if the rains continued our return might be impossible. We would be stranded and cut off like anybody else, obliged to wait until the waters receded or the coming again of some Moses to part the deluge. Consensus. We would press on and take our chances.

We arrived in Zinica one hour later. Blocking the road was a tree branch rigged as a gate. A dozen soldiers monitored our approach with interest. Hands on their weapons, they waited for their leader to finish his talk with Julie before relaxing their guard.

Villagers gathered on a rise above the road and watched us as if we were a traveling circus. Small wonder. The first WFP delegation to Waslala was in August 1987 and then again in January of this year. We were the first team to show up in Zinica. The sheer novelty of it must have been a clearing blow to their imagination.

David rolled off the truck taking his soccer ball with him. Kicking it around the dirt he soon had a cluster of children scampering down the bluffs to begin a game. Even the soldiers abandoned their serious demeanor and joined in, letting their rifles fall into the dirt to take up the round of kick and fetch. The youngsters too young and small to play ball gathered around Shuji who knelt down to meet them at eye level. Maybe these kids speak Japanese; giggling, smiling, cavorting in impromptu games, this soft-spoken man attracts children like the lure of an ice-cream vendor. If I were an anthropologist I would take those men with me into any out-back. These fellows can dismantle fears and draw warmth from that black hole behind the eyes of strangers whose first impulse must be to fight or flee.

The *asentamiento* of Zinica is home to 83 relocated families, each inhabiting nearly identical small cabins. In their spartan construction they were still superior to most of the farm labor camps I have visited in the States. Nonetheless the bivouac seemed barren. Each home was perhaps ten by fifteen-feet with a four-foot stack of cinder blocks supporting split bamboo siding and the customary galvanized roof. While concrete is expensive by comparison to bamboo, the families sleep on the floor behind the protection of the blocks to barricade themselves from assaults by snipers. The thin metal roof, while no protection from Contra mortar fire or a hand grenade, at

237

least wards off the flaming torch and incendiary debris thrown from the nearby jungle.

Our trucks were parked near the school where we would spend the night. The drivers worked quickly to unload our gear and then disappeared up the hill into the settlement. While they were always pleasant and helpful, they seemed a bit more enthused about arriving in Zinica than I would have expected.

Rhonda provided the answer; "We would have probably turned back at the river had they not insisted we come on. This is Francisco's home. His family is here, and since the drivers work for WFP they don't get home too often. We're having our noon meal at Francisco's home," and she pointed up the hill where a tangle of people were obviously enjoying a reunion.

Home is where the heart is and no river running strong was going to keep them from their heart's desire. I was happy for them but thoughts of my own home kept the edge off my appetite. More rice, beans and tortillas. I wanted to hug my wife, laugh with my children , run with the dog. Moreover, I wanted a hamburger, fries and a cold vanilla shake. Dream on, Donovan.

We brought the rice and beans with us so it took a while before lunch was ready. In the interval I slumped against the side of the cook shack and slowly slid to the ground. The sun was merciless and behind sunglasses, sunscreen, and a bandanna tied around my forehead, I was melting. I would simply dissolve into a bead of sweat, trickle into the dust and evaporate . . . disappear. Reality had become a cartoon.

Laura stepped outside and offered me a cup of coffee; just what I needed to bring my insides onto a par with the hot crust I was forming on the outside. In jest I accused her of being the kind of woman that would throw water on a drowning man. She hit me with broadside of Spanish that gradually fussed its way into my baking brain. Like a slow semaphore, it seemed she was saluting the fact that at long last I had found my place and was in good company. Turning back to the kitchen she said 'Adió' to the pig that unbeknownst to me was fast asleep against the building and not more than an arm's reach away.

The Child Development Center was clearly the finest building in Zinica. Eight-hundred square feet of concrete with wooden louvered windows, it contained an assortment of cribs, cots, and small desks. No toys. The snack room was filled with cartons of powdered milk.

The *Tienda Campesino* was a sharp contrast. Built by the State, the workers secured a three-million Cord loan to stock it with supplies. Behind a wire cage we saw a few clothes, pans, spoons, and assorted bottles of over-the-counter medicines. The village elder conducting the tour said it was rumored that soap and food were scheduled to arrive later in the afternoon. I recoiled at the thought that home in a camping trunk I have stashed more implements and commodities than this store displayed on its shelves! And this is supposed to serve the needs of eighty-plus families?

Back into the street and walking toward a bridge beyond the school, a soldier forced a halt while he gave instructions for crossing the trestle. We were to traverse the span no more than three persons at a time and keep our feet on the planks. It looked sturdy enough. Why the precaution, we asked? His one word reply was chilling; "Landmines." The army peppered the riverbanks and perhaps the bridge with explosives. If the Contra wanted to take it out, it would cost them dearly. Apparently livestock didn't get the message. A few days before, a cow wandered down to the river's edge and detonated one of these devices. To make matters worse, a trooper attempted to recover the carcass and salvage the meat. He met a similar fate. A cow, a soldier, how long before it was a child?

Two by two we made our way across, carefully, treading with exaggerated light steps, as if that would make any difference. Sure enough, there on the mud bank below we spotted a bright red disk with the black nipple protruding through the center. The old-fashioned landmine was even painted red and black, the colors of the FSLN. The evening rains unearthed the contraption until it just lay there looking raw and evil, waiting for the nudge that would shatter bone and flesh sending an unsuspecting traveler into an oblivion of bright pain and probable death.

Once on the other side we crossed a field to another building, this one housing a Sewing Co-op. Inside were four new treadle machines, donated by the Catholic Church in the U.S.A. Bundles of cloth and old clothes stood along the walls. There was no evidence of any work in progress or finished products. The machines were idle because of a lack of thread without which sewing remains an affair of the imagination.

Leaving the co-op, the majority of the team wanted to swim. Climbing down the steep banks to the river, my attention was drawn involuntarily to the bridge not fifty yards in the distance. Asking Dorothy if the soldier mentioned how far up-river they had planted the landmines, she shrugged her shoulders and, with a chilling jocularity, replied, "We didn't ask and he didn't say."

The quintessence of metaphysical pondering . . . to be or not to be . . . was being reformulated; stay hot and be, or cool-out and perhaps not be. My brain was not bright enough to unravel the conundrum. It definitely deserved a chilly respite. No towels, no soap, no change of clothes, it was into the water; not like dainty, cautious, pirouetting insects wary of the lurking fish, we hit that river with a yelp and looked like a herd of buffalo on stampede.

Returning to the village we were greeted by an elderly man who was the President of the Zinica's Roman Catholic Church Action Committee. Inquiring if we would like to visit the site where Carlos Fonseca was killed, we readily agreed. With his grandson, they climbed aboard one of our Toyotas and we passed through the checkpoint once again.

At a fork in the road we left the main route and maneuvered through a cut in the mountains. At our guide's instruction, the drivers pulled over and stopped in what appeared to be the middle of nowhere in particular. There was nothing discernible but the mountains wreathed in clouds, the surrounding jungle, and a small clearing covered with grass standing well over my head.

The old man weaved his way through the maze keeping to a barely detectable trail. A ripple of wind brushed across the stalks and spread them out in drifts like swells on the sea. Our approach ended in a clear-cut spot above a bluff that fell away steeply into a dark ravine. At the edge of the precipice lay a modest plaque dedicated to Fonseca. This was the spot where the *comandante* was killed in an ambush by Somoza's National Guard.

"I once met Fonseca," he reported, "when he was a chemist at a mine in Matagalpa. I recall him being tall, dark, a man with kindly features. He was the architect of our revolution and laid the strategy for guerrilla war."

As his stories unfolded he told us that an informer betrayed the *comandante*, telling the Guard when Fonseca would be passing through this valley. Fifty of Somoza's men took him by surprise and in the assault killed him with a bullet through the heart. The body was removed by helicopter and air-lifted to a secret place where several other eminent *comandantes* had been buried. Following the Triumph, the secret grave was located and their bones exhumed. Fonseca's remains were taken in a formal procession across Nicaragua to the tomb facing the National Cathedral in Managua.

All that remains on this spot is the plaque and six-foot tall cross made of galvanized pipe painted black. The cross was a gift from the people of Cuba. The cross, the plaque, the jungle on all sides, at the foot of the cross a cluster of flourescent crimson-leafed plants marked the place where the dark and kindly-featured man met his death. We were quiet, as if waiting for an oracle to speak. Then someone broke the silence, asking for the name of this unusual foliage, a variety that I had never seen before. The old man simply shrugged, said he did not know. He had never seen them except in this place. It was dull of me, but I asked who planted them here. Again he did not know but added, "Maybe God. Maybe it's God's homage to the *comandante*. They seem to be watered with blood."

Surrounding the grave we held hands around a circle and offered prayers or reflections. At the close, Julie meditated, "You can kill the good men, even Jesus Christ. But you cannot kill the living spirit of love for life and freedom. You can never kill that spirit.'' Finally each of us spoke our name followed by one word . . . *'Presente!'* One by one we retreated to the trucks and left the valley.

Back in the village two large IFAs filled with soldiers were stopped at the gate. Julie went forward to speak with the commanders. She knows most of them by their first name given her work in the mountains investigating contact between the Contra and the families who bear the brunt of this mayhem. The men in the trucks wore full battle gear; ammunition clips hooked to their belts, hand grenades dangling over the chest, and the ubiquitous assault rifle — the AK-47. As they spoke, two large Red Cross vehicles zoomed through the village neither bothering to stop nor slow down.

The Roman Catholic Chapel in Zinica resembled the houses with the exception that it is larger, open-aired, and has no side-broads; just a roof and rows of hard benches. We gathered there to meet with the Boards of Directors of the Agricultural, Production Service, and Sewing Cooperatives.

Fatigue was bearing down heavily and our questions seemed pro-forma, put forward out of an effort to be polite. Several times Laura nudged me when my eyes closed and I began nodding off into a doze. Not having eaten lunch was taking its toll and even though supper was less than an hour away, I had no appetite.

Returning to the school and our packs, I took a hammock and stretched it between posts at the far end of the porch. Arranging my pack and canteen so I could reach them without getting up, I crawled into the sleeping bag and relaxed. At the call for dinner I said, ''Pass,'' and chose instead to munch on the remainder of the trail-mix, my own private supply of *mono alimento*.

Darkness drifted down from the mountains and I lay there confounded by the elasticity of time; in the space of a short twenty-four hours I had witnessed a major disruption in the life of my Nica family, said goodbye to these marvelous folk, traveled deeper into the war zone, toured a refugee relocation camp, went swimming in a river laced with landmines, and paid my respects at Fonseca's death-site.

It was time to pray. With pencil and notebook in hand, as the shadows spread and deepened I wrote an evening letter to God.

REFLECTION: "Fussin' My Way Into Prayer as Combat"

I speak again, my No easy God,
    as my faltering practice leads me to do,
        because I'm tired and tormented,
        needing silence and stillness,
    yet unwilling to slumber before I struggle.
You have taught me that prayer is
    more a struggle than a sleep,
        for I remember a wrestling Jacob,
        an arguing Jeremiah,
        a complaining Moses,
    each of them living with prayer as a combat.
So, listen up, deal with me in this loving joust,
    this lively confrontation,
    and mind you,
        I seek no slouchy meditation,
        no quick slide into hand-holding ecstasies,
            no slick sweetness of picayune grace.
I'm willing to fuss with myself
    in my brokenness and distraction,
        out of my superficial faith,
    through the prides and comforts that taint me.
But that will have to wait,
    since now I'm going to fuss with you,
    lock horns and rise up
        on behalf of Enrique,
        and Zinica's 'least of these,'
    the people of this hard, hurting, beautiful land.
The smell of violence rides on the wind,
    this whore of the pimp called war,
    and I'm calling it out;

calling it to judgment
　　because it's not radical enough,
calling it the coward
　　because it's not rooted in love,
calling down the last count
　　because it never did anybody any good.
That son of yours struggled with the devil
　in the wilderness,
　　even with you in Gethsemane,
　and he admonished us speak up boldly,
　　to express our needs,
　　to ask, to beg, to plead.
Persistent as the widow,
　I pray for the hungry
　　who find in this village store no food,
　I pray for sick kids
　　whose bowels run like the river,
　I pray for the homeless
　　for whom a manger in a stable is luxury,
　And, yes indeed, I pray for the demented
　　who make war on these people
　　　to prove a point
　　that's not worth proving after all.
I'm simply telling it like it is
　because I am nestled here among folk
　　who need health and harvest and peace
　and I care . . . so deeply I can't contain myself.
I yearn and long for changes —
　so do they,
　and we find it intolerable
　　to be defeated.
So this prayer, this night, from this hammock
　is a rebellion,
　　not a resignation to some inevitable fate,
　but a declaration of intent
　　to get things changed.
And I will seek, knock, ask, and keep insisting

until we get what's fair.
But for tonight, give me yourself,
>   beyond whatever I think I need
>>   give me what I really need;
>>>   life and faith and rest,
>>   until in the morning I may open my eyes
>>>   and stand on my feet again
>>   going forth to work and struggle,
>>>   rejoice and be sad,
>>>   succeed and fail,
>>   and begin again.
In returning and rest I shall be comforted,
>   in quiet confidence shall my strength be found.
Let your compassion flow
>   round my incompleteness.
And around my restlessness,
>   your rest.

OBSERVATION: "A Gringo Gift — One Leather Ball"
June 22

After a two cup of coffee breakfast we loaded our gear onto the trucks and prepared to leave for Managua. David's soccer ball was missing. The elder who guided us to Fonseca's death-site climbed the hill into the village to search for the truant ball.

Within minutes a small boy returned; bashful and embarrassed, he held the ball forward, placing it in David's hands. Both the child and David stood there mute and uneasy as the boy told his story. Apparently he had taken the ball home to play with his friends and forgot to bring it back.

Would we believe his tale or take him for liar? Was he a thief? Did he deserve punishment? If so, who would deliver it — the village elder who stood there in stony silence behind probing eyes, the youngster's parents, our crew? It was a delicate moment, the air filling with an awkward tension thick as fog.

Not only was the ball now in David's hands, so was the decision. No one intervened to rescue either the boy or our team-mate from this dilemma. Finally David broke out in a grand smile. Handing the ball back to the boy, he announced, "I give you this ball. It is a gift. Enjoy it. Share it with your friends."

The black and white checkered ball cradled in his arms, the boy turned and dashed back up the hill. Only when he spotted the old man did he stop, turn around and blurt out his "Thank You," waving like a fellow with ants in his pants.

Walking back to the trucks David shrugged, kicked the dirt with his toe and said, "What the hell, it was only a ball. They don't have anything in this village."

Sweet Jesus, I was proud of my friend. I recalled when he bought that ball in Mexico City. It took him the better part of an afternoon to find it and since arriving in Nicaragua he paid more attention to it's whereabouts than where he stowed his shoes and socks. Treasured or not, how often do you get to feel that good?

A simple leather ball. Not expensive, it was something to kick around over the dirt, that tickles your laughter even when you stub your toe, eventually to be lost down a ravine or against a thorn. Maybe it would land on one of those red disks, right on the black bull's eye in the center and vanish in a thunderous roar, so much black and white leather confetti.

Was it just a ball? Perhaps beneath the surface David's gesture freighted the weight of another kind of gift — a new hope offered into a life where dreams are often desolate, a fresh sliver of trust for gringos, a moment for laughter instead of sorrow, a chance to see in one white face the profile of a brother.

Ready to leave, the diesels were idling at the gate but the sentry refused to lift the barrier. Soldiers from the garrison in Waslala had not yet arrived. A unit was dispatched each morning to sweep the road for landmines and make certain that the Contra had not demolished another bridge. Moreover, if they made it across the river, we could too. Not being the first over the road that day was a soothing thought. I felt more secure.

My contented frame of mind was short-lived.

As the truck with the dawn patrol approached the gate I saw two long poles lashed to the sides and extending forward over the road, like a charging bull with its head lowered, horns ahead. At the end and between the poles, a long thick shaft of bamboo was suspended from a rope and doing the cha-cha as it bounced over the ground. This was the mine-sweeping device. Low-tech? To be sure. Maybe even under-tech if the Contra rigged the landmines with a delayed-detonation device that would explode two seconds later when the truck's engine or cab was due overhead. That warm, comforting, secure feeling disappeared in an eyeblink.

Soldiers standing beside the gate were nonchalant, sometimes resting on their rifles with the barrels planted in the earth, sometimes letting them fall when they maneuvered to light a cigarette. Weren't these loaded weapons? Even if the safety gadget was locked, might they discharged on impact if they hit the ground just right, or just wrong? Whether you were close to them in conversation or standing a way off, you were likely to find the barrel of an AK-47 bisecting your body; not maliciously but casually . . . as in carelessly. How many people have been killed or dismembered as a result of this risky neglect of simple safety precautions?

I was edgy and ready to get back to Managua. Up to now everything was bearable; the hurdles of language had been managed, we survived the diet of rice and beans and tortillas. Nicaraguan cultural conventions and the protocols of WFP had been observed.

On the inside, however, I was feeling the emptiness of exhaustion. The dead weight of apprehension was eroding my serenity into shabby fragments, vexation mounting up until it became a burden that would not settle down. I wanted to bolt, to high-tail it out of the *campo*.

Inwardly wrestling with the moodiness that seized me, I needed to pin-point this malaise. Closing my eyes I ran an

247

inventory on my spirit, trying to locate a bill of particulars that would account for this low morale. Something was dingy, out of kilter. The head and heart began feeling for its source, yearning to bring wisdom to undisciplined emotions, understanding to chaos, a whiff of ammonia to my desultory temper.

It dawned on me that I had not been alone for nearly three weeks; twenty-one consecutive days of training, traveling, eating, sleeping, and working together as a team. I was peaking, achieving a threshold in my capacity for corporateness.

'Let me be,' something inside my head screamed. I craved aloneness, the chance to straggle off into a corner of the world and be unaccompanied. Looking around at the faces of the team in our truck, I knew some better than others and accepted the uneven camaraderie. Up in the mountains no one had teed me off. I wasn't carrying an unresolved grudge or a lingering resentment, the kind of internal garbage that needs to be composted fast before it rots the stuff of friendship.

Surrounded by dense jungle, I noticed a serrated ridge vaulting out of the canopy of green in the general direction of the gorge beside Fonseca's lonely marker. The urge moved within to wander and get lost within the shadows of those hills and make my way to that ledge.

Why? Was the schedule of our days becoming too monotonous, too commonplace? Had I lost the zest and vitality that comes from stepping outside the bounds of routine? Were the days coming and going, each one blending to the other like dough stamped out of a single cookie cutter? Something within was folding its wings, the bright light of adventure was dimming. It was a curious feeling considering I was in a strange land, in a war zone, with no guarantee that home was a place I'd ever see again.

When the gate was lifted and our trucks pulled out, it took a full thirty minutes before I managed to get comfortable on the tarps. Moving fast, the drivers lunged across the road unable to avoid hiting potholes that had been filled during the evening rain. How the hell did that ingenious mine-sweeping device manage to probe the holes to ferret out the possible mine nestled under the water?

I turned and put my question to Bard. "How do we know if there is a mine in the hole?" he said, repeating the gist of my inquiry. "It goes off," he said and then laid his head back down on the tarp. Some questions are best not asked, especially if you don't want to hear or deal with the answer. I decided to try and sleep all the way back to Managua.

I was awakened by the sound of our trucks slowing down and pulling off the road. In the distance, a procession of people were strung out in a long line. Walking slowly toward us I could hear the muffled sounds of murmuring. Or was it chanting?

In the middle of the crowd several men were carrying a make-shift stretcher on which lay the body of a woman. Hands foled across her breasts and a flower pinned in her hair, was she being conveyed to a rendezvous with a bridegroom and her marriage, to the hospital, or was she going to her grave?

From the looks and sounds of it, she was going to her burial. We said nothing, did nothing, and sat there silent as icons. In return we received nothing from that congregation; no waves, no smiles, no '*Adio.*' Under the windless high-noon sky, their eyes were sad, their stares blank as they passed and disappeared in the wake of our dust that was slow to settle. I felt like an interloper, an intruder on the sacred space of their lonely moment.

Death is no stranger. I arrived fifteen minutes after Dad died, fell on his chest and hugged him before his body got cold, became hard. I held Mom's hand at the bedside while she died. How many times as a clergyman have I stood or knelt while keeping the lonely waiting vigil and held the hand or wiped the brow of persons as they died? Accompanying people through their grief, having my chest pounded as their loss erupted in paroxysms of agony and all they could do was lash out in anger and smash their fist in fury — this I can handle.

But now both my useful professionalism and simple compassion seemed fragile, sloughing off. The will of my spirit and the chattering intellect rang like a hollow bell. My tongue was stilled. My felicitous roles were in a state of molting, shutting down, shedding.

Managua II

June 23

At 7:00 a.m. we herded ourselves into a bus and drove to the U.S. Embassy. The boulevard in front of the Embassy compound had been blocked off from vehicular traffic. A line of uniformed Sandinista Police stood silently in parade-rest formation protecting the main gate. Behind plate glass in the sentry booth, Embassy security officials peered at us through binoculars.

The irony of the scene was inescapable; FSLN military police protecting the U.S. Embassy, and on the inside, diplomats and bureaucrats scratching their heads trying to implement strategies for dismantling the Sandinistas.

As we arrived, Reverend John Long, a Presbyterian clergyman living in Managua, was addressing the assembly of perhaps one hundred persons.

"Here's how things stand," he said, speaking into the portable mike at a makeshift podium there in the middle of the boulevard.

"The U.S. Government has stopped the Veteran's Peace Caravan bringing genuine humanitarian aid, mostly for children. The Contras have destroyed the peace talks, apparently in collusion with the U.S. government. George Schultz is about the travel to Central America, carefully avoiding Nicaragua. The Nicaraguan government has taken radical actions to improve the economy, removing wage and price controls and raising the dollar exchange rate. Witness for Peace, for whom I work, has eight new 'Long-Termers' who arrived this week. And here we are, standing before the U.S. Embassy for the 241st time."

The Thursday morning vigil sponsored by the Committee of U.S. Citizens Living in Nicaragua inaugurated these weekly vigils over four and a half years ago.

Long asked the crowd, "Does any of this make sense?"

"Hell no," the crowd responded without having to be coached.

He continued, "One thing that unfortunately makes sense is that changing U.S. behavior in Latin America is not a quick and easy matter. It has not yielded to success, for example, the havoc of the Nicaraguan economy created by the embargo; nor to failure, the debacle of the Contras. It has not yielded to 241 vigils. It has not yielded to peace talks at Contadora, at Esquipulas, at Sappoa, nor at Managua. It has not yielded to Ben Linder's death, Brian Wilson's mutilation, or Paul Fisher and Richard Boren's kidnappings. It has not yielded to the Veternas' Caravan, nor to peace marchers, nor to delegations. Nor has it yielded in Congress.

If this tall and lanky preacher from Long Island was looking for a round of 'Amen's,' he got them. In spades.

John continued; "But another thing makes sense. Religion, morality, and the best instincts of humanity are against, not with, the U.S. government's behavior. It is clinics, cooperatives, schools, daycare centers, buses, homes, and men and women and children who are Contra targets. And this makes sense, too, that nearly seventy percent of the U.S. people oppose this war. It is the Roman Catholic church, the World and National Councils of Churches, nearly all the Protestant churches, and most of the Jewish community who seek peace here."

"Amen," "Right On!" the crowd shouted.

The man was getting into his stride. "It is the 'best and brightest' of U.S. youth, our war heroes, the middle age-ers, and the elderly who give of themselves and come here to learn, to work, to stand with the Nicaraguan people against our own government, and then go back and struggle some more."

"Preach it!" came the cry.

"And you know what else make sense?" but he didn't wait for us to tell him. "The Nicaraguan people, whatever their

251

political views, whatever their economic lot, whatever their geographical location, whatever their wants and needs, these sisters and brothers place peace above all else. Though the romantic shine may have tarnished from the dreams of revolution, the hope of Nicaragua is intact. So is its remarkable flexibility, responsiveness, and willingness to experiment. So is the openness, friendliness, faith, and love of these people who receive us into their country, their homes, their lives, and their selves; we who come to them from the country that is destroying them.''

John Long returned to the ranks of the crowd and several speakers stood to deliver their words of protest and share information about the state of the war.

A burly fellow in bib overalls started growling into the mike, translating his words from English into Spanish. ''A hundred and forty years ago, the U.S. government invaded Mexico. Now they're trying the same thing here in Nicaragua and some of us are saying, 'Get the hell out and go home, Yankees.' They're trying the old mo-jo fear tactic, trying to put fear into the hearts of these people. You know what fear is? It's when you get a man so scared that he says F __ __ __ Everything And Run. That's how you spell fear. But these folk aren't buying into it.''

FEAR. Interesting anagram. My chuckle was interrupted when I felt someone tugging on my sleeve. I turned and found myself face to face with George Baldwin.

Here was the man who told me to 'Come and see.' My delight could not be contained. I let out a holler and we clasped each other in a hug. He promised to come to the WFP House that evening to talk and give me some mail he wanted posted from the States.

George looks more like a Kansas prairie farmer than a former United Methodist clergyman and professor of systematic theology. Maybe he thought so too. A sturdy man, his sandy-gray hair and beard are the same color as mine. His brow is furrowed with three deep lines. The crow-foot wrinkles carved at the sides of his eyes suggest that he has paid his dues under the Nicaraguan sun. Sun-squint and laughter, both have left their indelible marks.

Twenty-six years a respected pastor, he relinquished his ordination, closed the book on his professorship, and directed that his pension checks be written to CEPAD in Managua. Pulling on his work boots, he divested himself of a life's worth of possessions, packed his suitcase with Levis and T-shirts, and shoved off for Nicaragua. It was a final vamoose. He didn't buy a round-trip ticket.

When Bill Moyers found him, he was living at Paiwas, an *asentamiento* in the lush mountain valley near Rio Blanco.

Against this background he told Moyers: "I was claimed by the invitation that Jesus gave the rich young ruler in Mark 10:22, 'Sell all you have, give it to the poor and come, follow me.' God has not called me to do something, even in the guise of servanthood; God has called me to be poor, no more, no less."[25] That's about as simple as it gets, especially from a former academician and professor of theology no less.

Moyers is himself theologically trained and a very astute observer of people and politics. But he appeared a bit taken back by this soft-spoken and remarkably gentle man with mud on his boots and dirt under his fingernails. Was Baldwin a literalistic lunatic, some born-again but muddle-headed leftist? Or was he just what he said he was, a pilgrim Christian willing to take Jesus at his word?

Baldwin suggested to Moyers, "As you read the Bible and read it from this base position, it's real easy to see that God takes sides. God takes the side of the poor . . . The threat south of the border is not Communism; the threat is that God takes sides, the side of the oppressed against the oppressor."

Like the rest of us, I suspect that George is a complex person. But he heard a word plainly spoken, made his decision, and answered with a simple 'Yes.' "Now I live a very simple life centered around the church and shared with these people."

Pulpits and lecture halls behind him, Baldwin was working at *Proyecto Christo Rey*. In fact, George was the catalyst that assisted the workers in creating a building materials and construction co-operative.

That evening the team was sitting on the porch debriefing the events of the day when I felt that old tap on the shoulder again. Pushing out of the circle, George and I moved down the veranda and sat down.

I asked about *Proyecto Christo Rey*. Workers from Paiwas approached CEPAD with a proposal to create the co-op. They needed funding. Since the ecumenical agency had already put up the money for building a water system for the settlement, perhaps they were good for another venture. The Sandinista government approved the scheme in concept but was unable to shake loose any money to back the enterprise. The function of the co-op was to secure construction materials and allocate them according to priorities determined by the people.

Proyecto Christo Rey needed $600,000 U.S.A. dollars to put wings on the dream. George thought they could find it. The government not only didn't have the money, it was unable to share assistance in developing a foreign grant proposal. However, a friend of Baldwin's was returning to West Germany in forty-eight hours. If he could put the request together, she agreed to circulate it in Western Europe.

With the help of a sidekick, the men spent long hours at the WFP computer. The result was a twelve page document, rough but adequate. Hand-delivered to the woman as she boarded the plane, she would translate their English into German during the flight.

"You know, Donovan, God works in strange ways," the twinkle in Baldwin's eye betraying an eagerness to complete the tale.

"Here's this lady, sitting on a jet translating the grant into German and a stranger seated next to her asked what she was doing. Well, she told him. And you know who this man was? The Executive Director of Bread for the World International. Right there on the jet he took our rough draft, read it and told her "We'll give the *Proyecto Christo Rey* cooperative $250,000.' Not, 'I'll think about it,' or 'Let me take it to our board of directors.' No sir. A plain, simple, 'We're in.' "

Seek — Knock — Ask! You bet! George sat there, glowing in the memory, marveling at the strange ways of Grace.

"The *Proyecto* was no longer an idea floating over a bottomless void." George continued. "The man from Bread for the World put a floor underneath it. A quarter of a million dollars is handsome seed money. A good start. And you know what? That stranger, the Bread for the World executive, offered to help her circulate the proposal around Western Europe. He was the contact with the West German Council of Roman Catholic Bishops who volunteered to put up the remainder. A dream pounded onto twelve pages of rough draft, typos and all, and presto, they shared $600,000 with the people. That's the kind of Grace Christian folk can shout about."

George directed the *Proyecto* for one year and left it in the capable hands of the people of Paiwas and the Co-op board. Like topsy, the gift continued to grow. From a water system to a construction co-op, and now a bakery. Next? The possibilities are limited only by imagination. That, and someone willing to say 'No!' to FEAR and, in its place shout, 'Let's get it on.'

And what is Baldwin doing now? "Since September I've been working with the Evangelical Church of the Insurrection. There are twenty-two priests in parishes here in Managua that are sympathetic to the Process. Some are on the faculty of the Jesuit's Central American University."

"What do you do?" I asked.

"Oh, not much. I drive one of the trucks for them; odd jobs when they ask."

Yeah, I thought to myself. That brother lives by a generous power and dances to the rhythm of a mighty melody. "Praise God from whom all blessings flow" . . . and for this plainsman from Kansas.

REFLECTION: "Christ the Failure"

Action is always superior to speech. Read the Christian Gospels. That's why the Word became flesh instead of newsprint. Even the language of Jesus is imbalanced. It's as if he proposed verbs instead of nouns as the linguistic linchpin. Come. See. Touch. Follow. Consistently the enigmatic emphasis rests on doing. Risk. Dare. Become.

Jesus didn't harangue the crowds about the dignity of labor; he worked at the carpenter's bench. He didn't talk about eternal life; he raised the dead. He didn't recruit students for seminars to elevate their self-esteem; he made friends with publicans and tax collectors and whores. He didn't sit down and write a thesis on the primacy of the spiritual over the material; he healed the sick and pled the widow's cause. He didn't analyze the glories of heaven versus the tribulations of hell; he offered water and bread to those who hungered and thirsted.

The world is full of words. Baldwin's words. Moyer's words. My words. Words flying helter skelter, falling like the buckshot of a hard rain. If you took all the Gospel's words directly attributable to the mouth of Jesus, how many would you have? From those three years you might have enough for a note, maybe a letter. The man wasn't simply telling the folk something. He was showing them everything.

Baldwin is half right; 'being' Christian is the bottom line, but on top of it, the pilgrim must write some words with the deeds of their 'doing.'

For all the fancy high-brow words spoken about this man who called the rich young ruler and my friend George, what are you left with?

The man of few words, the man from Nazareth, failed — failed miserably.

He accomplished hardly a single thing he set out to do and nothing that you would call successful.

In business he failed. Born poor, he learned a trade but abandoned it, held no regular job, begged his meals, and died a pauper leaving no property, no insurance, no pension, and was buried in a borrowed grave. No one gets a good credit rating on that kind of record.

In family life he failed. He never married though the Jews gloried in family and considered a bachelor a disgrace; no children, no heirs. That failure must have been accented when his mother doubted his sanity. It anyone should stand beside us, it is our mother, but Mary agreed with the crowd; "He is beside himself."

He failed in his pursuit of human betterment. Preaching good tidings to the poor, bread and justice did not become their portion. He proclaimed release to the captives but their shackles were not broken. He healed the sick and mostly they departed without so much as a Thank You. He was called King of the Jews, and crowned — with thorns.

As a teacher he failed. "Be not anxious about tomorrow," he taught, but his favorite disciples vied for seats on his right and left hands when he came into his Kingdom. "Lay not up treasures that moth and rust consume," he admonished, but men came to him asking that he arbitrate disputed inheritances. And the rich young ruler? Jesus' contemporaries never practiced what he taught. No reform movement swept the land as a result of his teaching.

As a leader of men he failed. Large crowds followed him from place to place but few became disciples. And of those that did, eleven forsook him and one betrayed him. For the price of a paper backbook at the corner store you can find better advice in the business of winning friends and influencing people. As for the church, he left nothing that historians of the period would mention for almost a hundred years.

An incredible life, a Horatio Alger story in reverse. Born under stars, he died under clouds. At that birth, angels sang and at his death crowds jeered. His path led not to triumph but to a tomb. His total assets could be summed up in the words, "They took him outside the city and hung him." That man ended up a tragic and pitiful failure.

As the world counts, that is; a pathetic failure and a dangerous man. Baldwin reminds us that Jesus was no stranger to the sight of crosses. They lined the highways and byways of the land like so many milemarkers. And on them were hung the dying and rotting remains of Rome's political enemies. The words, "Take up your cross and follow me" are an invitation to join the political struggle.

John Steinbeck once reflected on the persons who would be denied a visitor's permit to enter the U.S., not necessarily because they were guilty of criminal offenses; rumors associating them with misdeeds was sufficient: Adam — trespassing and theft; Saul — assault with intent to kill; David — revolution; Peter — civil disobedience and arson. Others would be barred had they not been born here: George Washington — insurrection; Lincoln — abolition of private property. Steinbeck went on to suggest that the person least likely to be granted a visa would be Jesus Christ. The charges against him would include inciting to riot, causing civil commotion, disturbing the peace, and being taken from jail by a mob.[26]

Baldwin said, "You have to decide where you will cooperate and where you will not." Take Jesus seriously, accept him for being a disturber of the established order, and you're on the scent of Steinbeck's speculation.

Raised in the Methodist church, the lens that Baldwin inherited for seeing the world was ground in that denomination's willingness to take Jesus seriously, to fashion its ministries into programs of justice. The Lord was prophetic and political; the mission and message of the Methodists was driven by a commitment to the Social Gospel where strong words were backed by expensive deeds.

Then something happened. The Church, including the Methodists — as far as George was concerned — reversed its judgment. By a subtle and cruel twist, they reversed it so far that Jesus eventually ended up sharing the fate of the prophets. The message of those flaming harbingers was initially taken seriously and they were condemned as being radical. They were heard, hated, and resisted for their hard words. But over time we became accustomed to their diatribes and denunciations and ended up respecting these outsiders and refused to listen to them.

Jesus gets the same treatment. The adoration given to Christ measures the failure of Jesus. Pictured in stained glass with a mellow halo round his head, choirs sing "King of Kings and Lord of Lords" while theologians rant about "Very God of Very God." Soon the man who walked among men becomes the Christ who sits at the right hand of God. The man who asked to be followed is worshiped by those who can't find

258

their feet. Unwilling to go with him into the streets, they bring him into the sanctuary.

Baldwin has a lover's quarrel with the Church — it is a lover's quarrel for the Church remains at the center of his self-consciousness, the hoop of flame in which he sees himself. At the core, George refuses to worship Christ in the company of people who never dare to follow Jesus, who have no doubt about the divinity of Christ and no faith in the teaching of the Lord, who believe that the Bible cannot be mistaken and that the Sermon on the Mount cannot be practiced, who are certain that Jesus was the Son of God and that his teachings would be disastrous if practiced in God's world. The continuing failure of Jesus is that the devout adore him when he asked them to follow and obey him.

Jesus looked over the great city and wept, "Jerusalem, Jerusalem, that does not know the things that make for peace." And Baldwin, the gentle soft-spoken man, weeps for nations that do not know the things that make for peace. When persons get clobbered on their march for decency, when right seems forever on the scaffold and wrong forever on the throne, when deserters pass themselves off as disciples, he looks to that man called Jesus and sees that the Cross holds up to heaven the earth's worst failure and its only enduring success.

OBSERVATION: "Rebellion on the Gatepost of Hope — Nicaragua's Feminists"
June 23

Sylvia Carrasco is Director of International Relations for AMNLEA, a Nicaraguan women's organization named after Luisa Amanda Espinoza, a heroine of the revolution. Nora Astorga founded AMNLEA and then served as Nicaragua's Ambassador to the United Nations before her death at age 40. Carrasco is the liaison between AMNLEA and feminist counterparts in the United States and Canada and refers to the federation as "our equivalent to your National Organization of Women." An umbrella association, its members are the mothers and women in the industrial work force, in the military and the militias, girl-children and professional women, the *campesinas* and *cooperativistas* and female members of Christian-base communities.

Prior to 1975 Carrasco worked as a domestic servant washing Somocistas' clothes. Refusing to let her life jell into the mold of a charwoman, during that year she joined the Sandinistas and was assigned to the rural areas surrounding Esteli. She put down the scrub brush and picked up an AK-47 to accompany tanks driven by women into combat that on occasion was fought hand-to-hand.

Some chauvinist stereotypes die a slow hard death in my head. It was difficult for me to imagine this young, lean, and urbane mother of three running a Guardia through with a bayonet, tossing a grenade over a barricade, or zippering an enemy's chest with a rapid-fire splay of bullets.

Pride emanated from her posture and attitude like boulders exploding from the volcano of Masaya. I stanched my curiosity. The Sandinistas eventually reassigned her to organizing women in the *campo* and then, noting that she was bright, following the Triumph they sent her to the university where she took a degree in history and graduated in 1983.

Carrasco emphasized, "Machismo is counter-productive, counter-revolutionary, and we struggle against it in both men and women." On July 20, 1979, the day after the Triumph, the Sandinista government declared that women were to be valued and treated as equal citizens. "A declaration is one thing," she added. "It is a good place to begin. But it did not have the force of law. Intentions don't stand up well against centuries of custom and tradition. They need to have teeth attached, something that can bite and chew its way through harmful attitudes. Some of the militant men in the Sandinistas thought that the women's movement wasn't necessary in revolutionary Nicaragua," Carrasco said, smiling. Laura laughed outright. I blushed. In the early 70s, equivalent words were in my own mouth but I wasn't talking about Nicaragua; I was speaking to my wife and referring to our marriage.

Necessary! Reminds me of a story told by a great and wasted friend of mine. After months of sobriety he went out on a binge. Telling a friend that he hadn't found it necessary to take a drink for a long time, the friend reported with having seen him drunk the night before. The hungover man responded, "But it wasn't necessary!"

Militant feminism isn't necessary, nor is revolution, but only if the antagonists are willing changed their spots. Without the 'necessary' teeth provided by the force of law, the women could be spoon-fed revolutionary rhetoric like pabulum, eat it indefinitely, and continue to choke, starve, and die.

Pressure mounted from the ranks of those same women who had joined the men in the jungles, who flew the planes and drove the tanks, women who earned and felt they owned the right to full partnership in the Revolution.

A word about the process of creating Nicaragua's Constitution was in order. While the FSLN intends to govern Nicaraguan life, it does so with a commitment to being open and straightforward which prompted an observation by Carrasco: "Sandinistas are interesting people. They take their promises to the people seriously. In 1979 they promised a free election within five years; it was held in four. Their national pride and desire to emulate General Sandino make deception and subterfuge impossible. It's a matter of self-respect and respect for the people. They take a stand on principle and prepare to defend it to their death. This applies to the work of creating a Constitution as much as building roads and homes and schools."

In 1988, the National Assembly is made up of 96 representatives from seven political parties. In 1985 it resolved to create and complete a Constitution during the same year. Work on the Constitution began in May of 1985 and in the context of establishing a representative democracy, the first draft stated that the State was obliged "to remove . . . obstacles that effectively impede the equality of Nicaraguans in their participation in the political, social, and economic life of the country," establishing "the right of all citizens to participate in the management of the country's public affairs and in the fundamental decisions of the State at all levels."

261

Lest someone snicker and challenge that as hollow rhetoric, it is well to reflect on the fact that covert wars conducted by the U.S. have not been subject to the scrutiny of Congress. They are not engaged with the knowledge and consent of our own people. We too live under judgment and must reckon with the distance between our professed principles of participatory democracy and the clandestine operations of a government that conducts many of its affairs under the shroud of secrecy in the name of protecting national security.

The National Assembly's Constitutional Commission studied 24 proposals submitted by the various political parties and other sources. From this array they produced a single rough draft. In order to include the Nicaraguans in the Process of creating their own Constitution, this draft was submitted to the people for popular inspection and searching evaluation. One-hundred fifty-thousand copies were distributed and 12 televised debates were aired between representatives of opposing factions. Since televisions in Nicaragua were scarce, a series of town-meetings called *cabildos abiertos* were scheduled where the public debated the proposal in open forum. In the months between May and June of 1985, 73 of these *cabildos* were held throughout the nation and involved 100,000 citizens, 2,500 of whom stood to speak their mind. A total of 4,300 suggestions were generated by the forums and returned to the legislative commission. A revised draft incorporated many of these and materialized in a document presented to the legislative plenary in September. One preamble and 198 articles equals one Constitution for Nicaragua, the 11th in that nation's modern history.

The Democratic Conservative Party (PCD) and the Independent Liberal Party (PLI) chose to boycott these *cabildos* protesting that the FSLN would manipulate the proceedings by saturating the gatherings with party faithful. Unfortunately, when you refuse to ante-up, you deal yourself out of the game. Charges of 'unfair' became more of a self-fulfilling prophesy than a legitimate assessment of the process, a fact that seems to have been lost on the press in the U.S. The bonafides of the *cabildos* were established by those who chose to include themselves in the process and by the extent to which these public opinions influenced the creation of a final product.

The role that women played in that Constitutional process was extraordinary. Nicaraguan women were posting their own Bill of Particulars on the gate post of the Triumph — getting their agenda on the docket of the Process. They objected to the language of Article 102 which used the term *patria potestad* referring to a man's power of life or death held over the head of his wife and children. A Constitution of, by, and for the people would include equal protections and secure the rights of these persons against ancient and despicable patrimonies. *Patria potestad* was eliminated.

Furthermore, an equally ancient and offensive machismo, in tandem with Roman Catholic Church law, perpetrated injustice against women by denying to them access to informtion and devices for birth control. AMNLEA sought remedy through a Constitutional provision guaranteeing this freedom of choice. Both urban and rural women were nearly unanimous in voicing this demand. They split rank on question of legalizing abortion. Professional and military women argued in favor of the provision while rural *campesinas* decried its inclusion. A powerful lobby mounted by the Roman Catholic Church succeeded in widening the wedge until the Constitutionally guaranteed right to family planning was defeated. The issue of legalizing abortion never came to a vote.

But a Declaration of the Rights of Women did materialize and the teeth of new law started to appear: (1) Women achieved both voice and vote in drafting and adopting the national Constitution. (2) Physical or psychological abuse of women became illegal. (3) The body of a women could not be used in advertisement. (4) Pornography and prostitution became illegal. (5) A pregnant woman was protected from being fired from her job, nor was it permissible to require proof of non-pregnancy as a condition for hiring. (6) A man was held financially responsible for the care of his children if the marriage dissolved and support payments were automatically deducted from his paycheck. (7) Male and female workers would receive equal pay for equal work.

"It is important that you understand the Constitution's position on Human Rights," Carrasco asserted. "Led by the Conservative Party in the Assembly, the new Constitution mandates that the five international treaties on human rights will be in force in Nicaragua. This is made clear in Article 46 which explicitly states that Nicaragua will honor and implement the Universal Declaration of Human Rights; the International Agreement on Civil and Political Rights of the U.N.; the International Agreement on Economic, Social and Cultural Rights; the American Declaration of Rights and Duties of Man; and the American Rights Convention of the Organization of American States."

Her recitation hung in the silence. Then, like a kite falling through a dead-air pocket, she asked, "And when did the United States sign the Universal Declaration?" Chagrin might describe the look on most of our faces.

While the nine-person Junta is all male, 34 percent of the elected National Assembly are women, most of whom are members of the FSLN. Women have been appointed Ministers in departments of government, for instance the Ministry of Social Services and the Ministry of Health. The Institute for Family protection within INSSBI assists women who have been abandoned. Female lawyers, of which there were none during the Somoza years, plead their cases before male dominated courts. In a majority of instances they win. If a woman is raped or battered by her partner, or abandoned and violated by a Sandinista husband, she has two avenues of recourse; through the civil legal channels and through the apparatus of the party. Since Doris Tijerino is Chief of the Sandinista Police, male party members don't regard that option as a convenient loophole.

Much of AMNLEA's work is focused around education: instructing women about the laws that are in place for them and how they can be leveraged; developing curricula for sex education in the public schools from the 4th grade onward;

mounting health campaigns to combat the high incidence of cervical cancer; advocating for therapeutic abortion to stay the rising number of deaths from non-sterile self-induced procedures; and increasing the numbers of child-development facilities within the workplace.

When asked to list the priorities of AMNLEA, she responded quickly: (1) the defense of the nation; (2) the emancipation of women; (3) its corollary, the emancipation of men; (4) increasing the participation of women throughout all realms and roles of Nicaraguan life and work; (5) establishing, with the force of law, the myriad rights of women; and (6) bringing peace to the hemisphere and throughout the world.

Carrasco has been especially successful in gaining financial support for AMNLEA from *Norteamericano* 'sister' organizations. MADRE in New York City contributed half a million dollars in support of hospitals for women. The U.S.A. Women-to-Women organization provides funds for legal and psychiatric services to Nicaraguan women beyond that which the government is able to cover. Typically, socialist-block nations provide technical assistance to women's projects and scholarships for professional study abroad. Capitalist governments that ignore Reagan's embargo offer material aid.

"Gifts from the U.S.A. sister organizations are appreciated. CIA meddling in our affairs is not. It's like the left hand taking back what the right hand gives," she remarked. "The CIA uses divisions between groups in AMNLEA and within factions to frustrate our progress. It's the old divide and conquer strategy. For instance, the CIA organizes among the mothers of men who are now in prison because of their crimes committed while they were members of Somoza's National Guard. These women infiltrate our membership and become informers passing on information about our work. They attempt to destablize our organization by frustrating the process of coming to decision about plans. One group in particular, the Mothers of the 22nd of January is paid by the U.S. Embassy. It is humiliating that they use this name for that is the date that the National Guard perpetrated a massacre against the people. The Guardia in prison are not political prisoners. They are there because they are killers!"

Nicaragua's Constitution abolished capitol punishment. Not only was the death sentence declared illegal but hard evidence from eye witnesses was required before persons accused of Guardia atrocities could be brought to trial, and if found guilty, sentenced to prison. Over 8,000 imprisoned Guardia have been released from Nicaraguan prisons because authorities could not document that they were personally responsible for heinous crimes against the people. Guilt by association or simply having been a part of Somoza's regime is, in and of itself, no warrant for imprisonment or other punishment.

Carrasco concluded with a reflection on the women who resist the Process and are counter-revolutionary; "From these women we are learning a hard lesson; biology does not make us political sisters. It makes us women but not necessarily *compañeras*."

REFLECTION: "Three Wise Women"

I think of the gifts that Nicaraguan women like Sylvia Carrasco deal into the Process, I remember gifts shared by their forebears centuries ago. Harrell Beck, my professor of Old Testament and preacher of rare gift, was a man of uncommon insight, a man with soul! The fact of his death cannot diminish the companionship I experience with him as a meditative presence, a spiritual bondsman and guide, traveling with me on the borderlands of faith.

Dr. Beck reminded us that beside the quaint stories of the Three Wisemen, we need to juxtapose three others. Call them the tales of the Three Wisewomen.

The first story begins right at the opening of the Gospel of Saint Luke. Elizabeth was descended from the ranks of priestly privilege, a caste with clout. Her husband Zechariah was one of the high priests of the Temple. At the point of the story, Zechariah and Elizabeth are vintage senior citizens. While the years may have been good to them in many respects, they have been hard in others. They are childless.

The priests take their turn in the liturgical rotations at the Temple and it falls to Zechariah to preside over the celebration of the high Holy Days. Zechariah enters the Temple before the worshipers and in the solitariness of that sacred sanctuary he presents himself before the Holy of Holies for a moment of personal devotion.

In the midst of this private audience he experiences a strange visitation. An angel appears and suggests that his prayer has been heard. But what was he praying for? He was praying for offspring, for descendants; a gift from God through his and Elizabeth's bone and blood, a child of their sinew and sweat, something to show for the long days of dreaming and nights in the bedchamber, a baby for layettes long since tucked away in dusty trunks, someone to wear the name haunting his dreams.

Selfish? Perhaps, though it is a yearning of the good kind, the type that doesn't steal from the font of a neighbor's blessing.

Apparently the prayer is not only heard, but the visiting angel suggests that God is willing to dispense a tender mercy and grant their petition. Zechariah and Elizabeth shall conceive.

The old priest is flabbergasted. Was it a turnabout that this relic of a man had not anticipated? Thousands of times, countless times, perhaps even by rote, perhaps as an unconscious mechanical gesture — the successor clause following 'Now I lay me down to sleep . . . oh yes, a child, please,' — perhaps this familiar and well rehearsed prayer knew its own way heavenward. And now God inclines the ear and kindly honors the request? Had he done something different? An instant-replay on the prayer searches for some word, a new word used or old words arranged in different sequence — what was it that turned the key in that old rusty lock, that tricked the ear or heart of deity?

Or were his prayers pale images and dim recitations of those persistently lofted by Elizabeth? Was the old man simply being let in on fringes of a formidable business that God had been conducting all along with his spouse? Was this another case of the priest functioning as a dull mirror for the bright faith of a stalwart disciple?

Perhaps God was simply in a jesting mood. Elizabeth was way past the point where women, or men for that matter, ought expect more than wobbly memories of the once-upon-a-time succulent comforts of trysting. Zechariah was dumbstruck and dumb-founded.

As if to drive home the bonafides, to assure the priest that indeed this is neither a fraudulent nor facetious mission, the angel opens a window to the future and confides to him God's plans for the destiny of this child.

Furthermore, the angel remonstrates with old Zechariah, until conception occurs, he will be speechless. What a thing to say to a preacher. Words are his stock in trade. Without them he may as well pack his duffel and disappear. "Old man, you will not be able to open your mouth or say anything until Elizabeth is with child."

Zechariah emerges from the privacy of the sanctuary, goes before the congregation, and you can imagine his consternation at not being able to disclose what he has heard and felt. He makes certain signs. Nothing. No stammer, no whisper. Cotton-mouthed and speechless, he reckons the angel was about some no tom-foolery business. Now both the crowd and the priest are bewildered.

Whether out of a desire to test the integrity of that heavenly promise or in the abandonment of an adventurous joy, the old couple shuffle to the boudoir where a renewed ardor is matched to a fresh hope. A child is conceived. The 'nephesh' of God is quickened with the breath of new life. And with it, the old man's mouth is unstopped. And whether his first words were 'Well, I'll be damned,' or 'Praise God!,' in time the child is born and his name is John.

The gift of Elizabeth, for I believe that Zechariah is only a bystander to that woman's deep desire, the gift of Elizabeth is that of persistent faith.

A second story. There was a younger woman, not high and lifted-up in the caste order of the day, a peasant woman whose name was Mary. She was betrothed, intended for marriage with Joseph, another commoner, a man little described, a prop on the stage in a drama that singularly unfolds around women.

Into the life of this young woman there is another visitation, another flippin' angel. A busy lot these celestial champions. We are familiar with this encounter. Again the preposterous suggestion; 'You will soon conceive and bear a son. Furthermore, his name will be Jesus. He will be great and bear the title, Son of the Most High; the Lord God will give him the throne of his ancestor David, and he will be king over Israel.'

Those words are worth pondering but not before she begs an appropriate question of clarification; 'How can this be, for I am yet a virgin?' When you are one of the righteous poor and don't have much, trading on virtue is not a frivolous proposition. Interesting, isn't it? The promise that she would become the mother of the Messiah and David's successor did not overshadow her desire to be decent. In the choice between dignity and glory she wouldn't sacrifice self-respect for self-aggrandizement.

God's power is inscrutable. As if to drive home that point, the angel told her, 'Moreover your kinswoman Elizabeth is herself conceived of a son in her old age. She who was reputed barren is now in her sixth month for God's promises never fail.'

A young woman, no doubt familiar with the Messianic expectation and the hopes of her people, is thrust into the midst of an experience that is incredible by the most bare of definitions. Was she hallucinating? Finally she hands it over with the words, "Here am I, thy will be done, I am the servant of the Lord."

And then what does she do? She hightails it to her cousin Elizabeth. What a remarkable blessing it is to have someone like that to run to when life throws a great big dose of confusion into your lap; a trusted friend, someone to commiserate with when it's all too big to comprehend. What a reunion.

The gift that Mary brings is obedient faith. "I am but your humble servant. Have your way with me Lord."

269

Now for the third wise woman, a woman on the stage only once throughout Scripture, a bit player. Called a prophetess, Anna was the daughter of Phanuel. A widow in her youth, now in old age she never left the Temple. She too is a forerunner, the first in that host of little old ladies seen hanging around the church, neither in the pulpit nor the choir, but sitting quietly in the corner, unobtrusive, praying or pondering, waiting for something or simply coming in out of the cold. With time on their hands they offer it to God. Nobody else wants it.

This time Simeon is presiding there in Jerusalem's grand Tabernacle. Like Zechariah, he has children on the mind, or more specifically, a child on the mind. He has prayed to God out of the dreadnought of his heart that he will not see death until he has seen the Messiah.

And lo, his prayers are answered. Mary and Joseph bring the baby Jesus to the Temple for consecration. As that father and mother lift up the infant child into the hands of this ancient priest, old Simeon, well, he knows that his prayers were not futile. God granted his request, gave him the length of days necessary to encounter the baby that was the Messiah.

And he prays, "Yea Master, this day thou givest thy servant his discharge in peace." He's willing to die now. "The promise is fulfilled for I have seen with my own eyes the deliverance which is made in full view of all the nations that will be a revelation to all and a glory for Israel."

You know who saw that? That little old lady sitting out there on the sidelines. Anna, the aged sentry, was watching. How many times had she sat through this play, observed the ancient rituals enacted over and over again? But this time it was different; in the dim light she strains to behold the look in Simeon's face, cocks the ear to catch the words from his mouth, attempts to put the pieces of an unfathomable puzzle into place. Do the flickering candles deceive her? What has she seen? What has she heard filtering through the muted silence of the old Temple? Can it be so, that this peasant couple are in fact presenting the Messiah to a wizened shambles of a priest? What confirms her against suspicions that she has gone round the bend, hit the wall of dementia, and is just another doting old woman on the down side of sanity? Who knows.

But we do know what she did. Needing neither her own visitation nor an invitation, she picked up her skirts and ran down the aisle and out into the street, smack dab into the middle of the market place. And she was shouting, "You all know what happened in the Temple just now?" As Luke tells it, "she talked about the child to all who were looking for the liberation of Israel."

I think of the women's work of Elizabeth, persistent faith. And the women's work of Mary, obedient faith. And the women's work of Anna, witnessing faith to the liberating power of God. I think of Elsa Aleman in Matagalpa beside Ben Linder's grave, Bertilde Cruz Pauth on the family *finca* in Waslala, Dr. Claire at the hospital, Sylvia Carrasco and AMNLEA. Who could help but conclude that they are about the business of women's work? Those who won't lend a hand had best get out of the way!

OBSERVATION: "Low Intensity War — Defined, Described, Decried"
June 23

Redolfo Castro, Director of the Regional Committee for Social and Economic Research in Nicaragua, was wearing a business suit; another first! Government Ministers, the director of a regional hospital, a Sandinista *comandante*, the administrator of CEPAD, the director of AMNLEA's international affairs, these men and women, by comparison, were unceremoniously attired, appeared and spoke in a relaxed manner. Dr. Castro, however, was wrapped with entitlement and projected the air of university faculty prestige.

In the fashion of formal pedagogy, Castro began: "Low Intensity War is the strategy that the government of the United States has applied to Central America over the past eight years. Why this strategy? What is it? What are its objectives and consequences? And what are its prospects over time?"

271

Low Intensity War is a name for three methods used to oppose revolutionary movements. Castro elaborated the point; "The war in El Salvador is a classic case of the U.S.'s counter-insurgency model. Siding with Duarte's puppet government, war is conducted against the insurgent rebels; the **counter-insurgent model**. In an effort to attract the *campesinos* away from the popular Farabundo Marti National Liberation Front (FMLN), the U.S. imposed a hollow land reform program. When that did not redirect their allegiance, massive aerial bombing was inflicted against the rural peoples. Then the U.S. arrived with aid called 'humanitarian assistance,' but even that has not diffused the people's support for the indigenous movement of national liberation. Nicaragua provides the example for a **pro-insurgency** use of that method. In this model, the U.S. sides with the minority that is opposed to the Revolution and the Sandinista government; hence they conduct a pro-insurgency war. Panama provides the third model, the **counter-terrorism** mode of LIW. It is unique because the issue of criminal trafficing in illegal drugs camouflages more substantial political objectives. In the name of conducting a war against narcotics, the U.S. attempts to overthrow Noriega for reasons that are entirely unrelated to illicit drugs. All three, separately or together, are types of 'limited conflict' that the U.S. government is using to press its power against the poor peoples of the Third World." He would amplify the Panamanian model later.

Castro stretched his neck as if getting a crick out, and continued; "Low Intensity War had its origins in the 1950s and '60s as your government worked to destabilize particular popular causes or governments in Latin America. For instance, in 1954 covert operations were effectively employed against the democratically elected reformist government of Guzman in Guatemala. In 1973, LIW was used to bring down the socialist government of Allende in Chile. I mention only these two so you can see that LIW can be used in either direction, against democracies or socialism, wherever the U.S. determines that its power or economic interests are endangered. Vietnam was not the first Third World intervention by your government, but it was the most expensive and the bloodiest. It was an over-priced lesson but it taught your civilian and military strategists that the use of massive conventional force in the Third World misses the mark. It doesn't work.''

Eight hundred thousand people died in Vietnam, most of them civilians. Of that number, 58,000 were U.S. soldiers. Another 360,000 of our men were wounded and how many remain MIA? Expensive lesson? Pity that we failed to learn that war is futile and a literal dead-end. Instead, in our un-repentance, we sifted through the economic and emotional rub-ble and deduced that we fought the right war but with the wrong methods. Back to the drawing boards.

There was a lull in Castro's lecture as he sipped water from a glass. I lapsed into a daydream and envisioned the strategists of war in those conference sessions; the old-guard advocates of conventional strategies on one side and the best and brightest of a new generation of warriors on the other: 'You blew it,' assert the young tacticians to their elders. 'Seven million tons of bombs or one 500 pound explosive for each citizen of Viet-nam, 40,000,000 pounds of napalm, the full mobilization and deployment of all branches of service equipped with the latest high-tech weapons and support systems that cost some 1.5 mil-lions of dollars per minute, and in nine years your program ended not in victory but in humiliating evacuation. Our turn!'

Castro resumed lecturing; ''The massive military and in-dustrial might of the U.S. with all its firepower was defeated by the strategy of guerrilla war and poor people who had learned the lessons taught by General Sandino, Chairman Mao, Ho Chi Minh, and Ché Guevara. A style of war suited to con-flicts between First World nations or as a threat in games of superpower deterrence was impotent against movements of na-tional liberation in the Third World. And this is the world of the enemy, at least for the next two decades. A new strategy and tactical system was required. You must know that the peo-ple of the U.S. would not support further interventions in the style of Vietnam.''

273

He reminded us of that with which we were too familiar. The extensive protests on college and university campuses, the sketchy and often half-hearted objections by the Christian Churches, the mobilizations that poured millions onto the streets decrying our infamy, the alienation of Middle America, the slow-in-coming disaffection of the corproate mainstream, persons like Martin Luther King Jr. eventually standing to challenge the fact that our war against the foreign poor was being fought and financed by our own poor, the fact that our foreign policy was but a mirror of our domestic policy . . . yes, we remembered.

"It was necessary to achieve the same ends but with different means," Castro continued. "War would continue but its profile would have to be subdued. So, LIW is a misleading term. It is not conventional war on a smaller scale. 'Low' is a military term and only refers to the level of troops deployed against the target nation; fewer troops, small arms, and less firepower. But the cost to the enemy would have to be high, intensely high in social and political damage. It would also have to be a war fought on the level of psychological impact as well."

The sledgehammer was replaced by the scalpel as the weapon of choice for waging Low Intensity War. And those who wielded it would be taken from the ranks of the indigenous population within the targeted country. U.S. military personnel would not storm the beachheads or sweep the cities and hamlets and blanket the fields and jungles in massive introductions of overwhelming kill-force. Let other people do the dying. Our policymakers were not willing to risk the escalation of our own casualties, another gruesome round of body bags, and the outcry of domestic resistance that this would trigger.

LIW is war Rambo style, superintended by the U.S. Army Special Forces with Rangers on the ground and the 160th Army Aviation Battalion in the air, the Navy SEALS underwater, Marine MAUs on the beaches and the Air Force Special Operations Wing soaring above. Experts in terrorism and counterterrorism, guerrilla and anti-guerrilla tactics, these multi-billion dollar products of highly specialized training are capable of orchestrating war in every corner of the globe; the attempted liberation of U.S. hostages in Iran, the invasion of Grenada, and the mining of the Nicaraguan harbor at the port of Corinto being examples.[27]

Castro's lecture was picking up speed, the words coming forth with arresting urgency. "The U.S. government is spending billions of dollars financing LIW, taking CIA recruits and training them in Brazil and Argentina and South Korea and Israel and then sending them into battle with conventional weapons supported by military intelligence and communications paraphernalia of the most sophisticated kind. Only rarely do the Special Operations trainers themselves kill the poor nonwhite people. The troops they direct do the dirty work and the work is dirty; they rape, pillage, and destroy all the things that make a nation work. And as long as their accomplices annihilate brown or yellow skinned people, that's okay. But the CIA's mining of Nicaragua's port of Corinto was a mistake. Twelve ships hit those mines, nine were destroyed, ships belonging to the Netherlands, the USSR, and even Great Britain. Many of them were insured by Lloyds of London. And you see, that capitalist company is owned by white rich people. When the U.S. stepped over that line it was forced by its allies to shift logistics. Nicaragua took this case to the International Court of Justice and when that court decided against the U.S., your country refused to acknowledge its jurisdiction. Eventually both houses of your Congress condemned the mining of our harbors and coasts and that particular tactic was suspended."

Castro continued; "The Special Forces' guerrillas alone are not enough of a threat to destabilize either an enemy government or dispose of an insurgent movement. They are only one element in a comprehensive strategy that is designed to keep the opposition on full alert. All of the enemy's resources must be mobilized to combat a larger threat. For this a rear-guard is required. In 1983 the U.S. sent nineteen ships carrying several battalions of Marines to Nicaragua's coasts. Understandably

275

we felt invasion was imminent. The armada grew to 25 war-ships with more soldiers and bombers lined-up on aircraft carriers while battalions of U.S. troops joined the Contras and the Honduran Army at the border, on the Honduran side of the Rio Coco. The U.S. State Department called it a 'training exercise' but we feared an invasion.''

And what does this kind of rear-guard intimidation accomplish? Castro elaborated the point. ''First it succeeds in keeping our nation, both the people and the military, on full-alert. That has an economic impact. It costs a great deal of money to keep a military system in a position to defend a nation at all its borders. When you spend precious limited resources to do that, you cannot disband or reduce the military and use those revenues to rebuild the nation and improve the conditions of the people. The second objective of this rear-guard harassment is psychological terrorism. How do you measure that? In order to succeed, LIW must also conduct a war of nerves and wear down the spirit of the people until they give up and no longer support the Revolution.''

When the gains in human services — the literacy campaign, health-care for the masses, building roads and homes and improving the efficiency of industry and agriculture — when this dwindles because money and human resources must be funneled into defense, finally the people begin to lose hope. At least that is the intent behind the strategy. It's a gamble that LIW tacticians take because it can also backfire. War and the threat of war can also drive people together and keep them united.

LIW intends to drive home the point that any nation seeking to challenge U.S. power and prestige will have to pay a great price.

Castro landed on that point like a hammer hitting a nail dead-center. ''But the point that your government hides from your people is that you pay a great price trying to keep us in what you think is our place. You have spent, directly and indirectly, three billion dollars in trying to teach Nicaragua this lesson and another seventeen billion throughout Central

America in support of that objective. In ten years, each citizen of your nation has paid $10,000 into this effort. If they were to be asked, the immorality of LIW not considered, do you believe they would think it worth the price? All of the nations of Central America are coming to realize that they too pay a high price for allying themselves with the U.S. in this LIW against Nicaragua. Not only do they forfeit their dignity and self-respect but increasingly their sovereignty as well. There is no civilian government in Honduras. The line of command for decision making in our neighbor nation follows this chain: (1) Washington D.C. at the top, followed by (2) the U.S. Military Southern Command headquarted in Panama, (3) the U.S. military themselves in Honduras, (4) then the Honduran military, and finally, almost as an afterthought, (5) their civilian government.''

In closing, Dr. Castro was asked to offer his interpretation of the situation in Panama. In his estimation, Noriega's role in the trafficking of drugs is a deflection from the real issues at hand which are twofold.

''First, the Panama canal is barely able to handle modern bulk transporters, container ships, and large petroleum tankers. Many vessels, including the largest of U.S. aircraft carriers and super tankers, are unable to make passage through the narrow system of locks and must detour around the Cape. The added expense plus loss of time makes necessary the consideration of building a larger size interoceanic waterway.''

Of the 29 conceivable routes across Central America, six are considered most feasible. Nicaragua heads the list. Using a route first established by Cornelius Vanderbilt during the California gold rush in 1849, ships enter Nicaragua from the Atlantic port of San Juan del Norte (Greytown) and proceed up the Rio Indio to Lake Nicaragua. Crossing the lake to the Bay of Salinas, it is a short distance to the Pacific Coast. Vanderbilt ran a stage for hauling passengers and cargo 12 miles over the mountains and down to the ocean. While building a canal across this terrain presents difficult but not insurmountable problems of engineering and environmental hazard, Castro was of the impression that Nicaragua was negotiating with Japan to determine the feasibility of establishing this intercostal channel.

Of course this was not the first time that the U.S. pondered the possibility of securing this access. The Bryan-Chamorro Treaty of 1914 ceded to the U.S. "in perpetuity and for all time . . . free from all taxation or other public charge, the exclusive proprietary rights necessary and convenient for the construction of a canal by way of any route over Nicaraguan territory." For this right, the U.S. government would pay Nicaragua three million dollars, funds which would remain in the U.S. against Nicaragua's future debts or credits.

Chamorro's deal with the U.S. was not only futile, it was illegal. Nicaragua's Constitution, then and now, expressly states that only the National Assembly or elected representatives of the people have the power to enter into treaty arrangements with foreign governments. Not easily defeated, Chamorro called three Constitutional Conventions for the express purpose of having this article deleted; he failed at each attempt. The treaty was declared unlawful and remains illegitimate.

Like the resurrection of an old dream, the Reagan administration picked up where Bryan failed and blew a fresh breath into the desire to secure "in perpetuity and for all time" ownership of a new interoceanic canal. In order to do so, however, they would either have to render Nicaragua more complaint to the notion or try another tact where Panama was concerned. Neither option would be easily leveraged. The attempt to bend the Sandinistas into subservience was stalemated. Moreover with respect to Panama, a tricky knot would have to be untied. It would require a step backward since, in Reagan's estimation, the federal government had recently shot itself in its own foot.

In 1978 President Carter signed and the U.S. Senate ratified the Torrijos-Carter Treaty. Among other things, it ceded to Panama full ownership and control of the canal by the year 2000. A time-line was established for the gradual transfer of canal operation into Panamanian hands. Moreover, Panamanian real-estate on top of which the U.S. built the Tyndall Air

Force Base, the Navy's Mine Defense Laboratory, and the headquarters of the Southern Command (the nerve center directing all U.S. military affairs in Central and South America) would be returned to Panamanian ownership.

Carter's decency was perceived by his successor to be nothing less than a moronic blunder. Since the clock could not be stopped and the year 2000 was less than two decades distant, the U.S. needed either a friend at the helm of the Panamanian state or, failing that, at least a docile and easily manipulated government. Since General Torrijos concluded the canal transfer treaty, it was not likely that he would back down and renege on the deal.

Enter General Noriega, friend and ally, a man willing to cut deals even when they overstepped the bounds of law and civility. As it turned out, however, the General was no easy mark. Unwilling to barter away Panamaian vested interest in the treaty, Noriega ceased to be a pal. Indeed hell hath no fury comparable to the wrath of a spurned suitor.

Panama is the most unrevolutionary nation in Latin America. With insubstantial agro-exports, its primary significance turns around the 'transit function' of the canal — that plus the free zone and its function as a global finance capitol. Myraid banks serve as stewards for foreign depositors including the laundrying of massive doses of cash from Colombian drug cartels. Seeking a safe haven for taxes and other benefits, many corporation around the world use it as the location for filing their articles of incoropration. Panama is safe turf since this Zurich of the Central Americas also bivouacs a greater concentration of U.S. military than anywhere else south of the Mexican border. Torrijos' occasional indulgence in inflammatory but empty revolutionary rhetoric notwithstanding, genuine instability in Panama would deplete the banks and close the canal.

Unable to cast Noriega in guise of a scurrilous revolutionary intent upon dismantling the capitalist machine, it became necessary to vilify him with other allegations; Noriega the pornographer, Noriega the sexual deviate abusing children,

Noriega the narcotics pusher in cahoots with the Colombian drug cartels.

While there may be truth in these accusations, were we to believe that these unsavory and deviant behaviors were recent character defects, perversions of a post-1982 and sudden sort that just happened to coincide with his ceasing to function as a U.S. ally on the payroll of the CIA? Or were we willing to overlook these debaucheries as long as he played ball in our game?

Castro concluded; "When General Noriega refused to resign his presidency and return to face the Administration's charges against him in U.S. courts, the federal government put the dollar squeeze on Panama. The U.S. shut down Panamanian access to cash in a move that made the people suffer but not the General. And the result? Anti-U.S. sentiments surfaced immediately and intensely. The people saw the pressure against Noriega for what it was, a reprisal for his not backing down from the Torrijos-Carter Canal Treaty. So, although the General does not deserve it, by manipulating the people's sense of nationalism and pride he became an instant national hero. And as for the dollar squeeze, Panamanians simply opened up the old market place, eliminated the middleman, and bartered and traded in arrangements of economic survival."

Third World peoples are poor, yes, but not fools. Neither are they blind. Because the lessons have been carved upon their flesh, they know in their minds and hearts that Low Intensity War is bankrupt and immoral. Bankrupt because it does not work. Not in the long run or in any run through any gauntlet. Immoral because it violates elemental human conscience. For a nation to violate the sovereignty of another and attempt to destabilize their democratically elected government is wrong. To terrorize civilians and decimate their dreams with torture and pillage, to destroy their homes and crops, to disrupt their shipping and trade, to shut the door on their access to capital and encourage the decapitalization of their own economy is immoral, is wrong. Moreover, the Administration's willingness to lie to Congress while violating our own laws is blasphemy.

Refusing overtures for peace which have come from Managua, again and again, is immoral, is wrong. We were wrong in 1854 and we are still wrong in 1988.

Daniel Berrigan, referring to Vietnam but equally appropro with regard to our Central American policy, remarked that "this rising tide of savagery and ruin which we have provoked and which we now sustain" is immoral and wrong. For 134 years we have pushed this madness and our only answer is more madness?

REFLECTION: "The Truth, the Whole Truth and Nothing but the Truth"

'Freedom fighters' or hired killers? 'Low Intensity War' or terrorism in verbal camouflage? 'Death squad thugs' or Special Operations Forces elite?

The Gospel of John recounts a curious conversation between Jesus and Pilate. The scene unfolds during the kangaroo-court that passed for a trial. Pilate inquired about the charges brought against the man from Nazareth asking, "Are you the king of the Jews?" Jesus replied, "My kingdom does not belong to this world."

Was the Roman procurator amused, in the mood for inconsequential sparring with words? "So you are a king," comes Pilate's retort. Jesus counterpoints, "King is your word. My task is to bring witness to the truth."

Like the cat believing that it has finally cornered the elusive and exhausted mouse, the sophisticated Roman bureaucrat yawns and slides in the metaphysical ruse, "What is truth?" Without waiting for a reply, he abandons the quaint diversion and goes about his business.

To Pilate's question "What is truth?" George Buttrick noted that there are three kinds of truth: courtroom truth, university truth, and Biblical truth.

The words of a critic come to mind: "Most friends of truth love it as Frederick the Great loved music. Strictly speaking he was not fond of music, but of flute, and not of flute, but of his flute." The mind reels — what music, which flute?

I abandon the mental courtroom with its legal truth and make my retreat to the dais of the university. It's an old haven, a safe refuge. Surely there, truth that is the result of scholarly work will assuage my tedious spirit. After all, the university's search for truth is in itself a work of liberation; the unbinding of ignorance, the emancipation from prejudice, the forfeiture of arrogance in the willingness to stand honestly and humbly before objective facts.

Against the hope that in the midst of this clamorous mess of a war there is some objective reality, I sit open handed attempting to sort and separate information from disinformation, fantasy from fact. Like a latter-day Diogenes with lamp in hand looking for a truthful person, I want to achieve a straightforward reckoning. The data coming at me from both sides is altogether unpleasant, the logic circular, the interests self-serving.

But what happens if truth turns out to be something dreadful, painful? When Oedipus learned the truth that he had killed his father and married his mother, he put his eyes out. When the truth hurts, when we hate it, often we will blind ourselves before acknowledging its claims and bending ourselves to its service.

While the jury of the court deliberates and the scholars wheedle and dicker, I pick up the option of laying the lens of Biblical truth into the balance.

Unlike university truth, Biblical truth is distressingly unphilosophical. I ask of the Scripture, 'Who is my neighbor? My countrymen or the Nicaraguans?' In reply I get no legal or scholarly definition but a story; the Good Samaritan. Strange but comprehensible. Leaping to the final object of my quest I ask, what is truth, and get another strange answer; Jesus saying, "I am the truth."

The Greek word for truth is *aletheia*, or 'unveiling.' The bride lifts her veil and 'the moment of truth' is at hand; the unseen and hidden becomes visible, public. The matador, poised over the bull, draws a visual line between the tip of his sword and one square inch at the nape of the beast's neck.

For an instant, it is 'the moment of truth' before the fatal thrust; the moment of destiny where life and death contend. In a 'moment of truth' the veil of the Temple is slashed in two and raw mystery is revealed in an eye-blink.

For Christians, the moment of truth is Jesus Christ. The Lord is not a legal fact or a scholarly analyzed proposition. The truth in Jesus does not consist of his teachings or proclamations from God. The truth is simply the man! And that man unveils the hidden, exposes the Mystery, and renders the ambiguous clear. Jesus is the man capable of bringing Diogenes' search to a screeching halt.

An interesting inkling. But strange?

Tutor and dear friend, Robert Hamill bid me to consider how strange other things are. Take a simple measurement for instance. Normally a yardstick is sufficient. But perhaps I want one that is precisely one yard, no more, no less. How do I gauge the accuracy of the device? The distance between the king's nose and outstretched fingertips will not do. It must be checked against the platinum bar in the Bureau of Standards, the keeper of one exact bar, maintained under constant atmospheric conditions, the standard and accepted definition of one yard — .9144 of a meter, one ten-millionth of the distance between the equator and the North Pole.

But I am a curious chap. I question the trustworthiness of that platinum bar. The answer? Whatever is meant by one 'yard' is the length of that bar; whatever the bar is, that is a yard.

According to Christian Scripture and faith, whatever Jesus is, that is truth! Is it any more arbitrary than the other? Biblical truth means tht Jesus is the yardstick; he is the measure of truth; we measure truth by him for he stands to us as our Bureau of Standards.

An interesting turn in the corridors of judgment. It is not that Jesus resembled God so accurately that he is therefore esteemed to be God's son. Instead, it is that God resembles Jesus so closely that we refer to God as the Creator of Jesus. "He who has seen me has seen the Father." Looking to

Scripture we say that whatever in this book witnesses faithfully to Jesus, that is authentic Scripture; it is inspired if it painstakingly points to him. The Church is of Jesus if it conforms to the mind of Christ and continues his ministry; he measures the Church, its mission, and its message. Where it fails to conform, the Church cannot legitimately wear his name.

And this truth called Jesus? It comes in many forms, but seldom in the shape of propositions to be memorized. It may come to you unannounced and unnoticed. It may come suddenly, like a thunderclap, or slowly like a lifting fog that reveals something beyond opinion and prejudice. It may come through reading or listening or seeing or on the heels of a shattering engagement with yourself. It may happen in a glad or fearsome act of obedience. And always you hear those words; "If you continue in my word, you will be my disciples, and you shall know the truth and the truth shall make you free."

Perhaps Albert Schweitzer said it best at the conclusion of his **Quest for the Historical Jesus**:

> *"He comes to us as One unknown, without a name, as of old by the lakeside He came to those who knew him not. He speaks to us the same word: Follow thou me! and sets us to the task He has to fulfill in our time. He commands. And to those who obey him, whether they be wise or simple, He will reveal Himself in the toils, the conflicts, the sufferings which they shall pass through in His fellowship, and, as an ineffable mystery, they shall learn in their own experience, who he is."*[28]

OBSERVATION: "Interview Inside the Citadel — The U.S. Embassy"

June 23

Entering the U.S. Embassy reminded me of going into the maximum-security federal prison in Walpole, Massachusetts. The prison erupted in a major riot and teams of civilian observers were called in to evaluate the situation with an eye to documenting alleged violations of the inmates' civil rights.

While my father had been chaplain at San Quentin during the 1940s this was my first experience inside a federal penitentiary. It was a chilling encounter. Surveillance was monitored by the omniscient electronic eye. Men sat behind bullet-proof glass controlling your movements by throwing switches to open and close doors. Commanding voices came at the ear from remote speakers directing you to turn, pass, halt, be seated.

At Walpole, the last room you passed through before crossing the yard to the prison cell blocks was a windowless chamber of solid steel, ten by twenty-foot with a fifteen-foot ceiling. Everyone entering or leaving the penitentiary was forced to linger in this gauntlet. When the great slab of a door at the rear slid shut you developed an immediate visceral kinship with the steer in a sorting chute waiting its turn to be dehorned, branded, castrated, or slaughtered. The wary eye involuntarily looked overhead into a plexiglass dome and the barrel of an automatic rifle mounted on a swivel. Anything moving through that crypt without permission would quickly be reduced to hamburger.

Here in the Managuan embassy, after passing through the check points, we entered a large circular room with wooden chairs set in parallel lines at the center. Behind the plate glass windows on the perimeter, the offices were empty. Involuntarily, my eye scanned the ceiling and walls for the port that deals in more than warm welcomes. Likewise missing was Walpole's strip-down cavity search for weapons and contraband.

Two men entered. The man in his forties looked like a Marine Corps drill instructor without the uniform. His younger cohort had the squeaky appearance of a recently recruited graduate student fresh from the halls of an Ivy-league academy. Taking a seat at the wall, the man with the crew-cut and loose fitting Hawaiian-print shirt slouched into a chair, stretched his legs forward, and leaned back against the glass. His arms folded tightly across his chest, his smirking cockiness bordered on contempt. I wagered that the buldge under the shirt at the belt-line concealed a revolver.

The younger man walked to the chair between our rows and sat. No hand-shake, no smile; it was a sharp contrast to the affable hospitality of the Nicaraguans who had shared their time with us.

Introducing himself as John Shearburn, in the same breath he added that he was a 'career-service diplomat.' I smiled. Twenty-five years ago following my ordination I relished being referred to as Reverend Roberts and later, Doctor Roberts. Shearburn's in his second tour with the department. His first assignment was Mexico City. He has been in Nicaragua for six months.

Following our standard introduction, Laura made it very clear that we desired to use his time for question and answer purposes. Perhaps sensitive to his green-horn status and the fact of a supervisor hovering in the wings, Shearburn ignored the request. It was his time, he was in charge, and he would set the agenda. Moreover, this thirty-minute incursion into his busy schedule would begin with a lecture in Nicaraguan history.

Turning my head, the widening grin on the face of his supervisor convinced me that the young man had scored his first point. Lesson number one when dealing with critical customers is to let them know who's in charge . . . right off the top!

Resisting an urge to protest this unsolicited if not cavalier tutorial, I resolved to listen carefully and probe his recital with an ear to detecting discrepancies or diversions from fact in his touting of the State Department's rendition of the truth, the whole truth, and nothing but the truth.

Instead, and as far as it went, Shearburn's account did not play fast and loose with the facts. One, two, three: the dictatorships and cronyisms of the Somozas were a rip-off of the Nicaraguan people; the 197[3] earthquake reduced 90 percent of Managua to rubble and the $200 to $300 million of relief aid never reached the people for whom it was intended; the government's assassination of Charmorro in 1978 clinched the Sandinista's alliance with the middle-class and hastened the overthrow of the corrupt dynasty.

The young man was chewing up our thirty minutes with his soliloquy, running down the clock. Since he wasn't the only one with other things to do, we pressed an interruption.

"Describe U.S. policy toward Nicaragua during President Reagan's administration," we queried.

The man in the Hawaiian shirt wasn't smiling now.

Shearburn began: "The $118 million allocated to Nicaragua in 1980 by the program of U.S. Aid to Developing Nations was curtailed in the spring of 1981 when it became obvious that the Sandinistas were commiting violations of the peoples' human rights. Concern for human rights was a theme of President Carter's administration and protecting those rights was a condition of that Aid package."

It's hard to pin Ronald Reagan's hostility toward the Sandinistas to abuses of human rights. Less than two weeks following the Triumph in 1979, and six months before he declared his candidacy for President, Reagan went on record as being opposed to the new government in Managua. Two weeks is too short a period for the new government to establish a history of human rights abuse. His bias against them was transparent.

The young diplomat continued. "President Reagan's policy toward the Sandinista government has four points: (1) They must stop their aid to guerrilla movements in El Salvador, Honduras, Guatemala and to a lesser extent in Costa Rica. (2) They must cease their ties to Soviet-block nations and Cuba. (3) They must reduce their military strength to a level commensurate with their neighboring nations. (4) They must produce evidence of a real mixed economy."

"You forgot to mention the President's concern for their human rights," we noted without sarcasm.

Unbelievable. Incredulous. The man's capacity for nonsequitur was appalling. When has a nation ever reduced the size of its military and increased its capacity for democracy while being invaded? Given the success of our economic embargo and the collaboration of our allies in curbing trade with Nicaragua, were we not forcing their dependence on the Soviet-block and Cuba as a matter of sheer survival? Merchants hawking their wares and haggling prices in Managua's *Mercado Oriental*, Circles Robinson's work with farming cooperatives,

Juan Pauth's insistence that he was an independent business-man, Esperanza's ownership of her cantina, garbage workers striking for higher wages, if this was not some indication of a mixed economy, what was?

Undaunted, he continued, "We have used two methods to pressure the Nicaraguans into compliance with these objectives. Diplomatically, the Mission and Embassy attempt to persuade the government to negotiate with other nations. Military intervention is no longer possible after Congress cut-off financial support to the Contras in February."

"Is the economic embargo a diplomatic tactic or part of the military strategy called Low Intensity War?" we asked.

"The United States has not tried to destroy the Sandinista government militarily and neither will the Contras come to power militarily. As an aspect of our policy, their only role is to pressure the government to the negotiating table."

Disinformation was being pandered as fact; Low Intensity War is an attempt to destroy a nation by methods that include military interventions, and, as he noted, the Contras will never topple the Sandinistas by sheer force of arms.

We tried to refine his focus, sharpen it up. "So the Contras and the embargo are part of a military strategy to prompt negotiation?"

"The Nicaraguan government's economic experiment has failed. The centralized plan is not working and they blame it on the embargo which was simply an attempt to get the world's attention and make it known that we did not like the Sandinista's policies. But the embargo has failed as well. It only increases the cost of importing goods by 25 percent."

If inflation is part of an index reflecting the impact of the embargo during the period of our short visit, the Dollar to Cord ratio soared from 1 to 13 to 1 to 187; the 25 percent estimate seemed ludicrous.

Why an economic embargo? By law, the President of the United States can inflict economic embargo upon a nation at the point where our national security is perceived to be imminently threatened. Consequently on May 1, 1985, President Reagan stipulated the following:

"I, Ronald Reagan, President of the United States of America, find that the policies and actions of the Government of Nicaragua constitute an unusual and extraordinary threat to the national security and foreign policy of the United States and hereby declare a national emergency to deal with that threat."[29]

Noting that fact, we inquired, "Specifically how are the Nicaraguans threatening our national security? What behavior of theirs warrants economic warfare against these people?"

Shearburn bristled. "Managua is the center for terrorist training that reaches out to instigate communist revolutions in El Salvador, Honduras and Guatemala. In addition to training terrorists, the Sandinistas supply these groups with arms and other forms of material support. In September of 1987, President Ortega announced in Mexico City that Nicaragua was supporting guerrilla forces in El Salvador."

The Sandinistas were responsible for 'instigating' armed insurrection in El Salvador? Either that was a poor choice of words or the man had slept through one of his tutorials. On the face of it, that represented a curious ignorance of historic fact. Salvadoran land-less poor mounted their first armed revolt against the oligarchy in 1932, years before the birth of the Frente Sandinista! In 1982 *La Prensa* printed a story claiming that the government was raising its production quotas in order to aid the Salvadoran guerrillas, a surprising feat since it implied a control over the economy that the government did not possess. Nicaraguan agriculture was experiencing critical shortages in the production of food to feed its own people. Moreover, the U.S. military, with all of its sophisicated communications and surveillance technology, was never able to produce convincing proof that arms shipments were being funneled to the rebels by their southern neighbor.

The uncritical assumptions within Shearburn's recital sounded as if they were taken from the Santa Fe Document created in 1980 by the Council for Inter-American Security, a group of conservative businessmen intent on shaping

President Reagan's policy toward Latin America. The report stressed the threat to our security posed by insurgent revolutionary movements throughout the Americas and recommended overt military reprisals to counter this menace.

In November of that same year a Dissent Memo was prepared by anonymous members of the CIA, Pentagon, and State Deparment. It called the Administration to consider what was termed 'the Zimbabwe solution,' an alternative approach to dealing with Central America. The model would utilize a negotiated settlement patterned after Britain's role in the successful resolution of the Rhodesia-Zimbabwe conflict, one that made possible the election of Robert Mugabe's Marxist government while affirming the independence of the new nation-state. The Dissent Memo failed to generate interest within Reagan's policy-making circles.[30]

The cold-war mentality prevailed with its perception of Nicaragua as a 'Soviet surrogate,' a puppet in the hands of Moscow, a pawn in the game dominated by superpowers playing out their roles in the conflict between East and West. Unwilling to refocus their lens and comprehend the matter as a dispute between the rich North and the poor South, the new administration wanted to send a quick and clear message to Moscow and the Central Americas: We would not be thwarted in our control of the hemisphere.

As if to credential the Santa Fe Document, Presidential 'findings' and 'white papers' began appearing. Within a month of Reagan's inauguration the new administration produced a 'white paper' claiming evidence of arms being shipped from the soviet-block through Cuba and Nicaragua destined for El Salvador. On close inspection the captured guerrilla documents used to substantiate these allegations were found to be inadequate, false, and probably forged. In the three months between November 1980 and January 1981, the Salvadoran army assassinated four American religious women, murdered persons at a Jesuit high school, and killed the Salvadoran head of land reform programs plus his two U.S. labor advisors. At home, the public outcry ran against the administration and the prospect of another Vietnam war.

Central America ceased to be front page news for approximately one month, the length of time it took for Mr. Casey at the CIA to produce another 'presidential finding' once again alleging covert operations flowing from Nicaragua in support of Central American rebels. This time the President suspended Nicaragua's $15 million credit for purchasing U.S. wheat, a gap that was quickly filled by Canada and the USSR. Since the Soviets had just been relieved from their own ban on the export of our grain, in all likelihood they simply diverted a portion of that supply to the Sandinistas.

Ten months later, in December 1981, the President authorized $19.5 million for aid to our new Nicaraguan allies, the 'freedom force' known as the counter-revolutionary Contras. While it was contemptible for Nicaragua to offer any form of material or encouraging support to Central American indigenous rebels, it was neither beneath us nor a contradiction for us to export counter-revolution into Nicaragua from neighboring Honduras.

Obviously, what's sauce for the goose is not always sauce for the gander! Since the U.S. decided that it would be the only dealer in the Central American game of power poker, it insisted on the right to determine the rules and order the deck. The folk at the White House, the Pentagon, Langely, and Foggy Bottom love white hat/black hat dramas. Never mind that the dangers are trumped-up, the enemy weak, and our goals vague, limited, and self-serving. In the name of hope, our foreign policy inflicts suffering on the poor and then runs away. I wince in chagrin when my government's foreign policy is noticeably absent of moral principles. I am embarrassed when it lacks coherence or consistency. I am outraged when it fails minimum standards of justice as fairness. Reagan's politics and Rambo-style war are indulgences in lethal narcissisms parading as patriotic nationalism.

The delegation attempted to refocus the interview back to the issue of human rights violations. It was a legitimate concern, possibly mutual, and one that might serve to move the session out of the rut it had landed in.

One of the team reiterated Shearburn's remark that in 1981 President Reagan had suspended U.S. Aid funds to Nicaragua because of alleged Sandinista violations of fundamental human rights. Indeed, during the intervening seven yeas, organizations such as Americas Watch paid careful attention to violations of human rights. Charges against the Nicaraguan government have included limits to the freedom of expression, interference with the practice and profession of religious faith, the imprisonment of political opponents, restrictions of due process of law including the limitations on Habeas Corpus, and violations of the laws of war such as the forcible and involuntary relocation of thousands of its citizens. Given the seriousness of these charges, simply raising our concern felt like offering Mr. Shearburn a splendid opportunity to join issue with us on a serious front and change the character of the briefing.

He didn't have to be asked twice to leap into the subject. "The Sandinistas have made lots of stupid mistakes and have utterly failed to do any right or decent thing. Just yesterday they kicked Gary Moore out of the country. He had been documenting human rights abuses in Zalaya with a video camera and turned up evidence that the government did not want to deal with."

Who was Gary Moore? Whom did he represent and to whom were his findings being delivered? Was he working for *The Unión Nicaraguense de Oposicion* (UNO) the political organization uniting the principal Contra forces and recently the recipient of $5 million in U.S. funds? And, simply, what did he discover? When pressed for further comment about Mr. Moore's case, Shearburn declined, remarking that the situation was still in process and could not be discussed.

We took another tact. "Since our government has been the principal powerhouse behind the Contras — organizing, funding, training, arming, and directing them — are we willing to share the responsibility for their human rights abuses?"

Witness for Peace and Americas Watch both have been keen in their investigations of Contra abuses and such facts are a matter of substantiated as well as substantial record.

Shearburn's reply ended the session. Looking at Julie, Rhonda and Tito he said, "You would have to ask your Sandinista tour guides about that."

Sandinista tour guides? Before we could launch a correcting rebuttal, both Shearburn and his cohort were out of their chairs and ready to leave. No pro-forma Thank You. Nothing. The End was writ large to our session as these men walked briskly into the outer offices.

"You may exit through the doors that you entered," came the anonymous voice over the loud speaker. Obviously our briefing at the Embassy was over.

REFLECTION: "Watchman, what of the night?"

On leaving the Embassy I felt bogged in a morass, sucked into a quagmire of painful memory. The parallels between what we are doing in Nicaragua and our experience in Vietnam were inescapable and haunting. In both instances offenses against sanity and decency added up to madness.

There and then, here and now, each time we became engaged in conflicts far beyond our original intent. Each time we abandoned a decent regard for world opinion and strained relations with our allies. In their collective judgment, we were wrong and set on the path of a hopeless effort. Each time we appeared unable or unwilling to recognize that an indigenous government represented a genuine social revolution. We misjudged their popular support within a large portion of the civilian population. Each time we refused to recognize internal strife as simply that, internal strife or civil war. Instead, we chose to intervene on one side hoping to determine the outcome. Each time our direct or indirect military presence disregarded the ancient rule of war that civilians be protected and non-combatants be excluded from violence. Each time the war has been expanded to intensify the battle on military and economic fronts. Each time the war sacrificed significant rapprochement with potential allies, in the Asian case forcing the Soviet Union into open support for North Vietnam, and in Nicaragua, isolating us further from the peoples of the Central and Latin Americas. And each time, our policy of war has caused terrible disruptions at home; in a society of extravagant wealth, the costs of war has impacted severely on domestic programs of health and education and welfare making it, once again, the children, the elderly, and the poor who continue to pay at home for our madness abroad.

The United Nations charter declares that "wars begin in the minds of men." My nation's wars begin in the minds and hearts of our people and in our laws and institutions. The obstacles to peace are more formidable than critics would suppose who blamed the Vietnam War on Kennedy, Johnson, or Nixon, and Contra War in Nicaragua on Reagan. It is not the villainy of the villains that makes for war but the acquiescence of the righteous. It is not a demonic President but a morally calloused people who allow wars to happen.

So when I ask, as the prophet Isaiah asked, "Watchman, what of the night?" I hear Isaiah's reply, "The morning comes, also the night." The night. It was Charles Beard that said, when it is dark enough you can see the stars. And what do we see by the light of those stars? Beard said it again, whom the gods would destroy they first make mad with power. His final thought, summing up his vast study of history, only deepened my mood; though the mills of the gods grind slowly, they grind exceeding fine.

Walking the streets of Managua I wanted to turn and find that young diplomat and delivery a soliloquy of my own. We North Americans cannot play God, nor even policeman; not in Central America, not Asia, not anywhere. We have neither the power, nor the wisdom, nor the right. Sandinista abuses of human rights constitute no justification for our management of the Contras or Low Intensity War and its scurrility. We have a clear choice: we can play the game of violence with all its insane consequences, or we can use the methods which eventually make for justice and welfare and decency.

One of the ancient prophets declared to a people in their day of decision, "I have set before you this day life and death, blessing and cursing. Therefore choose life, that you may live." Choose life, for yourself, your children, for humankind. All of us belong to God.

And what do I see by the light of that star? I see a day coming round when my nation will no longer define its boundaries by the Gross National Product at the top and Social Security at the bottom, with the Pentegon on the right and the Constitution on the left. I dream of a whole human family bounded on the north by the aurora borealis, on the south by the changing seasons, on the east by the primeval mysteries, and on the west by the Day of Judgment.

OBSERVATION: "La Prensa: Discrediting the Sandinistas" June 24

Chamorro and *La Prensa* are two names often spoken in the same breath. Outside of Nicaragua they are frequently regarded as interchangable. Founded on March 2, 1926, by the late Pedro Joaquin Chamorro, *La Prensa's* international reputation as a newspaper was hinged to its founding editor's 30 year opposition to the Somoza dictatorships.

In 1988 the name Chamorro is still synonymous with publishing, but no longer exclusively associated with *La Prensa*. Of Nicaragua's three rival news dailies, each are published by a Chamorro. The resemblance ends there. Pedro Joaquin's widow, Violeta Barrios de Chamorro, owns *La Prensa* in partnership with her eldest son, the founder's namesake. Another Chamorro, Pedro Joaquin's brother Xavier, is editor of *El Neuvo Diario* which came into being in May 1980 when a majority of staff at *La Prensa* became disenchanted with the paper's conservative editorial policy and jumped ship to establish their own press. Carlos Fernando Chamorro, the youngest of Pedro and Violeta's sons, eventually became editor of the Sandinista daily, *Barricada*.

To say that the Chamorro clan is deeply divided would be an understatement. *Barricada* is regarded by *La Prensa* staff as the "public wife of the Revolution." Although they disagree with its ideological bias, the fact that its political point of view is openly declared is respected and commended. Conversely, they have nothing but contempt for *El Neuvo Diario* and call it the Sandinista's "back-street mistress." Parading itself as politically independent while touting the government's party-line is journalistic subtrafuge. As if to return insult for insult, Xavier Chamorro regards *La Prensa* as the mouthpiece of the CIA and "Reagan's rag."

Taking a cue from their intensely political mother, Violeta's daughters are likewise strongly opinionated and divided in their ideological loyalties. Cristiana works at her mother's side at *La Prensa* while Claudia served as the Sandinista ambassador to Costa Rica.

Late in the morning of the 24th we arrived at the *La Prensa* offices for an appointment with Cesar Rojas, an Editor of the paper. With revolutionary graffiti generously applied to the exterior walls, this headquarters hardly appeared adequate for a paper boasting a daily circulation of 50,000. Inside there was a noticeable absence of the scurry and muffled din normally associated with newsrooms. The place looked sleepy, almost comatose. In the conference room, pictures of the late founder covered walls including blow-ups taken during riots following his assassination.

After a fifteen-minute wait, Rojas entered and sat down heavily in a soft leather chair. Laura's introduction of the delegation made a special point of thanking the Editor for granting this interview, the first WFP group had managed in a six-month period.

Rojas paid polite obeisance to the memory of the paper's founder. Asserting that *La Prensa* has always been committed to advocating the themes of justice and liberty, he said; "We opposed Somoza's dictatorship and now we oppose the Sandinista government because it has founded a communist totalitarianism that is worse than the Somoza's. During the nine years of the Sandinista's rule, we have been shut down by the government more times than during all of the Somoza dictatorships. Like any dictatorship, the Sandinistas maintain their power with the bayonet.''

Since March of 1982, Nicaragua has been governed under an imposed state of emergency decree. Certain rights secured to the people in the Statute of Rights and Guarantees of the Constitution have been suspended. Included in the 1982 'exception legislation' was the authority of the state to censor the publication of information considered to be sensitive to military or economic affairs. In October of 1985, President Ortega announced a decree that provided the state with additional power to restrict freedom of association and expression.

Opposition parties in the National Assembly, factions within the Sandinista camp, and a majority of the Nicaraguan Supreme Court, criticized this new state of emergency legislation. Likewise, many nations within the international community denounced this apparent totalitarian tendency. Nonetheless, the proposed measures were approved by the legislature. The Sandinista executive board was given sweeping powers to restrict freedom of movement, expression, and association. They further curbed the right to strike and gave the police permission to intrude on personal privacy.

The decision of the government to call for emergency measures may be justifiable in defense of the nation. It is disturbing, however, that they were instituted without carefully prescribed limits to defend the people against abuses.

The fact that they functioned to thwart legitimate political dissent was editor Rojas' most strident complaint: ''There is no political freedom when you do not have an unnrestricted press. Every night we submit the inside pages of the paper to the censors at the Office of Communications and Media. About noon the next day we get back notations marked in red of what they demand be excluded from an edition or changed in wording. Censored material varies from about 25 to 50 percent of what we submit. The front page was going to the censor about the time you arrived. That's why it is so quiet in here right now. When it returns early in the afternoon, we finish making changes and then run the presses. We write articles, send them away, and wait. You can look at recent examples of their work if you choose to. The penalty for violating their restrictions is severe. The government accuses you of being traitors or agents of the CIA, or, as has happened, they jail reporters, confiscate their cameras and film, and finally lock the press and shut you down."

The gaps created by the red pencil-wielding censors are replenished with innocuous pre-approved fillers. Even these must be cleared by telephone prior to being inserted in the paper. The presses do not run until the censors are satisfied that everything in an edition has come under their scrutiny. Normally, the government does not attempt to force the paper to print articles favorable to the Process. On the other hand, in 1985 the Sandinistas squelched the publication of a Roman Catholic periodical that advocated resistance to the draft. It also revoked the broadcast license of *Radio Catolica* when it refused to air a speech by President Ortega. At the bottom line, the government, through the office of the censor, arrogates to itself the right to determine what is newsworthy and fit for public consumption.

Examples of censored materials in Rojas' files included reports with photographs of accidents involving Sandinista Police vehicles, coverage of the war in Afghanistan, news of the breakdown of conversations between the government and a local garbage collectors labor union, stories about the Pope, and the dispute between Solidarity workers and the state in Poland.

Rojas was indignant. "It is not only Nicaraguan military and economic news that the censors prohibit. They censor copy from the AP, UPI, and Reuters wire services that might be seen as critical of communism anywhere in the world."

Rojas clarified the difference between information articles and editorials: "Since the Esquipulas Accords in August 1987, international opinion and hemispheric pressure has forced the Sandinistas to permit some level of criticism of the government in the press, but only by publishing information articles that are the public statements of opposition parties. When the

Communist and Socialist parties declare that the Sandinistas are opportunists and have a criminal strangle-hold of power over the people, we can print their positions. But editorials challenging their censorship, or the leadership of the FSLN, or exposing the disasters of their economic programs, these are not allowed. While the Sandinistas were very good guerrillas, they are lousy governors. For a regime that claims it must be very discreet with their successes and very critical of their errors, they are unwilling to have these neglects or failures challenged publicly in an independent press."

"Yesterday the Sandinistas announced the decommissioning of 400 Contras," Rojas noted with tight-lipped aggravation. "We prepared a story about the politial squabbling among the political directors of the counter-revolution and the censors refused to let us print that saying it was not newsworthy."

Asking whether it was possible to appeal the decision of the censors, Rojas was emphatic; "No. Theoretically Tomas Borge at the Ministry of the Interior has the power to override the decision of a censor. But that presents two problems. First you have to be able to reach Borge and that is not always possible. Second, by the time you get the copy back from the censors you have just about enough time to cut and paste and get the edition to the press if you want to make the deadline for putting the paper on the street in the evening. Practically speaking, making an appeal is not possible. Only rarely have we succeeded in overturning their decision."

To the question of whether a reporter or a paper can be sued for libel in Nicaragua, Rojas responded that indeed there were laws against spreading false information. He went on to attest that "In a totalitarian state, the laws of libel do not operate the same way they do in a democracy. In Nicaragua, the government has used these laws to close down independent presses and radio stations without a court trial to determine whether in fact someone has been injured by a malicious or false statement. This is a deliberate violation of our Constitutional rights that guarantee our freedom of speech."

As far as Rojas was concerned, nowhere was this more evident than in the case of the 1984 national elections which he regarded as a despicable fraud. Likening the Sandinista-managed electoral process to that of the Somozas he stated, "The Somozas held elections and always won. The Sandinistas do the same thing. The opposition was a facade, actors in the government's pocket playing parts in a script written and directed by the Sandinistas."

The editor appeared unmoved by our reminder that foreign observers monitoring the election were nearly unanimous in their appraisal that the process was possibly more fair than any other in Latin America. "The Frente Sandinista was the single political party controlling the entire electoral process. Through the office of the censor they also control the flow of information to the people. Without a free press or radio or television, how can you be sure that 80 percent of the people supported the election and gave the Sandinistas their backing? Was this a fact or carefully manipulated hearsay?"

Recalling the historic literacy campaign, what was its actual significance? The question began to trouble me. Empowering the people with the ability to read is as dangerous as it is commendable. It confirms the dignity of the human person to equip them with tools for making rational choices. Opening the door to an unlimited range of ideas and ready access to the pleasures of culture is a noble enterprise. On the other hand, when artificial limits are imposed on access to information, it is appropriate to question just how far that door has been opened. If the intent of the campaign was simply to increase the ability of propagandists to communicate, then the people have once again been tricked and victimized. Not empowered.

To the question of *La Prensa's* receiving financial backing from the U.S. government or the CIA, Rojas was categorical in his repudiation of that rumor: "We are not Chile's *El Mercurio* taking money from the CIA. We have always been independent, supporting ourselves from advertising funds. In fact each day we must reject ads because we do not have the paper or space to print them. We are the only independent paper in Nicaragua since *Barricada* and *Nuevo Diario* are subsidized by the government. Both these papers come out in the morning while we come out in the evening. If Nicaraguans only wanted to hear what the governemnt wants to tell them, they would buy these less expensive papers and leave us alone. But that doesn't happen. So what does that tell you? It tells me that every time they buy our paper they are voting against the Sandinistas, day by day.''

REFLECTION: "Censorship — An Issue of Hot Debate"

Censorship. Even the word leaves a bitter acidic residue on the tongue. Leaving the offices of *La Prensa*, the swelter of a tropical afternoon hit me like a blast from a furnance. Both the air and my mood were heavy. Censorship is as detrimental to the breath of a free society as it was hard to catch an invigorating gulp of air under the parching weight of the breezeless sky. While nature may often be unpleasant, it must be accepted. As an instrument of social policy, applying a tourniquet against the freedom of the press was quite another matter. A poor nation became poorer; information-poor.

Ideally law is regarded as the guardian of liberty. In fact, however, they are in tension and sometimes conflict. Since arriving in Nicaragua, nowhere was this tension more clearly evident than with the issue of state imposed censorship of the press and media. At the bottom line, when the state of emergency authorized the government to become a censor, the people were deprived of the freedom to decide for themselves what to believe.

Censorship rests on the assumption that a powerful person or party possesses political truth and is the manifestation of social justice. Consequently it has the authority to be the final judge of righteousness. It vests itself with the responsibility to see that false or misleading doctrines and information are not transmitted for public inspection. That is indeed an awesome power, one that has been historically associated with totalitarian regimes from the time of Plato's **Republic** to the present moment.

Sandinista claims that the Process or Revolution is about the business of being the 'architect of the reign of God' is a dangerous assumption. It is a notion that follows from an estimation of politics as a form of social engineering: those in power possess the correct blueprint for the perfect society; their task is that of constructing a new social order on the basis of that design.

Engineers manipulate inanimate materials. Politics deals with persons. When the two are confused and persons are dealt with as if they were so many bricks to be laid according to the lines of a blueprint, the very essence of liberty and freedom has been assaulted. It is one thing to aspire to do the will of God on earth; it is quite another to identify one's own will with that of God, an error frequently made by those who regard politics as a means of attaining spiritual salvation. The state is the servant of justice, not the source of truth or goodness. While it must promote conditions conducive to the public good, it is not capable of defining it. And never can it bring into being the Kingdom of God.

Alternatively, when politics is seen as an arena of moral endeavor, when the leaders of government are less driven to make anything and more concerned with inspring the cooperation of those whom they represent, only then is freedom preserved and protected. Suasion prevails over subtle or overt coercion. Citizens remain free to obey or disobey, cooperate or rebel. And that right to choose between alternate ways of acting is both the source of human greatness when used well, and of human degradation when abused.

When the state claims a monopoly on political truth, asking probing questions, raising doubts about the system or its values are forbidden. The government behaves as if it is ordained by God or history as the court of first and last appeal. Censors, as special agents of the state, are those persons presumably equipped with sufficient insight to understand the highly complicated operations of the public good. All others are discouraged from inquiring too deeply into matters of statecraft. To do so might lead to a loss of confidence in the state as the final arbiter of truth. If common citizens are allowed to determine for themselves what to believe, they may also decide how to behave which can lead to subversion, rebellion, and anarchy. Doubt leads to heresy, inspires madness, and renders society vulnerable to destruction. Such is the fear-driven rationalization on the part of those who use censorship to maintain power within a closed society.

Biblical realism accepts the place of conflict in society. It does not cower before the fear that the social order will disintegrate when conflict is allowed to take place. Peace and stability are never superior to the demands for justice. No person or party is either perfect or indispenable and neither will they ever possess an ultimate understanding of justice. Conflict is controlled not by denial, suppression, or limits imposed by censorship, but by the building of a political tradition of comity. The open society cherishes an atmosphere of civility between those who disagree and assures the provision of opportunities for those out of power to compete in open forum for the representation of the public will.

It is an odd twist of fate that revolutionary movements touting 'power to the people' should end up distrusting the very people they sought to liberate from tyranny. Restraints on the voicing of opinions, no matter how radical or apparently heretical, simply trade one estimation of infallibility for another. In the end, both liberty and the people are compromised. Mental development is cramped and the human character is robbed of that healthy skepticism and robust spirit of enquiry that is never welcome where oppression reigns.

Apologists for censorship in Nicaragua are quick to claim that placing strict limits against the free flow of informtion to the people is not a goal of the revolution. It is an interim measure, a constraint made necessary by the state of emergency forced upon the people by Contra war and U.S. aggression. The ability of a powerful enemy to manipulate economic conditions in Nicaragua by spreading disinformtion to the people must be checked. Since the state has no leverage over the source of misleading information, they are forced to control its target; the people who would be harmed by its impact.

Either way the Sandinistas appeared caught in a zero-sum game; whatever choice they made they came up a loser. Without censorship, the security of the state might be jeopardized by the spreading of false or destabilizing information. If it were announced that critical shortages existed in the production of vital commodities, the people might over-react in a panic difficult to manage. Building a new nation while simultaneously fighting a war was hazardous enough. Opening themselves to more problems would be foolish and not prudent. On the other hand, the use of censorship gave the enemy the perfect example it needed to buttress its claim that the Sandinistas were in fact evil totalitarians.

Extremely sensitive to this issue, one pro-Process person I spoke with translated his defense into an offensive counter-charge. By comparison to Nicaragua's up-front and public use of censorship, he suggested that North Americans were subjected to equivalent strictures. Citing the news black-out following our invasion of Grenada, one aspect of our censorship operates by omission. For instance, it we didn't read about it, hear about it, or watch it on TV, it didn't happen. It's the solipcism of the ostrich with its head buried in the sand. The second dimension of censorship was of another kind; our intoxication with trivia. Familiar with U.S. publications like *The National Enquirer*, he charged that our fascination with stories alleging the impregnation of women by extra-trestrials from Mars left no room for interest in hard news and worthy topics. Info-deluge, Info-trivia, Info-tainment.

It was an interesting point but a fatuous diversion from the issue at hand. Some people only read the sports pages, and in Nicaraguan press that is possibly the only section never red penciled by the censors. Of course there is propaganda in the free society, obsessions with trivia, and attempts at news black-outs or cover-ups. But where the press is free and functions within a rigorously competitive market for information dispersal and readership, the right of the people is preserved in their choice of reading and believing what is reported in *The*

Wall Street Journal, The Washington Post, or *The National Enquirer.*

When the state resorts to censorship, the implication is clearly drawn that it no longer trusts the people. It doubts their capacity to determine truth from falsehood. It assumes they are without faculty to detect accuracy from error, one bias from another. Uncritical adherence to the orthodoxy of an official party-line is not freedom. Unexamined beliefs are not finally protected from becoming empty and meaningless slogans, platitudes, or cliches. Censorship is not only a disparaging evaluation of the capabilities of the citizenry, but the absence of tensions between the state and the media makes totalitarian abuses almost inevitable.

For myself, I choose to maintain that truth must always be subjected to trial by ordeal. If we are to be practitioners of freedom, ideas and ideals contrary to our own must always be provided an open hearing; even if they cause pain, are disruptive, or threaten to destroy institutions. Not to do so is to let the enemy of an open society define the rules and manipulate outcomes. Arguments about the theory or practice of governance in war or peace must be heard and considered. That is the only short-term and long-term means for protecting public safety and programs of self-government.

The freedom of speech and press are not absolute rights. Freedom from all restraint is not freedom but anarchy — the war of all against all. A free press has both an obligation and a right to cultivate the minds of its readers and to seek and publish the truth wherever it may be found. To knowingly use the press for purposes of deception, to spread known falsehoods or bigotry or hatred, to pander to the lowest of human emotions, these are abuses of freedom. Conversely, to promote rational discussion and deliberation, to air legitimate grievances, to organize opposition to injustice and irresponsible government, this is the vital work of a responsible press in an open society.

By monopolizing the means of mass communication and using censorship to control those media, governors of a closed society seek to manufacture a consent for their rule. The rightness or desirability of policies are not left to the checks and balances of public opinion. Propaganda predominates and where it fails or falters, the enemies of the free society resort to terror, the use of secret police, and the threat of imprisonment for crimes labeled 'political.'

In an open society governed by the rule of law, with laws of libel in place, those who engage the important work of information distribution must be free from legal restraints. If they accept the responsibility to print or proclaim the truth without the deliberate distortion of facts, they make a vital contribution to the health, economic well-being, and the freedom of an independent political community. And if they betray that trust, ultimately they defeat themselves. They destroy the very foundation upon which their usefulness rests.

As we settled in for the flight from Managua to Mexico City and home, I asked myself, what are the intellectual virtues that I cherish? Honesty. Fearless inquiry into the most dangerous ideas. Humility to sit down respectfully before the facts. Openness to both criticism and confession. Sharing the thoughtful company of people who do not answer finally to any national cause. A confidence that in the very nature of things, deceit and violence and trickery will succumb to the rigors of reason and the demands of justice. These are virtues to be defended.

In the laboratory that is Nicaragua, we witnessed many obstacles thwarting their experiment in revolutionary social change. Our Low Intensity War against this nation is an industry, a political institution. It is a massive enterprise causing untold misery and death and justified by our abstract appeal to 'necessities of state.' In its conception it is an enemy of freedom, democracy, and the open society. It is an across-the-board censorship every bit as despicable as any attempt to limit a free press. And even more disturbing is the fact that it is lethal. In its practice it is murder. Confronting and challenging this evil is our work, our responsibility.

But in Nicaragua there are internal obstacles as well, factors within the Process that block the achievement of the goals of the revolution. Some are inevitable, like the tremendous burden of the task itself which often seems overwhelming. Always there is a demand for fresh ideas and the need to test alternative methods. Sharp and vexing ethical issues call for sensitivity and the willingness to go forward with ideological revision. Against this there is the tendency to absolutize positions, to be uninterested in critical judgments that would haul the government into accountability. The task seems Herculean, but unless the Sandinistas can achieve a certain degree of detachment, admit their errors, laugh at their foolishness, and maintain a critical attitude toward revolutionary thought and action, well, the people and the land would remain subjected to cycles of creation and destruction in violent collision. Perpetual war.

As a Christian, I read the Gospels as an essay in freedom. From the beginning to the end, Jesus is without fear of freedom. He accepts it, uses it, begs no special dispensation from it, and fulfills it. There on the anvil of the desert wilderness he chooses the manner of his obedience to the will of God. As a teacher he suggested how we may all live within the matrix of our freedom. And finally, when the terms of freedom are literally life or death, he rendered himself the supreme teacher of what it is to be free by going to the Cross.

Finally, it is my hope that Christian persons, never an insignificant part of the revolution in Nicaragua, will continue to combine their participation in the effort to transform society with a final allegiance to a point of reference beyond the immediate social struggle.

Remembering George Baldwin, Fernando Calmoer, Roger Valesquez, I began to sense a new form of Christian community emerging on the front lines of revolution. It is a community carrying on a running conversation between its theological and ethical heritage and the major human issues embedded in social transformation. These Christian political activists do not pretend to possess a homing instinct toward the good. Nor do they claim that their built-in moral compass naturally turns them to the right. Neither do they boast an intuitive grasp of some divinely inspired mandate for the new Nicaragua. In the company of other Christians they patiently and often painfully ask what are the claims of Jesus upon those who call him Lord? They believe that his claims have the authority of excellence. The answers stand outside of these individuals. Together with their sisters and brothers in the struggle they rely on what they know of him, breath by breath, heartbeat by heartbeat, and what 20 centuries of experience has taught about the cost of faithfulness.

Feed the hungry. Clothe the naked. Release the captives. For while there are victims, we are not free. Where suffering abounds, our conscience is not clear. Where hurt and deprivation prevails, our work is not finished. When any are deprived of their rights, our liberties are endangered. Against these convictions, no earthly principality or power can ultimately prevail. Thanks be to God.

What Time Is It? Time For Dancing On The Promises!

Sermon/Reflections from June 1988
in Nicaragua
And
Witness For Peace
"What Time Is It?" Ecclesiastes 3:1-9
"Time for Dancing On The Promises!"
The Beatitudes — Matthew 5:1-10

"Blessed Are The Peacemakers"
"Blessed Are The Meek"
"Blessed Are The Merciful"
"Blessed Are Those Who Mourn"
"Blessed Are The Poor In Spirit"
"Blessed Are The Persecuted And Reviled"

"Blessed Are The Peacemakers"
Sermon

A time for loving, a time for hating, a time for war, a time for peace.

Ecclesiastes 3:8, 9

Blessed are the peacemakers, they shall be called the sons of God.

Matthew 5:9

"A time for love, a time for hate, a time for war, and a time for peace." These are familiar words in the hymn of Ecclesiastes, 'The Preacher.' Love. Hate. War. Peace. But remember the leitmotif, the catch; 'A time . . .,' A time for . . .,' that haunting refrain coming at the ear like an echo until the point is driven home in a throb of consciousness. The wisdom of the Preacher's words is unveiled only to those who know **what time it is!**

The Nicaraguan village of La Dalia is roughly half-way between Matagalpa City and the resettlement township of Waslala. It's a dusty little town. Crouched at the foot of mountains vaulting into the clear blue tropical sky, it is the only interruption visible in an unbroken wall of jungle and up-thrusting rock. We stopped there for our noon meal. We also spent two hours with the Waslala District Political Education Secretary of the FSLN, the *Frente Sandinista*, the National Army.

Fernando Torres is handsome, in his 30s, and wore his authority loosely, like his clothes. The cotton slacks and short-sleeved shirt were an odd camouflage; the man is a guerrilla warrior. Soft-spoken *Compañero* Torres reminded us that the surrounding mountains have been the focal point of revolution and Contra-war. They also mark the birthplace of Nicaraguan heroes Sandino and Fonseca. These are the buttes and shears,

311

the mosquito infested forests and battlegrounds that gave title to *Comandante* Omar Cabezas' now famous guerrilla autobiography, **Fire From The Mountain**.

Great chunks of rocky chaos pounded the horizon. In the loamy-aired jungle, flowering bromeliads and epiphyte abounded. Silk-cotton trees stood on trunks thirty to forty-foot in diameter. Streams erupt out of crevasses and cascade through canyons toward tributaries and meandering rivers. This most spectacular panorama of majestic rock, greenness, and sweet air has not been a refuge of peace. No. They have been bombed and strafed, burned and pillaged for over sixty years. The capacity of the land to absorb violence and remain lovely is unnerving.

The Nicaraguan people don't fare as well. For three generations the war's impact on the humanity of the district, Torres' people, his kin and neighbors, has not been small. Flesh and the psyche are more tender than a tree's bole or a rock's cleft. I ask myself, what must it be like to live among uncanny natural beauty and at the same time endure unnatural hazard and terror?

The roads we traveled were swept each morning for land mines. Machine-gun turrets and light artillery were banked into nests besides the few bridges that were not collapsed into rivers by the Contra. IFA transport trucks careened over treacherously narrow hard-packed roads. Their living cargo — teenagers my son's age — were wearing cartridge clips laced into bandoleers. Their AK-47 assault rifles were slung low over the shoulder. Grenades swung from their utility belts. No frisbees, no skateboards, no sun-screen tucked into their trucks, they were not heading for an afternoon at the boardwalk.

In this war, Torres is an 'old man' at 30; most *compas* die young. They died young in Vietnam, too; nineteen was the average age of those 58,000 U.S. soldiers now buried under gardens of stone.

A large reconnaissance map on the Director's wall indicated the parameters for Contra and Sandinista occupations.

Red lines, the color of fresh blood, marked the corridors the Contra use on their northerly trek from the interior to the Rio Coco and the sanctuary of camps in Honduras. There were 1,600 known Contra in the surrounding mountains. Torres said that in the next 48 hours, 800 of them would cross the road we were on.

Our journey to Waslala would take us across those corridors; but not after sundown. By day, the land and the roads belong to *campesinos*. Their *fincas* produce rich and aromatic coffee and the surrounding jungles share their bounty of bananas and cacao, hardwoods and bamboo, mango and papaya.

The Janus-face of Nicaragua shifts with the setting sun. Under moonless and ethereal night skies, bottomless black with cold stars, the sounds and smells and shadowy phantoms of terror and death emerge. War is the nighttime reality of this mysteriously beautiful land.

Hanging on another wall were a series of posters. One bore the inscription from the ancient Preacher: "A time for hate a time for love, a time for war a time for peace." Other posters with biblical verses stressed the need for forgiveness. The young *comandante* asserted, unequivocally, "It is a time for peace. And before we can secure the peace, we must learn to forgive one another."

A poster declaring Amnesty hung near the door. Similar posters hung on cafe walls, in churches and cantinas, on shop doors and utility poles. Posted bulletins announced free vaccinations, anti-malarial drugs, and medical assistance for the Contra and their families. Fiestas were scheduled; the Sandinistas provided the music and the free beer for the Contra who were their invited guests. No ambushes, betrayals, or dirty tricks. The Sandinistas were extending the hand of hospitality to the men who were handing them terror and death.

It occurred to me that this was a strange way to conduct a war. No depiction or reference to the enemy as some less-than-human alien or wayward prodigal. It was a plea for reconciliation between brothers.

313

It also occurred to me that this is not at all a strange way to approach a 'time of truce' leading toward pace.

Two Men, Two Eras, Two Styles, Two Graves

As I contemplate 'what time it is,' I think of two men, two different times, two differing styles, and two graves. Visit their graves with me, learn something about the men and something about their commitments. Listen for that refrain: "A time for . . ."

Managua is a city of graves sprawling around its own corpse. On the western shore of tremendous Lake Managua, the hollow ruins of the National Cathedral tower like a silent ghost above the bleached cobbles of an empty plaza. Roofless, windowless, its gutted insides grow weeds where once there were pews and altars. Seagulls perch on the ragged empty ledges that formerly cradled the prisms of stained glass windows. No longer venerated by faithful patrons, in shadowy nooks and corners the statues of the saints look more dead than inanimate. Pathetic and crumbling, the chalky stains of bird droppings replaced the offerings of flickering votive candles and fragrant flowers.

The cathedral was not the victim of violence during the 1979 'Triumph' of the revolution. It was the victim of natural causes. The earthquake in December of 1972 centered in downtown Managua. Eighty percent of the city's buildings became tombstones of rubble. The world was appalled and wanted to do the right thing, the decent thing. Three hundred-million dollars poured into Nicaragua from the international community. It was money on a mission, shared for the purpose of reconstructing lives and homes. Less than five percent of that vast sum ever touched the victims of that calamity. The majority went into the personal coffers of Anastacio Somoza Debayle and his cronies. This was the last straw, the cap-stone in the long history of the Somoza dynasty's criminal pilfering of the people's wealth and Nicaragua's natural bounty.

Betrayal, treason, tyranny, could things get worse? In Somoza's Nicaragua, that is a question best left unasked. Of course they could get worse. And they did. No stranger to the politics of murder, Somoza added one more assassination to a long history of tyranny and horror. This time the victim was the popular *La Prensa* Editor, Pedro Joaquin Chamorro, a man of world reputation for his fearless denunciation of the dictator. His murder was the last straw in the alienation of the Nicaraguan middle-class. Many closed rank with rural *campesinos* and students dissidents and joined the Sandinista guerrillas to overthrow the ruthless dictatorship. On his way out the backdoor, Somoza ordered his Air Force to bomb Managua while he exhumed the graves of his family. He fled with their caskets plus all but $20,000 of the national treasury. Nicaraguans were left with their dead, their poverty, a capitol in ruins, and bankruptcy. Such were the thumbprints of his family's 45 year bequest to the people.

Revolutionary Warriors: Sandino and Fonseca

Across from the National Cathedral is the grave of Carlos Fonseca Amador. Working in the laboratory of a U.S. owned gold mine, Fonseca picked up the mantle of Augusto Cesar Sandino. The Nicaraguans revere Sandino as a 'Freedom Fighter.' Fonseca was his spiritual son.

Nicaragua has lived with intense strife between liberals and conservatives for over 150 years. In 1909, President Zayala refused to grant the U.S. interoceanic canal rights down the Rio San Juan, across Lake Nicaragua and the few short miles beyond to the Pacific Ocean. In reprisal, our State Department supported the conservatives to force Zayala's resignation. Within three years the U.S. Marines arrived to secure our control of Nicaraguan finances, railroads, and communications, not to mention our corporate investments in the mining of precious metals and the sugar, banana, cattle, cotton and fishing industries.

General Augusto Cesar Sandino's resistance began in 1926 when he refused to accept further U.S. intervention in Nicaragua's internal affairs. While other factions in the liberal resistance caved in and signed the peace treaty, Sandino continued his revolt. The State Department found in Sandino an indomitable nationalist. His conditions for disbanding the guerrillas were similar to the Contadora proposals fifty years later: U.S. Marine evacuation from Nicaragua, the appointment of an interim civilian government, and elections for a full-term president supervised by representatives from other Latin and Central American countries.

Sandino was an elusive and intractable warrior. The architect of modern guerrilla jungle warfare, his rebels stole military supplies from Somoza's regular army, lived off the land, and swam in the sea of the peasantry. Unaccustomed to these tactics, in 1928 the Marines employed aerial bombardment against the General's cadres. The use of Voughts and Corsairs to drop bombs from the sky was a record-making first in the annals of world military history. It was also a pitiful failure. Moreover, we ignored a significant lesson, one that we still had not learned some forty years later; technologies of superior firepower are no guarantee of victory in jungle warfare where a well-organized and motivated people are defending their homeland.

Unable to snare Sandino in the rhetoric of diplomacy or vanquish him in battle, the U.S. Marines left in 1933. Sandino signed a truce and returned to the mountains to organize peasants into argicultural cooperatives.

It was, however, a hollow armistice, empty of integrity. The Marines were replaced by a new police force — the U.S. trained Nicaraguan National Guard, General Anastasio Somoza's private army. When Sandino returned to Managua as the guest of President Juan Bautista Sacasa, Somoza ordered the General's capture and execution. Sandino's body was never recovered. Perhaps Somoza fed the corpse to the panthers in his private zoo; not an uncommon practice since he was fond of torture and gruesome sport. What Somoza and his U.S. allies could not accomplish by negotiation or force of arms they accomplished by treachery.

Twenty-two years later, in 1956 Carlos Fonseca became the founder, strategic architect, and leader of the resistance — the

Frente Sandinista. Twenty more years and Fonseca was dead at the age of 40. It waited another two and a half years before the 'Triumph' of the revolution in July of 1979. Fonseca's body lies beneath a simple monument across the plaza from the National Cathedral.

Within the week we would stand beside a simple cross made of galvanized pipe. This gift from the people of Cuba marks the lonely spot in the jungle where Fonseca was killed. Ambushed by 50 of Somoza's elite *Guardia*, the young but seasoned warrior fought to the death with an empty shotgun; another martyr in this land of 50,000 martyrs, this beautiful green land, a land of widows, a nation of orphans.

For Carlos Fonseca it was a time for war, a time to pick up the sword, a time to cast down tyranny before building freedom on the victory of liberation.

Revolutionary Accompaniment: Ben Linder

Another man, another grave. A different work, a different sense for what time it is in Nicaragua. This man was a citizen of the United States; his name was Benjamin Linder. We visited his grave in Matagalpa City on the first night of our journey into the mountain District of Waslala near where Fonseca died.

This was an especially significant pilgrimage for me. In May of 1987, I placed a white wooden cross in the front yard of the parsonage. Ben's name was inscribed on that cross; it is still keeping its lonely vigil in the flower garden. In Matagalpa I was visiting the ground of his burial some fourteen months after his death.

Ben Linder was an electrical engineer who had been working in Nicaragua since 1983. Designing and supervising the construction of a small hydroelectric plant in the town of El Cua, the project was completed in 1985. At the time of his death he was at it again, building a facility to serve the small village of San José de Bocay.

A fun-loving young man, on the tombstone beneath Linder's name is the carved image of a unicycle. Above the

317

seat, balls in mid-air circle a dove of peace. Ben would ride into a village and instantly the children gathered; Lord they loved him! A few clown routines, some juggling and magic, the young gringo was welcomed into their homes and lives.

But not everybody loved Linder. Ben knew that his work was hazardous. The Contras marked him for death with personal visitations, with notes, through rumors. These mercenaries have killed many health-care workers and doctors, ministers and priests, school teachers and others laboring to build and reconstruct this poor and tired and torn land.

Why? The rationale is as simple as it is diabolical. If you cannot defeat the people with superior fire-power, use another strategy. This one is called Low Intensity War. Doesn't that sound benign? Low-Intensity-War.

But if you unpack the oxymoron, this is the tactical fall-out: avoid direct contact with the *Frente*; assassinate civilians who are leaders in the work of reconstruction; destroy ambulances and busses and farm equipment and roads and bridges and schools and industry; apply economic embargo as the external means to cripple the nation's infra-structure; set land-mines on trails to kill cattle and *campesinos*; mine the roads to market and the riverbanks where villagers must go to gather daily water; kidnap or slit the throat of heads of households leaving refugees and orphans; and, burn the crops, burn the warehouses, burn the homes. In short, do your level best to generate a reign of terror. That, my friends, is the sweet business of Low Intensity War. Low? In the vernacular of my people, we call that 'low-life.'

Linder was helping to rebuild the nation. He worked to improve the material conditions of rural life. He nourished and nurtured a solidarity of spirit among the poor. The Contra regarded him as a dangerous enemy. Consequently Ben became a target for the Pentagon and Langley's Low Intensity War.

Nonetheless, he peristed with his work. Ben looked at the clock of his spirit and saw that it was time to build; a time for placing stones together, a time for making a dam to generate electricity, a time to place a light in the darkness, a time to pump water and bring power into homes, into schools, into hospitals. Ben was a gentle friend of creation, the juggler with the unicycle; he was a builder, not a destroyer. Ben was not a violent man. He was a dedicated man, a compassionate man. And now he is a dead man.

On the morning of April 28, Ben and his two Nicaraguan co-workers were unarmed as they worked beside a mountain stream. Twelve Contra launched their attack. Hand grenades were tossed onto the work site immobilizing Linder with wounds to his legs and left arm. Both Pablo Rosales and Sergio Hernandez, Ben's co-workers, were also wounded. Crawling toward the jungle cover they were overcome by the enemy. Linder was shot at point-blank range with a bullet through his skull. Sergio suffered a similar fate. Pablo Rosales was fatally stabbed in the chest. The bodies of all three men were subsequently recovered and brought to Managua for a period of national mourning.

Linder's corpse was later taken to Matagalpa City. President Ortega and Ben's father carried the coffin and led a procession of thousands to the small mountain-side cemetery where we now stood.

Standing in a circle, holding hands, we were offering our silent prayers when an older woman approached. Accompanied by her children, in her arms Elsa Aleman cradled a bouquet of cut blue flowers. She wanted to join Ben's friends around the circle. Following silent prayer we knelt to place the flowers in the sign of the cross over the grave.

In the quiet talk that followed, we discovered that Elsa was Ben's 'Nica Mother.' Every week she comes to this simple plot. She prays and places flowers upon the tombs of six *internacionalistas* killed by the Contras while pursuing their development projects. We paid tribute at the graves of the young men from France, Switzerland, and Germany.

Finally, we joined her beside another grave. This one belongs to her daughter. In 1979, Martine was a second-year student at the University Medical School in Leon. As the revolution moved toward Managua, she joined fellow students at the barricades and died on the cobbles.

We may not like it, we may resist it, but it is a fact written in blood; both Christians and Revolutionaries preface 'Triumph' with Tragedy.

We accompanied this Nica mother's tears with our own, quietly. In the silence I tried to imagine what the young woman once looked like. It is impossible to undo some damage, to recall to our presence that which has been banished forever. For some of us these were tears of penitence.

Elsa inquired about Brian Wilson and the convoy stalemated at Laredo on the Texas/Mexico border. The State Department at Foggy Bottom has prohibited them from bringing a caravan of medical and school supplies to Nicaragua. Brian had been a guest in her home on a previous visit just as the Linder family has shared her home. I recalled Brian and the three vets fasting on the steps of the Capitol in Washington D.C. I remember meeting him at the Concord Naval Weapons Station weeks after the munitions train rolled over his legs.

Elsa asked, "Why won't President Reagan allow them to share these simple things that we need so badly for our children?"

What could we answer? It was a hard-hurting silence that stopped our mouths from chattering explanations. Some grief is best respected by silence. And in that silence the unanswered question lingers, What time is it?

Two men, two different approaches toward the liberation and reconstruction of this war-torn land. Both men died violent deaths. Fonseca the soldier died with an empty weapon in his hand. Linder the non-violent unarmed engineer died trying to bring electricity to a village. Both were brave, principled, committed. Each of them looked at the clock and made personal decisions about 'what time it was;' "A time for hate, a time for love, a time for war, a time for peace." One picked up the sword of war and died by the sword. One picked up the tools of peace. He also died by the sword.

Killing Begets Killing: The Non-Violent Cobra

Who was right? Killing begets killing. Both the gun and the sword, in whose-ever hands, stand under the judgment of God. And where in the Gospel do we find vindication for exacting blood from enemy or defender, combatant or bystander?

I shall not be silent. For while there need be 'a time for keeping silent, and a time for speaking,' there is too much blood on the earth, spilt over stones that do indeed cry out.

A story told by Howard Thurman: In Buddhist writing there is the tale of a particular village whose inhabitants were being destroyed by the attacks of a death-dealing cobra. Finally an old holy man came to the village. The people gathered and told of their plight. The old man sought out the snake and urged it to discontinue its destruction. The snake agreed. Gradually the people discovered that the cobra was no longer dangerous. Their attitudes began to change and instead of fear they became bold. Tricks were played on the snake. Stones were thrown, scalding water was poured over its body, its tail was pulled; the snake's existence became imperiled.

Finally the old holy man returned. This time it was the snake that sought him out. In its bruised and pitiful state, it said with great bitterness, "I did as you instructed me and look what has happened. What am I to do now?"

The old man replied, "You did not obey me fully. True, I did tell you not to bite the people. But I never told you not to hiss at them."[31]

Until those who export war decide that now is the time to build up, the time to heal, the time to love and hate no more, there will be some of us hissing like hell. And through our clinched teeth we shall pray that they consult a different clock.

What time is it? Another ancient preacher tells us. It is time that "none shall hurt or destroy in all my holy mountain." In the name of the non-violent Jesus, Amen.

321

"Blessed Are The Meek"

Sermon

A time for tearing, a time for sewing, a time for keeping silent, a time for speaking.
Ecclesiastes 3:6

Blessed are the meek, for they shall inherit the earth.
Matthew 5:5

"Blessed are the meek; for they shall inherit the earth." Familiar words, "Blessed are the meek." What does it mean to be 'meek'? Is it the same as being humble, without arrogance, tolerant, unpretentious? I wonder.

Now, let's take a glance at Jesus. Mind you this is only a glance; not a complete picture. Jesus wheels on one of his disciples and exclaims, "Get thee behind me Satan." Again, in a heated debate with the Pharisees he shouts, "You brood of vipers." Again, in a scene that might resemble a rampage, Jesus moves through the Temple courtyard like Sherman marched through Georgia. Brandishing a whip, he upsets the tables of the money changers saying, "You have made of my Father's house a den of thieves."

Calling a friend the 'devil,' calling his enemies 'snakes,' this eruption of violent anger — the glance is turning up something other than a tolerant Jesus, something alternative to quiet decorum, something alien to humility and perhaps tinged with arrogance. This behavior does not reflect the mood of meekness. It is not mildness of temper or long-suffering patience under injury. In fact the Lord seems filled with intense passion. Gone are equanimity and composure. He appears to have lost his cool, and his temper.

I take comfort in that. Once again I am reminded that Jesus knew in gut and spirit that life is both playful and intense, that there is a time for jest and a time to be in solemn incomprehensible earnest.

The Challenge to Meekness

The challenge of meekness, of being centered and balanced, is, for many of us, just that; a challenge, a labor. The ancestral Celt in me savors the brooding muse and a marauding fiest. And when that spirit was bred to the raw sun and chili diet of my Texan forebears, the yield is a person that on occasion forfeits composure in a flash of acute hot temper. I feel a strong affinity with Jesus in those intervals of trembling tension. Inevitably, however, there is a price to be paid for these indulgences. Excessive emotions are so patently painful and harmful to us as a species, it is hard to believe they have survived the winnowing work of evolution.

Perhaps this shadow side, the dissonant un-meek side, was a condition of spirit that Jesus sought to address with the disciplines of his own meditation and contemplation and prayer. Psychology only reminds us of what we sense on the fringes of our waking dreams or taste in the metallic adrenalin residues at the corners of a dry mouth; in our depths are both terror and violence.

But if we move with these spiritual disciplines to the substratum of the soul, we find there the power that gives goodness its good and evilness its evil. Choice is that power. We can choose to be a victim of life or a warrior of the spirit accompanying the Lord of life. Meekness sees clearly and accepts the gifts and limitations, the strengths and weakness of life and persons. It resolves that fear, hypocrisy, and hatred — the three persistent hounds of hell that track the trail of the victim — shall have no dominion over its spirit.

Life may be as hard as crucible steel but the meek find in their spirit no room for cringing or for cowardice. Meekness breathes confidence because it is the soul's answer to the love of God. And sometimes meekness compels a solemn incomprehensible earnest such as Jesus' reading in the Temple from the prophet Isaiah; "The Spirit of the Lord is upon me . . ."

323

or the Song of Mary; "He hath scattered the proud in the imagination of their hearts . . ."

A baseball story makes the point.[32] It involves two of the legendary titans of the game. Leo Durocher, the former manager of the Brooklyn Dodgers, was a rookie playing in a game between St. Paul and Toledo. As was his habit, he mumbled some unkind remarks at a certain Joe Kelly who feigned a hearing problem. Approaching Durocher, Kelly said, "What did you say runt?" Leo played the fool and repeated himself. Kelly replied, "That's what I thought you said." A moment of stunned silence and Kelly hit him with a roundhouse. Durocher and several teeth hit the dirt.

Well, a certain Charlie Stengel was watching the incident and filed it away for future reference. Years later, Durocher and Stengel's teams squared-off in the World Series. Tension was running high at the beginning of a crucial game when Charlie recalled that incident from years ago and called out, "Hey Leo, who's your dentist these days?" Durocher's temper flared and the old warhorse started kicking up the dust. Sent to his dugout, Leo spent the afternoon in a fuming rage. Charlie's barbed remark was right on target. Leo pitched a fit, threw a tantrum, and not only lost his composure but his concentration for the game as well.

Inward Togetherness and Personal Power

A person has the key to your lock if they can spin you around with a word or memory, if they can sucker you off balance. When you wobble, you're at their mercy, vulnerable. We are not wrapped very tight if our equilibrium is left to the whim of forces and fortunes external to ourselves. As social creatures our feelings are conditioned by the external environment. But if our behavior is determined by the external environment, we have traded action for reaction. Our destiny is no longer our own. Durocher lingered in anger the afternoon of that crucial game and it cost him dearly.

When another person or circumstance can leverage us into losing our temper, the logic of bitterness and the desire for revenge is a frequent result. Why? Because we have handed over our personal power into another's keep. Then we fume. Like the victims we are in that moment, we resent having sloppily surrendered our autonomy. Later perhaps we recoil in smoldering rage, angry with ourselves for going out of control, and angry at the vulnerability it signifies. Once again, if somebody else has the power to manipulate our thinking or feeling or behaving, we are neither in charge of our own life nor living our own life. We have become a marionette dangling on strings held by hands not our own. Behind that, our emotion is humiliation, not humility.

It is also self-destructive. I'm wary of rattlesnakes, a fact of life learned lickety-split in West Texas. And I've learned something from watching them. During the late summer, that reptile goes through the dangerous ritual of molting. It peels the old skin forward like a sweater being pulled over head. While this happens the snake is blindfolded and fearful. A breeze stirs the brush and the rattler panics, lashes out in sightless terror. But if its body is touched, the snakes strikes the spot of contact. The result? It poisons itself with its own venom; a macabre suicide.

We shoot ourself in the foot, or worse, when we throw away our personal power in a tantrum. Sometimes we cannot unwind the damage. Always we suffer a vital exhaustion of the spirit.

The best use of the emotions of temper is as a fuel for God's light. If that lights burns in us, by its guidance we may find the path to live our way into God's will for our lives. We want light for the path, and courage to pay with our lives for the kind of world we so deeply desire.

Scenes from Nicaragua: A Pentecostal Excommunication

A story from Nicaragua. Two congregations, two persons, one problem and one solution. On Sunday night June 19th we worshipped with one of the five noisy and active Protestant congregations in the village of Waslala. Considering President Reagan's allegation that the Sandinista communists have eliminated freedom of worship in Nicaragua, Waslala may have been an exception. But it wasn't; it was the norm. Nicaraguan churches are alive and Christian faith vitalizes the culture.

The Pentecostal chapel was crowded and filled with the more affluent of the village; shopkeepers, merchants, families not living in abject poverty and destitution. On hard benches the men sat to one side, the women on the other. Eight men in comfortable chairs surrounded the pulpit beneath which a small cross and Bible rested on a table. Quite Protestant in choreography — the sermon over-shadowing the Cross and the Scripture!

One by one for two hours, the male elders whipped the assembly into a raucous session of hymn singing. Only the accordion and guitar made an attempt to stay in key. After loud prayers and long sessions of speaking in tongues, a sermon followed.

Conspicuous by its absence was any word in hymn or prayer or sermon acknowledging the fact that the congregation was living smack on target in the middle of a war zone. Worship, for me, is the rehearsal of the drama of my life before God, the giver of that life. Apparently they did not share that assumption. But how could the common life be so remarkably absent? Was it denial? Was it delusion? Their sleep and mine was sometimes interrupted by the sound of mortar fire in the night. We all dodged troop trucks as they rumbled through the village shuttling soldiers or ferrying wounded to the hospital. Not 50 yards from the chapel and huddled in a small shack was another recent widow and her hungry children. The Contra forced the entire family to watch as they killed her husband. I did not meet a family in Waslala that had not lost a loved one in some action of this war.

We were siting in a sanctuary, but it felt more like an escape hatch. I came standing in the need of prayer, seeking courage for my fears, longing for a thread of sanity in the skein of war's insanity. Instead, for me, this worship felt like a close encounter with an alien and separate reality.

Finally, the presiding deacon made his move. A male member of the congregation had 'fallen out of grace.' Within the week he started smoking tobacco, drinking bootlegged corn liquor, and listening to rock and roll. To say the least, it must have been a hell of a week. The preacher's cant chastised the man's errant and sinful ways. His voice rising in crescendo, he alternately decried the evils of alcoholic, fulminated against nicotine, and launched himself into a tirade against perverted and sex-driven rock music. As if on cue, the congregation raised their hands and delivered a litany of 'Amens.' The men in the audience were a little more subdued than the ladies. The deacon was for the moment their ally. Perhaps this heavy dose of fear-of-god public humiliation might dissuade their own men from likewise abandoning rectitude for debauchery.

The target of this oration was not present. It was not clear to me if he had been invited. Somehow the excoriating words and the ritual of excommunication seemed a bit like a sucker-punch without the culprit there to suffer his stripes. Maybe he didn't care and was simply glad to be shed of their cant. But his wife and daughter were there, sitting quietly, heads bowed, listening to the enumeration of this husband and father's sins and the verbal trashing of his faithfulness.

Lord knows how they were feeling. The Lord also knows how I was feeling. Outraged! What cowardly perversion of Christ's Gospel of Grace was this? What meekness, what generosity-in-attitude-toward-others here? My temper was not composed; it was sizzling like the Coleman lanterns that lit the hall. Something counterfeit was being traded for Christ's Gospel. While pretending to offer salvation they were in fact selling the terrible havoc of hate. Building fear and panic in the common life is not the work of meekness. Images of an angry Jesus pumped through my recollection.

Perhaps it was the hissing sound of breathing through my teeth, or the snap of my jaw cracking, or the fact that the knuckles on my fists were turning white. My friend turned and touched my knee. When she asked what was going on with me, I answered that I was furiously composing a challenge to this rubbish and mentally translating it into Spanish. I was every bit as willing to rampage through this charade as Jesus was to create commotion there in that courtyard. Her reply was chastening, "We're here to stand beside them non-violently, to be with them as guests, to accompany them. Not judge them," she said.

A moment later, by the time I got to the door, I had a cigarette in my mouth, was thinking about a drink, and wondered if Laura had any rock and roll tapes in her portable cassette. While I sometimes tempt the patience of God and chafe my fellows by my lack of meekness, I am learning to pray for its benedictions.

Meekness is remaining centered and not throwing away personal power. Meekness is remaining calm so the dust can settle lest decisions be clouded. Meekness is withstanding the mood of malevolence and the urge of vindictiveness. Meekness is pausing to breathe and focus so that actions taken in haste do not yield irreparable harm.

What I needed in that moment was to surrender the hard place of my heart to the softening influence of the non-violent Spirit of God.

Radical Love: "The *Misa Campesina Nicaraguense*"

How different our experience that same morning when we worshipped with the village poor. The farm workers of the Roman Catholic congregation sat on hard benches and sang marvelous folk-hymns loud and off-key. End of similarities! In the spirited *Misa Campesina Nicaraguense*, men and women sat together as families. Soldiers in uniform with their AK-47's slung over their shoulders were there and so was a Contra who had accepted amnesty during the week. The young widow was there. So was another young mother we met the day before. Recently reunited with her children, her past two years had been an odyssey in hell following her kidnapping by the Contra. Held prisoner at their Honduran camps, she was tortured and frequently raped.

328

During the service children roamed freely, often going to stand beside Father Enrique and touch the bright colors on his stole. The young priest has been hostaged twice by the Contra, once for nineteen days. A North American bishop's influence with our State Department finally secured his release; a rather telling maneuver which ought to suggest something about where this Contra-war finds it direction.

Lay Delegates of the Word led most of the service. Reports were made on the progress of the new sanctuary building program, the women's sewing co-op, the needs of the newest refugee families, and an upcoming regional training conference for the Delegates. These are the laity who carry the Bible, the Sacrament, literacy programs and health-care into the remote hamlets and distant corners of the district. Father Enrique is fortunate to visit each of the sixty-odd satellite congregations once a year.

Sitting behind me during morning worship was Santos and his family. We spent two hours the day before talking with Santos and his wife. Recently displaced from their farm by Contras, all their worldly goods were stolen. Deprived of a livelihood, they were forced into the village. He peddles firewood for pennies and his wife works in the sewing co-op.

In addition to being poor and a refugee, Santos is abusing 'El Alcohol.' That is a problem. He knows it. So does his wife. Probably everyone in the congregation if not the village knows it. So does Father Enrique who talks with Santos about the healing power of a loving God and the gift of 'El. A.A.' which presents a strong program in Nicaragua. When it came time for the offering, Santos helped pass the bucket. And when Father Enrique broke the bread of Christ's body for the forgiveness of our sins, Santos and I were both in line waiting to have the mercy-filled host placed upon our tongues.

Two congregations, two persons, one problem, two solutions. One congregation, bogged in the corruption of fear masquerading as faith, destroys the fabric of its own community in self-righteous indignation. Hyped on the emotional gas of an arrogant and zealous false-pride, they exploit human weakness and needlessly distance themselves from the tender mercies of the God they pretend to preach. When the mood of retaliation and revenge rides high in the spirit, persons and communities yield to evils every bit as cunning, baffling, powerful, and destructive as those which the Pentecostals sought to root out and exorcise in the habits of the 'fallen' brother.

The Roman Catholic congregation, penitent and hope-filled, did not underestimate the destructive power of sin. They did remain open to life and persons, ever learning and growing in the perfection of a loving compassion which is the tender mercy of God.

Meekness as a Communitarian Ethic

Meekness is a quality of spirit much to be desired by those who model their lives by the influence of Jesus Christ. But what about nations? Is it possible that our life in community demonstrates a need for the redemptive power of meekness? Of course I am thinking about relations between Nicaragua and the United States.

In July of 1986, Nicaraguan President Daniel Ortega appeared before the United Nations. He charged the United States with gross violations of international decency and law by forming and supporting the mercenary Contras. Under orders from the highest U.S. authority they have destroyed Nicaraguan property, mined the nation's harbors, killed or kidnapped its people, and fomented rebellion among the indigenous Miskito Indian populations.

A lawsuit brought to the World Court in 1984 found for the Sandinistas and ordered the U.S. to cease and desist from these actions. President Reagan refused to obey the order of the court. Without any semblance of meekness and filled with arrogant false-pride, the President told us that he acted in accord with a 'higher law,' that he was compelled by a greater cause — 'stopping world communism.'

Meekness disciplines us not to think higher, or lower, of ourselves than is appropriate and responsible. To gain such a perspective it is often helpful to stand present before history.

In that regard I fear that the President's and the nation's memory is tragically flawed. Saul Landau reminds us that in 1776 the British Crown acted in response to its own perceived 'higher cause.'[33] Thomas Jefferson charged King George III with gross violations of decency and law. He insisted that the King had "plundered our seas, ravaged our coasts, burnt our towns, and destroyed the lives of our people." In fact, the Declaration of Independence accused the King of "transporting large armies of foreign mercenaries to complete the works of death, desolation, and tyranny, already begun with circumstances of cruelty and perfidy scarcely paralleled in the most barbarous ages and totally unworthy of the head of a civilized nation." This same document also expressed indignation at the British strategy of stirring resentment among the indigenous Indian nations against the colonial settlers.

What a remarkable parallel. King George III and President Ronald Reagan are classic despots. Each retaliated with imperial righteousness against 'upstarts' who sought liberty from external oppression and were willing to fight for it if necessary. Notions of nationalism and revolution send shudders through despotic rulers of Empire. Consequently King George justified the denial of sovereign rights to the fledgling colonies. King Reagan forecasts a parade of horror should insurgencies toward independence succeed. And in each case, the only 'falling dominoes' on the horizon were the credibility and integrity of those who arrogated to themselves the prerogative of being 'king makers' of the world.

'Revolution,' was once an inalienable right. Now it is regarded as pornographic. Those who desire 'national liberation' are fiendish enemies out to profane the very liberties we cherished as sacred and once were willing to die for.

Be it a person, a congregation, or a nation-state, the virtue of meekness is menaced by stubborn refusals to cultivate a fair-minded and humble spirit. Similarly, both are thwarted by arrogant self-righteousness and harmed by resentments that seek revenge and give vent to rage.

When arrogant self-righteousness justifies deceit, hypocrisy, and lying as acceptable behaviors of statecraft, not only is meekness sacrificed but the republican principles of democracy are undermined. When undisciplined resentments guide the workings of diplomacy, retaliation becomes an obsession and a nation 'under law' becomes a nation led by outlaws. When we believe that our freedoms are menaced by a poor nation of less than three million persons who must devote 60 percent of their G.N.P. to defending themselves against aggressions which we pay for and direct, we have become a nation of fools. The menace is much closer to home!

"Blessed are the meek; for they shall inherit the earth." Indeed blessed are the humble who will not be humiliated. Blessed are the honest who sense a sure responsibility to God and to their fellows for the power that they use. Blessed are those who neither fear nor cringe nor cower before the haughty tyrant. And most blessed are those who recognize with authentic realism that anyone who permits another to determine the quality of their inner life has given away the keys to their destiny.

God help us! Christ guide us! Amen.

"Blessed Are The Merciful"

Sermon

A time for killing, a time for healing, a time for knocking down, a time for building.
Ecclesiastes 3:3

Blessed are the merciful: they shall obtain mercy.
Matthew 5:7

"Blessed are the merciful." But what is this 'mercy' we are called to be?

Last Sunday I meditated with the word 'meek.' This morning, as I continue reflecting on the significance of the Beatitudes and Ecclesiastes' call to timeliness from the vantage point of my experience in Nicaragua, the word is 'merciful.'

Often I wish that Jesus were more clear, more direct, less obscure, less inclined to play hide-and-seek with the meaning of his messages. Or, said another way, I wish Jesus used words more a part of the non-vocabulary functions of my life.

Late at night when the light grows dim and my mind becomes weary with the effort of it all, when my jaw rests uncomfortably in the palm of my hands, I hear myself muttering, "Open unto me. Open unto me with clarity. I would not miss the meaning of the message." And still I find myself struggling, stammering, trying to bring vibrancy to the silence.

Mercy: The Same As Kindness Or Justice?

In the aloneness of the waiting moment, my mind hums with questions. Is mercy the same as kindness? There is in kindness a warm and welcome quality of character; the quality of graciousness and gratuity. A kindly person is less inclined to be bored and blue. They are thankful and open in their affirmation of the goodness of life. A kindly person is a sharing

333

person. They share of themselves, their spirit, perhaps their possessions.

But here I have a problem, a problem called to my attention by Dean Howard Thurman.[34] Mercy as simple kindness implies the act of sharing which further implies the fact of surplus. I offer something from my cup that overflows. Mercy as simple kindness means that I yield to you that which is extra for me. And if I give to you out of my abundance, while that may be benevolent and philanthropic, is that mercy?

Perhaps not, or at least not altogether. My kindness in sharing is an act of generosity which is itself a significant moral attribute. But I sense that mercy is something else, something more.

Once again, in the silence, I hear the hum of a question: Is mercy the same as justice? I wonder. 'Stubborn Ounces — Just Scales.' The symbol for justice suggests balance, a squaring-up, a setting-right of things off kilter. Something I do or say causes you injury or harm. Whether the breakage is that of my promise or an expectation of decency, the air between us is heavy laden, filled with the ache of fracture. The need to make amends becomes apparent, at the level of feeling, at the level of law. The work of restitution must commence before reconciliation can be achieved. The rift between us must be mended. All of this is reasonable, is fair play, is just. But is this mercy?

The merciful person is concerned for that which is right, for that which is just, for that which restores balance and wholeness. But is my obedience to the moral law of justice the same as being merciful? I wonder.

I fret with these efforts. As the words chatter forth, they sound like the cant of a moral philosopher. How to salvage the effort?

An image occurs. In a space shot, the surest way to miss the moon is to set course directly toward it. The long way round, the way of trial and imagination and parabola, that alone has the chance to touch down on the unknown. No wonder Jesus taught in parables!

Perhaps an illustration will illumine a path through the far country and bring us home to the gist of 'mercy.'

First, a story from Nicaragua. The depraved barbarism of Somoza and the National Guard generated an abundance of opportunities for Nicaraguans to make choices between mercy and justice. During the 1970s, 10- and 12-year-old *campesino* children were kidnapped by the Guardia and trained to torture captured Sandinista guerrillas. Youngsters this age are not by nature extraordinarily vicious; however, they can be made that way. One of the Guard's training procedures involved giving each child a dog. A period of time was allowed to permit the animal and child to become attached, to trust each other and build expectations for future companionship. Finally, the children were told that they must torture their pup; they were to poke its eyes out, cut off its tongue, skin it alive, and, finally, kill it. If a child refused to inflict this cold-blooded torture on its animal, they were denied food and drink until they complied. If they were extremely non-cooperative, they were forced to watch while another child mutilated their dog to death. By these methods the *Somocistas* were able to produce dozens of juvenile criminals capable of heinous crimes.

By 1979 the FSLN was faced with a hard decision; what would they do with these young but villainous agents of torture, these youth conditioned into hardened murderers? Both socialist and capitalist representatives of state advised that the youth be executed. They reasoned that their very consciences had been warped to the point of obliteration; they were sociopaths and poor candidates for rehabilitation.

Comandante Tomas Borge, Minister of the Interior, announced the decision of the Revolution concerning these youth:

> *"Perhaps the worst crime of Somoza and his son was not to have killed Nicaraguans, was not to have converted the guards into criminals, but to have converted our children into criminals. Those children that are now detained were trained to take out the eyes of prisoners with a spoon. This was one of the techniques used by these*

*monstrously deformed children. The revolution has made
the political decision to rehabilitate rather than send them
before the courts.''*[35]

Indulge my fancy for a moment. How would these youth
have felt had they been remanded to the courts for trial and
punishment? Life had been hard for them and they had become hardened. Generosity and kindness was not a part of
their experience; neither in the receiving, nor in the giving. I
fancy that into such a life mercy and forgiveness must come
as a staggering blow, a force of emotion stronger than hate,
a breath of air against an asphyxiated heart.

When violence is met with violence, the citadel of the spirit
is not invaded. On the other hand, when dealt with merciful-
ly, the security these youth came to feel in their violent pasts
deserted them; they were thrown back upon the naked hunger of their heart to be cared for, to be understood, to be in
harmony with their neighbors.

Such can be the quality of mercy when put alongside the
demand for justice. Retribution breeds the desire for revenge.
Mercy relaxes the spirit and makes room for healing. Or is
that simply the naivete of a romantic and indulgent liberal *Norteamericano*? At least Borge and the Sandinistas were willing
to try it. And who calls them naive or romantic or indulgent
liberals?

The second story is different, though coincidentally it also
involves a dog. The point here is to see the work of mercy as
a compliment to compassion. Howard Thurman tells of a man
finding an ordinary dog in distress.[36] They were strangers to
one another with no prior histories between them. Struggling
for its life in a bog, the dog's body was covered with a thick
coat of oily mud. Stopping his car, the man jumped out and
called to the dog but soon discovered that the animal was too
exhausted to make the shore. Quickly he went into the murky
water and to the rescue. At first the dog tried to swim away.
Eventually the frightened animal realized that the man intended
help and not harm. As its body relaxed, shivers of relief

passed again and again through its terror-filled fur. Together they came to the shore, man and dog, wet, oily, exhausted. Taking the animal to the nearest veterinary, arrangements were made to wash and mend and feed the dog.

Perhaps this sounds like the story of the Good Samaritan. Jesus shared that parable as an example of the supreme law: Love God with all your heart, mind, soul, and your neighbor as yourself. Certainly the Good Samaritan and this man were kindly persons. They responded to another's need with compassion and generously shared their resources. In the example of the parable we discern an element of justice insofar as meeting human need may be regarded as an act of self-defense. Doing unto others as we would have them do unto us is simple fairness. Kindness generates the expectation of reciprocity; we hope that what goes around comes around. After all, next time we may be the one in the ditch. It's a bit of insurance against our own uncertain future.

Sensitivity Of Spirit: Muted Tenderness, Mellowness, Quiet Softness

But the story of the man and the dog is different. It illuminates the subtle distinction between justice and mercy. Kindness was offered to a strange and so-called 'dumb animal,' and that takes a special calibre of compassion. Perhaps it suggests a sensitivity of spirit that resembles mercy.

Mercy has about it a muted tenderness, a quality of mellowness, of quiet softness that often is not apparent in kindness as simple generosity. There is no concern for fairness here, no sense for calculating costs or figuring rewards. Mercy has about it something that absolutely goes beyond our understanding of 'just desserts.'

Another story. Once again it involves Tomas Borge. As one of the original founders of the FSLN, this rugged guerrilla *Comandante* stayed out of Somoza's hands until 1977. His reputation as a fearsome warrior is the stuff of legend. The dictator was so exasperated in not being able to find Borge that he ordered the National Guard to arrest his wife and children. Señora Borge was raped, tortured, and murdered.

Eventually the guerrilla *Comandante* was captured. Held incommunicado for seven months, Borge was beaten 24 hours a day for the first 15 days of imprisonment. Forced to stand without sitting for 60 days, the Guardia kept him handcuffed for 28 weeks and his head covered with a hood for nine months. Borge was released during an exchange for members of Somoza's National Assembly that the Sandinistas had taken hostage. Later, the *Comandante* encountered the man who murdered his wife. It was his prerogative to prescribe punishment. Tomas Borge looked upon this man and said, "The vengeance I pronounce is this; I forgive you." Was that mercy?

The *Comandante* is not a non-violent man. But he is a civilized man. That fact distinguishes him from the Contra. The barbarian separates from the civilized person in the priority given to the use of violence. A civil person postpones violence until all other methods have been exhausted; the barbarian, resorts to violence as soon as its will is thwarted. My hunch is that these distinctions hold true whether the person be a soldier in the field or an executive directing policies of hate and strategies of destruction from the safe comfort of offices in the Pentagon, the CIA, the National Security Council, or White House.

Mercy Is A Vehicle For Reconciliation

The civilized person keeps alive a sensitivity for the power within works of mercy. Mercy as a vehicle of reconciliation creates a climate in which our human need to be cared for and understood can be nourished and nurtured. Mercy inspires wholeness and integration within persons and between persons. The merciful person looks upon life with quiet eyes and touches the world gently, peacefully.

A different war, a distant place, another story offered by Howard Thurman. Standing in the lee of a South Pacific island, a Navy chaplain was completing the burial of 60 U.S. soldiers who had lost their lives that afternoon in a fierce battle at sea. As they started toward their landing crafts, one of the sailors said, "Sir, there is another body over here." The chaplain was tired, nauseated, exhausted in body and spirit. He bent over to examine the corpse and discovered that very likely it was the pilot whose plane had done so much damage to their ship. The men were all for throwing the dead man in the bush or leaving the body to rot on the beach. It became a moment for great searching of heart. Finally the chaplain's mind was made up. He called the men together and spoke these words:

> *"Men, we must find the right thing to do this afternoon. The right thing in the light of eternity. I know that you say he was the enemy, a suicide, a man ordered to dive his plane into our ship. But in a sense, I am the same kind of suicide. So I have a kinship with this fellow. He too is a human being. I find no hatred in my heart for him, and, if you search your own hearts you may not find hatred for him either. I ask you to help, not because of any future that we shall have together. Rather I want you to know that in a God-forsaken island in the Pacific, you and your chaplain, faced with the naked challenge to the essential humanness of mankind, sought a level of rightness that transcends the vicisitudes of fortune and circumstances. I shall not give him a Christian burial, because that would profane his own religious faith that differs from our own. But this we will do — let us kneel and pray to our own God in the presence of this dead man, as an act of reverence in our own hearts. This act will unite us beyond all conflict and all madness. When this is done, we will bury him with a headstone that bears no name, because we do not know his name, but with the simple inscription, "Japanese Pilot," and the date. Perhaps this act of reverence is an expression of the right thing in the eyes of Eternity."*[37]

"The Right Thing In The Eyes Of Eternity"

Listen to the words, "the right thing in the eyes of Eternity." The right thing. The right thing to do this day.

Our evolutionary ancestors were not passive, fruit-eating primates. They were predators living by tooth, nail, and bloody claw. Beyond our social niceties, in the bio-logic of their legacy, we share similar conditionings. When an enemy sheds our blood, the desire for vengeance rises with our blood pressure. Driven by the need to survive, resentments simmer with the desire for revenge.

But the chaplain invoked the spirit of decency. "He too is a human being . . ." In death, the pilot deserved respect. In life, the men on that beach needed to behave responsibly. And I am certain that they twisted and turned, juggled and shifted their ground until at last they each came face to face with their own sense of ultimate worth. Then they buried the Japanese soldier. Ah, the mystery in the gentling touch of mercy whereby the spirit of retaliation is relaxed and overcome!

A mellow sensitivity, a softened compassion, the muted act, no particular interest in fairness — in measured dealing, of such is the quality of mercy.

But I am not finished with the beatitude. "Blessed are the merciful; for they shall obtain mercy." Is that a paradox? I don't think so. Whether it be love, or kindness, or mercy, we cannot share what we do not already have. We are what we share with others. Whether we receive back in kind what we share, that is beside the point. We are only asked to do 'the right thing in the eyes of Eternity.'

Instead of executing them, a state takes the chance that youth trained to torture can be rehabilitated. A stranger puts himself at risk and rescues a foundering dog. Putting down the desire for revenge and risking the possibility that the enemy who has murdered his wife may kill again, a civilized man offers forgiveness. A man puts his reputation and the esteem of his fellows on the line and pleads that an enemy soldier be buried with respect.

Four stories. One lesson. Mercy challenges the spirit. It offers no guarantee of kindred pay-back. It's risky business and not for the faint-hearted.

In the meditative silence, I hear the hum of Dean Thurman's lingering question: 'Am I merciful or just decent?' Are you?

"Blessed Are Those Who Mourn"

Sermon

A time for tears, a time for laughter, a time for mourning, a time for dancing.
Ecclesiastes 3:4

Blessed are those who mourn; they shall be comforted.
Matthew 5:5

In the distance a long line of people walked slowly toward us down the dusty narrow Nicaraguan mountain road. Our trucks pulled to the side and stopped. When the drivers turned off the diesel engines, like a clearing blow to the gut we could hear the sounds of their anguish carried to us on the hot dry afternoon air. It was the unmistakable cacophony of distress and melancholy; the world dismantling and tumbling back through a back hole. In the middle of the passing procession six men carried a make-shift litter on their shoulders. Above the heads of the crowd we saw the body of a woman laying on the stretcher, clothed, still, lifeless. A bright flower was pinned in her hair and others were held in hands folded across her breasts. People from the village were processing the last lonely mile to bury their dead. They were not being quiet or composed; they were grieving and lamenting their loss.

Every separation causes a wound. The injury occasioned by death is painful. The whole range of activities and functions characterizing the life of the dead person are stopped, cut off, finished. There on that dusty road the last page in the book of the woman's unique, distinctive, and unrepeatable life had been turned. The village was facing up to the fact of that death by writing 'The End' with song and tears. According to their custom, in a fashion appropriate to the moment, they were throwing down the burdens of time and reason; they were

341

opening out to the fact that the delicate network of living relations had once again been ruptured. They were mourning her death, mourning the life-fact of mortality, remembering and mourning the fact that they too shall die and return to dust. It's a recollection worth a tear and a moan.

Nicaraguans are experienced in mourning; some 50,000 of them have died during the years of this revolution and counter-revolution. With a population of less than 3,000,000, death in such magnitude seems like a monstrous gaping invisible mouth with an insatiable appetite for blood. Poured into the earth like so much sacred food, their blood can no longer vitalize and invigorate the celebration of life as a wonderful gift, God's most precious miracle.

"*Sandino Vive!*" a wall shouts in blood-red graffiti. Street names enshrine the memory and pay tribute to heroes; the people speak the names Mayorga, Pomares, Valdivia, Rodrigo and they remember. Each village has its women's organizations. Normal enough. But here they are called "Mothers of Martyrs and Heroes."

Nicaragua is a people, a culture, a nation in which life and death are inseparable, where Nicaraguan death is a mirror of Nicaraguan life. When they explode, "*Patria Libre, O Morir!*" they touch the highest point of that tension. They graze the very zenith of the arc between mortality and freedom. These are a people who understand the meaning within the words of Octavio Paz:

> "*Death is a mirror which reflects the vain gesticulations of living. The whole motley confusion of acts, omissions, regrets and hope which is the life each one of us, finds in death, not meaning or explanation, but an end. Death defines life; our deaths illuminate our lives. If our deaths lack meaning, our lives also lacked it . . . Death like life is not transferable. If we do not die as we lived, it is because the life we lived was not really ours; it did not belong to us . . . Tell me how you die and I will tell you who you are.*"[38]

Contempt For Death, Contempt For Life

I am the child of a society that regards death as a disagreeable fact, the inevitable conclusion of a natural process. Like other unpleasant facts, North Americans attempt to cope with the reality of death by denial, avoidance, and flight. Mortality is the bane of 'polite culture:' absent in political speech, banished from advertising, masqueraded by morticians, death is excluded from our images, our words, and our popular customs. For instance, in our thralldom with high-tech medical science we anticipate that arteriosclerosis and internally generated diseases such as cancer will surely be eliminated, and soon. Finally, we pray, it will be hard to conceive how anyone can cease to live, except for murders and suicides and accidents.

But a civilization that denies death also denies life, and that's the stubborn unavoidable fact of the matter. Our attempts to mask death succeed only in transforming its power, and us in the process, until the same society that abhors death glamorizes war. The hypocrisy of our disdain for a natural fact becomes transparent in our fascination with the unnatural, witness Rambo cinema and the tabloid-press substitution of grotesqueness for reality. Best-selling author Stephen King, master of violence and the macabre, takes our measure when he asserts, "Horror is the church of Twentieth-Century America."

Death as a natural fact is exchanged for death as fodder for the pornographic imagination. Middle-American culture is enamored with health spas and marathons, with miracle drugs that retard wrinkles and hair-loss and aging. It is the culture of precision diets and synthetic fast-foods, all of which banner the 'good life.' It is also the political culture responsible for death beyond number in Hiroshima, Vietnam, in El Salvador and Nicaragua. The calculus of death in this magnitude is literally mind-boggling. Confronted with atrocity and death in mega-volume, the brain benumbs itself in defiance of sheer pain. Consequently we detach from death. We reduce it to numbers-play and chatter about 'body counts.' Unfortunately, when death becomes impersonal and stripped of meaning, life becomes equally meaningless.

One reason for my journey to Nicaragua was to somersault out of a death-dealing but death-denying culture into one where people do not turn their backs to death out of fear. I hoped to find in Nicaragua a people who did not idealize death. Why? Because they affirm life as too precious to be discarded lightly. I wanted to look into the mirror of Nicaragua where death and life are sacred opposites that compliment each other. I wanted to look deep down into the heart of this people who know that they already belong to death, and that each day is a miracle, a gift as undeserved as this life itself. I wanted to see if death in dedication to the noble cause of freedom and liberty from oppression was different from the death which I see and touch and live with here in North America. I hoped to sense something different in the Nicaraguan spirit, to discern how it enabled them to face death freely, make of death what it can be, and accept death with dignity. And I journeyed to accompany them, to stand beside them and make a witness to the carnage of war, that insane and obscene sacrilege. It was a pilgrimage to grieve my complicity with the evil afflicting them.

Grief-Work, An Enlightened Science

The questions linger, what are you capable and willing to mourn? Who would you mourn for or with? How would you do it?

We have witnessed a new and enlightened self-consciousness in this business of handling death. Books are written about dying, death, and the work of grief. Some of them become best-sellers. Seminars on the subject attract wide notice and participation. Therapists and preachers rattle on about the stages of grief. Following death, the common reactions include denial and isolation, anger and lashing out, a desire to bargain with the Fates, depression, and finally some measure of acceptance.

We are discovering that bereavement and the work of grief is by nature sacred. It is governed by its own special rules. It has a logic and a bio-logic infused with a unique potency. It

344

behaves according to an uncommon gravity where things merge, lose shape and return to the primordial mass. In mourning we leave our every day norms, we cease our preoccupations with hyper-rationality, we stop the world of business-as-usual, we stand in a sacred pause beyond all taken-for-grantedness.

But to put a name on stages, to talk about death and grief, this results in a certain taming of the subject. We want to handle our grief before it handles us. The thought that mourning may reach explosive, dramatic, delirious, or even suicidal extremes horrifies our Western European natures. We want to manage it. Well and good. But the thought occurs that what we may gain in effective management we may lose in the touch of soul with its colors and voices of deep unregulated emotions.

What Is It To Grieve, To Mourn?

As is my custom, I turn to words. Both the Preacher in Ecclesiastes and Matthew avoid using the word grief. Instead they say, "a time for mourning," and "blessed are they that mourn."

Are the words grief and mourn synonymous? Are they interchangeable? I wonder. What does it mean to mourn? Is it the exhibition of grief as in weeping, in wailing, or collapsing in bereavement? This is the most obvious meaning. But then what is grief? Is it merely a fervent reaction to the separation caused by death, the pain of an emotional amputation? Or is it an expression of sorrow, growing out of a profound sympathy for or identification with someone in distress?

Perhaps that holds forth a clue. Grief is a feeling, deeper than sadness and more like the sorrow occasioned by enormous loss. Mourning is an expression, a demonstration, the activity of giving vent to our feelings of grief. Freud says that "the work of mourning is difficult, slow and involves an extremely painful, bit-by-bit inner process of letting go."

I recall that Nicaraguan procession. People were weeping, some uncontrollably. Others staggered under the impact of a cruel blow and neighbors were supporting them physically.

Since mourning is what you do with your grief, they were mourning. A person can keep silent, remain composed even to the point of being stoic, can be holding the grief or holding it in. But that is not the same as mourning. Mourning means tears, it sounds like nausea and crying, looks like weakness and exhaustion and falling down, faintness or trembling, collapsing inward or outward, however a person may express that in their behavior.

To grieve is to struggle with how things will be and feel now that a loved one is no longer a part of our life. We grieve for ourselves. We are sorrowful and sad because we are painfully deprived. It is trying to think of life without that companionship, a thinking that often leaves the mind blank and unable to imagine anything. We remember the goodness and the safety that they brought into our lives, gifts that empowered us to move freely and fearlessly across the hard stretches of troublesome days or into the beckoning future raw with open unknown. And now we wonder how it will be for us. We grieve out of our fear because we do not know what is ahead for us in the unrevealed future. How will life be when they are no longer present on the horizon of our days, moving through the corridors of our thoughts, touching our flesh, and stimulating our emotions? We grieve because the earth beneath our feet seems to be crumbling. We have less to hold on to. Order has turned into the insecurity of disorder. Once again and most assuredly we have been confronted with the bold fact that things happen in life and to us over which we have no control, can exercise no leverage, and against which we are powerless.

Mourning becomes the physical and emotional act that opens us to the awareness that we must grow-on, slowly, gently, carefully, and very patiently. We let down before we can let in, not thoughts or insights, but a new love. Old boundaries formerly defined by the presence of another are relaxed. The distances we kept with others are lifted so that new intimacies can grow.

Mourning precedes the recovery of stability, precedes the generation of new energy, precedes the invention of new hope and our capacity to enjoy and invest in life.

Mourning accepts that, despite dreams and fantasies, the dead will not return to us in this life.

Mourning requires enormous adaptation, the altering of our circumstances of living, our behavior, our expectations, our self-definitions.

And we have choices. We decide what to do with our dead. To die when they die, to live crippled, or to forge out of the pain and memory new adaptations. And if we choose to live, we also choose to feel that pain and live past it before recovering the emotional capital we invested in the person now dead and investing it again and anew in another life.

So my question lingers, what is it, what are the things capable of making us mourn? On the other hand, what things, however terrible they may be, are incapable of affecting you?

You are blessed, in the words of the beatitude, if you mourn over situations that are worthy of the outpouring of your spirit. And that is a hard test.

Jesus Wept!

Indulge your fantasy for a moment; in your imagination, turn the inward eye to picture yourself a person of flourishing popularity. Your reputation preceeds you. Crowds gather eager to hear you speak, to teach. Some look into your eyes, listen to your words, and equate your personal power with the miraculous. They crave a moment of your irreplaceable time. Circling you in the press of profound needs, they reach out with the desperation of the hungry grasping for food, with the recklessness of the thirsty yearning for water, with the clumsiness of the sick seeking the graze of a healing touch. All around you, a sea of rising expectations. Amid the accolades and the heartbreaking anticipation, you come to be identified as the brightest hope of the people, the nation, the race.

You travel in the company of few close associates, carefully, if not curiously chosen persons, whose talents may be useful to your mission, to your message.

The adulation of the masses, a coterie of disciples, what's missing?

Perhaps the missing ingredient is simply a friend.

Now consider Jesus. He was such a man. And he had a friend; a man named Lazarus. Why did he choose Lazarus for the crucial office of friendship? The question is misplaced. Beyond calculation, we do not select friends like we create a list for a dinner party, attentive to details like compatible interests, how they voted in the last election, the sports they enjoy, their manners at table, or their conversational dexterity. Friends are walking miracles in our lives, a gift utterly unrelated to reward or justice. Where they come from, or why we seek each other out is a matter of mystery, the working of a power greater than our own.

Lazarus was a man with whom Jesus could simply be himself. With him there was no image to project or protect, no mission to describe or defend. Perhaps he was to Jesus as Jonathan was to David. They loved each other, savored the silent spaces of their togetherness, cherished the sharing of a sunset, the agony of illness. Friends want to be there when the one they love takes that last breath, holding a hand when they go forward into death.

Lazarus died. When Jesus arrived to stand beside the body of his friend, he was too late for holding his hand while the friend passed through death's door. But his tears were right on time. Caught up in the raw agony of his loss, the account does not report that he 'shed tears' or that he 'cried.' No. Jesus wept. Tears were simply the outward indications of the deep emotional pain wrenching his spirit, falling into an abyss that could no longer be bridged by easy access to his friend.

Frederick Buechner's insight is significant here, reminding us of our temptation to sentimentalize the scene, looking only at the emotion while avoiding the reality.[39] The demands of death are painful. Mourning is painful. We would deny, avoid, or flee from the disfiguring sight of such travail rather than encounter the spot where our kinship with that suffering finds its own match.

Mourn Your Own Death!

Have you ever mourned anybody?

Have you wept at anything during the past year?

Rilke said that nobody thinks about death, about their own death, because nobody lives a personal life. Have you ever thought seriously about the fact that someday you are going to die?

Is there anybody you know whose place you would take if one of you had to suffer great pain or go down to death?

If your answer to all or most of these questions is 'no,' the chances are you are dead already. You might consider mourning that.

On my last night with my host family in Waslala I was awakened very early in the morning. It was at least three hours before first light. The father Juan and mother Bertilde passed my hammock and went out onto the front porch. Someone was out there sitting with them. I heard low tones of conversation and then the unmistakable sounds of crying; the low moaning of a youth and a mother's tears.

Not wishing to interrupt, I remained still, listening and trying to grasp a sense for what was happening. Their 17-year-old son had been conscripted some weeks before and was now in basic training at a base near Matagalpa. Enrique's buddy from the village was in training with him and had been assigned for a routine training patrol. His unit emerged from the jungle into a clearing and suddenly encountered the Contra. Both groups were taken by surprise. In a spontaneous reflexive action they opened fire on each other. Enrique's buddy was killed. Later the Contra and FSLN would agree that this was an accident and not a violation of the truce. A tragedy to be sure, one of the unintended hazards of war, one of many regrets that adds one more name, one more body to the mountain of dead. How many regrets is the human spirit capable of absorbing before losing count, or consciousness? Nonetheless the young boy, Enrique's friend, was dead.

Enrique was terrified, in mourning, and now perhaps he was A.W.O.L. Having fled the military base, he returned home in the middle of the night to plead with his parents. He did not want to serve in the army. He did not want to be assigned so far away from the village and his parent's home. Most assuredly, he did not want to die! He wanted to learn bee keeping, work the farm, go to vocational school, court his girlfriend at the fiestas, and quit the insanity of this war. Finally, mother, father, and son all went into the family's sleeping quarters and the darkness closed in silence.

As I lay there looking out into the deep Nicaraguan night, Enrique's disillusion and despair was palpable. Bee keeping, the family farm, going to school, dancing with a sweetheart, how utterly clean, how utterly commonplace. Those have to do with the little graces by which life is dignified, is maintained, is sustained. But in the hurting moment they seemed unreal and ephemeral against the reality of death which was collapsing his hopes.

The Comfort Is In The Giving

Whether we mourn the death of a friend or the death of a dream, it is always the same; the heart needs to find some kind word or gracious gesture that reconnects us with the beauty that is still within reach. We need something to keep alive our sensitivity to the strengthening presence of God's moving spirit. When exhaustion has surrendered our last portion of endurance, when the inventory of our hope-against-hope is utterly spent, it is then, just then, that our spirit needs to be bottomed by the faith that life does move on.

By 4 o'clock the birds were singing and from the kitchen fires came the sweet smell of fresh coffee and tortillas. Soon 'first light' would be moving scantily through the mists of the valley. A new day was birthing. I'll never know what word was spoken or what prompted the young man's decision, but Enrique resolved to return to the army and basic training. There over the small portions of the family meal I saw sadness in his mother's eyes and stark seriousness in the hushed silence of his father.

Whether it's your mourning or mine or that of a people, sometimes we seem only to be stumbling in darkness through a long tunnel of tragedy and tribulation. The ultimate catastrophe, however, is to let life become reduced to a rubble of mourning; to allow a corruption of the spirit that poisons the soul with a contagion of inner distintegration. When that happens there is nothing left but emotional laceration and a pile of white ash where hope once kept house.

"Blessed are they that mourn; for they shall be comforted." They shall be reassured. They shall be consoled. They shall be solaced.

It does not mean, however, that they shall be tricked, granted some kind of time-warping reprieve, have the clock turned back and the cause of mourning removed. It does mean that the sweep and wash of mourning carries the seeds of healing and recovery.

Such paradox. We have compassion. We mourn. And in the doing, we are comforted. That is the promise. The results we trust to God. Amen.

"Blessed Are The Poor In Spirit"

Sermon

A time for embracing, a time to refrain from embracing.
Ecclesiastes 3:5

Blessed are the poor in spirit, theirs is the kingdom of
God.
Matthew 5:3-10

"Blessed are the poor in spirit." What does it mean to be 'poor in spirit?' Does it mean to be passion-less, empty of zest and vitality? Are the 'poor in spirit' drugged, siphoned and ready for the morgue? Perhaps they are merely stuck in the doldrums, without chutzpah, the victims of boredom. If you were to paint a picture of 'poverty of spirit,' would it be done in gray, grim, cadavorous monotones? I wonder. Maybe poverty of spirit is the product of a prophylactic lifestyle — the never take a risk or step up and stick your chin out safe life.

'Poor In Spirit:' Faded Worship?

We've heard it said that 'As a man thinketh, so is he.' It's also true that as a person lives, so do they worship. Consequently, it is no surprise that sometimes worship becomes a dull rational exercise, neither joyful or spirit-filled.

Typically, at the eleven o'clock hour on Sunday morning, established and mainline congregations know the meaning of Ecclesiastes' words, 'a time to refrain from embracing:' Right now this is the time and place to refrain from embracing! The liturgy is like fast-food; flavorless, routine, and guaranteed to leave you gaseous. Moreover, it's worship from the neck up. If the whole body of Christ can be squeezed into the helmet of rationality, you might as well leave the rest of the body at home, including your sex, wrinkles and warts.

352

Clergy preside in coal-black robes, resembling inanimate and denatured versions of that 'American Gothic' portrait. Were we all ordained to muteness and dipped in starch? Congregations often show up equally lifeless. Hands are neither raised in prayer nor slapped together in the smack of a clamorous joyful noise. In the presence of a burning bush, we might bow our heads; never would we remove our shoes or fall prostrate before the God the Inscrutable. We leave dancing to Zorba and suggest the public park to those who would make a joyful noise. Holy Communion is served in the pews to further insure against un-Protestant genuflections or the embarrassing sound of knees squeaking like rusty hinges. Altar candles are used sparingly as if in some commitment to Puritan thrift. If the smell of incense were to waft through the sanctuary, it would occasion ripples of horror born of a suspected hippie or harikrishna conspiracy. Charles Wesley inserted his lyrics into pop tunes sung in English pubs; now they are mumbled instead of sung and regarded as products of the Pleistocene theological era.

In this fog-shrouded worship, the congregation is securely fastened to the pews, more out of catatonic boredom than any need to be seat-belted for a wild ride in the spirit. The pews themselves are bolted to the floor, frozen in their march toward the altar, as rigid in their rank and file formation as the parallel lines of the graveyard. When children stray from their parents or fidget and cry, ushers move with SWAT squad dexterity shuttling troublemakers to that lock-up called the nursery. Should the liturgist be seized by a biazarre impulse and solicit thanksgiving for a healing, a victory over temptation, or a mercy-filled forgiveness, the result would be muffled coughs, shuffling shoes, and the deep breathing of an elder fighting sleep.

'Poor In Spirit:' Enthused Worship?

Let's look for a contrast. In another congregation, emotion carries the day. It's rock and roll for Jesus. The very windows threaten to crack in vibrations of holy ecstasy.

Responding to a heavy dose of spiritual amphetamine, the preacher bolts form the pulpit like a rodeo rider slamming out of the chute on a wild mustang; one hand clutches the Bible as if it were a cinch and the other jabs the air for maximum points. Going for blood and a wild ride, the preachin' deacon puts the spurs to the text and slides into the rhythms for a trip through the octaves. Turned-on, tuned-in, hip-slick-and-cool, someone with a guitar catches the beat and adds an electric jitter to the din. Hands clap and hips sway. The folk are workin' up a sweat under heavy spiritual currents threatening to overload. When it's time for prayer, palms are raised toward the ceiling as a sea of the faithful sway like the giant kelp under the waters of our bay. Oh, there are ushers alright. But not to shepherd children toward noise-proof rooms. These work like teams of emergency medical technicians making mad dashes to catch falling persons who have been slain in the Lord and are melting in rapturous swoons. Periodically someone is heard to say 'Amen' loud enough to ring the steeple bell above raucous choruses of 'Praise the Lord.'

Is that congregation, 'poor in spirit?'

Certainly these vignettes suggest something about passion.

The Bible Is A Passionate Book

Charles Bayer reminds us of that which we tend to forget: The Bible is a passionate book.[40] The creation narrative is passion on a cosmic scale. Big Bang or Garden of Eden, however God put creation together, passion was there. Do you doubt it? Ask any woman who has given birth. Moses leads the people of Israel out of bondage and into freedom. It's a trek born in Passion. David wept tears of Passion on hearing of Jonathan's death. Jesus faced-down a crowd intent on stoning a harlot. Once again, Passion. Faith and hope and love are words; add Passion and they become feelings; without Passion they're best left in the dictionary. In Gethsemane, Jesus sweat drops of blood; how's that for Passion? Jesus did not simply shed a tear at the tomb of his friend Lazarus; he wept. The difference between tears and weeping is Passion. Standing

354

on a bluff overlooking Jerusalem, he knew it didn't know diddly about the things that make for peace. He wept. He's still weeping. Heartbreak is an experience of Passion. Bayer suggests that the Lord's muteness during his trial was the Passionate fury of silence.

Jesus was not an emotional flat-liner. The Man, the Mission, and the Message bespoke of fire in the belly. At the core, his call is an invitation to Passion. Flinging open prison doors to liberate captives demands Passion. Nobody is going to go to the trouble of feeding the hungry or clothing the naked or sheltering the homeless unless they feel something akin to a Passion for 'doing unto others.' If someone smacks you upside the head and in the reeling instant it occurs to you to try something novel, like turning the other cheek, the energy required to relax the instinct for retaliation would score high on a 'Passion register.'

These pictures depict the path of the spirit warrior; they are not painted in gray hues. There is color here, vibrant primary colors that overflow with dynamism.

Let me paint you a picture of Passion. Actually it's a photo, one of my favorites, taken during the early days of the United Farm Workers grape strikes. In the foreground, a Kern County Deputy Sheriff is standing in a field in front of assembled strikers. His boots planted firmly in the earth, legs spread apart, a handgun and club dangle off his utility belt. And then, through his legs, in the background, you see it. This time Passion wears the face of Dorothy Day. Sitting quietly on a small stool and wearing a simple frock, a cheap straw hat shades her face from the sun and the Deputy's glare. Whenever someone starts singing "Like a tree planted by the water, I shall not be moved," I think of her and see that picture. This quiet, unpretentious, gritty saint is my working image of Passionate discipleship.

Passion ought not be confused with hyper-emotional fanaticism. When Paul talks about 'the foolishness of God' or invites us to be 'fools for Christ's sake,' he is not recommending that we 'play the fool' and become damned fools. Fanatics

355

are irrational emotionalists and notoriously, passionately, intolerant. Driven by fear they preach a gospel of hate. They make of their followers a herd of bleating sheep and those they can't corral they target for witch hunts, inquisitions, pogroms and holocausts. Whether it is the fanaticism of Washington's compulsive preoccupation with Communism, whether it is the fanaticism of Nicaragua's undisciplined Sandinismo, whether it is the sectarian fanaticism of Christian fundamentalists in the United States or Zionists in Israel or the zealots of Islam in Iraq and Iran, fanaticism always spells bad news for those who find themselves at the crackling end of its whip.

Job's Uselessness Provides A Clue

So what does it mean to be 'poor in spirit?' Jim Carroll suggests that in musing this question we think of the long dark night of Job.[41] This former Boston University Newman House colleague says that we should imagine a day overwhelmed by a 'worst possible case scenario.' Think of natural catastrophe like a flood, add wars, addiction, your children freaking out in mindless gang violence, muggers and pushers and pimps infesting your neighborhood, I mean, think awful! Job lost his job, his credit rating, his house, and the new BMW with the cellular phone. His ulcers were the least of his problems. His wife split, and his children died early and tragic deaths. We're talking a real bad day.

When everything around you has collapsed, fled, or otherwise turned into dust, what do you do? If you choose against suicide, the only thing left for you to do is to get to know yourself real well.

In this cosmic contest between God and the Devil, the objective is to see whether Job's happiness depends on what he **has** and on what he **does**, or whether it depends simply on the fact that he **is**. Subsequently Job loses all the conventions that structure meaning into his universe; his health, his material securities, his friends, his family.

Then something happened. Job was 'born again,' converted, which is another way of saying he arrived at a

356

turning point. He discovered that his life, his being, his Job-ness depended on no possession, no relationship, no position, no virtue. It depended on nothing. Literally, no-thing. With his clothes in shreds, his head shaved, standing there center-stage and bare naked, Job had to decide whether he liked what he saw. He was given the opportunity to say 'Yes' or 'No' to being Job — pure and simple.

Now I think we are getting close to the subject. When Job loses his job, so to speak, he begins to live. He begins to live close to the bone. When he stops his mad pursuit of riches and power, when he stops the deadly collecting of things, experiences, and people that keep him in debt and bored to tears, when he finally decides that he is not nearly as bad or unworthy or ugly as the hustlers and hucksters tell him, well, he has finally arrived at being useless. It is in radical poverty that Job meets God; in his uselessness, in his powerlessness. Now he's ready to become human. After all, uselessness isn't so bad. Art and poetry and laughter and everything lovely are useless — without productive utility.

'Poor In Spirit' and the Revolutionary 'God Of The Poor'

Having seen ourselves as useless and poor with our own eyes, we can begin to see ourself as through the eyes of God: For God sees from the point of view of the radically poor. In Nicaragua there are signs that quote 1 Corinthians 8:6, "*Para Nosotros no hay mas que un solo dios.*" ["For us there is no more than one single God."] After the 'Dios' someone was adding . . . "*El Dios de los pobres*!" . . . "The God of the Poor!" The first song we learned to sing in Nicaragua was by that same name, "*Vos sos el Dios de los Pobres*," from the *Misa Campesina*, The chorus goes like this:

> *Vos sos el Dios de los pobres,*
> *El Dios humano y sencillo,*
> *El Dios que suda en la calle,*
> *El Dios del rostro curtido.*
> *Por eso is que te hablo yo asi como habla mi pueblo*
> *Porque sos el Dios obrero, el Christo trabajador.*[42]

357

You are the God of the poor,
The human and simple God,
The God who sweats in the street,
The God with the weathered face.
That is why I speak to you like my people speak,
Because you are the laborer God, the worker Christ.

That *el Dios de los Pobres* should appear in the Latin American Roman Catholic Mass is remarkable — except for the fact that it was created in the *Misa Nicaraguense*. A church committed to the 'preferential option for the poor' has usually been bell, book, and candle committed to *el Dios de los Ricos*.

Nicaragua achieved something that Vatican II and the historic Conference of Latin American Bishops at Medellin would not have thought possible in their wildest dream — or nightmare; a revolutionary government, led by guerrilla commandos and four Catholic priests, believes that God takes the side of the poor. They believe that the religion of Israel and Jesus demands more than slavish bootlicking; it is a call to resistance. They believe that Israel's story and Jesus' example is more than a recommendation to obey external authorities; it is a call to conscience and social justice as articulated by the prophets. President Daniel Ortega preaches "*Pueblo de Sandino! Pueblo de Cristo!*" "People of Sandino, People of Christ," the potent juxtaposition and powerful conjunction of faith and fatherland. While this is no novel alliance, it is for Latin American. And that is the profound originality of Sandinismo with its *Cristianos Revolucionarios*.

That phrase, Revolutionary Christianity, is fashionable. And while it has distinct meaningfulness in Nicaragua and elsewhere in Latin America and Central America, when bantered about in North America clergy gatherings or seminary hallways, mostly it describes a new way of talking; not a new way of walking. The books I have read on the subject were written by professors and pastors comfortably situated in very middle class ivory towers. This sermon is written and preached by a well educated, secure, affluent gringo.

When Liberation Theology is not being written from the trenches like it is in Nicaragua, it is revolution at the level of argument; not action.

We are not in those trenches. So I will say a few words and leave the rest to the sisters and brothers who are walking the walk. Revolutionary Christianity is simply doing costly things for Jesus' sake. It is fundamentally the prerogative of the useless of the earth, the radically poor. They have little else to lose, save perhaps their life. And when you think about it, that seems very Christian. And very radical.

When I think of Revolutionary Christianity in our homeland, in this town, I think of the Salvation Army. There in that little building downtown across the street from the police station I don't hear talk about Liberation Theology. As a matter of fact the Army has never been any great shakes at theology. But it is a great Action Corps, content to throw its weight in practical service to *el Dios de los Pobres.*

The theological radicalism of Revolutionary Christianity is really quite ingenuous. It proceeds directly from the simplicity of the Gospel. It is totally lacking in ambiguity, irrelevancy, and dead-ends. From whatever point of the compass, in whatever time, out of whatever social strata and psychological type, when you come within hearing distance of the Gospel, if you have ears to hear, you are going to be taken to that spot where Job finally stood.

God promises to set us free. And that freedom always entails risk. Those of us who have gambled the risk and share our fears and heartbreaks, our dis-eases and addictions, our dreams and nightmares — not only before God but also one another — find that Christ makes good on the promises of liberation. We find tears that heal, we find companionship in laughter, we find folk willing to help with the chores that threaten to overwhelm, we find compassion growing out of passion, and we find that the Grace of God is glue for our brokenness.

'Blessed are the poor in spirit; for theirs is the Kingdom of Heaven.' Theirs is the rule of God. What a priceless gift. And we don't have to be perfect, sinless or holy to receive it.

359

All we have to do is hand it over and let the spirit of God invade our life, let the will of God direct our life. My desire, my prayer, my willingness to let the rule of God become the center around which my life moves, that alone renders me 'poor in spirit.' So be it. God help us. Amen.

"Blessed Are The Persecuted And Reviled"

Sermon

A time for giving birth, a time for dying, a time for planting, a time for uprooting.
Ecclesiastes 3:4

Blessed are you when men shall revile you and persecute you falsely for my sake. Theirs is the kingdom of heaven.
Matthew 5:10

This is one of my favorite passages in all of literature. Albert Schweitzer wrote these words at the conclusion of his **Quest For The Historical Jesus**:

> *"He comes to us as One unknown, without a name, as of old, by the lake-side, he came to those . . . who knew him not. He speaks to us the same word: 'Follow thou me' and sets us to the tasks which He has to fulfill for our time. He commands. And to those who obey Him, whether they be wise or simple, He will reveal Himself in the toils, the conflicts, the sufferings which they shall pass through in His fellowship, and as an ineffable mystery, they shall learn in their own experience, who He is."*[43]

The toils, the conflicts, the sufferings . . . is this what we inherit when we covenant with Jesus? Is sweat and struggle and pain the gauntlet we must pass through if we are to fellowship with Christ? Are these the tracks we must follow to the water's edge if we wish to encounter God? And if that be the case, who among us claims privy to this fellowship?

361

More likely we pride ourselves on being 'moderate' women and men; heirs to Aristotle's 'balanced humanism.' Jim Carroll explodes that corrupt myth by reminding us that in truth and in our usage, we are not so much balanced as paralyzed.[44]

Immobility, inaction, impotence, these are terms more apt to describe our condition. We are the Kitty Genovese watchers. Do you remember? It happened at the rump-end of those 'good old days,' that fashionably quaint decade, the marvelously secure 50s. Walking home to her apartment in New York City's Kew Gardens, she was attacked by a vicious knife-wiedling psychopath. Knocked to the ground and stabbed, her screams frightened the man way. But when it became clear to him that no one was intervening on her behalf, he returned and continued his murderous work. On and on it went. Stabbing, screams, running away, no interventions, his return, more stabbing, screaming . . . This continued for 45 minutes while 50 people in nearby apartments listened, watched and did nothing: No dramatic attempt at rescue, no call to the police, nothing. Zero. Kitty Genovese was murdered by 50 people — one of them used a knife. Speak to me of moderation, friends.

"Moderation: Our Own Slick Terrorism!"

Carroll calls this moderation "our own terrorism." Moderate operators in government, business, churches and schools all conspire in enlightened language to keep everything the same. And what stays the same? The systems of corporate power which feed on the powerlessness of the poor stay the same. Churches fret and whine about dwindling memberships — the statistics of decay — and then refuse risk-running missions that might attract on-lookers to join in something other than a tearful wake. The churches stay the same. But smaller. The dividing impulses which separate our society into keepers, the kept, and those who pay the bills, these remain the same. And so do the terrors of life that make of the old 'protection' racket a new growth-industry. The Defense Department's annual budget is literally out-of-sight and alarm systems and hand-gun sales are at an all time high. And the loneliness stays the same, though it looks different. The pointless parades of skinheads and yuppies and normies — all of this simply masks the gnawing sense that the old loyalties are fading because the old institutions are staying the same.

We question the justice of the judges. The competency of educators is no longer assumed. The corruptibility of politicans is taken for granted. We suspect that Tolstoy was right; behind every great fortune there is a crime. Pastors, preoccupied with their personal problems, are too busy to pray. We don't know our neighbor's names. We rent videos to dial-out, drugs to numb-out, and handguns to rub-out our enemies. Everywhere authority clings to its dignity like a pair of falling trousers and succeeds only in looking ridiculous. But the laughs stalls in our throats; the silly nakedness is our own.

Justice, Damnit! Now!

Yet every once and a while through the din and the clutter and the clatter we hear someone calling for 'justice.' Justice! Now! People of color, old people, women people, poor people, homeless people, all screaming for Justice! Damnit!

Then perhaps we remember that what little we know of God was taught to us by a Jew for whom justice and religion were inseparable. Biblical Israel was a community that defined sin as the surrender of freedom. To allow yourself to be abused in slavery was sin. To allow yourself to be violated sexually was sin. To allow yourself to be desecrated because of age or education or employment was sin.

Isarel's story is that of a people who became a fierce counter-culture of resistance to illegitimate external authority. A Jew was called to be 'a just one.' The 'just' share in the 'justice' of the Lord; they stand upright and are ready to create the future. The 'just ones' stood on their own two feet ready to move out of Egypt's oppressive slavery into the struggle for a liberated freedom. The Passover Meal was no 'fast foods' affair; it was to be eaten standing upright, the participants ready to go if summoned, to move out.

The 'just' are called to speak out; they refuse to stand by silent in the presence of exploitation. That's a dangerous

363

calling! You want to arouse the conscience of the crowds, not stir up more trouble. And here is Jesus saying, in effect, 'Blessed are they who side with Heaven when any fool can see it's on the losing side and all you get for your pain is pain.' They are blessed when they get worked over and cussed out on his account. And now he looks them straight in the eye and says, again, "Blessed are you!" Strange words.

Does this mean we are to take delight in our own suffering? That's morbid and masochistic; it's not healthy. We mistrust the mood. Rightly so. To do the right thing for the wrong reason is, as Voltaire said, the final treason. Taking pleasure in our own pain is sick. But the blessing does come. We rejoice and are exceedingly glad when we do not miss one opportunity to put ourselves at-risk for the sake of peace, when we hazard our security searching for truth, when we insist on fairness as elemental justice. We don't want to miss that chance. We want the sheer courage to declare ourselves on the side of decency. That's why we become glad. That's cause for rejoicing.

I have a friend who embodies this blessing for me. He has a 'free wheeling' and breezy manner. His interest is not primarily in making money. His passion is grounded in that old troika of righteousness; doing justice, loving mercy, walking humbly. Mistake me not. The man is no saint. Watching him in a meeting I relish the salty quality of his speech. I don't normally think of him as being 'religious' in the conventional sense. I am struck by his apparent lack of inhibitions.

His mind is like well-honed steel, vibrant, sharp, strong. In fact he pays considerable attention to what he calls 'the energy of mind.' In his estimation, the way a nation thinks determines the quality of its governance. "We should judge societies and their governments by the same criteria we use in estimating right conduct of mind," he says. 'Right conduct of mind' is no esoteric or obscure or mysterious matter for him. His mind is disciplined and ambitious. It is filled with variety and flexibility. His paradigm of the just society resembles this 'right conduct of the mind' when it includes the impulse toward inclusiveness and completeness, when it searches for coherence and uses power gently, responsibly, justly.

That may sound unnecessarily complicated. But the way he puts the bottom line is surely clear, at least for me: "Nothing can be done to ease injustice or oppression except with the aid of the flexible intelligence, the mobile imagination, and the will to self-sacrifice." And if you ask him, he says this is the 'next to the bottom line.' At rock bottom is what he calls the final truth, a simpler, deeper, and inexpressibly precious truth: "Honest shame is not to be mocked."

I like how he thinks, and how he looks. His face is that of a man who has seen much, understood even more, and remains completely unafraid. No piety there. I wouldn't suspect that he even kneels before an altar, but he does when he takes Communion. His best prayers are offered in silence, like the stillness betwen two waves on a rolling sea.

He possesses an authentic interest in people who are being harassed by life. His intelligent and informed good will finds him bending his life into solid advocacy on their behalf. He does not merely hear — he listens. The difference between them is a quantum leap. When asked, he offers his counsel by suggesting that 'you might consider this . . .' Faced with a complicated social problem at variance with his high sense of decency and human dignity, he becomes exhilarated. The tempo of his speech quickens and his eyes flash. He is willing to do costly things for the sake of *el Dios de los Pobres*. He is willing to stand-up, speak-up and pay-up dearly for what he believes. Lord, I love that man. God help me, he's even a lawyer!

Unlike armchair radicals and most theological liberationists, he is not bewitched, bothered, and bewildered by the intricacy of academic reflections of the faith. Instead, he simply clings to the minimum necessary intellectualizations that will support his recognizably Christian action. His imagination and conscience is fired by little ditties like "Jesus loves me, this I know." I am not surprised when I hear him whistling "Once to Every Man and Nation." In fact, of his several distinguishing gifts, those that mark him forever upon my heart are his ability to feel deeply the pain of others, to call things by their right name, and absorb significant punishment on behalf of justice.

Like Kazantzakis's Zorba, for him each day is ever a fascinating and eventful adventure. To be of service is a privilege and a joy. His life is an expression of his profound commitment to the purposes of God among the children of God. And he knows that the children of God is the single, indivisible, whole human family. He is tender without being soft, gracious without being officious, kind without being condescending. This is the fine art of his living. And it's contagious. He stimulates me to feel worthwhile, to touch my essential worth. To call him a friend raises a joyful shout in my heart.

The Daphne Blossoms in Struggle

In fact, my friend reminds me of a flower. Odd, isn't it. Once I tried to grow a garden. My neighbor was an old Portuguese farmer with a remarkable knack for growing magnificent vegetables and flowers. I asked him to come over and 'test' my ground. He took bits of earth here and there, rubbed them into his palm, smelled it, even tasted it with his tongue. Finally he recommended a recipe for planting. I followed his advice. I bought and planted an assortment of vegetables and flowers. My garden prospered. Varieties of tomatoes, beans, peppers, greens, squash, even egg plant. The flowers blossomed. Tony came over to inspect the yield.

Proud we were. Save for one pitiful plant. I inquired, "Why all this bounty and beauty save for this remarkable failure?" His reply was revealing. "This plant is called daphne. In your garden, it's too comfortable to do well. The soil is too rich, and it gets too much protection. It does not blossom without struggle." Given poor soil and rugged elements, it conserves strength, becomes hearty, and produces blossoms. In turn, these become seeds. In struggle it works to perpetuate its kind.

I think of the Beatitude. "Blessed are ye who are reviled and persecuted for my sake; yours is the Kingdom of Heaven." An easy life devoid of challenge and too much protection scatters the energy; it dissipates the resources that make for grit

366

and gratitude. Too much comfort works against higher purposes hooked to a dream. Without a dream, there are no fruits, no seeds, no future.

I think of my friends in Nicaragua. Many are flowering like the daphne through the struggles and the hellish horrors of an insane war. I remember a song, the first song we learned on arrving in Managua. It's called "*Nicaraguita:*"

> "*Ay, Nicaragua, Nicaraguita,*
> [*Oh, Nicaragua, dear Nicaragua,*]
> *la flor mas linda de mi querer,*
> [*the most beautiful flower of my love*]
> *Abonada con la bendita, Nicaraguita,*
> [*watered with the blessed blood, dear Nicaragua*]
> *sangre de Diriangen.*
> [*of Diriangen.*]
> *Ay, Nicaragua, sos mas dulcita*
> [*Oh Nicaragua, you are sweeter*]
> *que la mielita de Tamagas,*
> [*than the honey of Tamagas,*]
> *Pero ahora que ya sos libre, Nicaraquita,*
> [*but now that you are free, dear Nicaragua,*]
> *yo te quiero mucho mas.*
> [*I love you much more.*]"[45]

It is in the songs of Nicaragua and the worship of her Christians that I am beginning to track the scent of meaning within the Beatitude. It is out of the uprooting of Somoza and the Triumph over oppression that something new and fresh is being born.

Where the poor and the reviled and the persecuted struggle to endure our Low Intensity War, it is here that faith comes alive. Having spent themselves in labors of survival and compassion, they gather for worship unable to face another day unless their fatigued spirits are resensitized and their strength renewed. While they are not too hoarse to sing, they are too dog-tired to take any long homilies from the clergy. They listen as their neighbors read the Scriptures and then one by one rise to witness to what that means for their lives. High-brow and hoary preachment is noticably absent. The word hermeneutics may not translate into the language. Pretentiously ornate verbiage is heard no more. They speak their truth quietly and plainly. They testify to the pain and horror and misery they have experienced during the week and then they ask God to show them Jesus in it and to make known his will for them in the breathing moment. Finally they ask for the power to carry that out.

Colin Morris says that for folk such as these, what they know about crucifixion they have learned on the flesh of their own bodies; not from 'once upon a time' Sunday School lessons.[46] When they approach the altar for the Holy Eucharist, none are heard to complain that the Sacrament is observed too frequently. Indeed, they open their mouth to receive the bread of Christ's body like the hungry poor that they are. They reach for the wine of Christ's blood with the trembling hands of an alcoholic. Will they find the Risen Lord working his own mysterious alchemy in the flesh of their flesh, in the spirit of their spirit? Will they find him at work in the tragic mess to which they must return? And will he accept the concrete deeds of their faith as his due in place of some spiritualized devotion which they could not affect?

I am humbled in their company. In the presence of their faith I go through the double wringer, the upper roller of which is God's judgment and the lower roller of which is God's mercy. The experience is mind-stretching.

I think of the poor and oppressed of Mother Earth, in our own town and nation, women and men who labor and pray for liberation from the tyrannies of exploitation and disease and hunger and ignorance and unemployment.

I think of my friend who finds his life in the struggle to share it and spill it out for others. He has a taste of the Kingdom.

I think of the Church whose finest flower and most precious faithfulness is the product of simplicity; a base community forged in single-minded devotion to her Lord. Her mission is likewise simple: to feed the hungry, clothe the naked, release the prisoners, to set at liberty those who are oppressed, and to make music in the heart.

I think of the daphne. In rich soil and protected it becomes weak, it has a tendency to grow feeble and soft and is naught but wood and leaves. In struggle it yields the blossom of fulfillment.

Which am I? Which are you? Which?

God help us. Amen.

Postscript

Empires rise and fall. Political movments emerge, and whether they flourish or languish, eventually they disappear. Only stories remaining — memories and reminiscences, dreams and declarations — tales naming the past, asserting the present, conjuring a future. For a brief moment in time, my Nicaraguan neighbors touched my flesh and spirit with the images and poetry of their stories. I am grateful and humbled, inspired and terrified. Terrified? Of course. From now on, the story I tell myself about who I am, the story I tell you about Donovan Roberts, this story includes them. It cannot be otherwise.

And my story includes other people as well. In the turning moment, having concluded these Observations, Reflections and Sermons, I remember other storytellers, persons whom I owe a deep debt of gratitude. Had they not taken the time to make me a part of their stories, the Nicaraguans and their passion would not be a part of my life.

Is it coincidence? I don't know. But these storytellers were and are Christian clergy. I name them in my prayers. They are a brooding presence inserting themselves into the interval spaces within my meditative and contemplative moments, these shapers, trail-blazers and guardians of my spirit. Without them I never would have set foot on the trek to the water's edge. Had they not invited me, prodded me and chastened me, I would never had bothered to grope my way to the borderlands of faith.

Am I indebted to them? Hell yes. Indebted beyond the telling. Do I hold them repsonsible for my frailty, my foibles, my funny faith? No way.

R. Orman Roberts was my father, first pastor and first friend. Facing-down the House UnAmerican Activities Committee or knuckling a tear from his eye while telling the story of "To Kill A Mockingbird," a prophetic and passionate Jack

R. McMichael taught me that keeping silence in the face of injustice was heresy. A man of seminal intellect, J. Philip Wogaman was my first tutor in the rigors of careful, critical thinking. Handing me over to his former tutors, Dean Walter Muelder and Professor Paul Deats at Boston University, eight years and two degrees later their imprint on my life became indelible. Harrell Beck, a preachin' pedagogue without peer, gave me two gifts; a willingness to pray from the gut and a love for that mythopoetic treasure called the Bible.

While these friends disciplined me to think passionately and deeply about the complexities of the human condition, it waited for the Chaplains at nearby Marsh Chapel to lead me in the paths of spirituality. The School of Theology connects to the Chapel through a short corridor, a tiny isthmus bridging two worlds. While reason reigned as king, and sometimes tyrant, in the Academy, the Chapel was a realm of refuge, a trysting place, a place for encountering the domain of soul. Howard Thurman, and, later, Robert Hamill, were the Chapel's elders and sacred storytellers. And their gifts? 'Meditative thinking,' 'centering-down,' 'savor silence,' of such is the wisdom, the power and the incomparable majesty of Howard Thurman, the gentle brooding mystic. Bob Hamill taught me, no he showed me, that every person is a wonderfully unique, distinctive, unrepeatable story. A classic preacher, he was also a gentle listener. What a remarkable and rare combination.

The preaching poets were there, too, at least in the persons of Jim Carroll, Jim Kavanaugh, and Ted Lockhart; two Irish priests with whom I worked in Boston and Reno, respectively, and Ted, my best friend from the long days and short nights of graduate school.

These men, colleague pastors, companions, friends, they made the trek to Nicaragua with me. How could they not? Each have become homogenized into my spirit. They stand close-present to me when life threatens to overwhelm with chaos, each one casting their special light on the creative nerve within the breathing moment. They bid me to listen for the

371

faraway music that is forever singing softly at the heart of time, a gentle melody proclaiming that Life is Good.

Were it not for them, I would not hear the music. Were it not for them, I would not find my own feet, stand up, step up, and sing the melody of that gospel back home in a land that is very strange indeed!

Footnotes

[1]Martin E. Marty, *A Cry of Absence: Reflections for the Winter of the Heart* (San Francisco: Harper & Row, 1983), p. 16

[2]T.S. Eliot, *Collected Poems 1909-1962* (New York: Harcourt, Brace & World, 1970), p. 154.

[3]James Carroll, *Contemplation* (New York: Paulist Press, 1972), p. 78.

[4]Witness for Peace, "What We Have Seen and Heard in Nicaragua: On-The-Scene-Reports," 1986, p. 5.

[5]Howard Thurman, *Deep is the Hunger* (New York: Harper & Row, 1951), pp. 36-37.

[6] Commission on Human Rights in El Salvador (Non-Governmental-CDHES), "Affidavit of Mario Ossamu Nomura," Hospital Rosales — 4.C.H., San Salvador, April 15, 1987, p. 6.

[7]Ibid., p. 8.

[8]Peter Davis, *Where is Nicaragua?* (New York: Simon & Schuster, 1987), p. 288.

[9]Ibid., p. 22-24.

[10]Octavio Paz, "The Day of the Dead," in *Death and Identity*, ed. by Robert Fulton (New York: John Wiley & Sons, 1965), p. 387.

[11]Saul Landau, *The Dangerous Doctrine: National Security and U.S. Foreign Policy*, (Westview: Pacca Books, 1988).

[12]Alcoholics Anonymous, *Alcoholics Anonymous: The Story of How Many Thousands of Men and Women Have Recovered from Alcoholism* (New York: Alcoholics Anonymous World Services, Inc., 1976), p. 59.

[13]Salman Rushdie, *The Jaguar Smile: A Nicaraguan Journey* (New York: Penguin Books, 1988), p. 131.

[14]Wendell Phillips, "The Irrepressible Conflict," Speech at Rochester, New York, October, 1858.

[15]Inscription beneath the statue of Wendell Phillips, Boston, Massachusetts.

[16]Omar Cabezas, *Fire From The Mountain: The Making of a Sandinista*, (New York: Crown, 1985), p. 104.

[17]Sophocles, *Antigone* 1. 1, 1.

[18]William Shakespeare, *Hamlet*, III.i. 77-81.

[19]Dietrich Bonhoeffer, *Letters & Papers From Prison* (London: S.C.M. Press, 1953), p. 147.

[20]John F. Kennedy, "Inagural Address," January 20, 1961.

[21]Quoted in Conor Cruise O'Brien, "God and Man in Nicaragua," *The Atlantic Monthly*, August, 1986, p. 69.

[22]Kenneth R. Minogue, *Nationalism*, (London: B.T. Batsford, 1967), pp. 25-32 'The Anatomy of Nationalism; Three Stages.'

[23]Philip E. Slater, *The Pursuit of Loneliness: American Culture at the Breaking Point*, (Boston: Beacon Press, 1970), pp. 15-19.

[24]John Long, "A Statement," delivered at the U.S. Embassy in Managua, Nicaragua, June 23, 1988.

[25]"God and Politics: Part I," Bill Moyers, Public Television Documentary, 1987.

[26]John Steinbeck, "Editorial," *The Saturday Review of Literature*, April 3, 1965.

[27]Michael T. Klare and Peter Kornbluh, eds., *Low Intensity Warfare: Counterinsurgency, Proinsurgency, and Antiterrorism in the Eighties* (New York: Pantheon Books, 1988), p. 81, quoted in Jack Nelson—Pallmeyer, *War Against the Poor: Low Intensity Conflict and Christian Faith* (Maryknoll, New York: Orbis Books, 1989), pp. 4-5.

[28]Albert Schweitzer, *The Quest of the Historical Jesus*, (New York: The Macmillan Company, 1964), p. 403.

[29]Ronald Reagan, "Presidential Decree," May 1, 1985.

[30]Philip Berryman, *Inside Central America* (New York: Pantheon, 1985), pp. 44-45.

[31]Thurman, *Deep is the Hunger*, pp. 36-37.

[32]Ibid., p. 79.

[33]Landau, *The Dangerous Doctrine*.

[34]Thurman, *Deep is the Hunger*, p. 186.

[35]Quoted in Rosa del Olmo, "Remaking Justice and Rehabilitation in Revolutionary Nicaragua," in *Crime and Social Justice: Issues in Criminology* (Winter 1982) p. 103, quoted in Carter Heyward and Anne Gilson, *et al. Revolutionary Forgiveness: Feminist Reflections on Nicaragua* (Maryknoll, New York: Orbis Books, 1987), p. 83.

[36]Thurman, *Deep is the Hunger*, pp. 86-87.

[37]Ibid., p. 167.

[38]Paz, "Day of the Dead," p. 387.

[39]Frederick Buechner, *Telling the Truth: The Gospel as Tragedy, Comedy & Fairy Tale*, (New York: Harper & Row, 1977), p. 36.

[40]Charles H. Bayer, *A Guide to Liberation Theology for Middle-Class Congregations*, (St. Louis, Missouri: CBP Press, 1986), p. 153-160.

[41]James Carroll, *A Terrible Beauty: Conversions in Prayer, Politics and Imagination*, (New York: Newman Press, 1973), pp. 21-22.

[42]Carlos Mejia Godoy, "Vos sos el Dios de los pobres," **Misa Campesina**, in the Witness for Peace Songbook, "Songs of the Witness," 1988.

[47]Schweitzer, *Historical Jesus*.

[44]Carroll, *Terrible Beauty*, p. 110.

[45]Carlos Mejia Godoy, "Nicaragua," *Witness for Peace Songbook*.

[46]Colin Morris, *Include Me Out: Confessions of an Ecclesiastical Coward*, (Nashville: Abingdon Press, 1968), p. 36.